The House That Roone Built

The House That Roone Built

The Inside Story of ABC News

by Marc Gunther

LITTLE, BROWN AND COMPANY

BOSTON   NEW YORK   TORONTO   LONDON

First Edition

Library of Congress Cataloging-in-Publication Data

Gunther, Marc.
    The house that Roone built : the inside story of ABC News / by
Marc Gunther. — 1st ed.
        p.   cm.
    Includes bibliographical references (p.) and index.
    ISBN 0-316-33151-1
    1. Arledge, Roone. 2. ABC NEWS. 3. Television broadcasting of
news — United States. I. Title.
    PN4888.T4G86 1994
    384.55'4'092 — dc20   93-27259

10 9 8 7 6 5 4 3 2

MV-NY

*Published simultaneously in Canada by Little, Brown & Company
(Canada) Limited*

Printed in the United States of America

To my family

The world owes all its onward impulses to men ill at ease.
— NATHANIEL HAWTHORNE

CONTENTS

The House That Roone Built

INTRODUCTION

EARLY on the morning of September 5, 1991, three presidents stood together at one end of St. George's Hall in the Kremlin in Moscow. They were Mikhail Gorbachev, president of the Soviet Union; Boris Yeltsin, president of the Russian Republic; and Roone Arledge, president of ABC News.

The setting was magnificent. St. George's Hall, built in the 1840s and used as the stage for great celebrations, was an ornate gold-and-white room lit by six immense gilt chandeliers and three thousand lamps. Soviet dignitaries had gathered here to welcome cosmonaut Yuri Gagarin, the first man to fly in space, back to earth in 1961.

Thirty years later, the eyes of the world had again turned toward the Soviet Union. A clumsy attempt by Communist Party hard-liners to overthrow Gorbachev had just collapsed, giving way to renewed pressures for democratic reform, led by Yeltsin.

Now, for the first time since the coup, Gorbachev and Yeltsin were going to be interviewed on television. The interview had been arranged by ABC News for live broadcast in the United States and the Soviet Union, but interest was so intense that it had become a worldwide media event, to be seen in Japan, Germany, France, Great Britain, and Spain as well. Peter Jennings, ABC's star evening news anchor, would guide the discussion, and at ABC's urging, Gorbachev and Yeltsin had agreed to take questions from Americans in nine cities across the United States.

It was an extraordinary scene: the two most powerful men in the Soviet Union appearing on American television at a pivotal moment in their nation's history. Their presence before the ABC cameras spoke volumes not just about the revolutionary changes convulsing the Soviet Union but also about the growing importance of television as a player on the world stage.

No individual had done more to expand the role of television in world affairs than the third president in St. George's Hall, the man who greeted Gorbachev and Yeltsin that morning. He was a stocky, round-faced, red-haired man dressed in a dark blue suit and white shirt with pocket square. He smiled nervously and chatted with the Soviets, appearing on the television screen for an instant, but few of those watching could have known who he was. Although his face was not widely recognized, his name had become familiar to millions during a phenomenal career spanning four decades.

Roone Arledge: like so much about him, his name set him apart. It was Arledge who had brought Gorbachev and Yeltsin together — literally, by extending the invitation on behalf of ABC News, but also, in a more important sense, by dint of his impact on the world of broadcast news. He was a powerful man not simply because he ran one of the world's great news organizations but because of the way he did so — with absolute authority. To a remarkable degree, ABC News was Roone Arledge: he was the creator and the producer of its programs, the absolute ruler of its people, and the guardian of its independence. During stormy times for television, Arledge had turned ABC News into the dominant network news division of the 1990s. ABC News reached the most viewers, made the most money, and generated the most glowing accolades. Not since the heyday of Walter Cronkite at CBS had one network run so far ahead of the competition.

Thanks to Arledge, ABC News and its most famous anchors were known and respected by newsmakers not just in Washington and New York but also in Moscow and London and Tel Aviv and Johannesburg. Since taking command of ABC News in 1977, Arledge had assembled a galaxy of stars — Peter Jennings, Ted Koppel, Barbara Walters, David Brinkley, Diane Sawyer, Sam Donaldson, and Hugh Downs — that was unequaled in the annals of network news. He had invented "Nightline," the most important forum for serious journalism on television, and he had developed "World News Tonight," "20/20," "This Week with David Brinkley," and "PrimeTime Live" — all commercial successes. Each had its own identity, but every one concluded in the same way, with a video blessing that paid tribute to Arledge's news dynasty. "More Americans," an announcer said, "get their news from ABC News than from any other source." The boast was true.

By 1991, Arledge could lay claim to a place in a select circle of men who had created and shaped network news. Among them were William S. Paley, the CBS chairman who provided the support needed to begin CBS News; Edward R. Murrow, the revered CBS correspondent who set the standards for broadcast journalism; Don Hewitt, the shrewd innovator who produced CBS's first evening newscast and created "60 Minutes"; and Reuven Frank, the NBC producer and executive who paired Chet Huntley and David Brinkley, devised the format for election and convention coverage, and taught countless followers how to use pictures to tell stories. These were the men who invented network news in the 1950s and 1960s.

That set the stage for Arledge. His success at ABC, by itself, did not earn him a place in their ranks, but he had done more than revive ABC News. Arledge had come to network news as an outsider, with no stake in its traditions, and he had delivered a jangling wake-up call to an industry that had settled into a contented sleep after the pioneering days of Murrow and Hewitt. He arrived at the ideal time, when ABC was flush with money and ready to experiment with new technologies. He brought vision and energy and determination and ideas.

It was Arledge, more than anyone else, who created the expectation among viewers that they could rely on television to bring them live, immediate coverage of major news events as they happened anywhere in the world. It was Arledge, for better or worse, who did the most to generate the fame, wealth, and power enjoyed by star anchors at all the networks. It was Arledge who changed the look of broadcast news, experimented with new formats, and pushed news programs into remote corners of the broadcast day, from early morning to late night. And it was Arledge who helped make the global village a reality — by persuading world leaders to appear on ABC, by taking his programs to Moscow and South Africa and the Middle East, and by convincing Gorbachev and Yeltsin to talk with ordinary Americans. He had not only played the game of television news better than any of his peers, he had rewritten the rules.

As Gorbachev and Yeltsin took questions from Los Angeles, San Francisco, and Miami, Arledge knew that, no matter what was said, the town meeting would enhance the reputation of ABC News as well as his own stature. As it happened, the program was all he had hoped it would be — the town-meeting format produced compelling television as the Soviet leaders spoke for ninety minutes about everything from their personal spiritual beliefs to the future of their nation. The most striking moment came when they pronounced the death of Communism in the Soviet Union. "This experiment which was conducted on our soil was a tragedy for our people," Yeltsin said. Gorbachev agreed, saying, "That model has failed."

Watching the program on a monitor in St. George's Hall, Arledge was also pleased that the technically complex broadcast, linking Jennings in New York with nine American cities and the Kremlin, had gone off without a hitch — or at least without a hitch noticeable to viewers. The only problem involved commercial breaks, and it flowed from a misunderstanding involving Arledge and his corporate superiors at Capital Cities/ABC.

The incident occurred midway through the broadcast, when Richard Wald, an ABC News vice president in the control room in New York, asked out loud, "Aren't we going to break for a commercial?" Others assumed that Wald was speaking on behalf of Daniel Burke, the president of Capital Cities, and Steve Weiswasser, an assistant to the president of ABC, who were also watching from the control room.

But Arledge had issued his own orders, prohibiting any breaks after Gorbachev and Yeltsin had begun to speak, in part to make it harder for them to end the interview. When no breaks were taken, the Capital Cities men seemed to be irritated, and they left the control room before the broadcast was over. Later, they insisted they had not applied any pressure to get more commercials into the program, which cost ABC about $1.4 million. Wald confirmed their account. Their walkout had been misunderstood.

Nevertheless, rumors about the incident spread through ABC News, where, in fact, real pressures were being brought to bear on Arledge by Capital Cities. The glowing reviews for Gorbachev-Yeltsin would not protect him from the troubles awaiting him in New York. In a curious way, Arledge's situation resembled Gorbachev's — he was a visionary, but he was losing crucial support at home.

His problems were not new. Arledge was a self-centered man who drove his people hard, and as a result, he had never been beloved within ABC News. His problems with Capital Cities dated back to 1986, when Cap Cities took over ABC and stripped Arledge of his authority over ABC Sports, the organization he had built before taking over ABC News. Back then, Tom Murphy and Dan Burke, the cost-conscious managers who ran Cap Cities, also had tried to cut Arledge's $2 million salary. While Arledge eventually grew to know and like Murphy, who stepped down as CEO in 1990, he never warmed up to Burke and the other newcomers from Cap Cities. He felt that they never fully appreciated all he had done for ABC, and he hated it when they meddled in news operations. As long as ABC News brought profits and prestige to the company, Arledge argued, he should be left alone to run it, just as he always had.

Dan Burke would never agree to that. If anything, Burke faulted himself for not moving more decisively to curb Arledge's power. The problem was that Burke had very mixed feelings about Arledge. He had enormous admiration for his creativity, but he did not believe that Arledge had the management skills needed to lead ABC News in the 1990s: he was not sufficiently committed to cost control, he was inattentive to the details of administration, and he bruised people unnecessarily.

Nevertheless, Burke did not want to lose Arledge. He valued his talents as a programmer and worried that Arledge's departure would cause fallout inside and outside ABC News. If Arledge were forced out, he thought, some star anchors and producers might leave too. Discreetly, Burke took soundings around the news division to see how some of the most valuable people regarded Arledge. He kept his intentions to himself, but he could not hide his frustrations with Arledge.

Burke came away knowing that his misgivings about Arledge were shared by those who worked for him. He kept hearing the same things: that Arledge was a brilliant and creative producer, but that he was remote, indecisive, and bored by administrative detail. Nor was he a team player. The feeling was that Arledge put himself ahead of the needs of ABC News.

Burke decided he had to make his move.

With Arledge still overseas, Burke decided to give his news president a day or two to get over jet lag; then he would deliver the unpleasant news. Roone Arledge was about to face his own palace coup: his unchallenged rule over ABC News was over.

Chapter One

ARLEDGE ASCENDANT

MORE THAN ANYTHING ELSE, Roone Arledge needed sleep. As the president of ABC Sports, he had been working twenty-hour days, producing coverage of the 1972 Summer Olympics from Munich. The schedule was grueling: Arledge would arrive at ABC's television center each morning by nine, supervise the taping of events during the day and evening, and return to his seat in the control room at 1 A.M. to produce and assemble three hours of coverage to be broadcast live in prime time in the United States. At 4 A.M., he would convene a production meeting to plan the next day's coverage. Although Arledge never seemed to need sleep, ten days of this regimen had left him exhausted. And on the previous two mornings, he had been awakened early by phone calls — one from a man in Arkansas who complained that his local ABC station had preempted part of the Olympics, another from Bing Crosby, who wanted tickets to see swimmer Mark Spitz go for his seventh gold medal.

Still, Arledge felt pride as his workday came to an end at dawn on Tuesday, September 5. These Olympics, he thought, had produced a wonderful mix of drama, excitement, controversy, and beauty. The stars of ABC's telecasts had included the muscular, mustached Spitz and tiny Olga Korbut, a seventeen-year-old Soviet gymnast, who caught the attention of the cameras not only because her performances were thrilling but because her emotions, in victory and defeat, shone through so clearly. These Games had their heavies too: boxing judges whose decisions penalized the Americans; an official who would not let pole-vaulter Bob Seagren use a fiberglass pole; and ABC's own

Howard Cosell, who had heaped abuse on an American track coach who failed to get his sprinters to the starting blocks for a heat, costing them a chance at medals. Cosell didn't like taking flak from critics and viewers, but Arledge didn't mind; the important thing was that people were watching, and talking about, ABC.

That morning at about 5 A.M., Arledge and Dick Ebersol, his young assistant, shared a quiet moment outside the Olympic Village before going back to the hotel. Ebersol was cold and bone-tired, but Arledge paused to admire the view. "There was a gorgeous moon," Arledge recalled later, "and the lights were on in the stadium."

Two hours later, the telephone rang again in Arledge's suite. His daughters Betsey and Susie were under orders not to wake him, but an ABC executive named Marvin Bader told them they had better get him up right away. When Arledge came to the phone, Bader reported tersely that gunshots had been heard in the Olympic Village and Israeli athletes might have been taken hostage. Arledge replied, "Find Peter Jennings and Jim McKay."

The response was swift and enterprising — true to the spirit established by Arledge at ABC Sports.

Jennings had come to Munich to contribute feature stories to the coverage; he had looked forward to a relaxing break from his duties as the ABC News correspondent in Beirut. Now he was thrust into the midst of an Arab-Israeli showdown. He worked his way into a building with a distant view of Building 31, the Israeli dormitory, and commandeered a telephone.

McKay had arisen expecting his first day off from the Games. With no competition scheduled in gymnastics or track and field, his areas of expertise, he was about to take a swim. He was told to report to work right away. Taking over for Chris Schenkel, who until then had been host of the Olympics, McKay threw on clothes over his swim trunks and took his seat in the studio, where he would remain for most of the next sixteen hours.

Howard Cosell, meanwhile, raced to the Olympic Village. The village had already been closed to the press, but Cosell shed his ABC jacket and talked his way past security by claiming to be a Puma shoe salesman who serviced the athletes.

With Arledge in command, ABC Sports began to cover the biggest story on the planet — and to cover it brilliantly. Effortlessly, Arledge's men made the transition from sports to news. Although Munich had become a story of life and death, not victory and defeat, the story was, like any other, composed of pictures and words, characters and action, all of which needed to be shaped into a coherent narrative. Arledge and his ABC Sports team had been doing that for years.

Arledge had also watched news for years, and not as a casual viewer. In the control room in Munich, he remembered how NBC had been the only network on the air with live coverage in 1963 when Jack Ruby had shot Lee Harvey Oswald. "That always stuck in my head," he said. He vowed to stay with the story until the siege was over. "The cardinal error is to be there with the only live camera, then miss whatever might happen," said Arledge.

ABC Sports didn't miss anything. The unlikely hero of the coverage was a twenty-eight-year-old producer named John Wilcox who had slipped past security into the village with a film camera, a still camera, and a walkie-talkie stuffed into an Adidas bag. His mission was risky, but Wilcox, posing as a U.S. boxer, got into a Bulgarian dormitory next to the Israeli quarters. He rode up to the second floor, walked into an empty room, and found himself staring across a walkway at a terrorist holding a submachine gun, no more than fifty feet away. No one else had a better vantage point — so Wilcox began filming the scene and, using the walkie-talkie, made arrangements to get his pictures out.

The images were gripping: terrorists carrying submachine guns, one wearing a mask, another wearing a white hat, poking their heads out of windows and doors. The contrasts were striking: where athletes once strolled in harmony, German police officers donned sweatsuits to blend into the crowd as they prepared for a possible assault on the commandos. The reporting was superb: Cosell tracked the movements of athletes and police, Jennings vividly described the scene around Building 31, and Wilcox provided close-up views, speaking over his walkie-talkie to millions of viewers.

McKay, too, rose to the occasion. For hour after hour, still wearing his swim trunks under his suit, McKay absorbed all the information flowing in and relayed it to the viewers calmly and carefully. He also conveyed the mood of Munich with clarity and occasional eloquence.

"My father once told me that our greatest hopes and our worst fears are rarely realized," he said at one point. "Tonight, our worst fears have been realized."

It was nearly 4 A.M. in Munich when a bloody gunfight between the police and the terrorists brought the saga to its terrible conclusion. All eleven Israeli hostages were slaughtered.

Soberly, McKay reported that a memorial service would be held the next day in the great Olympic stadium. He recapped the day's events and signed off by saying, simply, "They're all gone." Physically and emotionally spent, he left the broadcast center to get some sleep.

Arledge remained. There was work to be done. Wilcox had emerged from the village with more dramatic pictures of the terrorists, taken with his film camera, that had not been shown on ABC. He wanted to produce a program about the massacre for ABC News. First Jennings, then Arledge, called New York, but they could not get a commitment from the news division to run the program. Arledge was stunned.

He decided to produce the film himself. "The hell with it," he told Wilcox. "You guys make it. I'll give you half an hour after the U.S.-Russian basketball game."

The thirty-minute special report, anchored by Jennings, documented the events leading up to the deaths of the hostages and broke new ground in an interview with the Munich police chief, who explained why he had decided to open fire on the Palestinian commandos at the airport. By feeding the program to the prime-time audience that had come to the set to watch the Olympics, Arledge ensured that it would reach a huge audience.

Praise was heaped on ABC Sports. Arledge's men shared twenty-nine Emmys for their work in news and sports at Munich, and ABC's broadcasts were lauded in a speech on the Senate floor. Les Brown, the highly regarded television writer for the *New York Times*, saw the coverage as a great leap forward for lowly ABC, saying, "The achievement carries a special significance in the world of American television, as another milestone in the emergence of a full-fledged third network force." The ultimate compliment came from Walter Cronkite of CBS News, who sent McKay a telegram of congratulations.

In his twelve years at ABC Sports, Arledge had never before earned such accolades. The feeling was immensely gratifying.

There were two footnotes to Munich.

Afterward, Arledge realized that the spot where he had stood early that morning with Ebersol was just a few yards away from the place where the terrorists had entered the Olympic Village. He had nearly stumbled upon the commandos. "I've often thought that if, for some reason, we had wandered over there, we would have been killed," Arledge said.

Some time later, Arledge invited Jennings out to his weekend home in Sagaponack, Long Island, for dinner. Arledge, who liked to cook, made dinner, after which they took a long walk on the beach. The talk turned to Munich — and to the deficiencies of ABC News — when Arledge put an unexpected question to Jennings.

What, he asked, would you think about my taking over ABC News?

Roone Pinckney Arledge Jr. was born on July 8, 1931, in Forest Hills, New York. His father, Roone Sr., a native of North Carolina whose family roots were in Scotland, had come to New York to work as a lawyer for the Equitable Life Assurance Company. His mother, the former Gertrude Stritmater, remained at home in Merrick, Long Island, a comfortable suburb where young Roone spent his boyhood and graduated from Mepham High School.

Those are the bare facts about Roone Arledge's family and early years — topics he rarely discusses. This is partly because Arledge is a shy man who finds it uncomfortable to plumb his own emotions. And it is partly because he has little interest in the past.

One result is that confusion has arisen over even the innocent facts of Arledge's formative years. In *SuperTube: The Rise of Television Sports*, author Ron Powers wrote after interviewing Arledge that he wrestled, played baseball, and edited the sports page of the student newspaper at Mepham High. Arledge was, in fact, the sports editor, but he served as manager of the wrestling team and never played baseball for Mepham. The high school yearbook indicates that his favorite adolescent pastime was drama — he was president of Skull and Bones, the school drama club, and he acted in many school plays, performing opposite a pretty teenager named Joan Heise. Later, Arledge participated in many campus activities at Columbia University, where he was president of his fraternity, but he was never the president of his graduating class — as his ABC biography stated for years. These are the first, but not the last, examples of how Arledge tends to reconstruct his past — to produce his own history. Why, long after achieving success in his career, he would feel the need to embellish his earliest achievements is not clear.

Still, Arledge and others agree that his parents instilled in him a fierce determination to make something important of his life. Roone Arledge Sr. was a warm, outgoing, physically imposing man who retained the sweetness and character of a Southern gentleman. He was a devoted gardener who liked to hunt and fish and sometimes took along young Roone. Later, Arledge created a television show about outdoor sports, "The American Sportsman," and he relaxed by going big-game hunting in East Africa with pals like Curt Gowdy.

Golf was another passion that the elder Arledge passed along to his son, as was cooking, especially Southern dishes like turnip greens and collards. "He made cooking kind of a masculine hobby, as opposed to a female chore," said Arledge, whose own specialties as a chef include swordfish and pasta.

Arledge's father was engaged by politics and world affairs, and he helped stimulate Roone's curiosity. The family set aside time each night to follow the news of World War II over the radio, as well as listen to the fireside chats of President Franklin D. Roosevelt. "At our dinner table, the talk was always, 'I bet that Omar Bradley is thinking this right now. I bet President Roosevelt is planning to do that,' " Arledge said. Arledge never forgot his father's reaction after Japan attacked the Philippines. "He said, 'Oh, that's good. We've got MacArthur out in the Philippines. He'll be terrific.' And I thought, how the hell does he know that? Who is MacArthur, number one, but number two, how does he know that?" This hunger for knowledge, later transformed into his desire to explain the world to viewers, never left Arledge.

Arledge also learned a lesson in independence from his father, a fervent supporter of FDR in a Republican area. In school debates, Arledge recalled, "I was the only one who took the Democratic point of view and argued against Dewey or Willkie. You had to defend yourself against ten people and it was a good learning experience." This was a favorite Arledge image: he liked to cast himself as the underdog fighting long odds.

Arledge speaks less about his mother, whom others describe as an unusually demanding woman who was unsatisfied with anything but the best from her son. "She was a great motivator," Arledge said. "She was always interested in excellence. If I got an A minus or a B plus, I became impatient. In some respects, she made me too much of a perfectionist, because she always thought I could do better." His friends describe Mrs. A., as she was known, as tough to please and not especially warm or accepting. She was thought to be responsible not only for the restlessness that drove Arledge but also for his need to deny his own foibles and mistakes.

Columbia University also exerted a strong influence. Arledge arrived on campus in 1948, filled with energy, curiosity, and ambition. He joined the wrestling team, performed in the college theater, and became active in fraternities. In the Columbia yearbook, Arledge's entry stands out because he has twelve lines under his picture listing his activities; no one else has more than seven. Arledge, as it happened, also edited the yearbook — "the only campus publication that made money," as Richard Wald, his college friend and ABC News colleague, said later.

Arledge was not a scholar — he wanted to study journalism and majored in liberal arts — but the teachers who made a lasting impression on him were the stars of the English faculty, Mark Van Doren and Lionel Trilling. "We had a faculty that was incredible — name after name after name," he said. "It was a spectacularly exciting time to be at Columbia." Reading the classics with Van Doren left such an imprint that years later Arledge could recall class discussions and quote Shakespeare from memory. From Trilling, Arledge learned about the nature of narrative, the idea that artists must sift through events and incidents that are, by themselves, shapeless, in order to transform them into meaningful drama. From there it was a short leap to Arledge's idea that televised sports events be organized around what he called a "story line." He told his producers and announcers to open their telecasts by introducing the protagonists and identifying the obstacles they would face and to be alert for new story lines to follow as the game unfolded.

At Columbia, Arledge was drawn to an impressive circle of friends. Wald, a graceful writer with a biting sense of humor, edited the college paper; he went on to be editor of the *New York Herald Tribune,* president of NBC News, and eventually, Arledge's vice president at ABC News. Max Frankel was the scholar of the group; he became editorial page editor, then executive editor of the *New York Times.* Larry Grossman, a brash, street-smart kid from Brooklyn, became president of the Public Broadcasting Service and of NBC News.

While they enjoyed the usual pursuits of college men, Arledge and his crowd were, at heart, serious-minded. They were engaged by books, politics, and ideas and fascinated by the media, which were entering an era of explosive growth. "New York was a very exciting place to be," Wald said. "Radio was changing, television was beginning and growing up, magazines were sprouting all over the place, and newspapers were thriving. And there we were, the perfect raw material — reasonably well educated and cheap. We all got on the escalator and rode it up."

At first, though, Arledge wasn't sure where he was heading. He spent a few months at Columbia's School of International Affairs studying the Middle East, but he didn't have the patience to learn Arabic. He sought work as a sportswriter but was turned away by a Long Island daily. "I wanted to be a writer," he recalled, "but I couldn't decide whether I wanted to write sports, government, philosophy, or theater." His goal was to land a job at *Time* or *Newsweek*, where he could pursue his many interests.

An act of kindness to a stranger brought his job search to an end. As Arledge recounts the tale, he was working one summer as head-waiter at an inn on Cape Cod, when a family arrived late for dinner. They were told by a hostess that the dining room was closed, but Arledge invited them in to eat: "So they sat down — the place was deserted — and began rushing through their meal. I kept saying, 'Take your time. I want you to enjoy your dinner.' They were very grateful, and before they left they took my name." Months later, through one of his father's connections, Arledge managed to get a job interview with the head of programming at the Dumont Television Network. He walked into an office, where the executive studied his face for a moment and then said, "How's everything at the Wayside Inn in Chatham?" Naturally, Arledge got the job.

It wasn't much of a job. Arledge was a gofer, but he made enough of an impression that, after Dumont folded, he found work at a New York TV station owned by NBC. He began as a stage manager and, after a time, earned his first credit as a producer — and won his first Emmy — for a puppet show called "Hi Mom," with Shari Lewis.

His ambitions went well beyond puppets. While working at NBC, he hooked up with his college friend Larry Grossman, who had become a junior editor at *Look* magazine and Arledge's neighbor in Brooklyn Heights. Hoping to make fuller use of their Columbia educations, as well as jump-start their careers, they dreamed up a series of high-minded television programs that would dramatize the stories behind great works of art, from Beethoven's Eroica Symphony to Walt Whitman's *Leaves of Grass*. They spent hours in the public library and spread their scripts across the ironing board in Grossman's apartment, working for more than a year to perfect the idea. "We were two loony kids," Grossman recalled. "We were going to save television from triviality." They called the program "Masterpiece."

To get the proposal before the eyes of the right executive took a different brand of cunning, this time supplied by Arledge. In 1953, Arledge married Joan Heise, his old high school friend, who had become an attractive, effervescent woman with a good sense of humor. They'd lost touch for a while but had been reunited by a mutual friend after Arledge got into the television business and Heise was working, by coincidence, as personal secretary to the aging General David Sarnoff, chairman of NBC's parent company, RCA. Joan agreed to have the "Masterpiece" proposal typed on Sarnoff's stationery and then steer it onto the desk of NBC's president, Sylvester (Pat) Weaver. Even so, Weaver had no interest in "Masterpiece."

Arledge was undaunted. His next idea, "For Men Only," was not quite so lofty, although it had its own brand of originality: he wanted to develop a television version of *Playboy*, absent the naked centerfolds. This time, Arledge persuaded NBC to invest in a pilot episode, which included a track-and-field segment narrated by Marty Glickman, drawings of a boxing match by the artist Robert Rieger, a jazz performance, and a starlet in a bathing suit, all woven together with flair by a production crew that passed bottles of Scotch around the set while filming. "For Men Only" reflected a different side of Arledge — the man-about-town who enjoyed sports, music, and beautiful women, as well as fine food, drink, and conversation. Although television had never seen anything like "For Men Only" in the late 1950s, Arledge's boss rejected the show, and it never aired. This was the era when NBC earned its corporate reputation for caution.

But "For Men Only" turned out to be an important program for Arledge and for ABC, because Arledge got it onto the desk of an ABC executive named Edgar Scherick. Scherick was an astute judge of talent, and while he didn't want the show, he wanted to meet the man who had made it. Scherick had just made a deal to produce a package of college football games for ABC, and he was looking for talented young producers. He knew that he had found one in Roone Arledge.

It is almost impossible for the modern-day viewer who has seen sports on television — an Olympics, "Monday Night Football," or even a locally televised baseball game — to imagine the world of sports television before the arrival of Roone Arledge. Primitive would be a kind description of the production quality; prehistoric would be more apt. The zeitgeist of the sports establishment of the 1960s can be gleaned from a remark Ford Frick, the commissioner of baseball, made to Arledge after awarding a television contract to ABC in 1965. "One of the jobs that baseball has to do is keep television from making the show too good," Frick said. "The trouble is that television wants the viewer to see the game better than the fan in the ball park. The view a fan gets at home should not be any better than that of the fan in the worst seat of the park."

Arledge was too polite to laugh out loud at Frick, but he had already consigned the old man's ideas to history. By the time he produced his first event in 1960, Arledge had decided that the old way of producing sports was hopelessly outmoded, and he had come up with his new, radical approach. In Arledge's scheme, the game was raw material, unformed stuff, like clay in the hands of a sculptor, that had to be re-formed and shaped into art — or at least into exciting viewing. The game was just the starting point. It was the show that counted.

This simple idea began a revolution: the instant replay, stop action, slow motion, isolated cameras, underwater cameras, cameras on the helmets of race-car drivers, even a microphone next to a dead zebra, so viewers could listen to a hungry lion slurping lunch. It also led to intimate shots of the players, reaction shots of the coaches, "honey shots" of the cheerleaders, and ultimately to prime-time football on Monday nights with three men in the booth, one of whom turned out to be the redoubtable Howard Cosell.

"When I got into it in 1960, televising sports amounted to going out on the road, opening three or four cameras, and trying not to blow any plays," Arledge said. "They were barely documenting the game, but just the marvel of seeing a picture was enough to keep the people glued to their sets. What we set out to do was to get the audience involved emotionally. If they didn't give a damn about the game, they might still enjoy the program."

Arledge wrote those words in an article for *Sports Illustrated* in 1966, as he first emerged into public view. But he had written his most important manifesto, his own bold declaration of independence from the chains of sports television's past, much earlier, in a memo he prepared for Ed Scherick back in 1960. The memo helped persuade Scherick to make him the producer of ABC's package of college football games that fall. The memo is worth quoting at length because Arledge so rarely put his ideas down on paper — and because it so perfectly expressed his philosophy of sports television. Here, too, are the seeds of what would become Arledge's approach to programming ABC News.

Heretofore, television has done a remarkable job of bringing the game to the viewer — now we are going to take the viewer to the game!!

We will utilize every production technique . . . to heighten the viewer's feeling of actually sitting in the stands and participating personally in the excitement and color. . . .

We must gain and hold the interest of women and others who are not fanatic followers of the sport we happen to be televising. Women come to football games, not so much to marvel at the deftness of the quarterback in calling an end sweep or a lineman pulling out to lead a play, but to sit in a crowd, see what everyone else is wearing, watch the cheerleaders and experience the countless things that make up the feeling of the game. Incidentally, very few men have ever switched channels when a nicely proportioned girl was leaping into the air or leading a band downfield. . . .

We will have cameras mounted in jeeps, on mike booms, in risers or helicopters, or anything necessary to get the complete story of the game. We will use a "creepy-peepy" camera to get the impact shots that we cannot get from a fixed camera — a coach's face as a man drops a pass in the clear — a pretty cheerleader just after her hero has scored a touchdown — a co-ed who brings her infant baby to the game in her arms — the referee as he calls a particularly difficult play — a student hawking programs in the stands — two romantic students sharing a blanket late in the game on a cold day — the beaming face of a substitute halfback as he comes off the field after running seventy yards for a touchdown, on his first play for the varsity — all the excitement, wonder, jubilation and despair that make this America's Number One sports spectacle, and human drama to match bullfights and heavyweight championships in intensity.

In short — *we are going to add show business to sports!*

Immodestly, Arledge concluded, "We will be setting the standards that everyone will be talking about and that others in the industry will spend years trying to equal." Immodestly — but accurately as well.

For Arledge was no armchair theorist. When, a few months later, he stepped into a mobile-unit production truck to produce a sports telecast for the first time, he found a home. The game between "Bear" Bryant's Alabama and the Georgia Bulldogs, led by quarterback Fran Tarkenton, faded from memory long ago. But the men who witnessed Arledge's performance in the truck remembered years later the way he took control of the telecast as if he had been producing sports all his life. Seated before a bank of monitors, wearing a headset and speaking in calm tones to his production team, Arledge invented the future as they watched — showcasing the veteran coach and the exuberant young quarterback, weaving back and forth between tight shots of the men on the field and panoramic views of the crowd, locating coeds in the stands, turning up the sound to hear the thud of a tackle, all in an effort to capture the feel of the game, to do more than document the action. This *was* a revolution, and it was most certainly being televised.

The Arledge credo — that the show mattered more than the game — found its purest expression when he created "Wide World of Sports" in 1961. The show covered major and minor sports — baseball and barrel jumping, boxing and baton twirling, rugby and rodeo. Few involved big events and many were tape-delayed. Just about everyone bet that the show would flop. Years later, ABC's founder, Leonard Goldenson, said, "I thought it was the screwiest idea I'd ever heard."

But Arledge wasn't selling cricket or hurling to the audience; he was selling emotion. Emotion could be found at the World Barrel Jumping Championships as well as the World Series. "Trying to break the seventeen-barrel barrier is as big an event in a barrel jumper's life as Hank Aaron breaking Babe Ruth's home-run record or Roger Bannister cracking the four-minute mile," Arledge said. "If you can get that across to people, make it possible for them to recognize how difficult it is, give them a sense of where it is happening and a reason to want the person to succeed — or fail — then the viewer can become involved." That first season, Arledge traveled the world with host Jim McKay and produced many of the programs by himself.

"Wide World" led naturally to the Olympics. Until they were produced by Arledge, the Games held little appeal for television; they were regarded as a collection of mostly minor sports with limited interest to viewers. But Arledge saw the beauty in sports like gymnastics and figure skating, and he knew he could turn them into compelling television. In Arledge's hands, the Olympics became a spectacle — a dramatic, unpredictable, talked-about festival of international athletic competition.

Arledge wanted to own every event; he would not be satisfied until ABC Sports dominated sports television. He bought the rights to Saturday-afternoon baseball, NBA basketball, the Triple Crown of horse racing, and in 1970, he pushed sports into the brightly lit arena of prime time for the first time with "Monday Night Football." This was another leap forward for Arledge and ABC — sports as mass entertainment, a smash hit that made the football game the starting point for an evening of excitement, controversy, drama, spontaneity, and pure fun with Howard Cosell, Don Meredith, and Frank Gifford. Purists complained that the show had overpowered the game, and they were "exactly right," in the Cosellian argot. "Monday Night Football" became a national institution.

By then, Arledge had become an executive as well as a producer. But even after he was appointed president of ABC Sports in 1968, Arledge could be found in the mobile-unit trucks on many weekend afternoons. He thrived on the action, especially when it provided an escape from administrative chores or network meetings. This set him apart from other executives, as he liked to point out. "The image that ultimately appears on the tube is what TV is all about," Arledge said. "So, for me, the most rewarding and exciting part of my job is making pictures and words that move people. . . . During a major sporting event, the action isn't in the commissioner's box, where every other TV executive sits, but in the mobile unit. That's the place to be."

When Arledge wasn't in the truck, he was watching at home. Every ABC Sports control room and mobile unit was equipped with a special red phone, which became known as the Roone phone. It rang often. "I can't hear any crowd," Arledge would say. "You sound like you're broadcasting from a morgue. Get the crowd level up." He would tell an announcer to talk more or keep quiet, or he'd remind his producer to plug an upcoming event.

No matter where he sat, Arledge set high standards. He hated to be told that something couldn't be done — that it was impossible to obtain a camera angle or that a star athlete would not do an interview. "He always instilled that in us," said John Wilcox, whose derring-do in Munich proved so valuable to ABC. "There's nothing you can't do. You can move mountains." This spirit once led an ABC gofer, under orders to rush sportscaster Keith Jackson from La Guardia Airport to Yankee Stadium, to rent an ambulance, which made the trip with siren screaming and lights flashing.

While Arledge was a demanding boss, his hands-on approach won him respect. Chet Forte, the network's premier sports director, once said, "We really feel we're working for the best man in the business. On Monday morning, he walks in and tells you what he thought of your show. You never have the feeling you were working in a vacuum." Joe Aceti, another ABC director, said approvingly, "He wasn't some guy in a suit and tie."

He made the guys in suits and ties happy too. Unlike the rest of ABC, which lagged behind CBS and NBC in every way, ABC Sports made money even as Arledge spent vast amounts on rights fees and production costs. His success turned sports television into a big-money business, notably in the case of the Olympics — which cost Arledge a mere $200,000 when ABC broadcast the 1964 Winter Games from Innsbruck. Twenty years later, ABC paid $91.5 million for the Calgary

Winter Games and $225 million for the Los Angeles Summer Games. While Arledge was faulted as a wild spender by some critics, others were grateful that he came along and drove the industry to dizzying new heights. "The bottom line on Roone is that he made the sports television industry what it is today," said Barry Frank, a millionaire agent who once worked for Arledge at ABC Sports.

The problem was that Arledge never let anyone forget what he had done. Nor was he generous about sharing credit, an annoying trait, given television's collaborative nature. On the air, he literally took credit for everything; by presidential decree, each and every event broadcast by ABC Sports — every Olympics, football game, horse race, and bowling tournament — concluded the same way, with a benediction: "The executive producer of ABC Sports is Roone Arledge." Howard Cosell would say that Arledge produced more shows he never saw than anyone else in the history of television.

When confronted with the charge that he was stingy with praise for others, Arledge blamed the press. "My name is so memorable," he once said, "I get credit for a lot of things I was not solely responsible for." It was not that simple. The famous signature line of "Wide World," for example, about "the thrill of victory and the agony of defeat," was reported for years to have been scrawled by Arledge on the back of an airline ticket during a flight home from Japan; the story was so particular that no reporter could have made it up. The truth was that the billboard line was written in a New York studio by Arledge and McKay. "My recollection is that it was a joint effort," McKay said later. "I can tell you for sure that I was involved in writing it." Similarly, the history of ABC Sports according to Roone Arledge did not include the name of Edgar Scherick, the man who hired him, bought the first college football package, and helped to create "Wide World." Scherick resented it. "Roone has never once given credit to anyone else, in any way, shape, or form," he said. "This is something I've told him many times. He just shrugs and claims it's not his fault."

Arledge's management style also turned some people against him. His comings and goings were unpredictable; he would arrive at work late, disappear for hours, schedule meetings for the early evening, and call his aides at any hour of the night and on weekends, with little or no consideration for their lives outside ABC Sports. His reluctance to return phone calls became legendary.

To admirers, those habits reflected a conscious effort by Arledge to train his mind on things that mattered. "Everybody gets burned out by the minutiae of this business," said Dick Ebersol, Arledge's assistant in the early 1970s. "He doesn't get chewed up by the shit. He gives himself time to think."

Others were not so charitable. They saw only rudeness when their phone calls weren't returned, and some aides felt that Arledge's early-evening meetings were a needless imposition on their efforts to maintain a family life. While Arledge himself put work before family, they did not think that they should be required to do so. A few aides complained that he did not think of anyone but himself and called him "the pink pig," a reference to his ruddy complexion.

The Arledge they saw also seemed to revel in his power a little too much; he made a point of skipping network meetings and required that a hotel suite be booked in his name at major sports events whether he planned to attend or not. Sometimes he showed up, but often the suite stayed empty. "Working on a day-to-day basis with Roone was exasperating," complained Jim Spence, Arledge's second-in-command at Sports, who later turned against him. "He seemed to think speculation about whether or when he might show up increased his stature by emphasizing his power to go his own way." Of course, Arledge did have the power to go his own way; he seemed to answer to nobody at ABC.

By the mid-1970s, Arledge was the dominant figure in sports television. His power and reputation were secure. But he told friends that he was growing bored. While Arledge genuinely loved sports — he enjoyed the competition and the excitement, appreciated the physical beauty of athletics, and admired the discipline and the excellence required to perform at the highest levels — he felt confined. "Roone had done everything he wanted to do in sports," said Don Ohlmeyer, an ABC producer and friend. "He changed an industry."

The wide world of sports was no longer wide enough to satisfy the ambitions of Roone Arledge. He needed a bigger arena.

While Munich had whetted his interest in news, Arledge's first instinct was to try his hand at show business. Characteristically, he began with a big show, a Frank Sinatra concert at Madison Square Garden that he produced as a prime-time special for ABC in 1974 and called, simply, "The Big Event." With Howard Cosell as host, the concert was broadcast live, and the ratings were terrific. Rumors arose that Arledge, as ABC's star executive, would soon take over the network's sagging entertainment division.

Instead, Arledge and Cosell teamed up to produce a live weekly variety show from the Ed Sullivan Theater in New York. The idea was to make Cosell the next Ed Sullivan, and "Saturday Night Live with Howard Cosell" premiered in September 1975 with star-power galore. The first show featured cameos by Sinatra and Ted Kennedy, a performance by John Denver, a duet featuring tennis great Jimmy Connors and Paul Anka, and the American debut of the Bay City Rollers, a Scottish rock group who were billed by Cosell as "the next Beatles." Arledge was never shy about selling his product.

But in the weeks that followed, Arledge and Cosell proved unable to transfer their magic to the entertainment stage. For "Saturday Night" to work, Arledge had to create a new show each week from scratch. Guests had to be booked, sets built, scripts written and edited — and Arledge found it hard to plan. "We were always flying by the seat of our pants," said Don Mischer, the director. When the ratings slid, Arledge began to doubt himself and blamed others for giving him bad advice. Later, he said, "When the research people with little scraps of paper told me children and old people want Kate Smith and tigers jumping through hoops, I went along with them. And it was all downhill from there." The show hit bottom when Cosell and Barbara Walters sang "Anything You Can Do, I Can Do Better." Howard and Barbara were no Sonny and Cher, and the show died a merciful death after only four months on the air.

While "Saturday Night" was Arledge's first major flop at ABC, he had an immediate opportunity to redeem himself at the 1976 Winter Olympics in Innsbruck. The Innsbruck games were not expected to generate high ratings, largely because NBC had failed to attract viewers to its telecasts of the Winter Olympics from Sapporo, Japan, in 1972. Worse, there were no stars on the 1976 American team except for figure skater Dorothy Hamill, who was barely known outside the precincts of "Wide World of Sports." Even Fred Silverman, the president of ABC Entertainment and a corporate rival of Arledge's, predicted that the Winter Games would be a programming disaster — not the kind of talk the sports people needed to hear as they tried to sell last-minute commercial spots to advertisers.

Arledge could not afford another failure. Shortly after New Year's, he journeyed to Austria, rented a helicopter, and with his aide Geoff Mason surveyed the mountains and valleys where the games would soon begin. Neither man spoke during the flight, but when they landed, Arledge had a plan. "I'm going to send a postcard back to the United States," he said. "We'll do it to 'The Sound of Music.' " The idea, he explained, was to deliver "lots of gemütlichkeit and pretty singing" to viewers who were not sports-minded.

Innsbruck became an artistic and financial triumph. Each night, Arledge opened the coverage with spectacular aerial footage of the Tyrol Alps, as trumpets played the stirring Olympic fanfare made famous by ABC. As usual, Arledge and his crew worked around the clock, taping events during daylight and feeding "live" coverage home between 1 A.M. and 4 A.M. The Olympics concluded on ABC with a stirring package of highlights set to the music of Beethoven's "Ode to Joy." The following summer in Montreal, Arledge once again demonstrated his mastery of the Olympics and put on a spectacular show. By then, "Saturday Night" was forgotten and Arledge's stock at ABC had climbed to an all-time high.

It was time to cash in. NBC approached Arledge with a multi-million-dollar offer that would have made him a consultant in sports and a producer of entertainment shows. Later, Arledge claimed that he had "five unsolicited offers, any of which would have paid me far more than I could ever make at ABC." But as he told television writer Kay Gardella of the *New York Daily News* in the fall of 1976, money "isn't the only consideration. I would much rather have it on my tombstone that I did something important."

His intentions became clear soon afterward over a long dinner at P. J. Clarke's with Fred Pierce, ABC's network president, who was both Arledge's boss and his pal. They talked breezily about ABC and its problems until the topic of news arose, when Arledge brought an unexpected intensity to the conversation. He told Pierce he'd like to take a shot at running ABC News. Pierce voiced enthusiasm — he had enormous confidence in Arledge's talents — but when Arledge called the next morning to follow up, Pierce tried to dismiss their conversation as "mostly booze talk."

One problem was that the job was filled. A low-key executive named Bill Sheehan was the president of ABC News, and while ABC's news operation was weak, few blamed Sheehan for the deficiencies; news had never been a corporate priority at ABC. More important, Pierce knew that neither of his bosses, ABC Inc. president Elton Rule and Leonard Goldenson, founder and chairman of ABC, would like the idea of putting Arledge in charge of News. "When I proposed Roone," Pierce said, "Elton and Leonard rolled their eyes and asked me if I had a screw loose."

Rule was extremely negative. He liked Sheehan, and he thought that Arledge was a cavalier executive who treated people badly. He never forgot how Arledge had dumped Keith Jackson, the football announcer and a good friend of Rule's, from "Monday Night Football" to make room for Frank Gifford. What rankled Jackson — and Rule — was that Arledge never called Jackson, who heard about his demotion from the press. "Keith was treated shabbily and so, too, were others over the years," Rule said.

Goldenson's reservations were more substantive. While he admired Arledge's work in Sports, Goldenson did not believe that anyone should run two divisions of his network. Arledge had left no doubt that he wanted News *added* to his portfolio. Moreover, Goldenson did not think that Arledge had the training or the temperament to be president of News, a job that traditionally had been held by an experienced journalist or an executive schooled in public affairs. "Making Roone president of ABC News was like throwing the deed to the family farm on the table," Goldenson said. "I couldn't be sure we'd win, but if we did, I thought we would win big."

Eventually, Pierce presented Goldenson with a stark choice: give ABC News to Arledge or watch him leave the network. "Fred was very insistent," Goldenson said. With Pierce blocking for him, Arledge had maneuvered his way to the goal line. Elton Rule told him that he could become president of ABC News.

Now it was Arledge's turn to ruminate — big decisions often paralyzed him. He went to Beverly Hills to see his old protégé Dick Ebersol, and they talked all night, as Arledge weighed the lucrative NBC offer against the challenges awaiting him at ABC News. "The choice is as simple as this," he summed up. "Riches beyond what anyone could want, as opposed to making a contribution to American life, really being a player."

The money was alluring. By then, Arledge had a son and three daughters approaching college age, and he maintained two expensive homes, an apartment on Central Park South and the country place in Sagaponack, Long Island. He had substantial financial obligations to Joan, who had ended their marriage in 1971 after he had left her stranded during a Hawaiian vacation so he could produce a college football game. (When asked in one interview how he invested his money, Arledge replied, "Lately, I've been investing rather heavily in divorce.") And Arledge had just married a stunning young woman named Ann Fowler, seventeen years his junior, a former Miss

Alabama who had been his secretary at ABC Sports. He also lived well, dining at New York's finest restaurants — he named one of his cats Silvio after the chef at Le Cirque — attending the opera and ballet, and golfing at the exclusive Winged Foot Golf Club, in Westchester County, and at the Royal and Ancient Golf Club of St. Andrews, in Scotland, where he held memberships. NBC's offer would have more than doubled his ABC salary of $1 million a year.

More than money, though, Arledge craved recognition — not mere fame, but the sense that he was regarded as someone who had made an impact, whose job mattered. By this time, his friends from Columbia had made a mark — Frankel had won a Pulitzer, Wald was running NBC News, and Grossman had become president of PBS. Arledge had been just as successful and better paid; his impact had been great, but he lagged behind them when it came to public esteem.

In Sports, Arledge believed, he'd never received credit for all he had done — despite his self-promotion. He had fought on behalf of sports journalism; it was Arledge, for example, who insisted that ABC be free to choose its own announcers, while the other networks gave the leagues veto power. Arledge also gave free rein to Cosell, who, for all his excesses, was the preeminent sports reporter on television. But sports was the toy box of journalism, and Arledge's achievements were not well understood. Often, he was described as the master of glitz, the father of the instant replay, or the inventor of trash sports. Or worse yet, as *Esquire* magazine headlined a 1974 profile of Arledge: "That Wonderful Person Who Brought You Howard Cosell." He didn't want *that* on his tombstone.

He accepted the job of president of ABC News. It was a prestige job, one where he could make a difference as well as establish his importance and seriousness. Arledge cared deeply about his reputation. He was, an old friend said, "an actor who lived by his notices."

The notices that greeted his appointment as president of ABC News on May 2, 1977, would have closed a Broadway show on opening night. The press instantly judged Arledge unfit to run ABC News. He was derided as the P. T. Barnum of sports and painted as a charlatan who would do anything to achieve success. The *New York Times* reported the news under the headline "Arledge Will Head ABC News; Disclaims Theatrical Flourishes" and sniffed that he was "one of television's leading showmen." *Time* raised the specter of "Network," the Paddy Chayefsky movie about a corporate power-player who corrupts a network news division. And Robert Lipsyte, who worked briefly for Arledge on "Saturday Night," warned that the evening news "could easily be delivered by an anchorteam of John Denver, Mason Reese, and Farrah Fawcett Majors."

Arledge was shell-shocked. Never again did he trust the press. "I just could not understand people who thought I was going to come in and destroy ABC News," he lamented.

Through no fault of his own, Arledge had become a lightning rod for concerns about the future of network news. Television critics who decried the beginnings of a star system, the incessant drive for ratings, and the sensationalism of local news viewed Arledge's appointment as another break with tradition. In a sense, they were right: Arledge's arrival at ABC News meant that a whole new way of thinking about television news had taken hold at ABC.

In the old way of thinking, television news was regarded as a branch of journalism — news was news, and television, like print or radio, was a means of presenting it. Executives in charge of network news, as a result, were veteran journalists, often with a background in print. This mind-set also shaped the networks' hiring practice for years as they drafted reporters from print, assuming that their skills were easily transferable to television. Walter Cronkite, Chet Huntley, David Brinkley, John Chancellor, and Harry Reasoner had all worked in print, however briefly, as had most of the executives to whom they reported. Every network news president except Richard Salant of CBS, a lawyer, had been a journalist.

By turning ABC News over to Arledge, Goldenson and Pierce were putting the emphasis on the *television* in television news. Pierce made the point when he said that Arledge would "bring a different perspective to the network's news through the eye of a production expert, with journalistic leanings." He was betting that Arledge's talents as a television producer would transfer to news. The task of network news, in this view, was the same as the business of network sports or, for that matter, network entertainment: assembling audiences to be sold to advertisers. Arledge was a winner in sports, and ABC needed a winner in news.

That kind of thinking was what worried the critics. It also troubled the veterans at ABC News. Those who had followed Arledge's career had watched, and even cheered, as he had expanded "Wide World of Sports," mined gold from the Olymipcs, and turned ordinary football games into wild and crazy spectacles on Monday nights. They had seen him fulfill the promise he had made to "add show business to sports!" They were terrified he would do the same with news.

* * *

Inside ABC News, Arledge was greeted like a skunk at a picnic. Nothing about him — not the bold-striped shirts, safari jackets, and cowboy boots he wore, not the oversize cigars he puffed, and not his marriage to a former beauty queen — fit the mold of what a network news president should be.

"Universally, this was considered to be the single biggest insult that management could inflict upon the news department," recalled Charles Gibson, a Washington correspondent. "It was to say that you guys are so bad or this operation is in so much trouble that we have to bring someone in from Sports." To lighten their gloom, the veterans joked about how Arledge would remake ABC's newscast. "What are we going to do with the middle commercial in the show?" they would say. "Are we going to call it halftime? And put a band on?"

The naysayers included Ted Koppel and Peter Jennings, who did more than worry or complain. They requested a meeting with Fred Pierce to try to block Arledge's appointment.

It was a risky move. While Koppel and Jennings would someday exercise considerable power at ABC News, they had scant hope then of influencing a decision made at the highest levels of the corporation. Koppel, thirty-seven, was respected as a State Department correspondent and weekend anchor, but he was barely known outside ABC. Jennings, thirty-eight, had been ABC's top anchor briefly in the 1960s, but he had failed and been sent overseas to rebuild his career and self-confidence. They barely knew Pierce, a square-jawed, stone-faced man with no feel for news. But they had invested their lives in ABC News. They held a stake in the company. And they feared Arledge would destroy all they had built.

The reporters rode up to the thirty-fifth floor of 1330 Avenue of the Americas, ABC's corporate headquarters, where they were ushered into Pierce's office. Green grapes and brie were laid out on a table, and Pierce poured three glasses of white wine. The network president was a cordial host, as always.

Koppel and Jennings presented their case. They conceded that Arledge had accomplished great things in Sports, but they argued that he lacked news experience and that his appointment would drive good people away.

If Sheehan had to be fired, they suggested, Pierce could replace him with Av Westin, a well-regarded executive who had left ABC.

Pierce heard them out politely but declined to respond, point by point, to their concerns. He did assure them that Arledge had no intention of cheapening ABC News. Then he escorted them out.

Koppel and Jennings realized then that there was no stopping Arledge; now they had to worry that he would learn about their mission. And Pierce warned Arledge not to expect a warm welcome from the old guard at ABC News.

Chapter Two

LAST WITH THE LEAST

THEY CAME BY AIR, land, and sea. Traveling on chartered jets, seaplanes, and limousines from points far and near, several dozen ABC News executives, producers, and correspondents converged on the Montauk Yacht Club on eastern Long Island. They had been summoned to meet their new leader, up close and personal, and as they arrived, they got their first look at Roone Arledge.

They did not like what they saw.

He sat at the head of a U-shaped wooden conference table, with the hint of a smile on his thin lips, looking like a nervous host in a room full of strangers. He was forty-five years old, but his round face had a boyish, ruddy glow and his attire was mid-1970s trendy: a blue-and-white polka-dot shirt, short-sleeved, open to mid-chest, revealing a gold chain that hung around his neck.

This, they thought, was the getup of a showman, not a newsman.

The Montauk meetings were Arledge's idea. He had scheduled the gatherings for a weekend in May, just before he moved into News, and had selected a place where he felt comfortable, a posh yacht club at the tip of Long Island, about thirty miles east of his own weekend retreat in Sagaponack. When ABC veterans heard that a charter plane carrying Washington bureau chief George Watson from La Guardia to Montauk had touched down en route to pick up Arledge in Sagaponack, they could not miss the message — the penny-pinching days of ABC News were over. Some felt the display of conspicuous consumption was overdone.

Most of the ABC News veterans were already prepared to dislike

Arledge. Resistance was strongest in the Washington bureau, where men like Frank Reynolds, Howard K. Smith, and Ted Koppel saw news not as a business but as a calling, as a lifelong commitment that required seriousness of purpose and a devotion to public service. They could not accept the idea that they had to take direction from a novice.

If the veterans brought preconceptions about Arledge to Montauk, he, too, arrived with a bias. He looked around the room and saw only failure. ABC News, unlike his sports operation, lost money, and its ratings lagged way behind CBS and NBC. "No one in their right minds wanted to work at ABC News," he would say. "It was a graveyard." Arledge intended to overhaul the place, especially after he learned about the opposition to his appointment.

These mutual suspicions put everyone on edge. When Arledge began one session by remarking innocently that better days were ahead for ABC News, Frank Reynolds took that as a put-down.

"You think we're all losers, don't you?" Reynolds said.

Behind the resentments was a fundamental disagreement over how to measure success in television news. Men like Reynolds, Koppel, and Sam Donaldson knew all too well that ABC trailed the other networks in the ratings, but they did not regard that as defeat; they saw themselves as smart, scrappy underdogs who covered the news at least as well as CBS and NBC. "Up and down the line, man for man, we were as good and in some areas better than our competitors," Donaldson said. "We didn't have as many resources. We didn't have the clout or impact. But we covered the stories." To the old guard, that was what matterd most: covering the news.

Arledge was not so high-minded. He saw ABC News as the Cleveland Indians of network news, perennial also-rans who could not compete. By any measure that counted in television — ratings, profits, or prestige — ABC News was failing, and in Arledge's view, those who thought otherwise were deluding themselves. "Compared to CBS and NBC, it was like we almost didn't exist in news," he said. "It was third because there were only three networks. Otherwise it would have been fifth or tenth."

Try as he might to be diplomatic, Arledge could not hide those feelings. They surfaced again when he made a mildly disparaging comment about ABC's coverage of the political conventions in 1976. He was trying to be upbeat — he promised that ABC would provide more convention and election coverage under his leadership — but the effect was not what he intended.

This time, it was Wally Pfister, a vice president for special events, who bristled. Pfister remembered that ABC's 1976 convention coverage had been curtailed not by the news division but by the network — to accommodate the baseball All-Star game, which was being shown by Arledge's ABC Sports.

"We asked for more time," he told Arledge. "You were fighting us."

Smiling, Arledge promised to fight as hard for News as he had for Sports. But how would he deal with conflicts between news and sports? This was another worry of the old guard. The journalists believed they were entitled to a full-time leader.

Throughout the weekend, traditionalists also listened for any hint that Arledge would bring entertainment values to the news. With that in mind, Marlene Sanders, a serious-minded vice president for documentaries, spoke up.

"What do you think of Geraldo Rivera?" she asked.

It was a loaded question, and everyone knew it; everyone, that is, except Arledge.

Rivera had become a flash point for critics who saw show-biz values reshaping broadcast news, particularly the action-oriented, personality-driven newscasts on local stations. Rivera was more than a personality, but his work as a hard-charging investigative reporter had been overshadowed by his flamboyant, self-promoting style. Rivera appeared on ABC entertainment programs, but he had been rebuffed by Bill Sheehan when he sought work at ABC News.

Arledge flunked the test.

Without hesitating, he replied that Rivera was very talented, that he might need guidance, but that he was the kind of reporter who could be terrific and who would play a big role at ABC News.

Sanders was appalled. She decided she was unlikely to develop any rapport with Arledge — a feeling that was entirely mutual.

Only a handful of people at Montauk sensed that Arledge's arrival might present opportunities. Jeff Gralnick, an aggressive producer who had worked at CBS, chafed at what he regarded as the sluggish, backward-looking mentality of the old ABC News. Looking straight at Arledge, Gralnick launched an attack on the old regime even though he was flanked by two of Sheehan's vice presidents.

"I promised my wife I'd come out here and come home still employed," Gralnick said, "but I'm telling you, a lot of what you're hearing is garbage. What this is, is a third-rate news division, with third-rate salaries and third-rate equipment.

"There are some people who may be comfortable with that," he added. He glanced to either side of him, to erase any doubt about whom he had in mind, then turned back to Arledge. "That's what you're the president of right now. If you can fix those things, then you can have a news division. If you can't, we might as well go home right now."

Arledge loved every word of it. That was the kind of competitive fire he felt was lacking at ABC News.

That night, in a private talk, Gralnick told Arledge that he had a job offer from NBC and asked bluntly, "Why do I want to work for you?"

"You want to work for me," Arledge replied, "because I'll make you work harder than you've ever worked, and you'll be better than you ever thought you could be." Gralnick stayed after getting a hefty raise. He became one of the few incumbents brought into Arledge's inner circle.

Sessions with groups of ABC people, who were shuttled in and out, stretched over two days, through lunches, cocktails, dinners, and drinks, which were followed by more talk and a late-night, high-stakes poker game. Arledge would begin the evening at the bar, then retreat to a small conference room for a series of private talks. It reminded one executive of the wedding scene from *The Godfather,* when Vito Corleone held court in a back room with only the most privileged guests.

By the end of the weekend, those who had listened to Arledge were struck by how little he had revealed. He seemed to respond favorably to almost every idea without committing to anything. His comments provided few clues about his intentions. For a time during the sessions, Marlene Sanders and a colleague amused themselves by passing scraps of paper back and forth — she'd write "bull" on it, and he'd write "shit."

When they went back to work on Monday, ABC staffers who had been to Montauk found themselves hard-pressed to answer questions from colleagues about Arledge or his plans. No one had any idea what he was going to do with ABC News.

Roone Arledge had scant interest in what had preceded him at ABC News. He preferred to look ahead, not behind, and his willingness to discard tradition was one of his great strengths — it was part of what made him a visionary.

But Arledge's disinterest was also driven by ego — before long, he would imply that ABC News barely existed before he came on the scene. "Nobody watched it," he would say. ABC was "not compet-itive, it was not well regarded, it was not anything." This was simply not the case, and Arledge's failure to recognize the strengths of the old ABC News widened the gulf between him and the veterans who were proud of their accomplishments. In fact, by 1977, ABC News had come a long way from its humble origins, although it was not nearly the equal of NBC or CBS.

This was true, for much of its lifetime, of all of ABC. Indeed, ABC had begun as a stepchild of NBC, which was forced by regulators to sell one of its two radio networks in 1941. Edward J. Noble, the Life Saver magnate, bought the NBC Blue Network for $8 million and renamed it the American Broadcasting Co. Lacking the money to expand into television, he later sold the company to a theater chain run by Leonard Goldenson.

When Goldenson took over in 1953, CBS and NBC were famed brand names. ABC, unknown and broke, was dubbed the "Almost Broadcasting Co." "We had no hit shows, no stars, and nothing in prospect but struggle," Goldenson said. ABC couldn't even broadcast its shows across America. While the company owned TV stations in five big cities, the network had only nine affiliates. It would take ABC more than twenty years to build an affiliate base to match that of its rivals.

With no tradition to guard, Goldenson welcomed risk-takers and mavericks like Arledge who thrived in the company's informal, free-wheeling atmosphere. They had nothing to lose: desperation bred innovation.

Goldenson, for example, was the first television executive to con-vince the Hollywood movie studios to produce programs for the net-works, a breakthrough that brought such shows as "Disneyland" and "Cheyenne," the first TV western, to ABC. Programmers at ABC realized that, to create hits, they needed fresh concepts, shows that were so unusual and promotable that they would practically grab viewers away from the established networks. In the 1950s and 1960s, ABC put on "77 Sunset Strip," the prototype private-eye show; "Ben Casey," television's first medical drama; and "Peyton Place," the first soap opera to succeed in prime time. And even when it came to television violence, ABC ignored constraints and scored with "The Untouchables," the bloodiest show of its day. This environment was ideal for Arledge, whose departures from tradition at ABC Sports — "Wide World," "Monday Night Football," and Howard Cosell —

were welcomed. "We were gambling in our growth all along the line," said Goldenson.

The gambling paid off big when Goldenson made ABC the network of the young. In a landmark study done for ABC, Dr. Paul Lazarsfeld, a Columbia researcher, found that the most popular shows at CBS and NBC, which showcased stars from radio, appealed to older audiences. He recommended that ABC pursue the young, whose viewing habits were still forming. Conveniently, ABC's advertising salesmen found that they could sell young audiences to sponsors by demonstrating that their buying habits, like their viewing habits, were fluid. By the mid-1960s, ABC had a lock on the Clearasil crowd by showing "Gidget," "Shindig," "Tammy," "The Patty Duke Show," and "The Flintstones" all in prime time.

But the youth strategy that powered ABC's sitcoms and dramas stunted the growth of ABC News. Kids and teenagers who were drawn to ABC's prime-time shows didn't watch network news. Older viewers, who cared about news, had no reason to tune to ABC.

Besides, the habits of news viewers were notoriously hard to break. Loyalties formed early. CBS News, led by Edward R. Murrow, established itself during World War II, and NBC News created the team of Huntley and Brinkley at the 1956 political conventions — long before anyone paid serious attention to news at ABC.

For years, news was an afterthought at ABC. John Charles Daly, the network's first anchor, was better known as the host of the panel show "What's My Line?" on CBS. In the early 1950s, Daly served as an ABC vice president for news, sports, special events, and religious programming — all of them backwaters.

By his own account, Goldenson ignored ABC News until 1960, when U.S. Senator John Pastore, who chaired a committee responsible for broadcast regulation, urged him to develop news and documentary programs. News was then a money-losing prestige vehicle, albeit one that came in handy when the network owners needed to placate regulators in Washington.

Goldenson also found Jim Hagerty, the first president of ABC News, in Washington, where he was press secretary to President Eisenhower. Hagerty was a lifelong print man who hired newspaper reporters like John Scali of the AP, Bob Clark of the *Washington Star,* and Bill Lawrence of the *New York Times* and threw them on television. Lawrence, who covered the White House, was the most distinguished, but he was ill-suited for television because of his extremely raspy voice.

Hagerty paid no heed, blithely assuring his new men that they need not visit a voice coach or learn about makeup. He thought television put too much emphasis on cosmetics.

Elmer Lower, who replaced Hagerty in 1963, was better prepared for the job. A former news executive at CBS and NBC, Lower built the foundation of a worldwide news-gathering organization; he taught the mechanics of television to the old-timers, stationed ABC's first film crews overseas, and, most important, recruited talented young people. Lower hired Frank Reynolds, Peter Jennings, Ted Koppel, Sam Donaldson, Tom Jarriel, Steve Bell, and Barrie Dunsmore, all of whom later became star anchors or reporters. These were the men who bristled when Arledge said that "no one in their right minds wanted to work at ABC News." They loved working there.

"They were very heady days for young correspondents," said Ted Koppel, who at age twenty-six went to cover Vietnam. "I don't think CBS or NBC would have hired a twenty-three-year-old correspondent. But ABC had to take chances the other networks simply would not take. We took a perverse kind of pride in being the youngest, the poorest, and in many instances the hardest working of the news divisions."

Still, Lower's ABC News faced staggering disadvantages. His news budget was puny; in 1964, for example, ABC spent $5 million while CBS and NBC spent about $30 million apiece. Affiliate problems also persisted — for most of the 1960s, ABC's evening news couldn't be seen anywhere in Ohio. And airtime was hard to come by because the network was reluctant to displace money-making entertainment shows. "Goldenson was a bottom-line man," Lower said. "He didn't really care about news."

But Goldenson couldn't be blamed for ABC News's most visible problem — its failure to develop a stable anchor for the evening news. Neither Hagerty nor Lower could find anyone to compete with Walter Cronkite on CBS or the NBC team of Huntley and Brinkley, although it was not for lack of effort.

First, Hagerty experimented with a seven-man anchor rotation, including, among others, radio veteran Edward P. Morgan and Fendall Yerxa, a former editor at the *New York Herald Tribune*. They were followed by an anchor trio consisting of the hoarse-voiced Bill Lawrence, labor reporter Bill Sheehan, and NBC castoff John Cameron Swayze. Ron Cochran, an ex-FBI agent and CBS correspondent, was next into the breach, followed by Morgan and the opinionated

Howard K. Smith, another CBS veteran. In 1965, the season of "Gidget" and "Shindig," twenty-six-year-old Peter Jennings took over for an unhappy two-year stint. Bob Young, his successor, lasted just five months before yielding to Frank Reynolds. This parade of fresh and not-so-fresh faces put off the audience; these were the 1960s, when the news itself provided all the turmoil any viewer could want.

In the meantime, CBS and NBC grew rapidly. They opened bureaus around the world, exploited the new technology of satellites, and, sensing a growing appetite for news, expanded their evening newscasts from fifteen minutes to half an hour in September 1963. This was a pivotal moment for network news; literally within months, polls showed that television had inched ahead of newspapers as the primary source of news for Americans. With a nightly half hour, CBS and NBC could deliver more news during an era when the big stories — civil rights, Vietnam, space exploration, and urban unrest — were ideally suited for television. Not until 1967 did ABC introduce a half-hour newscast.

Only in 1970, by hiring Harry Reasoner away from CBS, did ABC truly enter the dinner-hour news competition. When Reasoner jumped to ABC for the then-princely sum of $200,000 a year, he brought a strong, stable presence to the anchor desk for the first time. A star at CBS, Reasoner had served as Cronkite's substitute on the "CBS Evening News" and, with Mike Wallace, co-anchored the first two seasons of "60 Minutes." His familiarity and credibility paid instant dividends, as those affiliates that had not broadcast any network news began to carry ABC's newscast.

With Reasoner and Howard K. Smith as anchors and Av Westin as the executive producer, the "ABC Evening News" won its first favorable notices. Westin, another CBS alumnus, brought energy, intelligence, and a sharp editorial focus to the broadcast. Ratings grew, as did commercial revenues. While CBS and Cronkite remained dominant, ABC closed to within striking distance of NBC. But the broadcast could not sustain its momentum, and the ratings faded, as did hopes of catching NBC.

When Elmer Lower left in 1974, his replacement, Bill Sheehan, found himself on the defensive. "The network was losing money and there was a very tight squeeze on our budgets," Sheehan recalled. When ABC's prime-time entertainment ratings fell, Sheehan had to lay off staff and fend off pressures to close bureaus. Getting airtime for special reports proved as difficult as ever, as Sam Donaldson learned, to his everlasting frustration, at the height of the Watergate scandal when he could not get onto ABC to break the news of the Saturday Night Massacre.

"We felt we had reached a plateau," Sheehan said. That was one view — to others, it looked as if ABC News had slid into a valley.

One dissatisfied viewer was Fred Pierce, who had been named president of ABC Television in 1974 and engineered a remarkable turnaround at the network. Pierce and programming whiz Fred Silverman put on such hit shows as "Happy Days," "Starsky and Hutch," and "Laverne and Shirley," and soon after, ABC became the top-rated network in prime time. Arledge's ABC Sports also made money and won plaudits. And Pierce launched "Good Morning America," which mounted a strong challenge to NBC's "Today."

All that was left was to fix ABC News. For the first time, the network had money for a rebuilding campaign.

Instead, Pierce tried a quick fix. In 1976, ABC hired Barbara Walters to co-anchor the "ABC Evening News." It was a high-stakes gamble in the ABC tradition.

Walters, then forty-six, was the most celebrated woman in television news, a highly promotable star who as co-host of "Today" had become famous for interviewing presidents, world leaders, and Hollywood celebrities. Pierce saw her hiring as a "double whammy" — her arrival would lift ABC's evening news, while her departure would damage NBC's morning franchise, which he had targeted with "Good Morning America." While Pierce was no feminist, he figured that ABC would get credit for being first to hire a woman as its evening news anchor. And he was sure that Walters would bring an avalanche of publicity — as, indeed, she did.

Pierce also planned to expand the newscast to an hour or, at least, forty-five minutes. A longer program, he believed, would allow Walters to do high-profile interviews and ensure that Harry Reasoner would not have to cede precious airtime. Bill Sheehan loved the idea of doing an hour; for once, ABC would lead the way in news.

So eager were they to land Walters that her demand for a $1 million salary, about twice the going rate for a network anchor, never became a significant issue. ABC News paid her $500,000, and the entertainment division put up another $500,000 for a series of prime-time interview specials.

Walters earned every dime — although her stint on the evening news proved disastrous. She would be faulted for many things during her years at ABC News, but no one ever accused Barbara Walters of not working hard for her money.

Somebody was trying to outmuscle Dan Rather. That, he vowed, was a mistake no one would make twice.

The CBS newsman stood outside a church on Fifth Avenue, where he had arrived early on a Sunday in 1969 to cover a visit by President Nixon. He was holding his ground against a crowd of reporters jostling for better vantage points.

As Rather recalled, he became aware that "someone was torpedoing toward the front at about knee height" and decided that whoever it was would "get crowned" if he got in Rather's way.

"Just as I figured," Rather said, "this intruder wiggled through the crowd, straightened up out of a kind of Vietnamese crouch, and stepped on my new shoes."

He looked down to see Barbara Walters.

Rather was irritated, but he stepped aside. Walters turned sweet as could be, even promising to have NBC pay for any damage she had done to Rather's shoes.

That was Walters — tenacious, competitive yet charming, willing to use whatever it took to get where she was going. Those qualities brought her success, and they were the qualities that irritated rivals and viewers alike. To some degree, she was the victim of a double standard. "People think Mike Wallace is doing a great, go-getting job, yet they think Barbara's aggressive and pushy," said Dick Wald when he was president of NBC News and Walters's boss. But by any standard, Walters drove herself — and those around her — relentlessly.

She never stopped working. Producers grew accustomed to taking her calls at all hours; she overscheduled herself and ran late for appointments. Flying home after a long day's work, Walters could not relax; she shifted into what a producer called her "woulda, shoulda, coulda phase," second-guessing her efforts, working on a script, or preparing for her next assignment.

Idle time left her fretful. Walters had planned to spend the summer between leaving "Today" and joining ABC "eating candy and reading trashy novels," she said. Instead, she appeared at both national political conventions, taped an interview with Barbra Streisand for a prime-time special, and helped to plan a party thrown in her honor by ABC. She chafed at being off the air and called it "the worst summer I can remember."

"One of the problems with my life," Walters said, "probably the only problem, is that I feel guilty doing anything just for pleasure. I have to learn sometimes how just to have pleasure." She enjoyed time with her daughter, but by the mid-1970s, she had been married and divorced twice.

What made her run? At first, Walters had no choice — not if she wanted to be taken seriously in a business that was notoriously inhospitable to women. But Walters's intensity persisted long after she had overcome the obstacles an ambitious woman faced in a man's world. Other forces were at work, forces that those who know her trace back to her early years.

Barbara Walters was born in Boston on September 25, 1929, two years before the date she gave as her birthdate. (She had a sixtieth birthday party in 1991.) Her father, Lou Walters, owned the famed Latin Quarter nightclubs in New York and Miami. Dena Walters was a devoted mother, especially when it came to Barbara's older sister, Jacqueline, who was retarded. As a girl, Barbara was pampered with expensive toys, fine clothes, and summer vacations in Europe.

But her childhood was also riddled with uncertainty. Lou Walters was rarely home. She attended five schools before she was fifteen, took refuge in schoolwork when she couldn't make friends, and recalled "being always on the outside." Her biographer, Jerry Oppenheimer, who interviewed childhood friends and relatives, wrote that "a sense of loneliness and rejection haunted much of her childhood, along with a craving for attention and an intense desire to prove herself worthy of it."

Financial insecurity also plagued the family. Lou Walters's nightclub business fell on hard times; people were staying home to get their entertainment from television. He declared bankruptcy in 1966, and he owed $100,000 in back taxes to the IRS. From then on, Walters helped support her parents and her sister. "What people don't understand is that I *had* to work," she said.

By then, Walters had practically forced herself onto the air on "Today." She had begun as a writer, at a time when the only women on the air were the actresses or models who hosted fashion and cooking segments as the "Today" girl. Walters was pretty enough for the job — a green-eyed five-foot-five brunette, she wore conservative but stylish clothes — but she was held back for a time by her lisp, which gave her trouble with her *r*'s and *l*'s. Nor did she have any desire to assemble casseroles on television.

But Walters wangled feature reporting assignments and handled them well. Everyone knew she was smart and dedicated. So, in 1964, she replaced the actress Maureen O'Sullivan as the "Today" girl — although no one ever called Walters that again. Walters rewrote the job description, doing field reports across America and preparing so thoroughly for interviews that she was accused of upstaging laid-back host Hugh Downs. Walters fought the patronizing attitudes of producers who pushed her to do food and fashion and scored such exclusives as the first extended interview with Secretary of State Dean Rusk about Vietnam.

Walters became the leading personality on "Today" after Downs left in 1970. Even then, she had to defer to new host Frank McGee, who treated her with scorn.

"If we did political interviews from Washington," Walters said, "Frank insisted on asking the first three questions. Then I was allowed to step in." Walters had no choice but to go back into the field. "If I were able to get them on my own and I could then do them on film, outside the studio, I could do more hard-news interviews, which I enjoyed," she said. She interviewed Presidents Johnson, Nixon, and Ford, their first ladies, cabinet members, foreign heads of state, and countless celebrities. These interviews, which began as a product of necessity, became her trademark.

Walters endured fifteen years of 4:30 A.M. wake-up calls for "Today," but the morning exposure was not enough for her. To prove she could carry a show on her own, Walters became host of a daily syndicated program called "Not for Women Only." It made money for her and NBC.

More than money, though, Walters hungered for approval. She needed constant reassurance that she was doing good work, to the point where co-workers joked with her about it. When *Newsweek* put her on the cover in 1974, she was thrilled but wondered out loud whether *Time* would sell more copies that week. A producer told her, "You're insatiable."

Her secretary, Judi Beck, once said, "If there are twelve good reviews on a special and one bad review, from Oshkosh or someplace, Barbara will feel terrible about the bad one and ignore the rest." Walters herself confessed to an interviewer, "I have forty years of feeling insecure. It just doesn't end." Her neediness sometimes left her insensitive to others, and she was harsh with those who did not live up to her high standards. "Without meaning to be, Barbara can be cruel," a longtime associate said.

Yet Walters had a generous and compassionate side, too, as

colleagues in trouble learned. She always sent cards or flowers when co-workers took ill, and her loyalty to friends was legendary. Her personal assistants got expensive gifts for the holidays, and kindnesses were extended even to their relatives; when a "20/20" publicist's father took ill, Walters sent him a lovely note in the hospital, thanking him for sharing his daughter with her and ABC.

She also displayed an endearing ability to laugh at her own foibles. Once, while preparing a newscast with Reasoner, she was called on to describe an event that happened at Mount Ararat, in Turkey. Why, she lamented, couldn't it have been Mount Kisco?

Virtually all these facets of Walters's personality came through on the screen. There was a restless energy to her questioning, an insistent tone to her voice, and when reading copy, a tendency to hurry, as if she were perpetually behind schedule. Her empathy and vulnerability showed through too.

Not surprisingly, she provoked passion among viewers. Mail to "Today" was divided nearly evenly between her fans and critics. "Either get rid of Barbara Walters or put a gag in her mouth," one viewer wrote. Walters was thin-skinned, so aides tried to shelter her from critical mail or unfavorable press.

That proved impossible when she was hired by ABC. For weeks, Walters was the target of outrage over her new job and million-dollar salary. Her decision to switch networks for a more visible, higher-paid position, as any man would, provoked nasty attacks.

Headline writers had a field day. "Doll Barbie to Learn Her ABC's," said the *New York Daily News*. The *Washington Post* called her "A Million-Dollar Baby Handling 5-and-10 Cent News." Even the *Christian Science Monitor* cast Walters as a fickle woman, saying, "Barbara Leaves Jim for Harry."

What hurt most was the response from the news establishment. Richard Salant, the president of CBS News, said, "This isn't journalism — this is a minstrel show. Is Barbara a journalist or is she Cher?" Walter Cronkite said he felt "the sickening sensation that we were all going under, that all of our efforts to hold television news aloof from show business had failed." Over at NBC, David Brinkley observed, "Being an anchor is not just a matter of sitting in front of a camera and looking pretty."

Walters could not believe how cruel people could be. Much as she tried to convince herself that the criticism was fueled by sexism and even jealousy, she took it personally. She was being treated, she thought, "like a Rockette dancing my way onto the stage, like some terrible show business figure." She was shaken. Was this to be her reward for working so long and so hard?

In no time at all, everyone could see that Barbara Walters was not going to save ABC News. The day after Walters's ABC debut, David Brinkley began NBC's "Nightly News" with a wry comment on her opening-night performance. "Good evening," he said, in his clipped style, pausing slightly. "And welcome back."

Viewers who tuned in to ABC News to see what a million-dollar anchor looked like soon returned to CBS or NBC. Walters was not especially good at reading the news, and the plan to showcase her interviews had to be dropped after Pierce's grand hopes for an hour-long newscast were dashed by ABC's affiliates. Reasoner was unkind and unhappy; he never thought that he'd needed a co-anchor.

The only person at ABC who stood to gain from the problems was Roone Arledge. The handling of Walters confirmed his belief that the management at ABC News was inept. He knew Bill Sheehan and his aides, and while he found them pleasant, he thought that they were dull and lifeless. He felt the same way about their programs. He did not see much talent in the news division, and the talent he saw was misused. All this led him to describe ABC News as "a graveyard."

The truth was that ABC News was anything but a graveyard. None of Arledge's predecessors could claim to be men of vision or ideas, but considering that money was always tight, they had built a solid, if colorless, news division. ABC News had a first-rate Washington bureau, strong producers and correspondents, and a good mix of veterans and young people in the field. As for future stars, Arledge inherited Walters, Jennings, Koppel, Donaldson, and Charles Gibson — albeit in the wrong roles.

This team had valuable players and even a few all-stars. What it lacked was vision and leadership, money, depth, and showmanship — all of which Arledge stood ready to provide. But his misreading of the history of ABC News meant that Roone Arledge would fail, for a time, to recognize all the talent he had sitting on his own bench.

Chapter Three

THAT UNCERTAIN SUMMER

ROONE ARLEDGE wasted no time making changes at ABC News, and there was no way anyone could escape the turmoil. Ted Koppel tried — he set off on vacation — but by the time the trip was over he was sure his career at ABC News had also reached its end. It was a vacation he would never forget.

Koppel's plans had been unorthodox from the get-go. Strapped for money — he had been working part-time while his wife, Grace Anne, went to law school — the Koppels had two weeks to spend with their four children. They found a week-long cruise to Bermuda available at summer bargain rates and arranged to take it twice. In between the two cruises, Koppel had an afternoon to kill in New York, so he stopped by ABC to see some friends. By the time he reboarded the ship, his vacation was in ruins.

Koppel had learned during the layover that Phil Bergman, who produced ABC's Saturday night newscast, had been removed from his job by Arledge. As the program's anchor, Koppel was distressed — with good reason.

For one thing, Bergman was a friend. An amiable old-timer, Phil Bergman had joined ABC in 1962, following his older brother, Jules, ABC's longtime science editor. As anchor and producer, Koppel and Bergman enjoyed an easy rapport; they shared a mild cynicism about the world in general and television news in particular.

Koppel was also disturbed because he had not been told about the change by Arledge. While he realized the new president could and would do whatever he pleased at ABC News, Koppel thought that he was entitled to be informed of a change of producers, simply as a courtesy. He felt snubbed.

Finally, Koppel figured that Bergman's removal was a prelude to his own. Anchoring the Saturday program meant a lot to him; he not only read the news and helped shape the lineup but also wrote a closing commentary each week. He had always wanted to be an anchor for ABC.

Koppel had no way of knowing what Arledge thought of him, but the evidence was not encouraging. In the three months since Arledge had taken over, Koppel had called him several times, hoping to begin a relationship. None of his calls was returned.

As their ship headed out to sea again, Koppel unhappily told Grace Anne that he didn't think he could work at a place where he could not even talk to the boss. He stewed for a few days, and by the time they reached Bermuda, he had made up his mind to quit. He cabled his resignation to Arledge.

Koppel's discontent had simmered for weeks. He was not alone. Few ABC News veterans enjoyed the summer of 1977, Arledge's first at ABC News. They feared for their jobs and for the news division. "The whole place became very paranoid," Phil Bergman said. "Doors would shut and secret conferences would take place. It was like you might imagine the change in power would take place in the Kremlin."

Koppel had special reason to worry. Except for anchoring on Saturdays, he'd been off the air for a year, giving him no chance to impress Arledge with his work. Koppel certainly wasn't going to wow the new boss with his looks: he had always looked younger than his age, with his lopsided boyish grin, bushy hair, and ears that stuck out so far he'd been teased and called Dumbo as a kid. How Koppel had become a network anchorman, even on Saturdays, mystified Arledge, who didn't care to investigate, not after he heard about Koppel's meeting with Fred Pierce.

When Arledge received Koppel's resignation, he ignored it. "I had other, more pressing things to do," Arledge said. "I didn't want him to resign, but I also didn't, at that time, value him as much as I later came to." Besides, Arledge was accustomed to the looser environment of Sports, where he moved people around at will, without elaborate negotiations; he saw no need to explain to Ted Koppel why he had taken Phil Bergman off Saturday nights. The fact was, he'd planned to remove Koppel, too, and soon did.

On his last Saturday newscast, Koppel quit once more, this time over the air. He wished his successors, Tom Jarriel and Sylvia Chase, good luck and signed off, he thought, for good. "I was quite choked up," he recalled, "because I had already been with ABC, at that point, for fourteen years." When he went into the men's room to compose himself, he was consoled by veteran producer Bill Lord.

There matters stood until others intervened. Bill Sheehan, the outgoing news president, tried to get Koppel to rescind his resignation. "I don't think we can work things out," Koppel told him, "because I don't feel that I can work for a man who doesn't return phone calls and with whom I have no contact." Sheehan also lobbied Arledge, as did Arledge's secretary, Carol Grisanti, a savvy woman who admired Koppel. Eventually, she arranged for Koppel and Arledge to have lunch.

They met at Alfredo's, Arledge's favorite restaurant in those days, where Koppel became one of the first people at ABC News to experience what he would later, with admiration, describe simply as "the treatment."

The lunch stretched over three hours. At the outset, Arledge said he'd like Koppel to stay at ABC News, which Koppel instantly agreed to do. Then, in response to questions from Arledge, Koppel talked on and on — about his experiences with Henry Kissinger and his views on foreign affairs, as well as his history at ABC, his own career goals, and his ideas about news. Arledge turned on the charm, and in a one-on-one setting few could be more charming. For all his power, ego, and supposed flamboyance, Arledge displayed a soft-spoken, inquisitive, and sometimes self-effacing conversational manner that most people found disarming. He was genuinely curious and a wonderful listener, content to offer perceptive reactions while allowing others to talk. Later, there would be times — when he was trying to woo a star from a rival network or meeting an important figure for the first time — when he would prepare for such talks. "Hostesses like Liz Rohatyn and Ethel Kennedy always get annoyed," he once said, "because if I go to a party, I always try to find out beforehand who's going to be there so I can get a bio on them and be able to make intelligent conversation." Since most people like nothing more than to talk about themselves, the technique was effective.

Koppel was bowled over. "It was one of the great experiences in life," he remembered. "I floated out of the room, absolutely convinced that my problems were over and everything was now going to be wonderful." It wasn't mere flattery; the truth was that Arledge was far more intelligent, thoughtful, and likable than people expected him to be in those days. Of course, Koppel had come to the lunch with minimal expectations — and no job — so the fact that Arledge wanted him back was enough to buoy his spirits. At the end of the afternoon, Arledge asked Koppel to send him a videotape of his work and promised to consider him for a role on a new prime-time program being developed by ABC News.

In the fall, though, Koppel returned to his old correspondent's job at the State Department. The cast for the prime-time program, "20/20," did not include his name, and after a while, his euphoria evaporated. He missed anchoring, missed the chance to present his version of the news to millions of Americans, and wished he could be a bigger player at ABC News. In Arledge's mind, though, Koppel was an able correspondent, no more and no less. The State Department was just where he thought Ted Koppel belonged.

Had Roone Arledge stopped to catalog the problems facing him when he arrived at ABC News, he might have been discouraged. The news division needed strong leadership and talented producers and correspondents to join the incumbents, plus vast amounts of new equipment. Ratings for the evening news were sliding lower, while the anchors, Harry Reasoner and Barbara Walters, barely spoke to each other off camera. Aside from an occasional documentary, the only other news program at ABC was a tired Sunday morning talk show called "Issues and Answers."

Arledge did not bring with him a master plan for ABC News. Nor would it have struck him as useful to draft one. That wasn't the way he worked. His methods were more haphazard. He would play with ideas — toss them out, see how others reacted, and, ideally, test them on the screen — and watch for opportunities, always staying "on the balls of his feet," as an aide put it. Like his father's hero, FDR, Arledge believed in "bold, persistent experimentation."

While Arledge had no roadmap to guide him, he was never short of ideas. He began lobbing them out as soon as he was named president of News.

"I would like to experiment with utilizing many anchor people," he told one television writer. "It would depend on where news is happening, but I would like to see us with anchors at least in New York, Washington, and Europe — either London or Paris."

He told another interviewer that television needed to explain the news, not just cover it. "It's perfectly valid to cover a war in Zaire if we're not just covering it because there are pictures of tanks," Arledge said. "But I think we have to tell our viewers what this is liable to mean to them. . . . What is Russia's role, what is our interest, and why do we care if there's a war in Zaire. What the hell does it mean?" Zaire, he figured, was the news equivalent of barrel jumping; viewers could be persuaded to watch if they were given a reason to care.

And Arledge always said that, to achieve success, ABC News would have to cover big stories better than anyone else. This, he thought, was critical, if only to shift the battleground away from the dinner-hour news dominated by CBS and Walter Cronkite. All-out, aggressive crisis coverage had paid dividends for Arledge and ABC in Munich in 1972; it would work again, he was sure, when another big story came along. "We're going to be the best," he said, "by establishing a reputation that if the world comes to an end, people are going to tune in to ABC to see if it really did or did not." He used to say, "The day after the atomic bomb hits, we want every television set to be burned in to Channel Seven."

The only drawback to that plan was that the world does not come to an end, or threaten to, very often. Moreover, Arledge arrived at ABC News during the summer, the slow season for news, when not much usually happens. Not much did. But Arledge wasn't going to let that stand in his way. In the line made famous by onetime ABC anchor John Cameron Swayze, he was about to "go hopscotching the world for headlines."

His very first week on the job, Arledge spotted an opportunity to test out his theory — and his troops.

Terrorists seeking independence for South Molucca, a cluster of eight hundred tiny islands in the Indonesian archipelago, seized a school and a train in the Netherlands. They released the children but held fifty-five rail passengers hostage while demanding freedom for Moluccan political prisoners and a plane to fly them to safety.

It was not the end of the world. It was not even war in Zaire. But it would have to do.

With unaccustomed force, ABC News attacked the story. Producers, crews, and correspondents were flown in from London, New York, and Chicago. "We steamrolled that story," recalled Pete Simmons, the producer in charge in Holland. "We had something like six crews and four producers, and we just beat the hell out of everybody."

Back in New York, Arledge took command in the control room as the news division broke into regular programming to present live blow-by-blow accounts of the hijacking, which lasted twenty-one days, until, to everyone's relief, the Dutch retook the train. Few Americans cared about South Molucca — no amount of explaining would change that — but Arledge had delivered a message inside ABC News that resources would be available to cover breaking news. That became even more clear when, in the midst of the Moluccan affair, another ABC army of crews and correspondents was airlifted to Tennessee to cover the prison escape of James Earl Ray, the murderer of Martin Luther King Jr. An enthusiastic Arledge declared that ABC might form a "flying squad of expert reporters" to cover big stories — expert at what, he didn't say.

In his search for an Olympic-size story, Arledge next settled on the arrest of David Berkowitz, the accused killer known as the "Son of Sam" who had been the target of a massive manhunt after murdering or assaulting thirteen people in New York. Arledge got so caught up in the excitement that he arrived at police headquarters at 3 A.M., according to the *Los Angeles Times,* which reported that he was dressed "as if for a touch football game, a glass of scotch in one hand, a portable two-way radio in the other." Arledge later denied having a drink, but he remained at the scene to oversee live morning coverage and then headed back to ABC to propose that all that night's "ABC Evening News" be devoted to Son of Sam coverage.

Fortunately for Arledge, he was persuaded to reserve a few minutes for other news — including, as Washington anchor Howard K. Smith slyly put it, "one item of truly historic importance," an agreement on the Panama Canal treaty. But ABC spent more than 19 action-packed minutes on the Son of Sam, while CBS did 8:40 and NBC 8:56. No angle was left uncovered — there were reports from police headquarters, a profile of Berkowitz, a Barbara Walters interview with the police chief, commentary from columnist Jimmy Breslin and psychologist Sonya Friedman, and, most memorable, a breathless report from Geraldo Rivera, who, wearing his customary jeans and T-shirt, cast aside the legal niceties to describe the accused as a "killer" and "fiend."

Rivera knew he was playing to the emotions of the crowd. "I wanted to remind our viewers that this butcher had essentially confessed to his crimes," Rivera said later. "I was excited and angry; there was a venom to my voice as I spoke of this killer, a disdain that told viewers what I thought of this man and what he had done."

In ABC's Washington bureau, producers and correspondents watched in silence; the Son of Sam coverage confirmed their worst fears about Arledge. With Frank Reynolds and his producers in the lead, they drafted a letter to Arledge deploring the excessive, tabloid-style approach. After delicate negotiations over the tone, a dozen or so correspondents signed on, including Reynolds, Smith, Sam Donaldson, and Brit Hume. They insisted that they wanted only to persuade Arledge to rethink his approach, but the letter made its way into the newspapers.

Arledge was incensed. He was always sensitive to criticism in the press, and never more so than during that summer. "This was a grenade that landed in his home," an aide said.

Still, he plunged ahead. Arledge was guided by his instincts, and his instincts told him that the biggest story in America on August 16, 1977, six days after the Son of Sam fiasco, was the death of Elvis Presley. Again, Arledge turned to Rivera, who was becoming his favorite reporter, this time assigning him to anchor an 11:30 P.M. special.

While the traditionalists hated seeing Rivera as a network anchor, a more significant controversy was set off by Arledge's decision to make Presley's death the lead story on the evening news. The other networks led with the news that President Jimmy Carter's Panama Canal treaty was opposed by Ronald Reagan but supported by former President Ford. From rival CBS News came the charge that Arledge was applying entertainment values to ABC's newscast, as critics had predicted he would.

"Elvis Presley was dead — so he was dead," declared Richard Salant, the president of CBS News, a man who took his news seriously. "Our job is not to respond to public taste," he said. Arledge replied that Presley "dropping dead of a heart attack at the age of forty-two was just a little less predictable than Ronald Reagan coming out against the Panama Canal treaty." Presley, he said, "affected the lives of millions of Americans who are clearly interested in him and his death."

Now Arledge found himself drawn into debate over a fundamental question: What is news?

Tradition at all the networks had long held that their primary obligation was to present stories of significance. By the 1970s, when television had become the leading source of news for most Americans, CBS News went so far as to codify that doctrine in a book of standards and practices. "We in broadcast journalism," the rule book said ponderously, "cannot, should not and will not base our judgments on what we think the viewers and listeners are 'most interested' in. . . . Our judgments must turn on the best professional judgments we can come to on what is important, rather than what is merely interesting." This was an admittedly elitist approach. As Salant said,

"Our job is to give people not what they want but what they ought to have." Putting on the "merely interesting" amounted to pandering for ratings.

Arledge was not constrained by such traditional journalistic values, which, in any event, were not strictly observed even at CBS. Beyond that, such debates held no interest for him. He was not one to theorize, and he would never dream of publishing page after page of rules in the CBS manner — that was the opposite of staying on the balls of your feet. While Arledge wanted public esteem, he needed competitive success, even if that meant breaking a few rules. "There is a beguiling kind of temptation to try and please your fellow broadcasters, your peers, and everybody in the news establishment," he said. "If I do that, then that's probably the worst thing I can do." Arledge preferred to approach the news without preconceptions. An aide from that era said, "He went in remarkably fearless, with an absolute blank-slate, open-mind, tabula-rasa attitude." Arledge's loyalists took to derisively calling the traditionalists the "Capital J's" — for journalists.

But if Arledge's approach differed from that of CBS's Salant or the "Capital J's" at ABC, it was not because he was trying to cheapen the news, as some charged. He learned from the reaction to such excesses as the Son of Sam coverage that there were limits beyond which he could not go. But Arledge *was* trying to find ways to connect with the viewers. As Dick Ebersol, his former Sports aide, put it, "Roone constantly thought about two things — show and audience." This could mean untangling a complex story or providing background on a world leader. Or it could mean satisfying public curiosity about the death of Elvis. Dick Salant could call that pandering, but to Arledge that was a producer's job — to package the news so that it mattered to viewers. Arledge's nose for news was untrained, but his instincts were sound — to go after stories with impact, stories that could be turned into victories for ABC News.

Soon after arriving at ABC News, Arledge took a tour of the newsroom with Jeff Ruhe and Peggy Brim, two young assistants who worked for him at ABC Sports. What he saw disheartened him: the people seemed listless, and the place didn't seem to have much spark. Afterward, the twentysomething Ruhe joked, "I'd like to have the Grecian Formula concession for this crowd." Arledge agreed, saying, "You could practically smell the formaldehyde."

Everyone from Sports felt the same way. At ABC Sports, Brim said, "there was not one person who was not a commando. Even the secretaries had a spring in their step." By comparison, she said, ABC News "was in decay. People were dispirited and lifeless, and the technology was from the stone age." Arledge badly wanted to bring the Sports culture to News — to energize the News people and demand that they work harder and smarter.

He began by importing a group from Sports: Ruhe, Brim, his finance man Irwin Weiner, and director Roger Goodman. Ruhe and Brim were typical ABC Sports hires — young, bright, well educated, hardworking, and loyal. "We did anything and everything that Arledge asked us to do," said Brim. Weiner, thirty-eight, who managed the budgets and negotiated with talent, was valued for his street smarts and his honesty; he was once asked by Arledge to look into morale problems in Sports, and he reported back that the biggest problem was Arledge's own failure to communicate with people. Goodman, thirty-two, came along to update the look and feel of news programming — the sets, lighting, music, and graphics.

None had news experience, however, so Arledge bought some: he brought back Av Westin as executive producer of the "ABC Evening News." Westin's rehiring cheered ABC veterans who had enjoyed working for him on the evening news in the early 1970s. "He was a fabulous newsman," said Peter Jennings. "Wonderfully supportive, marvelously intelligent." But Westin was more than a bridge to the veterans; he was an inventive producer who, like Arledge, was unbound by the past practices of network news.

Westin, forty-seven, was a native New Yorker who had worked at CBS News as an editor, a director, a field producer, and a show producer during the pioneer days of network news. An innovator, Westin once produced a morning news program for Mike Wallace that surprised some CBS old-timers by exploring such topics as alcoholism and infidelity. "I love your show," a sainted CBS veteran once told him. "When are you going to put news on it?"

After a stint in public television, Westin joined ABC as the evening news producer in 1969. There, he jazzed up the news with graphics, pushed producers and correspondents to use pictures better, and won respect as a gifted editor. He also created the lively "Close-Up" documentary series for ABC. "My persona generally is to be the iconoclast and the maverick," said Westin. "I'm delighted to be referred to as the guru of television. That gives me a license to be outrageous, rather than to be the defender of the flame." Thin, dark-haired, and handsome, Westin was a tireless self-promoter who wore his outsize ego and ambitions on his sleeve — even though he'd already lost his job once for plotting to become president of ABC News. Arledge valued his talent but kept him at a distance because he didn't fully trust him.

Instead, Arledge placed his trust in David Burke, who became his second-in-command and loyal friend. The two men were introduced by Stephen Smith, a friend of Arledge's and brother-in-law of Ted Kennedy, whom Burke had served as chief of staff in the U.S. Senate, and they hit it off right away. Burke was a shrewd, tough operative of rock-solid integrity who became known inside ABC as the "consigliere," because he handled Arledge's dirty work. He wasn't universally liked, but he could be trusted to tell the truth. "Someone who will stab you in the front" was the way one producer described him.

The son of a policeman and grandson of a fireman, Burke, forty-one, was an Irish Catholic who grew up in Brookline, Massachusetts, and devoted much of his life to public service. He soon carved out a specialty — as a reliable right-hand man to the powerful, working for Kennedy in the Senate, for Howard Stein, chairman of the Dreyfus Corp., and for New York Governor Hugh Carey, as his chief of staff, a job that thrust him into the midst of the New York City fiscal crisis. "Without David, I never would have made it," said Felix Rohatyn, the investment banker often credited with saving the city from bankruptcy. But Burke never sought credit for himself, a trait that endeared him to Arledge.

With his key executives in place, Arledge pursued on-air talent. He felt about stars as George Steinbrenner did about free agents when he owned the New York Yankees — you could never buy too many of them. Except for Jennings, Rivera, and perhaps Donaldson, Arledge didn't see any stars in the correspondent ranks at ABC. So he shopped elsewhere, particularly at CBS News, whose cachet and winning record meant a lot to him. "Those were the days when, if you used to take out the garbage at CBS, you were thought to be brilliant," said Tom Yellin, a CBS producer who defected to ABC.

Like Steinbrenner, Arledge spent freely. His aide Irwin Weiner said, "This was Butch Cassidy and the Sundance kid. Instead of banks, the other networks were where we tried to raid and rob." If that meant paying more than the going rate for talent, so be it — ABC was rolling in money, thanks to its hit entertainment shows. Later, Arledge likened his hiring binge to William S. Paley's talent raids on NBC in the 1940s when Jack Benny, Burns and Allen, and Red Skelton were all lured to CBS. "We had to make a fairly big splash to tell people we were serious," Arledge said. "I don't want to compare myself to Bill Paley. But I think that, in the early days when Paley raided NBC for Jack Benny and Amos and Andy, you can look at it that he spent lavishly — or that he was building a network that lasted for years."

Burke went after anyone from the front ranks of CBS, figuring that others would follow. "We courted Bill Moyers forever, to no avail," he said. He tried to recruit Fred Graham, the Supreme Court reporter, and Washington correspondent Bruce Morton, with no luck. The risks of being associated with Arledge and ABC were too great. "In essence, they were saying to us — how can I come to work for ABC News and still have lunch with my colleagues?" Burke said. The biggest name that Arledge and Burke could pry loose from CBS was crusty veteran Hughes Rudd, whose best days were behind him.

Their first big catch came from NBC. Cassie Mackin was a young, high-profile, golden-blond Washington reporter with brains and charisma. She had previously approached ABC, but Bill Sheehan turned her away because her price was too high — she wanted $100,000 a year and a promise that she be spared what she called "chickenshit" assignments. To Arledge, Mackin was worth it, even though six-figure salaries for correspondents were then unheard of. Arledge said, "We gave her slightly more money than probably what she should have gotten, but I wanted to ring a bell to people and say, ABC is here, and don't sign a new contract without at least talking to us." Bells were soon ringing, but Mackin's salary spread discontent among the ABC incumbents, most of whom earned much less.

Arledge scouted talent everywhere. An early target was Sander Vanocur, who as the television writer for the *Washington Post* had come to Arledge's home in Sagaponack to interview him on the eve of his appointment at ABC News. A former NBC News political reporter, Vanocur shared cocktails, wine, and dinner with Arledge, and they stayed up half the night talking. Vanocur's story for the *Post,* although prescient in some ways, was a valentine. Flattered, Arledge hired him as a vice president in Washington, in charge of investigative reporting.

Not that flattery was required to impress Arledge. He was watching television one day when John McWethy, a White House correspondent for *U.S. News and World Report,* forcefully and repeatedly pressed President Carter to answer a pointed question at a news conference. By his own account, McWethy was nervous during the confrontation, saying, "It's not fun, interrogating a president when you're a twenty-nine-year-old reporter." But Arledge loved it. Within a few weeks, McWethy was hired to cover the Pentagon for ABC News — although it wasn't until a couple of years later that he actually met Arledge.

Naturally, doors spun in both directions during Arledge's early months at ABC News: as newcomers were rushed in, old-timers were hustled out. Arledge, who hated to deliver bad news face-to-face, usually had David Burke fire people for him, although he often communicated his displeasure by other means. Sometimes he simply refused to see executives whom he wanted out.

Marlene Sanders, the vice president of documentaries, got the coldest of cold shoulders. Frustrated by her inability to make contact with Arledge, Sanders had her secretary keep track of their attempts to reach him; she logged four broken appointments, nine phone calls that were not returned, and ten unanswered memos. When she finally got to see Burke, Sanders was told that responsibility for documentary production had been transferred to Pam Hill, an energetic and flamboyant producer. Sanders left for CBS News without ever learning why she had displeased Arledge. "He probably thought I was part of the old Bill Sheehan tradition, boring and stiff and dull," she said.

Other Sheehan-era holdovers barely hung on. George Watson, the vice president and Washington bureau chief, didn't have a single private conversation with Arledge all summer, not even to be told why Vanocur had also been named a Washington vice president. Bill Lord, Sheehan's vice president for news, was stripped of his office and his executive role and sent off to produce news inserts for "Good Morning America." Bob Siegenthaler, another veteran, was vacationing in Maine when he was replaced by Westin as executive producer of the evening news. To Arledge, Siegenthaler's decision to take a vacation so soon after Arledge's arrival marked him as insufficiently dedicated to the new regime. He was named director of planning — but given nothing to plan.

Siegenthaler, Lord, and Watson were solid, but that was part of their problem; they lacked the flair and dash that made a strong first impression on Arledge. Nor did they labor to impress the boss. "I was a poor tribute-payer," Siegenthaler said. Not until years later were their abilities recognized by Arledge.

Arledge's manhandling of the veterans, each of whom had loyal followers, fueled resentment. "Good people got tarred with the brush of the old ABC," an insider complained. Arledge also irritated people because he virtually went into hiding after Montauk, leading some old-timers to compare him to Howard Hughes.

The lack of respect went both ways. Arledge was stinging in his criticism of the status quo, writing in one staff memo: "The 6 P.M. feed . . . was not worthy of a local station in 1948, far less ABC News."

And he was annoyed by the "Capital J's," with their fretting over standards; their complaints reminded him of the way his fellow students at Columbia had made excuses for the Lions' woeful football teams. "We developed this reverse snobbery," he said, "that if Princeton or Yale or Harvard had good football teams, that automatically meant their academic standards couldn't be as good as ours because they're clearly bringing in goons and we will never stoop to that. ABC News had developed, as a kind of scar tissue or protective coating, this idea that they were purer than anybody else. Really, they were afraid to compete."

"We didn't like the resistance," recalled David Burke. "And your feelings about that will heighten when you feel that the people who are not accepting you are people who have sort of dedicated themselves to being in third place."

Burke could not hide his disdain for the old ABC. He spoke his mind, no matter the consequences; the consequences turned out to be memorably unpleasant when Arledge and Burke made their first trip together to Washington, the heart of the resistance movement.

For the occasion, a dozen or so correspondents were invited to dinner at the Madison Hotel to meet Burke and discuss the evening news. First, though, someone brought up the death of Elvis.

"For God's sake," Arledge interrupted, "am I going to have to wear a hair shirt all my life over this one night's show? I mean, is this such a big deal to you guys?"

The debate was short-circuited, but bad feelings simmered. When the topic shifted to the newscast, people talked cautiously about doing longer spots and taking stories outside the Beltway.

When Arledge left the room for a moment, Burke weighed in harshly.

"I have never heard such a bunch of mundane, uninspiring ideas in my life," Burke said. "And I don't hear any enthusiasm here for what we're trying to do."

In a confrontational tone, he told the correspondents that they had better understand that Arledge had made a commitment to ABC management to improve the news division, and that he, Burke, had made a commitment to work with Arledge, and that they would all do well to make a commitment to join in.

Everyone was floored — except Frank Reynolds. He was furious. He was so sputteringly angry that when he stood up to respond to Burke he could not — or would not — speak Arledge's name.

"I don't know what, what . . . what your friend here thinks he's doing," Reynolds said, drawing himself up to his full five-foot-six height, "but we have been working hard all of our lives in this business. We've been doing good work, and we don't even know you, and we don't have any need to be saved. Who do you think you are to come down here and talk to us this way?"

Burke backed off. He hadn't meant to insult anyone, he said. He just wanted to get everyone on the same track. Later, Burke would joke that he felt like he needed a visa to get into the Washington bureau. The old-timers reminded him of children who were suddenly forced to accept new stepparents. In time, he thought, they would come around.

Reynolds calmed down too. He was an intensely proud man who could not stand to be insulted by new bosses he didn't like or trust or respect. But he had little choice but to make peace with Arledge and Burke. Besides, he told himself, he wasn't working for them. He was working for ABC News.

In a sense, Roone Arledge owed his job to Barbara Walters. Had she led the "ABC Evening News" to glory, Bill Sheehan would have been a hero and Arledge would have stayed in Sports, gone to Hollywood, or joined NBC. Instead, Walters flopped, Sheehan took the fall, and Arledge was sent in to clean up the mess. The evening newscast was his biggest problem, and it would remain so for years.

Putting Av Westin in charge gave the program a strong leader, but it was not going to solve the problems between Reasoner and Walters. Nor was Arledge's second move, although it helped: he ordered director Charlie Heinz to stop shooting the anchors on camera at the same time. Essentially, Arledge granted the bickering couple a separation; no longer would they have to appear in public together, pretending to get along for the sake of the viewers. Even so, Heinz said, both anchors frequently looked so disgusted on the set that "we were always careful to make sure we looked before we put either of them on camera."

The Harry and Barbara Show was doomed. Arledge had said as much when he hired Westin, telling the executive producer to find a way to gracefully get Reasoner and Walters off the air — once he figured out who to put in their place.

Insiders blamed Reasoner. It wasn't that he disliked Walters; he had been just as grouchy about sharing anchor duties with Howard K. Smith. That Walters was a woman and not a journalist of the old school was more than his bruised ego could handle. "Harry was not about to share what he considered to be the male anchor role with any woman," said producer Bill Lord.

Walters could not relax on the set, which was no wonder since she was a frequent target of Reasoner's undisguised barbs. His most famous put-down came when, after a story about Henry Kissinger, Walters said, "You know, Harry, Kissinger didn't do too badly as a sex symbol in Washington." He replied acidly, "Well, you'd know more about that than I would."

Off the air, it was worse. Walters and Reasoner were sequestered at opposite ends of the newsroom. "Harry stayed here, and Barbara stayed there, and they never came out and talked," said Mike Stein, a writer. "They were never, ever sitting around the rim at the same time." The rim was where producers prepared the lineup of stories and edited scripts as they came in.

Never a hard worker, Reasoner slacked off more than ever — except when it came to protecting his turf. "When I got there, I found Barbara Walters's producers, Harry Reasoner's producers, and they actually had a stopwatch," Westin said. "I was told that Reasoner was owed a five-minute, thirty-second piece because she had done a five-minute, thirty-second piece several weeks before. It was terrible."

Arledge had to decide what to salvage from the wreck. A study done for ABC by Frank Magid Associates, a consulting firm that specialized in broadcast news, found that Reasoner remained popular. But the research also found that he "falls just short of making the kind of impact on viewers that Walter Cronkite does." To Arledge, that was Reasoner's problem — he was too much like Cronkite to compete against him. "People like Harry, but they weren't going to leave Walter to watch Harry," Arledge said. He couldn't see building a future around Reasoner.

The Magid study had worse news for Walters. Viewers liked her interviews, but nothing else. "Participant reaction to Barbara Walters is consistently negative," the study said. "Viewers often volunteered that she is not worth the money she is being paid, that she appears lofty, 'stuck-up,' extremely difficult to understand and follow, has a bad voice, is not able to effectively handle the anchor responsibilities and, quite simply, is not the type of personality that viewers can relate to as an individual." Had Arledge followed the research, Walters would have been cast aside.

She feared the worst. "I felt my career was over," Walters said.

But Arledge was not going to abandon Walters. She was, for one thing, one of his few allies in the news division. They had met long ago when they both worked at NBC, and when she first arrived at ABC, he'd called her occasionally. Walters was one of the few people to welcome him to ABC News. "I just thought he was so smart and, selfishly, I knew it was only going to help me," she said.

Whether or not they recognized it, Arledge and Walters were soul mates: they were outsiders, scorned by the news establishment and the press, thin-skinned about criticism, but powered by incredible inner drives.

Still, empathy alone does not explain Arledge's support for Walters. Arledge didn't know much about journalism in those days, but he knew a television star when he saw one. He dismissed Magid's research — imagine, he thought, what the research would have said about Howard Cosell. His gut told him that Walters was the biggest star at ABC News, and he sensed she could become even bigger.

Roone Arledge made lots of rookie mistakes during his first season at ABC News. After all, he almost lost Ted Koppel. But there was no way he was going to lose Barbara Walters.

Chapter Four

WIDE WORLD OF NEWS

THIS WAS BIGGER than the Moluccans, bigger than Elvis, bigger even than the Son of Sam: Israel and Egypt were about to make peace. Roone Arledge wanted his biggest stars on the scene — immediately, if not sooner.

He located Peter Jennings in South Africa. Jennings was not only Arledge's favorite foreign correspondent, but Anwar Sadat's too, after doing a documentary about the Egyptian president several years earlier. Arledge, calling from an impromptu command post at Alfredo's, told Jennings to leave at once for Egypt. "Charter a plane if you have to," he said.

If only it were so easy, Jennings thought. Egypt did not have diplomatic relations with South Africa and would not allow even a charter from Johannesburg to land in Cairo. Arledge, as usual, didn't want to hear excuses. Just go, he said.

Jennings went. He flew to Geneva, stopping only to shower, and then to Cairo. No camera crew was waiting — no one back in New York had thought to arrange for one — but Jennings went to the presidential palace anyway and got in to see Sadat.

"Under what conditions would you go to Israel?" Jennings asked.

"If Begin invites me," Sadat replied.

That was all Jennings needed to hear. He sent a telex to New York, referring to Israel as "New South Wales" to get it by Egyptian censors, and filed a report for the evening news.

Within hours, Bill Seamans, ABC's Tel Aviv bureau chief, found Menachem Begin at the Knesset.

"Sadat will come if you invite him," Seamans said.

"Well, I invite him," Begin said.

They had a worldwide scoop. Arledge had the "ABC Evening News" broadcast the story at 6 P.M. — this was Monday, November 14, 1977, six months into his regime — and awaited the cheers.

They never came. Thirty minutes later, CBS News broadcast the same story, with spectacular results. Walter Cronkite had talked to Sadat and Begin via satellite, after which a creative CBS producer put the video of the two leaders side by side so it almost appeared as if they were talking to each other. For days, the newspapers ran stories about Cronkite and television diplomacy — stories that mentioned ABC as a footnote, if at all.

Arledge was crestfallen. "Walter's interviews were sensational," he told a reporter, but they "occurred after our contacts. We were first on the air on both radio and TV with the story." Selling that as an ABC coup was impossible.

Years later, Jennings recalled the incident as "typical Roone. The grand idea, the brilliant idea, but he hadn't put that one crucial detail in place" — getting a crew to Egypt so both leaders would be on camera.

No such details were overlooked as Arledge prepared for Sadat's visit to Israel five days later. Planeloads of ABC correspondents and crews were dispatched to the region. Airtime was cleared in New York. And Arledge positioned his stars like kings and queens on a chessboard: he wanted Jennings, who was in Cairo, to trade places with Barbara Walters in Tel Aviv, so that Walters could fly on the plane with Sadat from Egypt to Israel. They managed the switch even though no civilian planes had flown between Israel and Egypt in thirty years; Arledge persuaded the Egyptian ambassador in Washington to get permission for a charter with Walters to make the trip.

On the flight back to Israel with Sadat, Walters worked her magic. She passed a note to the Egyptian president, asking for an interview with him and Begin. She had scrawled four words at the bottom for his reply: *yes, no, alone, together.*

He had circled *yes* and *alone.* Once on the ground, she persuaded him to do the interview with Begin.

By then, Arledge was exactly where he wanted to be: in the control room, producing the coverage. ABC News swarmed over the story all weekend, except for a break on Saturday afternoon while Arledge's ABC Sports covered a Big Ten football game.

The coverage was notable for its backgrounders — profiles of Sadat and Begin and a long piece by Frank Reynolds on the history of Arab-Israeli tensions. These were Arledge touches, products of his insistence that ABC make the news meaningful to viewers. This was that hypothetical "war in Zaire" he spoke about; he wanted ABC viewers to know the players and understand the stakes.

ABC also stayed on longer than anyone else. While CBS and NBC carried Sunday morning speeches by Sadat and Begin to the Knesset, only ABC was live with President Carter at church, where Donaldson could ask, "You see the hand of God moving in all this, don't you?" Carter said he did, and at that instant, Arledge cut back to the Israeli parliament cheering Sadat.

This was no longer a meeting between two leaders in the Middle East. Arledge had transformed the Sadat-Begin summit into a drama of great characters unfolding live on a worldwide stage.

There was no mystery about the approach — this was the sports style of coverage brought to news, the same techniques Arledge had tried out on the Moluccans and the Son of Sam. Deploy your stars, cover the action, switch from venue to venue, and bring the viewers up close and personal, giving them not just the news but also the feel of the event. Sadat-Begin had become a spectacle, like "Monday Night Football" or the Olympics: the best seat for watching peace in the Middle East was in front of a television set tuned to ABC.

Walters's joint interview with Sadat and Begin put the finishing touch on the weekend. She chatted easily with the two leaders, and while she didn't break new ground, just the sight of Sadat and Begin talking to each other — and to "our good friend Barbara," as Sadat put it — lent it significance. The interview provided an enormous lift to the embattled Walters, who often cited the Sadat-Begin summit as the most exciting story she had ever covered; Sadat had a special place in her heart.

Once again, though, Cronkite played the spoiler's role. He arranged his own interview, which CBS showcased on "60 Minutes." Snippets of Walters's interview ran earlier, so ABC was again first, but Cronkite's interview had more impact. About the only solace the ABC people could take was that Cronkite ended by asking, "Did Barbara get anything I didn't?" — a question that was edited out of the broadcast, of course.

To Arledge, ABC's Sadat-Begin coverage was both gratifying and frustrating. He recalled the weekend as "the first time our people really understood how good they could be if they would just do what we told them to do and go all out after stories. Even though we didn't quite get credit for them." The absence of credit was what frustrated him. ABC's victories didn't register despite Arledge's effort to promote them. Viewers tuned automatically to CBS.

The lessons were unmistakable. Breaking news stories presented opportunities to ABC News to demonstrate its mettle. And Arledge's ability to produce live, dramatic coverage was ideally suited for special events. But special events coverage, no matter how well done, would not bring viewers to a network that lacked popular news programs. "60 Minutes," for instance, was not only a gold mine for CBS News, but a valuable platform; Arledge was impatient to get his own magazine show onto ABC. Even more important were the changes he wanted to make to ABC's evening news.

There, he knew, he would have to find a bigger role for the globe-trotting correspondent who had served him so well, first in Munich in 1972, then in the Middle East in 1977. Peter Jennings had been cast as ABC's star anchor before, with unhappy results. But Jennings was older and wiser now, and ABC News was stronger. And this time, Jennings would not have to carry the evening news alone.

Peter Jennings's first turn at the ABC anchor desk is not his favorite subject. "I've forgotten a lot about it and blocked it out," he says. But he remembers a day when the network anchors were invited to speak at an industry luncheon at the Waldorf-Astoria in New York. There were the veteran Walter Cronkite of CBS, old hand Chet Huntley of NBC, and from ABC, twenty-seven-year-old Peter Jennings.

When someone in the audience complained that anchors practiced show business, not journalism, Huntley bristled. "My only concession to show business is that I stop in the makeup room every day and have these bags under my eyes painted out," he said.

To which Cronkite added, "Yes, and Jennings stops in and has them painted *on*."

Years later, Jennings could laugh at the story and confess that, yes, he was "unbelievably unqualified" to anchor the "ABC Evening News" in 1965. Everybody knew it — his competitors, the critics, and most of all, his colleagues at ABC. They called him the "anchorboy" or "Peter Pretty," treated him like a male model, and when he left the room, made cruel jokes about Peter going back to his playpen. Everybody knew it, that is, except Peter Jennings.

Maybe that was because he was so young. Maybe it was because he was vain — "a bit of a peacock," said one veteran. Or perhaps he had dreamed so often of doing great things in television that he simply could not turn the job down.

Broadcasting, after all, was in the blood of Peter Charles Archibald Ewart Jennings, who was born into Canada's first family of the airwaves in Toronto in 1938. His father, Charles Jennings, was a famous radio announcer, the coast-to-coast voice of the Canadian Broadcasting Co., while his mother, Elizabeth, came from one of Canada's wealthiest families. Peter and his older sister, Sarah, enjoyed a comfortable childhood of riding lessons, cricket matches, and private schools.

Peter greatly admired his father and, after his death, sometimes described him as "the Edward R. Murrow of Canada." The analogy was strained: Charles Jennings was a gifted announcer and a dedicated programming executive, but he had never been a journalist. Where he resembled Murrow was in his commitment to broadcasting as public service; he was a decent, humane man who struggled gamely to defend the CBC against political and commercial pressures until, demoralized, he retired to his country estate and beloved dogs. Charles Jennings died in 1973 at age sixty-five, leaving his son to uphold his ideals. "He was the most honorable man I have ever met," Peter Jennings would say. "He was swallowed by the business. Sadly, the business got commercial and slick and swallowed him up."

Young Peter was only ten when he got his first anchor job, as host of a Saturday morning radio show called "Peter's Program." He was to be paid $25 a week until his father insisted that he turn the money down. His other love was sports, and he played cricket, soccer, and hockey with a natural grace. "It was of far greater interest to me to get out and play hockey or football than study literature or, God forbid, math and chemistry," he said.

He was not exaggerating. Peter was thrown out of an exclusive private school, then dropped out of a public high school before he finished tenth grade. Years later, Jennings was embarrassed by his lack of formal education — he told reporters in the 1960s that he'd graduated from college. But at the time, his parents were the ones who were upset. The teenage Jennings was sentenced to work as a bank teller, figuring balances and hoping to figure out what to do with the balance of his life.

He found the beginnings of an answer at a radio station in tiny Brockton, Ontario, where he spun records ("Good evening, it's your old DJ, PJ") and covered the news. A train crash gave him his first opportunity to do a story for the CBC; before filing it, he called home to read the script over the phone to his father, who was so overwhelmed that he could not speak. "He was seeing his life as a broadcaster begin again in the person of his son," Jennings said. "It was a very, very emotional moment for both of us." Soon he switched to television and CTV, Canada's first private TV network, where he covered Parliament Hill and co-anchored the news. There he came to the attention of Elmer Lower, who brought him to ABC News.

Within a year, Jennings was plucked from the ranks to anchor ABC's fifteen-minute evening news. He was chosen not for his reporting ability but because he looked great on camera: he was six feet one inch tall, strikingly handsome, with modishly long brown hair. The network hoped that the young viewers who liked ABC's prime-time shows — this was the era of "Gidget" and "Shindig" — would flock to see a young man with movie-star appeal read the news.

A part of Jennings understood that he wasn't ready for the job, but he tried to bluff his way through. "My greatest weakness, aside from my youthful arrogance, was that I really didn't know anything about America," he said. Worse, he did not know how little he knew.

His attitude irked the veterans. The crusty Bill Lawrence once snubbed him during a broadcast of "Issues and Answers," telling him that his question had already been answered. Behind the scenes, he was excluded from editorial meetings. Even his efforts to write his own copy were discouraged because his writing style ranged from the conversational to the convoluted; he wrote in circles that could not easily be uncoiled and resisted editing. Walter Porges, a producer, said, "You had to apply a lot of heat until he bent."

On the air, Jennings inexplicably insisted on retaining his native speech patterns, pronouncing "been" as "bean" and "schedule" as "shedule." His Canadian roots and patrician manner — he was compared to a young William F. Buckley — did not play in Peoria. One viewer with a sense of humor wrote, "Cut out the phony Britishisms. This is America, old boy."

Jennings has always said that he quit the anchor desk after two and a half years. According to Bill Sheehan, Jennings was asked to step down. Whatever the real story, the not-so-noble experiment had failed, and for a time, Jennings remained a figure of derision within ABC News. A colleague recalled an incident at the 1968 Democratic convention when Jennings proposed a story idea — and it wasn't a bad idea — that was literally laughed at by others in the room.

Looking back, Jennings said, "I never imagined I would be the anchorman again. Ever."

Soon after leaving the anchor job, Jennings sought an overseas posting. In 1969, he was sent to Rome; there he found a friend and colleague in fellow Canadian Barrie Dunsmore, and he found work he loved, as a foreign correspondent.

The Rome assignment was a dream job, a reminder of why he had been drawn to journalism in the first place. He was free to pursue stories through southern Europe, north Africa, India, and Pakistan, sometimes at a leisurely pace; there was time for dinner with the foreign minister or a cruise up the Nile. An intensely curious traveler, Jennings was the antithesis of the Ugly American; he sought to understand foreign cultures on their own terms, rather than to measure them against Western standards. Producers who traveled with him say he would arrive somewhere and envelop a story, talk to people around the fringes and slowly make his way to the core — although occasionally, his critics said, he never got there. While Jennings capably handled breaking news, he loved doing features that gave viewers a sense of place or a glimpse into the character of a foreign leader.

Jennings found himself especially drawn to the Arab world, with its tangled politics and rich history and culture; the very foreign-ness of the Middle East fascinated him. "For six years — six years — I never talked about anything but the Middle East," he said. "It's like taking drugs — you never get it out of your system." He relocated to Beirut when the city was still a cosmopolitan Mediterranean port, before the Lebanese civil war, and eventually reported from all nineteen Arab nations. "I was getting my first honest-to-God education," he said. Jennings traveled with a satchel of books, magazines, and newspapers, trying to make up for the formal schooling he never had.

His immersion in the Arab world became complete when he married Annie Malouf, a young and vivacious Lebanese photographer, in 1974. This was his second marriage to a beautiful woman — his first, to Valerie Godsoe, a Canadian debutante who worked for the CBC, ended after he moved to New York — and it contributed to Jennings's image as a playboy. A producer who traveled with him in those years said, "He was notorious for all the women he had hanging over him." He came across as immature and insecure, and the result was he was not taken seriously by some ABC colleagues. One ABC critic said, "Peter enjoyed life. You wanted to go to dinner with Peter because he knew the best restaurants and the headwaiters knew Peter."

His friends call such sniping unfair. "Sure, he would go to restaurants in Beirut, but he would go with half the Lebanese cabinet," said Barrie Dunsmore. "Peter was extraordinarily curious and interested and energetic. He worked very hard." Jennings became a first-rate foreign correspondent, producing not only news reports but also documentaries about Sadat and the Palestinians. Those were programs that made a difference, he thought, programs that would have made his father proud.

Nevertheless, still not quite sure what he wanted, Jennings gave up his foreign post in 1975 for another anchor job, this time in Washington, where he delivered five-minute newscasts for "A.M. America," a forerunner of "Good Morning America." He gained new visibility but, predictably, found the work suffocating. Before long, Jennings returned overseas as ABC's chief foreign correspondent, based in London.

Once again, life was good. It got even better when he was named the roving foreign anchor of Roone Arledge's new and improved three-anchor evening newscast. Jennings could continue to cover stories as a reporter, which helped satisfy his natural curiosity and his desire to do meaningful work. And, as an anchor, he was assured of a daily dose of airtime to feed his ego.

"I have the best job in television," Jennings said, even if he was anchoring one-third of a news show and not the whole thing.

Before settling on a three-anchor format, Arledge had spent months testing new approaches to the evening news. He wanted to reduce the roles of Reasoner and Walters, to pick up the pace of the broadcast, and, always, to set ABC apart from its competitors. With the help of his executive producer, Av Westin, he soon achieved all his objectives.

Together, Arledge and Westin invented "whip-arounds," a technique that strung together reports from correspondents without cutting back to the anchors to introduce each one. A package about the economy, for example, included a Washington story about inflation, a Detroit story about the auto industry, and a piece from San Diego about home prices — throughout which Reasoner and Walters would disappear.

Arledge also experimented with "sub-anchors" — correspondents who would introduce stories from the site of an event. Jennings would sub-anchor a package from the Middle East, while Reynolds or Donaldson sub-anchored from Washington. This also cut down on "face-time" for Reasoner and Walters and gave Arledge a chance to see how his favorite correspondents would perform as anchors.

Finally, Arledge insisted that when Reasoner or Walters had to introduce stories, he or she do so quickly. In a memo to correspondents, Westin wrote, "You can't expect the anchor to spend 30 seconds or more to set up your piece."

Everything was being written shorter. Where possible, pictures, graphics, and natural sound were used in place of words. This, Arledge thought, served viewers who had come to expect fast-paced, visual storytelling. "The ability of people to absorb facts has grown tremendously," Arledge said. "Commercials have done this to a great degree. They have thirty seconds to get a message across, and they use that time very judiciously."

Westin, too, urged the correspondents to think visually. In a memo reflecting his impatience, he wrote, "Almost all our reports lack style and fail to take the fullest advantage of the marriage of picture and narration." He recommended that stories begin by "concentrating on the smallest element." A congressional hearing, he said, could begin with a close-up of a witness adjusting a microphone, while a piece about car prices could start with a customer embarking on a test drive ("A key in the lock will cost 10 percent more in 1978 . . ."). Westin railed against "wallpaper" — generic pictures of faceless people that were used to cover narration — and he told photographers to avoid panning and seek well-framed close-ups. This put him in sync with Arledge, who put handheld cameras on the sidelines at football games and told a "Monday Night Football" director, "If a guy wears a mustache, I want to see the goddamn thing."

Over time, they saw progress. Westin again put his thoughts in writing: "The number of stories used on an average broadcast has gone up; the use of the 'whip-around' and the 'sub-anchors' has moved from theory to reality; the program is faster and by many accounts, more interesting and informative." Best of all, though Westin didn't say so, viewers were seeing less of Reasoner and Walters; they appeared for about three minutes a day, compared with Cronkite's six minutes on CBS.

That was still too much for Arledge, but he wanted to strengthen the corps of producers and correspondents before replacing his anchor team. In the past, he thought, ABC News had expected too much of its anchors, hiring a Reasoner or adding a Walters but never making a full-fledged commitment to build an organization. "People would tune in out of curiosity and then find the news program lacking, and so they wouldn't stay," Arledge said. This time, he wanted to solidify the structure before giving the house another new coat of paint.

But Reasoner forced his hand. When Bill Sheehan brought on Walters in 1976, he had promised Reasoner that he could leave in two years if things didn't work out. They had nothing in writing, but Reasoner informed Arledge that he intended to return to CBS in June 1978. Reluctantly, Arledge agreed to let him go.

As the deadline approached, Cronkite loomed large in Arledge's thinking. Uncle Walter had become a national institution, more trusted than presidents, more famous than movie stars. "We didn't have anyone in that league," Arledge said. Besides, Arledge had no desire to produce the same newscast his competitors did. "CBS is delighted at having us be just like them," he would say. "It's only if we change the rules that they have to worry."

So Arledge changed the rules. He declared the concept of the solo, fixed anchor to be outdated. He had no anchor better than Cronkite, but he could have more anchors, who would be scattered far and wide to report as well as read the news. For a time, ABC even sought to replace the term "anchor" with "deskman." As Westin told a reporter, "The deskmen will be at the scene, rather than reading regurgitated wire copy."

The new terminology was partly a response to the sticky problem of Barbara Walters. Her contract, which Arledge described as "the William Morris Agency at its worst," guaranteed her the New York anchor job for five years, as well as the right to be consulted about co-anchors. By changing the title and job description, Arledge could argue, in theory, that he had no anchors at all. It never came to that because Walters chose not to hold ABC to the contract — "to Barbara's everlasting credit," Arledge said.

Still, Arledge took pains as he constructed a new format to minimize damage to Walters. He considered trying to keep Reasoner but did not, to avoid the appearance of demoting Walters. He also decided not to base an anchor in New York because that might embarrass Walters. "We did all of that, really, to save Barbara," Arledge said. Walters's fragile ego was battered anyway, but she never blamed Arledge.

Eventually, Arledge settled on a three-anchor format, with anchors in Washington, London, and Chicago. They were to cover the news, as well as introduce stories by others. Arledge wanted them in motion, and it was said in jest that his ideal format would put the anchors into a jet plane that circled the globe and touched down wherever news happened.

"I recognized that, short of Walters, we had no stars," Arledge later explained. "So I decided to do what we did with 'Wide World of Sports.' We would make the presentation of the news the essence of our program, instead of building it around personalities, as the other networks did. Out of this, the personalities would evolve."

The London slot belonged to Jennings. He had all the necessary journalistic skills, plus he looked great in a trenchcoat, which mattered to Arledge. Jennings's trip to Fred Pierce's office to try to block Arledge's appointment had been forgotten.

The Washington job required more debate. Arledge wanted Dan Rather or Roger Mudd from CBS, or Robert MacNeil, from public television. Only MacNeil was prepared to join ABC, but he was unwilling to move from New York to Washington. That left Frank Reynolds, an experienced anchor and reporter but a leader of the old guard. He got the job mostly by default.

Filling the third slot was tougher. Arledge wanted a new face, someone who, as he put it, "had not been a failed ABC anchor." He looked at local anchors Max Robinson from Washington and Mort Crim from Philadelphia, mixing and matching them with Reynolds and Jennings on tape to see how the combinations looked.

Arledge leaned toward Robinson, a popular anchorman for WTOP-TV, CBS's Washington affiliate. Robinson lacked network experience, but he was a superb newsreader, as well as a handsome, well-spoken black man. Putting a black anchor on the newscast might attract black viewers, who tended to watch less network news than whites, as well as draw attention to ABC. Arledge never forgot the importance of promotion.

Before making up his mind, Arledge had ABC's consultants, Frank Magid Associates, test Robinson's appeal. Using Magid was controversial — back then, employing market research to make journalistic judgments was anathema to news traditionalists — but Arledge wanted to know how Robinson would play outside Washington. Magid reported back that Robinson was "praised for being very easy to understand and follow, dynamic in his speech and comfortable to watch." That was all Arledge needed to hear.

The cast of the revamped program, which was christened "World News Tonight," included two more principal players. Howard K. Smith would provide commentary from Washington, and Barbara

Walters would run a "special coverage desk" in New York. Walters, in effect, had become a correspondent, albeit a glamorous one.

While Arledge created the new format primarily to avoid a head-to-head battle with Cronkite, "World News Tonight" was nevertheless an interesting journalistic experiment — a gamble only a third-place network would take. Without meaning to do so, Arledge had developed an approach that, in its way, offered an alternative to the traditions of objective reporting, embodied on television by the all-knowing, all-seeing anchor. Cronkite's trademark sign-off — "that's the way it is" — was a nightly tribute to objectivity, reflecting his grounding in neutral, wire-service reporting. But by the 1970s, many journalists scoffed at the ideal of objectivity; they argued that the best way to capture events was not with a single, omnipotent voice but through many personal points of view. Multiple anchors were a step in that direction, as was Arledge's willingness to allow some ABC personalities — Cosell in sports, Geraldo Rivera in news — to mix reportage with opinion. He spoke of encouraging more "personalized reporting" and less "regurgitating" of news from the wire services.

With the new format, Arledge had also unwittingly created a metaphor for America's diminished role in the world after Vietnam and the Mideast oil shocks. This was "*World* News Tonight" — not solely the American establishment view of the world from New York or Washington, but also the view from the heartland and from London or Moscow or Tehran or wherever news happened. Arledge did not conceive of his broadcast in those terms, but he sensed that ABC News could make its mark by covering foreign news more aggressively and, in that way, bring America closer to the rest of the world. He'd learned from the Olympics that Americans could be made to care about Russians and Rumanians.

Arledge did recognize the risk built into his newscast of multiple perspectives: viewers accustomed to getting their news from a single trusted authority might tune out. Skeptics were everywhere, even inside ABC. "We're told the day of the all-knowing anchor is over, yet now we have five," complained Howard K. Smith. "You don't give the public a Punch and Judy show with a new face after every commercial." Others saw the format as smoke and mirrors, reflecting "Arledge's naked desperation," one critic said.

If only because of his experience with "Monday Night Football," Arledge understood another, more mundane problem with the format. On Monday nights, Arledge put three men in the announcing booth, only to find that someone was unhappy afterward because he had not had time to say his piece. This happened, inevitably, even though the "Monday Night" trio had three hours to fill. The "World News Tonight" trio had twenty-two minutes. What's more, Jennings, Reynolds, and Robinson each believed he could carry the program on his own.

Of the three anchors, Frank Reynolds was literally the most battle-hardened. As an infantryman during World War II, he was shot in the leg, sustaining a wound that took him out of combat. As a commentator, he came under attack from Spiro Agnew, then vice president of the United States. And Reynolds had been bruised by the network news wars, rising once before to anchor the news on ABC, only to abruptly lose the job.

But Reynolds was a survivor. Gray-haired and a mere five feet six inches tall, he was not a physically imposing man, but he conveyed the sense that he was not to be taken lightly. In his private life, he was a churchgoer with deep family ties; as a reporter, he cared deeply about the news and stood up for his beliefs. "A tough little Irish Catholic mick" was the way Sander Vanocur once described him. His oldest son, Dean Reynolds, liked that, saying, "That was Frank. It wasn't that he had a chip on his shoulder. He just didn't take shit from anybody."

A decent, sentimental man in an often-cynical profession, Frank Reynolds was a product of America's heartland. He was born in 1923 in East Chicago, Indiana, a steel town where his father, Frank Sr., was a mid-level executive and his mother, Helen, a strong-willed woman, drilled the traditional Irish Catholic values of family and church into her son and three daughters. Frank Jr. attended Wabash College for a year before dropping out to enlist in the army.

During the early days of television news, Reynolds worked as a reporter and anchor in Chicago, where he fit right into the city's "Front Page" style of aggressive street reporting. He joined ABC News in Washington in 1965, taking a hefty pay cut because he wanted to cover national stories. He was assigned to the Johnson White House until he was named ABC's evening news anchor in 1968.

His first go-round as an anchor was an unhappy one. "I remember reading the daily situation report, and I'd read about here is Joe in Bangkok and Anita is out in Abu Dhabi and somebody else is on the campaign trail and there I was sitting on 66th Street and not really having very much fun," Reynolds said. He missed reporting and did not like sharing the anchor desk with Howard K. Smith. His son Dean said, "Smith was a rabid right-winger and my father was on the left, and they didn't get along."

In 1970, ABC decided to replace Reynolds with Harry Reasoner. "It was a total shock to him," said Bill Sheehan, who gave him the bad news. "I thought he was going to have a heart attack." Ratings for the evening news had been steady, so Reynolds had no inkling he was in trouble.

Had other factors come into play? Reynolds, for one, thought that he was a victim of politics — not ABC politics, but the pressure politics of Richard Nixon and Spiro Agnew. When Agnew launched his stinging attack on the news media in November 1969, he singled out Reynolds for one of his anti-Nixon commentaries. Unafraid, Reynolds had fired back over the air, but he was strongly urged by his ABC superiors to tone down his opinions.

"It was not a very proud time in the history of television," Reynolds said, years later. "I paid a price for stating my views. I was taken off the air. I believe it was definitely a factor. I think there were other factors, too, but Howard K. Smith was retained and he endorsed Agnew's views."

He did not go quietly. Being fired left him with an abiding distrust of management, some of which surfaced during a blunt commentary that took parting shots at ABC and Agnew and spoke volumes about Reynolds.

"I'm not going to suggest that I'm completely happy about what has happened to me," Reynolds told his viewers. "I don't like it one bit and see no reason to pretend that I do.

"I suppose I ought to say I hope I have not offended anyone in the last two and one-half years, but that's not really the truth either," he went on. "Because there are a few people I did want very much to bother, and I hope I have."

Reynolds had the script framed and hung on his office wall, as a reminder of how perilous life as an anchor can be. Next to the script was a telegram from a reporter in Tennessee, who told him, "Don't let the bastards get you down." He didn't.

Indeed, he emerged whole — partly because he had the perspective to see that life did not begin and end at the anchor desk. He was devoted to his wife, Henrietta, and their five sons. He cared not about celebrity but about the news. And he cherished the friendship and support of colleagues at ABC News.

Indeed, as a leader of the troops, Reynolds was peerless. His intergrity was unshakable, and he was valued as a critic and cheerleader.

"There was a wonderful quiet dignity to Frank," said reporter Charles Gibson. "He's the best I'll ever work for." After Reynolds lost the anchor job, Ted Koppel wrote to say, "I respect and admire you. You demonstrated courage which, contrary to popular opinion, is not one of the more sought-after virtues in this business." Reynolds wrote back, "It's a lousy business, Ted, but a great profession." He described himself as "battered but by no means beaten."

Back in Washington, where he felt at home, Reynolds covered George McGovern's presidential campaign in 1972 and Ronald Reagan's in 1976. Afterward, both men remained his friends — a measure of his fairness as a reporter.

Always, Reynolds took his work seriously. The worst thing anyone could do was to treat him like "talent" that needed handling. Once, while taping a documentary, a stage manager approached to ask, "Mr. Reynolds, do you have any lines in the next scene?" "I don't do lines," Reynolds replied, with a baleful stare.

Reynolds worried more than anyone else that Arledge would bring show business values to news. "I got the feeling almost every time there was an ad with Frank's picture in it, he felt uncomfortable," said Gibson. Reynolds refused to think of himself as a personality. "One of the things I deplore about our current milieu of broadcasting," he once said, "is there has been so much emphasis placed on who delivers the news, who the messenger is, rather than what the message is."

This was Reynolds at his stiffest, a quality that sometimes came through over the air. Critics complained that he was stern, that he looked as if he carried the world's weight on his shoulders. To some, he was pompous and self-important. Certainly he lacked the reassuring warmth of Cronkite, the model anchor of his time. Sam Donaldson said, "You had to get through the fact that beneath what appeared to be a rather cold, forbidding presentation was a very warm, caring heart and a very decent individual."

No sooner had he made Reynolds an anchor of "World News Tonight" than Arledge wanted to soften him a little. They quarreled over cosmetics — Reynolds's makeup, his haircut, and the color of his suits.

This was hardly a matter of journalistic principle. But Frank Reynolds could be as stubborn about his clothing as he was about his commentaries. He was not about to change his style — or his suits — to please anyone, least of all Roone Arledge.

*　　　*　　　*

While Jennings and Reynolds had spent years as reporters, the knock on Max Robinson when he arrived at ABC News was that he had not paid his dues. That, he thought, was grossly unfair. He felt that he had been forced to work harder than anyone else to reach the top because he'd labored under the burden of racism.

Robinson never forgot how he broke into television in 1964, when he was hired by a UHF station in Portsmouth, Virginia, to read the news.

Read he did — and that was all he did. Viewers who tuned in saw just the station logo and the word NEWS. Robinson was a disembodied voice — a sonorous, made-for-anchoring voice — but just a voice.

He wanted to be seen as well as heard. "I figured I had relatives and all who wanted to see me on TV," he said, "so one night I took the slide down and appeared on the screen."

The next day, he was fired.

Robinson liked to tell the story about Portsmouth. To him, it was a story about racism in the Old South, about the obstacles he'd overcome, and about his refusal to accept second-class status. He ended with a punch line — "Portsmouth, Virginia," he would say, "was not ready for color on TV" — and so he seemed able to see the humor in his predicament.

But as years passed and troubles dogged Robinson, the story also could be seen as a cautionary tale about a man who was compelled to rebel, who would not play by the white man's rules, and who flirted with self-destruction. Hints of this dark side surfaced by the time Robinson was hired by ABC, but they were only hints. At the time, Robinson seemed to be on the verge of his greatest accomplishments.

Great success was expected of Maxie Cleveland Robinson Jr., who was born into a middle-class family in Richmond, Virginia, in 1939. His mother, Doris Robinson, was a schoolteacher. And, like Peter Jennings, Max Robinson grew up in the shadow of a legendary father. Maxie Robinson Sr. was an outstanding collegiate athlete who became the no-nonsense coach of the baseball, basketball, and football teams at all-black Armstrong High School. Maxie Sr. was a role model, career counselor, and father figure to his players.

To his children, he was a taskmaster. The Robinson kids were taught lessons about hard work, self-reliance, and racial pride. "There was this whole community of people telling us we were special and important and wonderful, and that we were destined to be the leaders, if you will, of our race," recalled Jewell Robinson Shepherd, Max's older sister, who became the first black admitted to Goucher College.

Young Max read widely and earned high marks in school, but he had one glaring flaw — a sickly child, he lacked the athletic ability to carry on the family tradition. That responsibility fell to his younger brother, Randall, who captained the Armstrong basketball team and won an athletic scholarship to college. The effect on Max was all too predictable. His mother, Doris, once said, "He always felt he was less in his daddy's sight than Randall, who played basketball. He never had the confidence that he could accomplish things that we knew he could do."

Still, sports was not the only arena in which a young man could become a star. After a year at Oberlin College, a stint in the U.S. Air Force, and a period of drift, Max Robinson discovered television. WTOP-TV, the CBS affiliate in Washington, D.C., hired him, first as a gofer and then as a news reporter. He looked terrific on camera, and his voice conveyed strength and authority.

"Max was a natural," said Jim Snyder, the WTOP news director who made the thirty-year-old Robinson the city's first black anchorman in 1969. "He always had great presence on the air." Robinson became co-anchor of the 6 and 11 P.M. newscasts, with Gordon Peterson, and together they dominated the ratings.

Robinson loved the spotlight. He partied with Washington's black elite, dressing in a colorful dashiki when he entertained artists and politicians at his home. When he took to the streets, he was swarmed by admirers. One reporter wrote that he had "a tall, almost regal bearing, like some African prince in pinstripes, set off by a disarming smile."

Like his father, Robinson became a role model. He helped start a national organization of black journalists and lent a hand to young reporters, dispensing advice and job referrals. He pushed WTOP to hire, train, and promote blacks and to be sensitive to minorities in its reporting. Robinson could be overbearing, chiding black reporters who, in his estimate, were insufficiently committed to "the cause." But he was driven by his own sense of responsibility and moral outrage.

"I have never felt any great joy in speaking out," he once said. "But I believe when there are fewer of us, we have to speak out. Malcolm once said, 'When it hurts, don't suffer quietly.' "

His private life brought little peace. Robinson was married and divorced twice when he met Beverly Hamilton, a social worker who shared his fervent commitment to racial justice. By the time they were wed in 1973, however, Robinson felt burdened by his success, tormenting himself because he was not doing enough for blacks. To measure his dedication, he had only to turn again to his brother Randall, a Harvard-educated lawyer who had devoted his life to fighting apartheid in South Africa.

Occasionally, Robinson's demons surfaced. One night in 1973, Robinson came home with friends, obviously depressed. He found a pistol, walked onto his balcony, and fired more than twenty rounds of ammunition into the ground. Friends said Max was despondent over his father's death three weeks before. On the air the next day, Robinson apologized. "Even a newsman gets out of joint once in a while," he said.

The truth was that he had been drinking heavily, as he often did. Robinson was frequently late for work and occasionally did not show up at all. His boss, Jim Snyder, felt there was little he could do. "It never got to the point where it was damaging the operation," he said. Robinson had gradually detached himself from news gathering; he came in, read his lines, and went home.

In fact, Robinson had never cared much for reporting — as anyone who had checked his background could have learned. Sam Donaldson, who worked at WTOP in the 1960s, had tried to teach Robinson to operate a film camera so he could gather his own footage, but got nowhere. "He was not interested in the menial work of learning the business," Donaldson said. The ABC newsman was appalled when he heard that Robinson had been given a job on "World News Tonight" that required him to report as well as anchor.

All the warning signs were there, but Roone Arledge never saw them. Arledge, as usual, had focused on the screen; he had ordered tapes of Robinson's work and had liked what he saw. In particular, he was impressed by Robinson's work after Hanafi Muslims seized hostages in downtown Washington in 1977; he had been the first journalist to talk to the Muslim leader.

Arledge figured that his producers could teach Robinson anything he needed to know about reporting. Arledge knew that no one had to teach him how to read the news.

On July 10, 1978, ABC News broadcast the first "World News Tonight." In twenty-two action-packed minutes, Arledge and Westin found time to introduce their five major players — Reynolds, Jennings, Robinson, Walters, and Smith — and to present new music and graphics, field reports from seven correspondents, a whip-around from the White House to the Knesset, and a dozen zippy "tell" items. The show was everywhere and nowhere, hopscotching the globe for news.

Reynolds, characteristically, began by noting the seriousness of the enterprise. "We are aware of our responsibility to you," he intoned, "and we intend to meet it." In London, Jennings introduced a story about the trial of Soviet dissident Anatoly Shcharansky. Reports and reaction followed from Moscow, Washington, Tel Aviv, and Paris. Walters interviewed law professor Alan Dershowitz, while Smith weighed in with an anti-Soviet commentary. No angle was left uncovered — although, for all the talk about not chaining anchors to their desks, Reynolds, Jennings, and Robinson sat in studios that looked remarkably alike.

The format's awkwardness was evident. In the *Washington Post*, television critic Tom Shales wrote: "Within the first ten minutes, there were at least seven shifts of location . . . Reynolds threw the ball to Jennings in London just so that Jennings could briefly introduce a report from Moscow. Then it was back to Washington, and time for a commercial. It should perhaps have been a commercial for Dramamine, but it wasn't."

Inside the network, the practice of having one anchor lead into another became known as layering. Arledge wanted Reynolds to open the broadcast by saying good evening and then yield to Jennings to introduce a foreign story or to Robinson for a domestic report. But Reynolds did not want merely to say good evening; he wanted to deliver some news too. The other anchors felt the same way. So the top story each night often was introduced twice; by the time the correspondent on the scene in Warsaw or Atlanta got on the air, half the story had been told.

Further confusion arose as the world was carved up into spheres of influence. Jennings, based in London, claimed Japan and South America, as well as Europe, Africa, and the Middle East. But stories from Canada, Mexico, Central America, and the Caribbean belonged to Reynolds. "We had some clumsy moments," said producer Walter Porges. "Some places are overseas, but they are not over seas." Reynolds and Robinson also clashed over who would get to say what.

A month or so after the debut, Arledge and Westin brought the three anchors to New York to work out some ground rules. They wanted the anchors to air their grievances face-to-face, to ease tensions that had begun to simmer. "We had thought we were getting together to iron out kinks, to work out different procedures, all that sort of business," Westin said. "Instead it erupted."

Over dinner at Alfredo's, Arledge and Westin said they wanted Reynolds to open and close the program each night — making him first among equals. That was acceptable to Jennings, who valued the freedom to report as well as anchor. But Robinson, who defined himself as an anchor, feared he was getting second-class treatment. As he drank more, he grew vehement; he argued that waiting in line behind Reynolds each night to have his say amounted to being forced to the back of the bus. Reynolds thought that was ludicrous, and when he said so, Robinson lashed out, calling him a bigot. Westin did his best to smooth things over, but the damage was done.

After the dinner — which became known around ABC as "the last supper" — Jennings suggested to Robinson that they talk some more. For an hour, as they paced the streets of Manhattan, Jennings tried to persuade Robinson to seize the opportunity to travel around America, pursuing the most interesting and exciting stories he could find. Jennings wasn't selling him a bill of goods; he later thought that if he tired of London, he would enjoy Robinson's job. "You could take the Midwest and pretend it's Hungary, Egypt, the West Bank, India," Jennings would say. "I thought it would have been a fabulous way to get under the skin of America."

Robinson could not be convinced. Who was looking out for his interests? he wondered. First, he'd been ripped out of familiar surroundings, cut off from family, friends, and fans, and forced to relocate to an unfamiliar place, all so that Reynolds could anchor from Washington. Then he'd been forced into a secondary role on the program, again because of a desire to showcase Reynolds. Now Jennings was telling him to spend more time in the field — even though his strength was anchoring, not reporting. It was no wonder Robinson thought that he was being sabotaged.

"Max was convinced that everyone was screwing him, which was partially true," said one insider. "But he was dealing with two other anchors, both of whom had extensive experience as major reporters for the network, writing their own stories, putting together their own television pieces. Max was essentially a local anchor who had gotten himself thrust into this. He was in so far over his head it wasn't funny."

Arledge quickly grew tired of Robinson and his complaints. He turned the problem over to David Burke, who tried to develop a rapport with Robinson, and to Westin, who sent some of his best producers to Chicago to work with the unhappy anchorman. At least "World News Tonight" was getting on the air every day without embarrassing Arledge or ABC. The same could not be said about "20/20," the other program Arledge had introduced that summer. ABC's new prime-time magazine was dying — and Arledge had no one he could turn to to save it.

Chapter Five

20/20 HINDSIGHT

GRAB A DRINK ."

Roone Arledge issued the command, but the staff for "20/20," his new prime-time magazine show, declined to obey.

Six days after the premiere of "20/20" on June 6, 1978, Arledge was visiting the production offices near Columbus Circle. He stood at the top of a circular staircase beside a fully stocked trolley bar complete with bartender. But the people at "20/20" were in no mood for a party.

"C'mon, have a drink," Arledge said.

He was practically pleading.

The resistance appeared spontaneous, but it was not. Harold Hayes, who had just been fired as the host of the first "20/20," had told everyone that he had no desire to share good fellowship with Arledge. He was furious. So were many of his colleagues.

It was bad enough that they had labored for months to produce a flop. The first episode of "20/20" had been the most ill-conceived hour of broadcast news ever seen on ABC, a shapeless hodgepodge that included an overblown exposé on rabbit killing, a fear-mongering story on terrorism, and several pointless features, all presided over by two anchors whose thickly accented speech could barely be understood. The "20/20" debut was so awful that it had to be seen to be appreciated and, unfortunately for ABC, the critics had tuned in. "An animated smudge on the great lens of television" was the way the *Washington Post*'s Tom Shales described it. Another critic wrote, "Ick, ick, poo, poo!"

But the critic who mattered most was Arledge, and it was his handling of the "20/20" debut that really upset the troops. He had been inexplicably absent from the show for weeks until, at the last possible minute, he stepped in with a vengeance — ripping up the entire show and growing so disgusted that he told his executive producer, Bob Shanks, to leave the control room.

When the show bombed anyway, Arledge tried to distance himself from the fallout and blame everything on Shanks.

"I hated the program," Arledge told the *New York Times,* saying that he had not seen the show until it aired. Technically, this was true — the last-minute changes meant that no one saw the entire program before airtime — but he implied, wrongly, that he'd played no part in producing the premiere.

"Frankly, I was appalled," Arledge told the *Washington Post,* as if he'd had nothing to do with the show.

The "20/20" staff members were left to twist in the wind.

Later, Harold Hayes said, "The most unforgivable thing about that man was his failure to take responsibility for something in which he was involved."

Small wonder no one wanted to join the party.

One self-appointed critic who watched "20/20" with more than passing interest was Don Hewitt, the executive producer of CBS's "60 Minutes." Hewitt said afterward that ABC would be fine "if they had Morley Safer, Mike Wallace, and Dan Rather, my producers and film editors." He was smug about "60 Minutes," and with good reason — no one had come up with another successful news magazine since he had invented the genre ten years before.

Hewitt dreamed up "60 Minutes" after CBS put him in charge of documentaries, which he hated. "Nobody likes to read documents, so why would anyone want to watch something called a documentary?" he said. Seeking an alternative, Hewitt, who was easily bored, decided to tell three stories in each program; he picked Mike Wallace and Harry Reasoner as his hosts. He understood that he was producing not the news but the adventures of Mike and Harry and Dan and Morley. "There are TV shows about doctors, cowboys, cops," Hewitt would say. "This is a show about four journalists. But instead of four actors playing these four guys, they are themselves." He had struck prime-time gold. "60 Minutes" cost less to produce than an hour-long drama, and it was owned by CBS. And unlike sitcoms or dramas, "60 Minutes" could — and did — run forever.

Naturally, every network wanted its own magazine. Arledge promised to create one for ABC by the summer of 1978. With time running out, he met with Bob Shanks, a vice president of ABC Entertainment, to see if he could recommend an executive producer.

Shanks nominated himself. He had been a producer for public television's innovative "Great American Dream Machine" and executive producer of "The Merv Griffin Show" before joining ABC, where he took credit for launching "Good Morning America." Shanks also wrote a book, *The Cool Fire,* explaining television in mind-numbing detail. ("There is much to learn about being a good director. On the other hand, there is much that is either in you or not, an inherent talent. A director's sense of visual rhythm or pacing is best when it is part of his personality. Still, a lot can be acquired through training.") Shanks had no news experience, but Arledge could hardly fault him for that.

Shanks went to work in a hurry, coming up with the name "20/20," which stood for perfect vision, and a logo, a pair of spectacles inspired by his own steel-rimmed glasses. A decent, low-key man, Shanks wanted to stretch the boundaries of commercial television to create a show with a hip, contemporary feel. He was inspired not by "60 Minutes" but by the "Dream Machine," a free-form mix of news, features, music, drama, and humor. He also hoped to draw on print models, especially after he made Harold Hayes, the legendary editor of *Esquire,* his second-in-command. Like every producer of a new show, Shanks promised that his creation would be different from anything else on the air. That promise he kept, in spades.

To begin, Arledge and Shanks assembled an eclectic group of correspondents. They included Geraldo Rivera and Sander Vanocur, Sylvia Chase from CBS, Dave Marash, a New York anchorman of varied interests, the astronomer and writer Carl Sagan, and Thomas Hoving, the flamboyant former director of the Metropolitan Museum of Art. "These weren't Ken and Barbie dolls," a "20/20" producer said.

Behind the scenes, Hayes was the major influence. He hired two magazine writers, Brock Brower and Ed Tivnan, who with Shanks looked for new ways to present information — a gossip-column segment called "Cries and Whispers" featuring an unseen couple chatting in bed, an offbeat review of the news called "The Wayward Week," animated political cartoons, even graphics to help the viewers expand their vocabularies with words like "arcane" and "exegesis."

But the print men, while bubbling with ideas, could not persuade the television people that they knew what they were doing — probably because they didn't. Hayes, who looked down on television, wanted to send the correspondents out to gather footage for stories that would be written and produced by the editors in New York. The correspondents resented being treated like glorified legmen. "You can't take stars with defined personalities like Geraldo Rivera, Sander Vanocur, Carl Sagan, and Sylvia Chase and expect them to be field hands for people who've never done TV," Chase said.

Hayes, in turn, resented the correspondents, who he thought acted like children. He mistakenly ignored their warnings that the production process was unwieldy and the show understaffed. But his worst miscalculation came when he agreed to host as well as edit "20/20."

His promotion came about by accident. Looking for fresh faces, Arledge and Shanks auditioned a vast number of prospective hosts and reporters, including Robert MacNeil of PBS, Ben Bradlee and Carl Bernstein of the *Washington Post,* politician Julian Bond, writer Pete Hamill, television critic Marvin Kitman, and Samuel Dash, the former Watergate lawyer. Ed Tivnan, who had worked for *Time,* recommended *Time*'s art critic, Robert Hughes, an outspoken Australian who had done television commentary for the BBC. Hughes delivered "a magnificent winking, smiling, ad-libbing audition" that, by Tivnan's account, earned him a second tryout, this time paired with Hayes. Shanks was captivated by the duo and anointed them his anchor team. "Our culture doesn't produce men like this," he enthused.

By this time, the television veterans were convinced that Shanks had gone nuts. Hughes's Australian accent was hard to decipher, while Hayes, a North Carolinian who had studied at Cambridge, spoke in a mannered style reflecting both locales. Shanks insisted they refer to each other as Hayes and Hughes, which added to the confusion. Said Marash, "Anybody who had screened their audition tapes would have to say, if these guys can get through to the American public, I personally am a Congolese anteater."

Arledge was warned that a disaster was brewing, but he did nothing. No one quite knew why. Later, he explained that he was preoccupied with "World News Tonight" and a series of high-impact documentaries. "I just didn't assert myself," Arledge said. That hardly sufficed as an explanation of how he could permit a program as important as "20/20" to go awry.

At the time, Arledge confided in aides that he was worried about the show and uncomfortable with Shanks. But with "20/20" housed in its own office, a few blocks from ABC News, the warning signs were easy to ignore. "Roone realized that something was wrong, but he didn't know how to fix it," said his assistant Jeff Ruhe. Others thought that by keeping his distance from a show that smelled of failure, Arledge would be in a position to disown it — as he did — and escape blame.

The day before the premiere, Arledge finally stepped in. To mark the tenth anniversary of Robert Kennedy's assassination, he ordered up a graveside interview of Ted Kennedy by Sam Donaldson. He buried deep in the show a sophomoric bit with a Jimmy Carter claymation doll singing "Georgia On My Mind." And he had the anchor lead-ins rewritten, to give them more punch. When Arledge left the studio, after chewing out Shanks, a couple of young staff members broke down and cried.

More tears were shed on premiere night, these by Flip Wilson, when he confessed, during a mawkish segment, that he had spanked his daughter with a belt. The less-than-dynamic duo of Hayes and Hughes chatted ineptly with California Governor Jerry Brown. But Geraldo Rivera's lead story, an overlong, overheated, overhyped exposé about the killing of jackrabbits by greyhounds, provided the most bizarre touch. Rivera's so-called special report consisted of bloody, stomach-turning visuals and a narration delivered at an emotional pitch suggesting he had uncovered a new Willowbrook, if not another Watergate.

The viewers that night included ABC News people working late on the format for "World News Tonight." "You know the worst thing about that program?" producer Walter Porges said afterward. "The part where it says at the end that it's a production of ABC News." Naturally, the traditionalists blamed Arledge.

At a photo session afterward, Arledge tried to avoid having his picture taken with Hayes and Hughes. By then, he knew they wouldn't last. But Arledge could not avoid the opening-night party at Alfredo's, where everyone tried gamely to celebrate, until Shanks began to drink and complain about Arledge. He recalled how he tried to call Roone, how Roone would not respond, how Roone had his chance to reshape the show. Shanks's wife, Ann, tried to shush him, as did Irwin Weiner, Arledge's moneyman, but he could not be deterred. Finally, his voice booming, Shanks declared, "You know, he doesn't return anybody's phone calls. He doesn't even return his daughter's phone calls." If Arledge harbored doubts about whether to dump Shanks, that erased them.

Arledge took home a cassette of the "20/20" premiere, hoping to screen it before taking action, but he was busy the next day going over his contract with Fred Pierce. Even after moving into News, Arledge had not signed a contract to replace the one that had expired in 1975 — he hated committing to anything. That night, Arledge kept a promise to his friend Ethel Kennedy to attend a benefit dinner and a Neil Simon play, but he left early to go home and screen the show again. "It was even worse than I imagined," he said.

The next morning, he flipped on "Good Morning America." Filling in for David Hartman was Hugh Downs, who had been host of NBC's "Today" for most of the 1960s. Arledge called "GMA" and arranged to see Downs at the ABC suite at the Dorset Hotel. The two men had never met.

When Downs arrived, Arledge skipped the formalities.

"Hugh, have you seen '20/20'?" he asked.

"Yes," replied Downs. He thought it best to say nothing more.

Arledge told him, unnecessarily, that Hayes and Hughes were not working out as hosts.

"Are you interested?" Arledge asked.

Downs was interested. Even better, he was available — "20/20" needed a new host in five days. Arledge figured he wasn't going to do any better than Hugh Downs.

Hugh Downs had enjoyed a remarkable television career. He had done morning and late-night shows, prime-time and daytime shows, news shows, talk shows, game shows, commercials, and documentaries. He would appear on national television for 10,000 hours, a feat that earned him a place in the *Guinness Book of Records* as the most durable performer in the history of the medium.

His longevity was not easily explained. Downs had no formal training as a journalist or entertainer. He could not report a complex news story or tell a joke. Nor was he sexy or handsome. In the idiom of television, Downs was a "personality" — a utility man with a pleasing voice who was famous for being well known.

Downs himself was forthright about his talents. In his autobiography, *On Camera,* he wrote: "In a medium full of flashy entertainers, brilliant comedians, superb actors and honey-throated announcers, I was none of the above. I was a well-spoken kid from Ohio with an absolutely ordinary personality."

He explained his enduring appeal by saying, "The less talent you deploy, then the more you are just a person, the more acceptable you are, the less danger there is of burn-out and over-exposure."

He was as mainstream as Hayes and Hughes were offbeat.

And yet it was a mistake to underestimate Downs. He dropped out of college but educated himself. He was a gentleman, but he could be tough. And he was popular with the viewers.

"Hugh is twice as intelligent as he's ever let anybody notice," said Brock Brower, his "20/20" colleague. "Dumb Hughie? He's a very smart guy."

Born in Akron, Ohio, in 1921, Hugh Downs got his start in radio but soon moved to television as an announcer for soap operas, news shows, and the kids' show "Kukla, Fran & Ollie." He first emerged as a personality while playing second banana to Jack Paar on NBC's "Tonight" in the late 1950s and early 1960s. There, Downs was cast as the house intellectual — "Paar's Plato," one columnist called him — because he had read the great books and could discourse at length about astronomy, aeronautics, and theoretical physics. Comic Red Skelton once said, "Ask Hugh what time it is and he'll tell you how to build a watch."

Meanwhile, Downs became television's premier pitchman. He possessed one talent without which no one can survive long on the air — the ability to project sincerity — and so he sold lots of Alpo and Brylcreem. His believability helped land him another job as host of "Concentration" in 1958, at the height of the quiz show scandals.

When Paar quit in 1962, Downs wanted to take over "Tonight." When he lost the job to Johnny Carson, NBC found a place for him at the other end of the broadcast day, as host of "Today." He brought a calm, relaxed mood to the mornings, and unlike his predecessors, Edwin Newman and John Chancellor, who were journalists, Downs was willing to read the commercials. He did the NBC dawn patrol for nine years, serving as an easygoing counterpoise to his intense co-host, Barbara Walters.

His gentle on-air manner hid his stubbornness. In 1968, Downs refused to sign a new contract until NBC dumped Al Morgan, the "Today" producer, with whom he was feuding. A few years before, Downs threatened to quit NBC if he wasn't named host of a new nighttime version of "Concentration." In a letter to his boss, Downs wrote: "From a legal, profit and ownership standpoint, 'Concentration' belongs to NBC. But from a moral, audience and entertainment standpoint, 'Concentration' belongs to me."

He could stand up to the network because, unlike many television performers, he was not wedded to his job. If anything, he was less involved than his bosses liked. Al Morgan once called him "the laziest man in television," and while that was unfair, Downs was no workaholic. He had seen "hot" personalities like Paar burn out; he trusted others to do their work and, sometimes, his as well.

Personally and financially secure, Downs enjoyed his private life. He and his wife, Ruth, traveled widely. He sailed, flew planes and gliders, and enjoyed deep-sea diving. In fact, Downs developed so many outside interests that he quit "Today" in 1971 and moved to Arizona. He wanted to work less.

Then Arledge called. Downs wanted the "20/20" job, but on his terms. He insisted on being sole anchor and working no more than four days a week, so he could honor a commitment to PBS. Downs also wanted a management role on "20/20," but on that point Arledge would not yield.

As host, Downs was an inspired choice. Calm and credible, he brought an immediate touch of professionalism to "20/20." He was not called on to do much, but his presence helped viewers accept the rest of the unconventional cast. Downs provided, in his words, "a stable center around which fiery segments can spin."

Indeed, Downs's hiring began to pull "20/20" back from the edge of television and toward the safer middle. As envisioned by Shanks, the program would have tested the boundaries of prime time; it was an experiment that, given time, might have produced fresh and provocative television. Even Arledge would later concede, "They fervently believed they were going to change television, and this was a great program. And in some respects it was avant-garde." But after the premiere, Arledge felt he had to take drastic action; this was not the time to try to lead viewers to places they didn't want to go. By hiring Hugh Downs, who was the antithesis of avant-garde, Arledge was responding to the commercial pressures of television. This began a process of narrowing the scope of "20/20" that has continued for the rest of its life.

When Roone Arledge was asked how long it would take to turn ABC News around, he would always tell a story. Before taking over, he would say, he had talked to Morley Safer and John Chancellor; Safer had told him it would take seven years to have an impact, while Chancellor had said it would take five. Then Elton Rule, the president of ABC, had assured him, "I want you to understand that we're not expecting miracles — it might take a year." Finally, Dick Beesemyer, an ABC executive in charge of affiliate relations, had grabbed him at a meeting to say, "Hey, if we could turn this news thing around in a couple of months, there's about six stations I could grab for us."

The story cast Arledge in a favorite role: the underdog fighting against long odds. It served him just the way that downplaying the achievements of the old ABC News did, by calling attention to the obstacles he faced. In this instance, though, his point was well taken — no formula could bring instant success to ABC News. After a year on the job, Arledge had learned that running news was tougher even than he had expected it to be. But he also had discovered that the job brought him the excitement and impact he had wanted.

Some of the problems came as no surprise: news viewing habits were ingrained, he knew, and, unlike in sports, an up-and-coming network could not buy a news audience by outbidding its rivals for major events. But Arledge was not prepared for all the criticism he was getting from both inside and outside ABC; he'd never suffered such bad publicity in sports, and the attacks only reinforced a tendency he already had to feel misunderstood and unfairly victimized. "Everything you do is (a) covered and (b) interpreted, usually wrongly," he would say.

The criticism upset him so much that he asked his secretary, Carol Grisanti, not to give him any more negative press clips; one day, he opened his *New York Post* and found a big hole cut out.

"What the hell is going on here?" Arledge asked.

"You wouldn't want to know," Grisanti replied.

It wasn't just the press that judged him harshly. Rivals were also quick to rebuke Arledge for his excesses. After ABC boasted about its Sadat-Begin coverage, Walter Cronkite said, "I hope for the good of broadcast news that those who lean more toward the values of Broadway than those of journalism will eventually put behind them the unseemly, undignified and unprofessional scramble for self-promotion." Arledge took that as a compliment, saying, "All of a sudden, it gets competitive, and it's like I've walked in and broken the rules of the club."

Still, Arledge made some concessions to tradition; he no longer came to work in bold polka dot shirts and beige safari jackets, replacing them with navy blue suits and conservative pin-dot ties. And he never again went as wild over a tabloid story as he had over Son of Sam. Mostly, though, his critics drove him to work even harder, to prove them wrong. "It was one of those things that made you realize that you could never quit," he said. At forty-seven, Arledge was energized by his new responsibilities, which was fortunate, since running both the news and sports divisions would have tested the endurance of any man.

His management style was freewheeling. Titles and organization charts meant nothing to him, and he never held formal meetings or wrote memos. "If Roone would call a meeting it would be for effect," said David Burke. "And he never wrote anything down. He knew everything, and he had complete deniability." Many nights, a small group of aides would gather in his office after the evening newscast; people would help themselves to drinks from Arledge's well-stocked bar, and they would talk, sometimes for hours. Late at night, Arledge might have another idea and ring up Burke, who got so used to taking his calls that he put a long extension cord on his bedroom phone; that way, he could sit outside the door and talk without keeping his wife awake.

Arledge managed by crisis. He ignored problems that did not demand action, hoping they would resolve themselves, and put off decisions until the last minute. He was harder to reach than ever, especially when problems arose in Sports, which clearly had become a secondary concern. His calendar was in perpetual flux: appointments could get canceled on a whim, and he'd run consistently late. When Sally Bedell, a *TV Guide* reporter, asked him how he managed his time, Arledge replied, "It depends on where the fire is. I am hard to get, but once I get there, I get immersed down to much more detail than an executive normally would."

While Arledge often managed to set aside a few hours for his passions — a round of golf or a concert at Lincoln Center — he was working all the rest of the time, even when he seemed to be at ease. One weekend, Arledge was watching "World News" at his place in Sagaponack with his daughter Patty when a report came on about the strategic arms limitation talks, known as SALT. "Do you know what the SALT talks are?" he asked her. She didn't, which prompted him to call the control room to tell the producer to provide more background next time. "That's the problem," Arledge would say. "We never explain things. If you don't watch the news every night, it's like coming in in the middle of a book."

For all the setbacks, the criticism, and the long hours, Arledge never doubted that he had made the right decision to move to News. His competitive juices flowed all the time. "It was exciting, it was intellectually stimulating, and it was frustrating," he said, "but overall, it was sensational fun." Beyond that, Arledge felt that he was doing work that mattered. He had toyed with the possibilities of producing entertainment shows or even running a network, but in his heart he knew he was ill-suited for a conventional executive role. "I didn't want to spend my life with affiliates and sales meetings and budget meetings and all of that," he said. Instead, he wanted to bring new viewers to news, to tackle big stories, and to create programs with impact. "It was a very, very important thing to be doing," Arledge said. All the attention that ABC was getting reminded him that he had become a major player in the world of broadcast news. That was a feeling he liked.

Hiring Hugh Downs gave "20/20" a lift, but his arrival only began the process of saving the show. The program was under pressure to generate strong ratings; even after ABC became the top-rated network in prime time in 1977, Fred Pierce was unwilling to concede an hour of prime time each week. To put numbers on the board, the magazine show needed more than good stories; it needed stars.

Downs was a familiar face, but he had never been accused of displaying excessive charisma. Geraldo Rivera, by contrast, could become a star. Rivera was a hot personality, an ethnic New Yorker who, like Howard Cosell, was plucked from local television and given a national stage by Arledge. Like Cosell, Rivera had the ego, the talent, the ambition, and the outsize personality to stand out in the bright lights of prime time. "Roone loved Geraldo," said Dennis Sullivan, a "20/20" producer. "They were very, very close." Rivera recalled, "He praised my reporting, my instincts, even my occasional emotionalism."

Rivera, who was only thirty-five when he signed on with "20/20," had grown up on Long Island, the first-born son of a Puerto Rican father and a Jewish mother. An underweight child, he suffered from acne, asthma, and allergies — which, he said, forced him to develop "an engaging, resourceful personality to get people to look past the pimples." He was raised as a Jew and was first known as Jerry; he had a Star of David tattooed on his hand to celebrate Israel's victory in the Six-Day War. Later, Rivera's Puerto Rican roots came to the fore as he plunged into the maelstrom of New York City politics, and he insisted on being called Geraldo.

A creature of the 1960s, Rivera was thrust into the public eye as a lawyer for the Young Lords, a radical Puerto Rican group. Hired as a reporter by WABC-TV in New York, he was a newsroom renegade, an iconoclast who brought passion and point of view to his stories. Rivera was the video equivalent of a newspaper columnist — like Cosell, he freely mixed reporting and opinion on the air, upsetting the traditionalists. When he sought work at ABC News, Bill Sheehan offered him a job but said he would be paid only $50,000 a year, $30,000 less than his salary at the local station. Naturally, he turned it down.

But Rivera would not be confined to the local news for long. He broke out by hosting "Good Night America," a late-night talk show aimed at young viewers and produced by ABC Entertainment. Rivera did everything he could to make the program a hit, once going so far as to smoke marijuana on the air to hype the show, but he was no threat to Johnny Carson. After the late-night show was canceled in 1977, Arledge was delighted to hire him at ABC News. Together they would take on the news establishment, although, like Arledge, Rivera craved respect as well as fame; he once confided to a colleague that he dreamed of becoming the next Edward R. Murrow.

Rivera, though, was far too much the rebel to win over the journalistic establishment. He flouted the rules, insisting, for example, that he could join in political campaigns while working as a reporter. His flamboyance also offended traditionalists: he was a notorious womanizer who gloried in the spotlight and boasted about his celebrity. "Like a rock star with a hit record, I would stop traffic, turn heads and start a crowd," he boasted in his autobiography, *Exposing Myself*. On the air, Rivera never passed up a chance to expose himself. The joke at ABC was that if Geraldo had been sent to Vietnam, he would have opened his story by saying, "Behind me, the Vietnam War."

Yet the precise qualities that were unacceptable in a straight reporter made him ideal for "20/20." Arledge wanted a well-defined character for the show, and Rivera obliged him — he would be the street-smart crusader fighting for the underdog. With the help of his own unit of intensely loyal producers and researchers, Rivera churned out hard-hitting stories on such topics as Agent Orange and drug company rip-offs, letting nothing stand in his way. Tracking the Agent Orange story to a Missouri farm, for example, Rivera and producer Charlie Thompson brawled with field hands who didn't like a TV crew nosing around. "Geraldo broke the jaw of the guy who owned the farm," recalled Thompson, a savvy but hot-tempered Vietnam veteran who did nothing to quash rumors that he carried a pistol when traveling with Rivera.

Arledge and Dick Wald, his Columbia friend whom he'd hired as an ABC News vice president, thought Rivera was invaluable. Wald, who was assigned to watch over "20/20," said, "He was the center of the show. He provided the burning energy that made it different from other news magazines. He had good story ideas and he worked hard."

With a host and a star in place, Arledge still needed a program — or at least an executive producer to shape one. Jeff Gralnick, a young producer, took over for Shanks and brought some order to the place before giving way to an ill-fated trio of producers — Brock Brower, Dennis Sullivan, and Dan Cooper — who found it impossible to run a show by committee. "It was just a constant battle all the time over what we should do and how we should do it," said Brower, whose legacy to "20/20" was the tag line "We're in touch so you be in touch," that he wrote for Downs. The troika was replaced by Al Ittleson, an affable executive, who also proved unable to take command. "He was a sweet, nice, competent, wonderful person," an insider said, "but people were jumping up and down on him with cleats." With all the turmoil, "20/20" cast about for an identity and struggled in the ratings during its first season.

Nevertheless, the cast had talent, and the stories, while uneven, were unpredictable in the best sense. Rivera, Marash, and Chase produced solid investigations; Tom Hoving did lively pieces on discos and Broadway; and Carl Sagan drew on his knowledge of science to do a variety of stories.

Arledge took a pragmatic approach to "20/20," relentlessly focusing on how the audience would react. Often, after screening a segment, Arledge would say, "Why would I watch this?" The question was Arledgian in its vagueness, since it didn't reveal whether he liked or disliked the piece, but his point was that stories had to be more than merely interesting; viewers needed to be given a compelling reason to watch. Arledge pushed for segments with a hook, stories that could be sold in ten- or twenty-second promos. "I had the impression that he was hoping for something sensational, searching for some story that would immediately put the show in a high-wattage national spotlight," Downs said.

For a time, "20/20" went after names in sports. Leon Spinks, Pete Rose, Mario Andretti, Earl Campbell, Jim Bouton, Diana Nyad, and Bobby Orr were all profiled, but the ratings did not budge. When an interview with singer Rod Stewart got huge ratings, Arledge and Wald saw big-name rock stars as the answer to their problems. "Until people knew the program, they needed a hook to bring them in," Wald said. "And the hook was essentially glitter. And we did a lot of it. Unapologetically. It wasn't perfect, but it worked."

Entertainment value, not news judgment, shaped story selection, much to the chagrin, once again, of ABC traditionalists. In the space of one season, "20/20" did pieces on Donna Summer, Ed McMahon, Frank Sinatra, the Village People, Paul McCartney, Tammy Wynette, New Wave rock, Michael Jackson, George Burns, Liza Minnelli, Lawrence Welk, Blondie, Fred Astaire, Herb Alpert, the Swedish pop group ABBA, Andy Warhol, Wayne Newton, Billy Joel, Loretta Lynn, and Suzanne Somers. The ratings began to climb.

Arledge also got the high-wattage story he wanted: a dramatic account of the drug-induced death of Elvis Presley, reported by Rivera and produced by Charlie Thompson. Presley was a hero of Rivera's and a perfect target for Thompson, who had great contacts in his hometown of Memphis. They spent months interviewing witnesses and obtaining documents that detailed Presley's long history of drug use — so much of it new and exclusive material that they took over the entire hour-long season premiere of "20/20." On the air, Rivera delivered an eye-opening account of Presley's demise and blew apart the cover-up that followed his death. It was the perfect "20/20" story, applying the techniques of investigative reporting to a red-hot, sensational topic to produce huge ratings — the highest in the show's history, then and now. "The Elvis Cover-Up," which ran on September 13, 1979, became the most-watched news program of the year.

By then, "20/20" had a new leader. In desperation, Arledge had turned to a strong producer with proven talents — Av Westin, who had put "World News Tonight" on the air. He proved to be the right choice. Westin set standards of editorial quality, monitored stories through each stage of production, and imposed financial discipline. "The moment he got here, Av set up a system," said producer Jeff Diamond. "Everybody respected him, maybe feared him a little bit. He came in with a big reputation and he was going to make the show work."

Westin's system was expressly designed to shift power away from the correspondents to the producers. Rivera resisted successfully — his "20/20" unit operated almost as an independent production company — but the other correspondents were required to work with producers assigned by and responsible to Westin, who believed in centralized control. "This is a producer's medium," Westin said, "in which a correspondent plays a critical role, but only one role. The correspondent is part of the transmission belt." Under his scheme, the correspondents, who had to be on the air regularly to establish their characters, were to get involved in a story only when their presence was needed.

A few correspondents grumbled. Driven by his principles and his ego, Dave Marash insisted on taking lead editorial responsibility for his stories; he objected to what he saw as a production-line mentality that, when taken to extremes, reduced the correspondent to the role of actor. But because each piece took weeks or months to complete, he was unable to churn out the twenty to twenty-five stories a year that the system demanded. While Marash got a reputation for being stubborn and slow, he said, "One of the things that slowed me down was that I was always trying to find out what was new, what was different. Or what was wrong with the official or presumptive version of a story. To me, the whole joy of journalism is actually chewing on and digesting and tasting and ruminating in your second stomach the materials of the story."

Westin's push for control and efficiency meant that more stories had to be plotted in advance, presold, and market-tested before producers and correspondents could commit time and money to them. This drastically reduced the likelihood of embarking on an open-ended quest for a story and being surprised along the way; indeed, surprises were unwelcome.

But Westin's approach worked. The trains ran on time, and stories were well executed and polished, if not as daring or unpredictable as during the early days. "20/20" averaged an impressive 30 share during 1979–80 and 1980–81, his first two seasons; that meant the show reached 30 percent of the viewers watching television during its time period, Thursdays at ten.

By then, Arledge had reshaped "20/20" to meet the demands of prime time: the program had a recognizable host, identifiable stars, promotable stories, and an efficient means of production. "20/20" was also more predictable, more mainstream, and less inclined to challenge its viewers, none of which bothered Arledge. He had no interest in noble failures.

The payoff to ABC News was substantial: "20/20" became the news division's first profitable program, generating tens of millions of dollars a year in revenues. The program also gave ABC News a prime-time platform for high-profile stories and interviews that could not be squeezed onto "World News Tonight." Getting a news program established in prime time was no small feat, as all the networks would demonstrate in the years ahead as they struggled to come up with another one.

No one was more impressed by the rise of "20/20" than Dick Wald, who had been president of NBC News for four years during the mid-1970s. Wald had been fired, a victim of the corporate infighting that plagued NBC, and after a brief stint with media giant Times-Mirror, he had come to work for Arledge at ABC. Wald was the only aide to Arledge who had run a major news organization, so his experience was valuable.

But nothing in Wald's experience prepared him for the patience ABC's corporate hierarchy had displayed with "20/20." Arledge, he thought, deserved enormous credit for acting decisively to rescue the show. But Wald was equally impressed by the way Fred Pierce and the network had backed Arledge, especially after the opening-night debacle. The contrast to NBC's environment was striking.

"I had come from a place where people were working against each other, where they were very insecure," Wald said. "Here the company was committed to making news successful. Fred had made his commitment, Roone was holding him to it, and Fred was trying to make the thing work. Everyone was rowing the boat together and they were going to make it work. And they did."

Arledge soon would put the network's commitment to ABC News to an even stiffer test.

Chapter Six

FROM MORNING TILL NIGHTLINE

BOB DYK'S fifteen minutes of fame began on a Sunday afternoon in the fall of 1979 in London, where he worked as a radio reporter for ABC News. He had come into the bureau for weekend desk duty, when he spotted what looked like a big story on the wires: militant students had seized the American Embassy in Iran.

No one knew then how big a story it would become. Ten months earlier, protestors who had occupied the embassy were ejected after a few hours. This time, Iranian authorities assured the Carter administration that they would again wrest the complex away from the demonstrators.

Still, ABC needed to get someone to Tehran. Dyk began calling around, as did the assignment desk in New York. Peter Jennings, who had covered Iran, was on home leave in Canada. Nobody else with a visa could be found.

Reluctantly, Dyk volunteered. He had a visa, but he also had two young children and no desire to revisit Tehran. Besides, Dyk, forty-two, was a radio man. He wanted to work in television, but he was not sure he was ready for the network.

Ready or not, Dyk was ordered into the breach by Stan Opotowsky, who as ABC's director of news coverage in New York was responsible for deploying correspondents and crews around the world. Opotowsky knew he needed to get someone, anyone, in quickly, if only to protect ABC against getting beat. Bob Dyk would have to do. "He was the only guy who could make the plane," Opotowsky said.

Long before that Sunday — this was November 4, 1979 — Roone

Arledge had often said that what ABC needed was to get ahead of everybody on a big story. He would say, "Sometime, somewhere, a story will break, and we'll be in position to cover it better than anybody else, and then people will say, how did they get to be as good as they are?"

That sounded great, but Opotowsky, a veteran, knew that "to be really exclusive on a huge story requires two things — that you do the right thing and the other guys do the wrong thing. Part of it is luck and part of it is sticking your neck out, taking a chance you don't think the other guys will take."

As it happened, CBS and NBC — concerned about the potential dangers — hesitated. Dyk and veteran photographer David Greene left London by plane that evening and found, to their surprise, that no one from CBS or NBC was aboard. When they got to Tehran, they went immediately to the embassy and came upon an unforgettable scene.

Thousands of people surrounded the embassy, spilling out of the gates, shouting anti-American slogans. "Death to America," they chanted. "Death to Carter." Their screams made a hellish din. Stunned, Dyk was hustled into the building to tape the first news conference by the militant students. On the way out, he spotted an American flag in flames, an image captured by Greene. The story dominated Monday's "World News Tonight."

In the meantime, Iran temporarily closed its borders to Americans. Over the next few days, five CBS crews and three from NBC were turned away at Tehran's Mehrabad Airport. Walter Cronkite was so envious after watching ABC that he placed a congratulatory call to the ABC assignment desk, in front of his CBS people — "more to humiliate them than to congratulate us," Opotowsky thought.

For a week, Bob Dyk owned the biggest story on the planet. He was given a battlefield promotion to television correspondent and filed stories for "World News Tonight," "Good Morning America," and "20/20." Over the air and in print, ABC promoted its exclusive. "We moved faster than anybody else," Arledge boasted. "We just sensed it was a bigger story than the other two did." The Nielsen ratings for "World News" jumped by two points, which translated into 1.5 million new households.

Four days into the crisis, ABC News broadcast a late-night special, a forty-five-minute report anchored by Frank Reynolds. Jeff Gralnick, the producer, gave the special a catchy title: "The Iran Crisis: America Held Hostage."

"Look at this," Reynolds began, "one American, blindfolded, handcuffed, today in the courtyard of the American Embassy in Tehran." ABC had the most explosive pictures yet from Iran — footage of hostage Barry Rosen, an embassy official, paraded in humiliating fashion before captors and cameras. Blanket coverage followed: Dyk's reports from Tehran, a profile of the exiled Shah by Barrie Dunsmore, a look at terrorism by John Martin, a report on U.S. diplomacy by Ted Koppel, and a poll reported by Sam Donaldson.

ABC did not present another special for six days. The story's full import was not yet clear. "This was a bunch of weird people holding a bunch of Americans," Gralnick said. "Diplomacy is going on, and it takes time to understand that this is really serious, that those bastards really have us by the balls."

At about this time, Arledge went to Lake Placid, site of the upcoming Winter Olympics, to promote the ABC Sports telecasts of the games. He took questions about skating and skiing, but most reporters wanted to talk about the hostages. When Arledge got back to New York, he suggested to his news executives that they do a special every night. "Look," he said, "my elevator man, the taxi driver, the pilot on the plane, the people in Lake Placid who should be talking about the Olympics — all these people care about now are the hostages in Iran."

On November 15, eleven days into the crisis, Arledge and David Burke went to see Fred Pierce. They needed his approval before they could commit to a nightly special.

As usual, Pierce worried about dollars and cents. The ratings for the specials were good, but he wasn't sure that commercials could be sold on a nightly basis. "How long can this thing go on?" he asked.

No one could say. Arledge and Burke guessed that the hostages might be free by Thanksgiving and figured they would surely be home by Christmas.

Pierce gave the go-ahead. He assumed that the specials would lose money but thought that they would burnish the image of the news division and reflect favorably on ABC. Any financial losses could be absorbed by the network, which was earning more than $400 million in profits from its daytime and prime-time shows. Like everyone else, Pierce thought the story would go away soon.

That night, Reynolds signed off "America Held Hostage" by reminding viewers that ABC News would keep them informed of developments throughout the next day and "again at this time tomorrow night." Then, almost casually, he added, "In fact, we'll be on the air every night at this time with a broadcast about the crisis in Iran as long as there is a crisis."

Arledge was not satisfied with that. Unlike Reynolds, he was not shy about self-promotion. He had a press release issued declaring ABC's commitment to "America Held Hostage." He bought newspaper ads trumpeting ABC's late-night coverage and promoted the show on the air. This, he sensed, was the big story he'd hungered for.

Inside ABC, not everyone agreed. Bob Siegenthaler, who was assigned to produce "America Held Hostage," thought the open-ended commitment was foolhardy. He argued that ABC should do a program only when there was news. "When you say you're going to stay with the story 'until it's resolved,' it traps you," he said.

At the other networks, executives saw Arledge's declaration as showmanship and said so. "To commit in advance, not knowing what the news is, is obviously overkill," said Ed Fouhy, CBS's Washington bureau chief.

Even CBS's Dan Rather, one of the most aggressive newsmen in television, voiced doubts to David Burke, who had quietly begun to court Rather, hoping to lure him to ABC.

"Everyone in my shop says it's ridiculous, and I tend to agree with them," Rather said, over a lunch with Burke. "We know what you folks are going to wind up doing. You're going to wind up recutting tape from the evening news."

Burke assured him that ABC had other ideas. "Dan, we're going to explain the story," he said. "We're going to tell people what Shiites are, what Sunnis are."

Rather remained a skeptic, though not for long.

For in the weeks ahead — as the names and faces of the hostages and their families grew familiar, as the White House began to display anger, as the Iranians remained intransigent, and the image of burning American flags became a nightly staple on the news — the story grew. Competition among the networks intensified. Television would eventually devote as much intense, sustained attention to the hostage story as it had to any story in its history, including civil rights, Vietnam, the moon landing, and Watergate. Unlike, say, the eighty-two crew members of the USS *Pueblo*, who were held captive for eleven months by North Korea in 1968, the fifty-two hostages in Iran were a highly visible presence on television for all their time in captivity. Dramatic, emotional, and visual, this was a made-for-television story — a live, global miniseries with an unscripted ending. And the story belonged to ABC.

But the story had grown too big for Bob Dyk. Once Peter Jennings landed in Tehran, Dyk assumed a backup role from which he never emerged, although he was on hand to cover the hostages' release. By his own account, Dyk needed time to develop as a television correspondent, but he faded from view with the hostages and left ABC in 1983.

The Iran story was so dramatic that no one realized what Roone Arledge was really up to during the fall of 1979. He was covering the hostages, of course, and he was promoting ABC News, but above all, he was staking a claim to airtime. Arledge knew that power, in television, derives from control over airtime, and he wanted the half hour between 11:30 and midnight for ABC News.

Late-night television viewing had been dominated for years by "The Tonight Show" on NBC. CBS scheduled old movies against Johnny Carson, while ABC offered reruns of its prime-time hits — the fare included "Love Boat, "Police Woman," and "Charlie's Angels." The reruns were inexpensive, but ABC's ratings were weak, which left an opening for Arledge.

He had coveted the late-night time period ever since becoming News president. "If there was a plane crash, a key congressional vote, a visit by a dignitary, whatever it was, we would do a half-hour special," Arledge said. In the months before the hostage taking, ABC had run 11:30 specials on President Carter's energy program, the resignation of United Nations Ambassador Andrew Young, and for four days in October, the travels of Pope John Paul II.

Arledge had occasionally hinted at his designs on the time period, but no one took notice. It never occurred to anyone that viewers might be willing to stay up until midnight to watch news. "It was gutsy to go with news," said Bob Siegenthaler. "It flew in the face of programming logic."

With "America Held Hostage" Arledge set out to disprove the conventional wisdom. Not only was the story gripping, but the timing was right — he had spent more than two years remaking ABC News. By now, Arledge and Burke had hired dozens of people, producers and directors as well as correspondents, and their confidence in the holdovers had grown.

Technology had also transformed the news-gathering process by the late 1970s, making possible the immediate coverage of news around the world. The growth of air travel was one factor — it took less time than ever to get crews into out-of-the-way places — as was the expanded use of direct-dial telephones. The shift from film to videotape in the mid-1970s also speeded up production; film took an hour or more to develop, while videotape could be played back and edited immediately; portable editing equipment enabled correspondents to craft their stories in the field. But the most profound changes were driven by the spread of satellite technology, which made it possible to transmit footage instantly, live or on tape, from around the world to viewers at home. The technology eventually meant that the networks could transmit news instantly from a portable earth station that could be packed into suitcases and shipped anywhere.

The satellite transmission itself wasn't new — Arledge's ABC Sports had used satellites to broadcast a U.S.-Soviet track meet live from Moscow in 1965 — but for years relatively few countries had the facilities needed to uplink footage onto satellites. Throughout the 1960s, for example, the networks could not feed stories out of Vietnam or the Middle East — film had to be flown to Hong Kong or Rome — and until 1973 there were no reliable earth stations in the Arab world. But the technology spread rapidly as foreign governments recognized the financial and political benefits of permitting American networks to feed news out of their countries. Governments that were slow to catch on were prodded by the networks; ABC executives urged the Egyptian ambassador in Washington to have a modern uplink installed in Cairo, if only to ensure that all news from the region not be filtered through Israel. By 1979, the message had gotten out, and dozens of nations had uplinks. The Iranian television and radio facilities were among the most modern in the third world.

"The technology was improving so fast," Opotowsky recalled, "that I warned our foreign desk — never say you can't feed from a city because you couldn't last week. Check it again today." Just as Arledge had employed slow motion and instant replay to reinvent television sports, he would use satellite technology to transform news. Had the Iranians taken the hostages a decade earlier, "America Held Hostage" would have been unthinkable — pictures from Iran would have lagged days behind the news. The time had come to exploit the new technologies of the global village.

Arledge threw all his energies into "America Held Hostage." He held daily bull sessions to discuss the show, watched every night, and called on the red Roone phone with comments large and small. When Barrie Dunsmore used the word "xenophobic" to describe the Ayatollah Khomeini, Arledge phoned to object, saying too many viewers wouldn't know what the word meant. He frequently offered story ideas, particularly on slow news days, when he pushed for coverage that would help viewers make sense of events.

To a great extent, Arledge was guided by his own curiosity. His interests were so varied — they included foreign affairs, politics, sports, music, food, and architecture — that he found it hard to understand people who lacked curiosity about the world. Arledge read voraciously, working his way through stacks of newspapers and magazines, so many that his assistant, Jeff Ruhe, said, "You could live off his discards." And although he was too shy to strike up a conversation with a stranger, Arledge's curiosity went beyond reading, especially when he traveled. One night in Moscow, he came upon the Russian Army rehearsing for a parade and stood for a long time, watching, even after his companions returned to the hotel for a drink. "I thought — how can you walk away? When in your life are you going to have the opportunity to stand three feet away from the Russian Army and watch how they operate, what their equipment looks like, their faces and all," Arledge said. "I guess either you're curious about those kinds of things or you're not."

Not surprisingly, Arledge was filled with questions after the hostages were taken. To a reporter, he said, "What negotiations have been going on? What military prerogatives do we have? When you get a complex story like this, it's particularly important to explain to people the limitations — that if you blow up the oil fields, which is the first thing people think of, you're going to destroy the economy of half of our allies and we're going to drive the price of oil in the world up to an unacceptable figure. Or if you bomb Qum, you're going to unify the whole Moslem world against us and you're going to make Khomeini a martyr."

"America Held Hostage" examined the choices facing the White House, as well as the politics and culture of Iran. Correspondent Lynn Sherr did pieces on the history of the region, the nature of Islam, even a story that simply asked, "What is a mullah?" One critic wrote: "Americans are learning more about the temperaments, politics and geography of the Islamic world than they have ever had a chance to learn before."

The program strained the resources of ABC News. Arledge rotated correspondents into Iran, where the network had five crews, one of which staked out the embassy around the clock. "We were burning people up night and day," said Steve Skinner, a producer in Tehran. "There was tremendous pressure from New York to get ahead and stay ahead." Stateside, one of the first to tire was Frank Reynolds, who was anchoring "World News Tonight" as well as "America Held Hostage." After a few weeks, it was apparent that Reynolds, who took his editorial responsibilities seriously, could not continue to anchor two shows a day.

On November 29, his fifty-sixth birthday, Reynolds took the night off and was replaced by diplomatic correspondent Ted Koppel. Because he had all day to focus on "America Held Hostage," Koppel brought ideas and energy to the show; he became a frequent substitute for Reynolds. "Ted took what we were doing, built on it, and brought his own personality to it," said producer Mike Duffy. When Reynolds moved on to cover the 1980 presidential campaign, Koppel took over the program — although, by then, the hostage story and the campaign were inextricably intertwined.

Political calculations at the White House, in fact, had helped ABC launch "America Held Hostage." The Carter administration saw the hostage crisis as a way to unite the country behind the president, who faced a Democratic primary challenge from Senator Edward Kennedy. Barrie Dunsmore, who was given access to key State Department officials, said, "We needed a daily news peg. If they had said, 'No, we're not going to talk about the hostage crisis anymore,' that show would have ultimately perished." Hodding Carter, the State Department spokesman whose briefings became nightly television fare, even called Reynolds after the show one night to thank him for the coverage. Later, of course, Carter would come to rue the nightly focus on the hostages and especially the title "America Held Hostage" — because, as White House spokesman Jody Powell put it, "Demonstrably, neither the government nor the country was 'held hostage' by this."

By year's end, even with the daily satellite feeds, the frequent explainers, the commitment of resources, and the cooperation of the White House, "America Held Hostage" was flagging. Some nights, the show was cut to fifteen minutes, and the staff was overworked. Producer Bob Furnad had T-shirts made up saying "ABC Held Hostage," but Siegenthaler would not allow them to be distributed; he did not want it said that the network was making light of the story. Still, ratings for "America Held Hostage" were growing, and the show was a source of pride inside ABC. On New Year's Eve, the network had champagne delivered to the exhausted staff.

While the gesture was appreciated, few were in a mood to toast the arrival of 1980. Koppel recalled, "We went weeks not only without a day off but working eighteen hours a day. And assuming that one day Roone would come to his senses and say, 'Okay, guys, nice job,

but this thing's going to go on forever, so we'll go back to normal.'
Well, wrong. He had a strategy which none of us knew about."

When Ted Koppel first did interviews on "America Held Hostage,"
he followed the customary practice of talking face-to-face with his
guests. But there came a night when Ali Agah, the Iranian chargé
d'affaires, was unwilling to leave the Iranian Embassy for fear he
might be arrested by the FBI. The ABC Washington bureau sent a
crew to the embassy, put a camera on Agah, and rigged up a green
chromakey screen that appeared blank in the studio but, to viewers
at home, looked like a window through which Koppel could see Agah.

Arledge loved it. He called right away to say that the chromakey
window looked terrific, that they should use it again. The screen gave
the show a distinctive look; a similar window had been used by "The
MacNeil/Lehrer Report" on PBS, but most interviews were then done
in studios. The technology also had the effect of enlarging Koppel,
putting him in control and giving viewers a sense that he was directing
as well as hosting the show, which, of course, he was. "We began to
play with the formula," Koppel recalled. "It was clear to us that if
we could do it across town, we could do it cross country. And if we
could do it cross country, we could do it around the world."

President Carter's State of the Union address brought another
opportunity to experiment. That night, Koppel's guests included Defense Secretary Harold Brown, Soviet spokesman Vladimir Posner,
and Iranian foreign minister Sadegh Gotzbadeh.

Koppel remembered, "Rather than do what prior to that time had
been done on television — where if you had more than one guest, you
interviewed guest number one and you said thank you, then you went
to guest number two and then guest number three — I played them
off, one against the other, and had them respond to what the other
person had said. It ended up becoming a global village conversation,
sometimes even argument, debate. And it really was, for those days,
exciting television."

Again, Arledge loved it. He was the first to perceive that Koppel
had a talent for orchestrating a conversation, an ability, as Arledge
put it, "to take two cables and hold them together and strike sparks."
He could see all manner of possibilities for the format, telling aides,
"That's what this program is going to be."

Here Arledge was operating at the peak of his own abilities. He
had not dreamed up a new format in his head, but given the chance
to watch the show and see Koppel operate, his producer's instincts

took over. Arledge usually did not know what he wanted before he got it, a trait that frustrated those around him, but he had a superb critical eye, an ability to look at a program and see what worked and what did not. If he was a genius, as some ABC colleagues said, he was a reactive genius — an "inspired tinkerer," in a phrase minted by David Burke. Arledge's tinkering with "America Held Hostage" had led him to a new way of presenting the news on television.

It was time for another visit to Fred Pierce. Arledge wanted to turn "America Held Hostage" into a program that would remain on the air permanently. While Pierce was dubious about the long-term prospects for a late-night news program, he was again willing to trust Arledge. He decided to commit to a twenty-minute program on Monday through Thursday. That way, ABC could schedule reruns of "Charlie's Angels" or "Love Boat" at 11:50 P.M., getting some viewers aboard before midnight and enabling ABC to pad the hour-long shows with commercials, since they did not end until 1 A.M. Most ABC affiliates cleared the full ninety minutes of programming.

Work began in earnest on the new show in February. The Winter Olympics would provide a natural break in March between "America Held Hostage" and the program — whatever it was to be called. Arledge wanted a title that did not mean anything, an empty vessel that would fit whatever program evolved. "The truth about titles," said Dick Wald, "is if you take a relatively simple title, people come to accept it as an apt description even though it doesn't mean a hell of a lot."

Arledge could spend hours on these details — titles, sets, logos, openings, and the like. This time, Arledge, Wald, and David Burke went round and round on titles until Wald made two lists of words — news, late, night, tonight, midnight, time, world, word, wrap-up — and began to play with combinations. The horse-racing phrase "the morning line" led them to "the night line" and then to "night line," which provoked further debate about whether to write it as one word or two. They settled on "Nightline."

All that was left was to choose an anchor. Arledge would later maintain that Koppel was the only serious candidate, but others say that Arledge thought a star anchor would be needed to carry the show once the hostage crisis was resolved. Dan Rather, who was being recruited by ABC, was a possibility. So was his CBS colleague Roger Mudd. Koppel, for one, never felt he was the front-runner.

"I have a great deal of love and affection and respect for Roone," Koppel said later, "but if I was his first choice, he did an absolutely brilliant job of concealing it from me. It's fair to say that at that time, I was certainly not the first, second, or maybe even third choice."

But with time running out, Koppel was deemed the best available choice. The job offer finally came in a call, not from Arledge but from Wald, on February 8, 1980, Koppel's fortieth birthday. He accepted on the spot.

Against all odds, he had achieved a lifelong goal: he had become an anchorman for ABC News. What's more, he had overcome his "Roone problem," turning Arledge, who had scorned him, into a fan. That, by itself, was testimony to the singular talents of Ted Koppel.

He may not have been born cocky, but Ted Koppel developed self-confidence at an early age. He believed in himself, and just as important, he learned not to display his doubts. He was so self-assured that he turned down the first job he was offered at ABC.

Koppel, then twenty-three, had returned to New York after graduate school to seek work in broadcasting. His efforts had produced a $90-a-week job as a copyboy and enough rejection letters to cover a wall of his den, when he heard about an opportunity at ABC Radio. The radio network was hiring reporters at $375 a week for a program called "Flair Reports"; Koppel wangled an audition, where he read his own scripts. When the producer called afterward, he told Koppel that his audition was very good but that he was too young to go on the air. He offered him a job as a writer for $175 a week.

Koppel declined. He recalls saying, "I didn't apply for that job. I don't want that job. I want the on-air job, and I think you are being shortsighted because no one is going to know on the air how old I am. Either I can do the job or I can't." After he hung up, Koppel felt awful — he had turned down a big raise, after all — until the producer called back a few days later to tell him the reporter's job was his.

He'd learned a valuable lesson. Projecting a sense of security, he saw, could be as effective as possessing the real thing.

"No one is that confident in reality," Koppel said, "but ours is a business of appearances, and it's terribly important to appear to be self-confident. The minute you give evidence of doubt, people are going to eat you alive."

Koppel almost never showed doubt, especially not after others came to share his own estimate of his talents. One writer dubbed him "Koppel the Great, Emperor of 'Nightline,' Grand Inquisitor of the United States," and he was often called the smartest man on TV.

Richard Threlkeld, an ABC correspondent in the 1980s, went further, saying, "He's the smartest man I've ever met — no contest." In truth, Koppel was exceptionally intelligent, but he came across as even smarter because he had about him an aura of almost frightening certainty.

"It is not arrogance," he said. "It is just — and I truly do regard it as God's gift to me — it is just that I know I'm good at what I do, and I've always known I'm good at what I do."

Besides, he added, "This industry never has been, and I guess never will be, overpopulated with brilliance."

Koppel traced his self-control back to his British boyhood. Edward James Koppel was born in Lancashire, England, in 1940, the only child of wealthy German Jewish parents who had been forced to flee the Nazis in 1938. His father, Erwin, who had owned a rubber-tire factory, was harassed and jailed briefly before friends helped him escape from Germany. His mother, Alice, was a gifted singer and pianist.

The Koppel family listened to Ed Murrow's radio broadcasts in England during the 1940s. Ted was too young to have understood much about Murrow, but, he said, "There was something about it that I admired very much. I told people I wanted to be a broadcaster from the time I was about eight or nine years old and have never wavered in that."

In England, he spent three years at boarding school, where he was subject to the Victorian-era rituals that required new students to serve the older ones, making their beds, fixing them tea, and the like. "I got self-control the hard way," he said. "Nothing makes you more vulnerable than a perception of weakness among ten-, eleven-, and twelve-year-old English schoolboys."

The Koppels moved to New York in 1953. One of Ted's earliest impressions of the United States was triggered by a radio jingle for a stomach-pain reliever — "eat too much, drink too much, try Brioschi, try Brioschi" — that brought tears to his eyes the first time he heard it. Food rationing in England had ended only a few years earlier, and the thirteen-year-old Koppel could not believe that people had to worry because they ate or drank too much. Again, it was a matter of self-control. Nobody's forcing them to eat or drink, he thought.

After graduating from the private McBurney School, Koppel went to Syracuse University, best known in the 1950s for its powerhouse football program. Koppel's sport was soccer — he'd made the all-city team in high school — but he wandered over to the football field to see if he could be of assistance to Ben Schwartzwalder, the legendary coach of the Orangemen. Koppel had seen football players kick field goals, and he was sure he could do it better.

Koppel pulled himself up to his full five feet nine inches — he weighed about 135 pounds at the time — and told Schwartzwalder in his British-accented English, "That business of kicking a ball between the goalposts, that's a piece of cake." Coach Schwartzwalder had to laugh, before telling the young man to stick with soccer. He had Jimmy Brown. He didn't need Ted Koppel.

As it turned out, college and professional football would soon welcome the first soccer-style kickers, Pete and Charlie Gogolak, brothers who, like Koppel, were European immigrants. Later, Koppel would joke, "The Gogolak brothers, I have always felt, appropriated my place in football history."

In graduate school at Stanford, Koppel met his future wife, Grace Anne Dorney, a doctoral candidate who impressed him as being smarter than he was. Their parents initially opposed the wedding because she was Roman Catholic and he was Jewish, but the marriage has lasted more than thirty years and Koppel remains a devoted husband.

From his radio job at ABC, he moved into television. He was the youngest television correspondent at ABC News during the era when correspondents traveled without producers; he wrote his scripts, edited film, transmitted stories, and when called upon, took his own pictures. Later, Koppel ran bureaus in Miami and Hong Kong, where he was regarded as the wunderkind of the correspondent corps — a young guy who looked even younger but was cocksure and smart.

"Some of the happiest memories I have," Koppel said, "are being out in southeast Asia and covering a story with a cameraman and a soundman and coming up against a CBS unit that would be two crews, one correspondent, and a producer. And when we kicked ass on those occasions, and sometimes we did, it was very, very sweet."

In 1971, he was named ABC's diplomatic correspondent, based in Washington. He wanted to spend more time with Grace Anne and the children. Instead, he traveled the world with Henry Kissinger, logging close to 500,000 miles of air travel over the next five years. Koppel became a friend and admirer of the secretary of state, who tried to hire him as State Department spokesman. When he was later faulted for being too close to Kissinger, Koppel conceded the point, calling their friendship a mistake. But he defied anyone to point to an instance in which his affection for Kissinger colored a story.

While covering Kissinger, Koppel trained himself to become a good listener. "If you listened very carefully and learned to unravel the double negatives and qualifying phrases he puts in, you could read extraordinary stories in what he was telling you," Koppel said. "If someone is trying to do a verbal dipsy doodle around me, I don't miss it very often, because Henry Kissinger is the best dipsy-doodle artist in the world." He also honed his interviewing skills at State Department briefings, which required reporters to gently poke and probe for news.

By this time, Koppel was a valuable player at ABC News, although Bill Sheehan, the News president, thought he would be most valuable behind the scenes. In 1976, Sheehan offered him a choice of jobs — executive producer of the evening news with Harry Reasoner and Barbara Walters, or senior vice president of ABC News, a job that might lead to the News presidency. Unbeknownst to his boss, Koppel had other plans; he wanted to take a year off so his wife could attend law school. Eventually, he worked out an arrangement that allowed him to anchor the Saturday evening news, do a daily radio commentary, and spend the rest of his time keeping house and writing a novel with his friend Marvin Kalb. Koppel's willingness to take time off was another reflection of his confidence and stability, but it cost him with Arledge, who expected a total commitment.

With Arledge's arrival, Koppel's career thudded to a halt. Arledge dismissed his Saturday-night producer, replaced him as anchor, and sent him back to the State Department. "What that said to me was 'Sonny, I don't care who you think you've been here, under me you're nothing,'" Koppel said. "I'm sure now that he didn't mean any cruelty by it, but I sure took it that way." Reportedly, Arledge joked that Koppel looked like Howdy Doody.

Koppel and Donaldson measured their status daily on the "Roone stock barometer." After Koppel had a piece on the evening news, Donaldson would call and say, "Ted, you're at forty-six and a half today, up three-quarters." Koppel would reply, "Well, I saw your piece and I think you're down a half today." The gallows humor did nothing to overcome their belief that they had been passed over by Arledge, who looked to CBS and NBC for stars. "I was more or less resigned to the fact that, under Roone Arledge, the most I could really hope for was to occasionally do some sub-anchoring," Koppel said. As a rule, once Arledge made up his mind about someone, there was no changing it.

In the spring of 1979, however, Koppel embarked on a project that sent his stock price skyward. With producer Mike Von Fremd, Koppel reported an eleven-part series for "World News Tonight" called "Second to None," about the military readiness of the United States and the Soviet Union — a subject Koppel feared would bore viewers unless it was spiced with drama. They spent months on the series, visiting military installations around the world, collecting hundreds of tape cassettes, and spending what seemed like a fortune to Von Fremd, who'd come from CBS. What made the series memorable, though, was a nine-minute segment — one of the longest ever on the evening news — in which they created World War III, using graphics and visuals to show how a nuclear war would unfold. Behind the razzle-dazzle was solid journalism, and the series won several awards.

Arledge was so thrilled that he put ABC's promotional juggernaut behind the series, buying print ads and holding screenings for TV writers and defense experts. "CBS wouldn't have dreamed of doing anything like that," Von Fremd said. The week the series ran, "World News Tonight," whose ratings had been climbing, overtook NBC to finish second in the weekly Nielsens for the first time. Champagne flowed in the ABC newsroom. "Ted could walk on water after that," said Von Fremd, who was rewarded himself with an unsolicited raise.

Six months later, the hostages were taken. First from the State Department, then as anchor of "America Held Hostage," Koppel was able to display his anchoring and interviewing skills. Everyone was impressed with his command of the story, his intellectual agility, and the elegance of his presentation.

What few saw was that Koppel was also a gifted performer, as he was the first to admit, quoting a line from George Burns about sincerity: "If you can fake that, you've got it made." Koppel said, "I don't think there is anyone who has ever been good on the air who doesn't have a certain theatrical ability, and it is the ability to convey sincerity."

Koppel recognized the hostage crisis as his big chance. "It was a very tense time, one of the few times I felt a little less secure," he said. "But it was also not a time to let people know you're feeling insecure. I had to seem more self-confident than anyone around me, because if I wasn't going to be self-confident, sure as hell nobody else was."

Arledge was sold. He set aside his doubts and entrusted his most important creation, the breakthrough show he had nurtured lovingly, to a leader of the old guard. This pleased Koppel's ABC colleagues and left them slightly in awe of what he had done. "The greatest success story of diplomacy in broadcasting is how Ted turned Roone Arledge around," one veteran said. "Ted deserves an Emmy for that performance alone."

"Nightline" had an advantage over every other new television program. The show had been shaped by an on-the-air tryout, three months of dress rehearsals that were used to test formats and ideas. The result was that the first "Nightline," on March 24, 1980, looked much like the last "America Held Hostage," and the premiere arrived with minimal fanfare.

That was deliberate. Koppel had gone to see Arledge, to urge him not to raise expectations for "Nightline." Koppel thought that "the most dangerous thing you can do in this business is to come on and beat the drums and play the trumpets. Whereas if you come on and say, folks, this is just a modest little show, nothing special about it, then people will sit there and say, actually, it's not bad."

So Koppel, controlled as ever, began the program by matter-of-factly informing the viewers that "this is a new broadcast in the sense that it is permanent and will continue after the Iran crisis is over." Then he moved on to the news.

Koppel might not have been so cool had he known that Ali Agah, the Iranian chargé d'affaires and a guest on the show, was at that very moment throwing a fit in the Iranian Embassy.

Susan Mercandetti, the first "Nightline" booker, had persuaded Agah to come on the show, but she had promised that he would have to talk only to Koppel. But Koppel, in his introduction, had said that Dorothea Morefield, the wife of an American hostage, would speak directly to Agah.

When Agah heard that, he removed his earpiece and fixed his stare on Mercandetti, a personable young woman who was already fighting opening-night jitters. "You told us we weren't going to do that," he declared. He began speaking loudly in Farsi to his entourage.

Mercandetti was terrified not only for the show but for herself. The Iranians, in her eyes, were fanatics. On the phone to Bill Lord, the executive producer of "Nightline" in New York, she pleaded: "Bill, you can't do this to me. You cannot do this to me."

"Oh yes we can," Lord replied calmly. "Blame it on New York."

That was the only way out. Mercandetti began to yell at her boss on the phone, surprising the Iranians in the room, who buzzed around her. She yelled some more. Then, to the Iranians, she denied that she had promised anything at all.

Agah stayed put.

After a setup piece from Bill Blakemore in Tehran — the Shah had arrived in Egypt, complicating efforts to free the hostages — Koppel interviewed Agah and talked with Morefield. Then he got them talking to each other.

Morefield asked, "How can you continue to hold these innocent people?"

Agah set off on a long discourse about the U.S. government's role in Iran, said he was "humbly sorry for your feelings," and even expressed gratitude that the show's title had been changed from "America Held Hostage" to "Nightline." Koppel interrupted, to give Morefield another chance.

"Why are we not being allowed to hear from the hostages?" she asked. "Why are there so few phone calls coming out? Why isn't there mail coming out of that embassy in Tehran?"

Agah, flustered, suggested that the CIA might use the mail or phone calls to communicate with the hostages.

The confrontation was so compelling that plans for a second story on the show, about Democratic primaries in New York and Connecticut, were dropped.

As Koppel signed off, Mercandetti was thrilled. "We knew something electric had just happened," she said. "It was hot. Ted was really, really good." Others agreed. Stu Schwartz, a senior producer, thought "Nightline" had done exactly what they all hoped it would do — "bring people together who would not have spoken to each other in any other way."

Arledge, too, called with praise, but he worried that the show had stayed with one topic for too long. He had hoped, on the first "Nightline," to break away from the hostage crisis, if only to make the point that this was a new program. And Koppel thought that the show had been just okay. The next morning, he wasn't willing even to go that far. He read Tom Shales's review in the *Washington Post* and felt "absolutely shattered."

Shales had been brutal. He described "Nightline" as "at best a great leap sideways and at worst a pratfall backwards for network news." The exchange between Morefield and Agah, he wrote, had been "cheaply theatrical, hokey, mawkish and self-promotional. It wasn't news, of course; it was the new news, neo-news, non-news, a sugary news substitute."

Koppel was so distressed — he liked Shales, and he knew Arledge read all his press clippings — that he called the critic to say that he thought it was unfair to pillory a new show after one night. Shales promised to take another look, after time passed.

"Nightline" needed time to define itself. "A week before we went on the air, we didn't have a clue what the program was going to be," said Koppel. That was an exaggeration, but up until the debut Arledge had talked of including a newscast, sports, or weather in the format. The second "Nightline," much of it anchored by Frank Reynolds in New York, was a hodgepodge, with reports on the primaries as well as on Iran. Before long, though, "Nightline" settled into an uncluttered format — an opening tease, a setup piece by a correspondent, and Koppel's live interviews.

Koppel credited Arledge. "Roone is the ultimate production tailor who is watching the product on the air and saying, nip it in a little bit at the waist and he needs a little more padding on the shoulders and, you know, that particular color looks good on him," Koppel said. "He's watching night after night and he knows what he likes and he knows what he doesn't like. He has tremendous endurance, patience, and creativity, and he'll keep fiddling until he gets it right." Arledge never missed "Nightline," and for a time he made a habit of riding his exercise bike at night while watching.

"Nightline" also needed time to become established among the newsmakers who were needed as guests. Official Washington had been conditioned to get up early for "Today" or "Good Morning America," but politicians were initially reluctant to stay up until midnight for a shcw nobody knew. Arledge insisted on doing the interviews live; he was always partial to live television, and he figured that if word got around that "Nightline" had allowed one senator or White House aide to tape in advance, then everyone would want the privilege. He would tell the "Nightline" staff that the program would someday be the most important show on television and that people would clamor to come on, but everyone dismissed that as cheerleading.

For weeks, Mercandetti had to explain the show to potential guests. One night, she recalled, Koppel paused by her office as she told someone, "No, no, it's ABC. He used to be the State Department correspondent . . . K-O-P-P-E-L." Koppel smiled at first, but after he listened for a while, his head and shoulders drooped.

Typically, though, when they encountered setbacks, the young and eager crew at "Nightline" only resolved to work harder. They were led by executive producer Bill Lord, who, like Koppel, had come out of the old guard — he'd joined ABC News in 1961 — and initially opposed Arledge. Lord had worked as a reporter, writer, producer,

Washington bureau chief, and vice president at ABC News, before being demoted by Arledge. He'd worked his way back up, winning respect for his news judgment, toughness, and mastery of technology, all of which he needed to get "Nightline" on the air.

Lord inspired fear as well as respect. A New England WASP, he was tightly wound and quick-tempered. "There was an obsessive side to Lord. He had to have his own way," a colleague said. Lord was once so brusque with reporter Bob Clark, an old friend, that the mild-mannered Clark slapped him in the face. Clark could have been fired, but everyone figured that he had been provoked by Lord, so he got off with a two-week suspension.

At "Nightline," Lord was so pleased to be running a new and important program that his mean side rarely surfaced. If anything, his toughness helped the show get the support needed from the rank and file. Unavoidably, "Nightline" was a burden because crews and correspondents, accustomed to finishing work after the evening news, had to stay on for hours, to file new footage or arrange a late-night satellite feed. In Europe, this literally meant staying up all night to serve "Nightline" — or "nightmare," as some called it. But, with Arledge's backing, Lord rode over all resistance. "He would pick up the phone and just obliterate people," an aide said.

In the control room, Lord was fearless. He was so comfortable with technology and so sure of himself that he would change the topic of "Nightline" at the last minute, even shifting gears on the air. "Lord was extremely adept at putting people on two tracks to do two 'Nightlines' and then deciding very late what he wanted," said correspondent Jeff Greenfield.

A month after the "Nightline" premiere, Lord's ability to crash a show was tested when the news of a failed attempt to rescue the hostages broke after the 11:30 P.M. feed. Although Lord, Koppel, and others were on their way home by then, they returned to work to produce a new show for the West Coast. To Lord, it was never too late or too much trouble to get news on the air. Like Arledge, he hated to be told that anything couldn't be done.

Lord also turned out to be an ideal complement to Koppel. Lord had gut instincts about news, while Koppel was cerebral. Lord's technical know-how was vast, Koppel's limited. And Lord's tastes balanced Koppel's — he liked Washington stories, politics, science, pop culture, and music, while Koppel's interests lay overseas. "There was a fear that, if left only to Ted, we would do esoteric foreign policy stories every day," said producer Lionel Chapman.

Lord, for example, was the first to see that "Nightline" need not always be issue-oriented. When Mount Saint Helens erupted, Koppel did not want to devote the show to a volcano, thinking there was nothing to analyze. But Lord crafted a program that explained the eruption, examined emergency preparedness, and showed spectacular live pictures of the mountain at sunset. Koppel saw he'd been mistaken.

For two such strong-willed men, Lord and Koppel worked well together, although they worked apart. Because Arledge wanted his executive producer close at hand in New York, Lord supervised one "Nightline" staff there; Koppel led a group in Washington, where he preferred to live. Workdays began and ended with a conference call, with all staff members invited to participate.

"Nightline" was an unusually democratic shop. Ideas percolated upward, from researchers and editors as well as producers. Kyle Gibson, a twenty-four-year-old production associate who had studied Korea at Yale, suggested doing a "Nightline" on the thirtieth anniversary of the Korean War in 1981 and then helped produce the show. "Every day was an adventure," she said. "It didn't seem as if there was any place on earth that could be as exciting as 'Nightline' in those days."

Producers competed to come up with the most creative setup pieces. A story exploring the Jews' historic claims to Israel was narrated, in part, by readings from the Old Testament. A Rashomon-like piece looked at the war in El Salvador from the points of view of a colonel, a businessman, and a priest. "We were never satisfied with the thing that worked well yesterday," said producer Tom Yellin. "We always wanted to try something new."

Lack of money never stood in the way of new ideas. Getting the story was everything. "We could go anywhere, do anything," said Lord. "We never had a financial problem or a crisis." Once, when producer Lionel Chapman requested permission to rent a helicopter to take aerial pictures of Mount Rushmore, which he regarded as a luxury, he was told not to waste anyone's time asking, just to do what was necessary. "Nightline" producers flew hundreds of miles to get a sound bite for a piece and took weeks to craft stories.

This, too, was by design. Arledge had decreed that "Nightline" should have all the money it needed. The theory, an insider said, was that "if you have a new program and you want it to succeed, you throw money at it. Because the potential benefit from success will justify that expense. It seems to people on the outside to be a mindless strategy of extravagance. In fact, it's a tried-and-true formula for producing success. The last thing you want when you're trying to create a new program is to worry about whether or not you should do something because it might put you over budget. You can't afford to have that thought. Because, if you start thinking that way, you will, in fact, fail. You will always be holding yourself back." Later, as the television environment changed, Arledge denied that he had given "Nightline" a blank check, but no one who worked there could remember any spending limits.

It's no wonder "Nightline" was a happy place to work. Staffers had money to burn, the freedom to innovate, and the fun of creating something new. "It was like the excitement that goes with freshman year in college," said correspondent James Walker. "There was constant cheerleading, fountains of ideas spouting all the time, and everyone enjoyed each other." The hours — most people worked from 11 A.M. to midnight — were the only drawback, although some staffers took perverse pride in their all-consuming commitment.

"Nightline" people were smart, aggressive, energetic, inventive, arrogant, extravagant, and competitive — exactly the kind of people Arledge loved. The feeling around "Nightline" was nothing like the feel of the old ABC newsroom. The "Nightline" culture, instead, rewarded big ideas, bold execution, and brash approaches. It was the culture of Arledge's ABC Sports, rebuilt from the ground up on what would become the signature program of ABC News.

On January 5, 1981, ABC extended "Nightline" from twenty minutes to half an hour and announced that the program would now be seen every weeknight. The show had attracted sizable ratings, running behind Carson on NBC but ahead of CBS's movies. No longer could anyone doubt that there was an audience for news late at night.

A few days later, Koppel opened the *Washington Post* and saw his portrait on the front of the Style section. Tom Shales had kept his promise to revisit "Nightline."

This time, Shales called the show "smart" and "classy" and "the most successful programming initiative in ABC News history." He ignored Arledge, gave a brief nod to Lord, and gushed over Koppel. "He's a smoothie. He's a pro. He's a rocket," Shales wrote. "What makes 'Nightline' click is Koppel's bulls-eye interviewing style, a verbal and rhetorical combination of Sugar Ray Leonard and Mikhail

Baryshnikov — a succession of jabs, rejoinders and judicious-to-delicious interruptions: Koppel a cappella." The Shales article began a decade of unqualified raves for Koppel and "Nightline."

"It meant a lot to me when I saw that he had changed his mind about the program," Koppel said. "Then I knew that we were home free."

But the magnitude of what Arledge and Koppel and Lord and the rest of the "Nightline" crew had accomplished became apparent only slowly. Since the early 1970s, the presidents of all three network news divisions had labored to expand their evening newscasts to an hour. Network executives, if they were honest, admitted that the twenty-two-minute format made it nearly impossible to present a national newscast of depth and seriousness. Men like Richard Salant of CBS News and Reuven Frank of NBC News had lobbied their corporate bosses, begged their affiliates, and talked the idea up in the press, to no avail. Now Arledge had found a second half hour; perhaps it was not quite as good as having a full hour at dinnertime, but in some ways it was better, because "Nightline," unburdened by tradition, broke away from the format of the evening newscast.

"Nightline" was the most significant addition to television news since "60 Minutes." It was also a new way to present news, a form original to television. Unlike the evening newscasts or Sunday morning talk shows, which were created for radio, or the prime-time news programs, which were inspired by magazines, "Nightline" had no antecedents in radio or print. "Nightline" did things print could not — it set off sparks, permitted glimpses of character, made the world feel smaller, and now and then made news of its own, live, as viewers watched. "Nightline" was pure television.

The program was Arledge's greatest accomplishment as well as his most unlikely coup. He had the vision, the creativity, the corporate clout, and the will to get "Nightline" onto the air and keep it there. After David Burke grasped what they had accomplished, he liked to joke about it with Arledge.

"Imagine," Burke would say, "that you and I, absent the hostage crisis, went over to ABC and said, 'Hey, Fred, we've got a great idea. Every night at 11:30, we'd like to have the State Department correspondent, you know, the one whose ears stick out and has the funny hair, doing talking heads against Johnny Carson.'

"Roone," he'd go on, "they'd call security. First they'd take a urine sample, then they'd call security, and then they'd fire you. They would think you were crazy."

Chapter Seven

THREE'S A CROWD

THE END of the Iran hostage crisis, like the beginning, brought glory to ABC News. While all the networks covered the release of the hostages and the inauguration of Ronald Reagan, ABC News alone broadcast the results of an extraordinary investigation into the U.S. government's secret negotiations with Iran. The investigation was led by Pierre Salinger, one of Arledge's prized hires.

Salinger's name was often cited by Arledge's ABC critics when they accused their boss of behavior inelegantly known as "star-fucking." Arledge enjoyed the company of famous people, even after he'd become well-known, and he had a peculiar attraction to those, like Salinger, with ties to the Kennedy family. Salinger had been JFK's White House press secretary, a U.S. senator, and a corporate executive, but he had never worked in television when Arledge hired him as a "contributing correspondent" in 1977. Two years later, he became ABC's Paris bureau chief.

His television skills were minimal. Salinger liked to shout at the microphone, and he had no aptitude for blending pictures and narration. Once assigned to cover a papal trip, he began his story by saying "This is Pierre Salinger in Rome" — just as the screen showed a close-up of the Pope getting off an airplane. What's more, Salinger's opulent lifestyle — he lived in a nineteenth-century chateau, two hours from Paris — and limitless ABC expense account provoked jealousy. An ABC colleague griped, "Roone has made it possible for Pierre to live in the style to which he always wanted to become accustomed."

But Salinger functioned not so much as a reporter but as an

emissary on behalf of ABC and Arledge. He was not on the air much, but his value, Arledge said, was that "he was the most important American journalist in France and, by extension, in much of Europe. Pierre Salinger could get us in to see Giscard d'Estaing, and other American journalists might not be able to." Salinger could also get Arledge, a gourmet, into France's best three-star restaurants, a courtesy appreciated by the boss.

If months passed when he rarely appeared on the air, Salinger's contacts paid off in a big way on the hostage story. A lawyer he knew in Paris tipped him off to the Carter administration's secret negotiations in November 1980, and after a quick trip to New York to secure Arledge's approval, he set to work with enormous energy on the project, code-named Tango Delta. The investigation, which was coordinated by a cerebral London-based producer named Robert Frye, drew on the worldwide resources of ABC News, as producers and correspondents interviewed sources in Iran, France, Egypt, Pakistan, Austria, Algeria, West Germany, Switzerland, Great Britain, and Panama.

By January, ABC had gathered so much information that Arledge approved a three-hour broadcast. He was so fascinated by the story that he screened every segment with executive producers Av Westin, Bob Roy, and Frye. "Roone was totally involved," recalled Frye. "It wasn't a matter of his position as president of the news division. He was functioning more as a colleague. It was as pure as it gets in this business."

With the release of the hostages on Tuesday, January 20, 1981, Arledge asked for three hours of prime time on Thursday night for "America Held Hostage: The Secret Negotiations." This time, he could not persuade Fred Pierce. Instead, the program began at 10 P.M., in the hour that belonged to "20/20," and continued for two more hours beginning at 11:30 P.M., in the "Nightline" slot.

Salinger began the tale by revealing the contents of a secret note, handwritten a year earlier by President Carter and signed "J. C.," that was given to a left-wing French lawyer to deliver to the Iranians. The documentary went on to chronicle, in meticulous detail, the Carter White House's efforts to free the hostages. "The story has all the elements of a fictional spy thriller," Salinger said, "but it is all true." He was not exaggerating — the program was broadcast journalism at its best and a rousing finale to ABC's coverage of the hostages. Arledge had begun to win the respect he had desired for so long, as some critics noted.

"From the start of the hostage crisis, ABC dominated news coverage," wrote William A. Henry III, the Pulitzer Prize–winning television columnist. "Roone Arledge's organization sent the first correspondent and camera crew into Iran, even before the embassy takeover. It triumphed again at the end, with full details of the hapless secret negotiations. The prestige has spilled over into everything else ABC News does. In the eyes of the industry and the public, Roone Arledge, 'that man from sports,' and his staff, the former 'Almost Broadcasting Company,' have come of age."

"Nightline," special events coverage, and documentaries such as "The Secret Negotiations" brought recognition to ABC News, as Arledge hoped they would. They were the evidence he needed to show the corporation, the affiliates, and the press that ABC News was getting better. They also helped buy him the time he needed to improve the evening news — still his most important show.

Gradually, "World News Tonight" was getting better. Arledge and his deputies had redesigned the show and improved the quality of the reporting. While Cronkite's "CBS Evening News" still dominated the ratings, "World News" had pulled into a virtual tie for second with NBC's "Nightly News" with John Chancellor.

Arledge's slick, fast-paced, three-anchor news package offered viewers, particularly younger ones, an alternative to Cronkite and Chancellor. For one thing, "World News" was visually arresting, for Arledge took full advantage of new video technology, as he had in sports. His favorite director, Roger Goodman, served as Arledge's personal shopper, buying the latest in gadgetry, from computers that generated graphics to tiny cameras for undercover reporting. Together they set out to remake the look of network news — and they accomplished nothing less.

In 1978, for example, Goodman bought for $150,000 the first video product made by a company called Quantel — the machine literally had the serial number of 001 — after he saw that it could take a picture, shrink it, expand it, and move it around on the screen. After playing around with it in Sports, Arledge used the Quantel to frame images in a box that appeared to float over the anchorman's shoulder, a look that was then new but soon became standard on all the networks, as well as on local TV newscasts everywhere. The Quantels were also used to enliven stories with freeze-frames, wipes, and dissolves, editing techniques that had not previously been used in news.

Goodman also bought Chyrons, machines that generated brightly colored maps, charts, graphs, and illustrations and imposed text over pictures. A red slash, like the one on the cover of *Time* magazine, was superimposed on stories, in an effort to give ABC's newscast a distinctive identity. Hours were devoted to debate over the slash — whether it should be used simply as a dateline or to give viewers a zippy headline (e.g., "Car Wars") about the story. "The slash was indicative of the kind of detail Arledge paid attention to," said producer John Armstrong.

Neither CBS nor NBC paid as much attention to visuals — not then, anyway. "It jarred the hell out of me at first," said Hughes Rudd, the veteran correspondent who'd come from CBS. "At CBS, I'd sit down and write a piece, and it was their problem how they would illustrate it. You can't do that at ABC. If you say that 'a lot of water has run under the bridge,' then, by God, you've got to see a bridge with water under it. You've got to try a little bit harder at the typewriter to make the copy fit the picture. At first I thought it was too simple-minded. It was too much like a comic strip. But they're right, you know — it's a comic-strip medium in the first place."

Rudd was not exaggerating — at its worst, ABC resembled a Monty Python spoof of the news. Once, as reporter Bettina Gregory said, "The scales of justice tipped the other way on appeal," a picture showed the figure of Justice, her scales flapping wildly in the wind. Another time, Capitol Hill correspondent Don Farmer and producer Stanhope Gould set out to do a long piece explaining why President Carter's energy program had failed in Congress. With no pictures to illustrate the story, because cameras were then barred from the Senate, Gould built a collection of life-size cardboard cutouts of senators to use as props. Staffers watching the newscast that night in the Washington bureau stifled their giggles when they first saw the cutouts, but they lost control when, to illustrate the idea that Vice President Walter Mondale had been sent up to Capitol Hill, Farmer appeared on the screen lugging a Mondale cutout onto what looked like the Senate floor. "The whole place collapsed," recalled Brit Hume. "We were not laughing, we were screaming. We were doubled over."

Critics complained that the visual razzle-dazzle was designed merely to stimulate the audience. "World News" began each night, for example, with an elaborate opening, dividing the screen into four squares, each previewing a different story. Upcoming segments were promoted with snazzy "bumpers" and "teases" that ran before the commercials. Neither innovation served a journalistic purpose, and the new electronic toys were overused for a time. "It got out of control," said producer Stu Schutzman. "All we were doing was watching things squeeze and zoom and bounce and turn and spin and freeze."

But even traditionalists came to value the electronic graphics, which became known, ironically, as "ca-ca." (Goodman was called Mr. Ca-Ca around ABC.) Used judiciously, Goodman's machines did wonders to enliven stories that were otherwise hard to illustrate, stories like the four-minute piece that once ran on "World News" explaining the Federal Reserve banks, the money supply, and interest rates. Graphics could be generated on deadline to show the path of a hurricane, the mechanics of Pentagon weaponry, or electoral vote projections. Before long, ABC's techniques were copied widely.

With the graphics came music — which before Arledge had been a rarity on news programming. While the first four notes of the "World News Tonight" fanfare — E-flat, A-flat, high E-flat, B-flat — reminded some people of the "Laurel & Hardy" theme, the music was actually written for ABC News by Bob Israel, a gifted New York composer, who produced numerous arrangements of the ABC leitmotif, including a brassy, patriotic version for election nights, a fife-and-drum tune for Inauguration Day, and a tinkly, futuristic sound for space shots. Arledge liked having a theme that was identified with ABC News, although traditionalists again voiced displeasure. "I don't like it," said Richard Salant, the former president of CBS News. "I always used to say that on the day that the *New York Times* is delivered to my home accompanied by a chorus of a hundred, I would have music on my hard news. I think it's a distraction." CBS had barred music on the evening news for years as part of its attempt to separate news from entertainment programming, but to Arledge, music was one more way to get people's attention.

Arledge expected his correspondents to be able to grab people's attention too. As he built his "A-Team," a group of regulars who could become known and trusted by the viewers, he was not just looking for good reporters — he was casting a show. He wanted his top correspondents to have a distinctive presence, one that would pique interest and inspire confidence among viewers. In this, Arledge insisted that he was no different from a newspaper editor who cares about the layout of the front page. "All these people who say looks don't mean anything are full of baloney," he said. "If you don't have the ability to hold people's attention on the screen, that's almost a fatal flaw."

Those who lacked the right stuff, as he perceived it, suffered. Barrie

Dunsmore was considered a top-notch reporter by his peers, but he was shoved aside at the State Department so that Arledge could make the better-known Sander Vanocur ABC's chief diplomatic correspondent. Arledge disliked Dunsmore's reedy voice, his slightly foppish on-air look, and even his name. "Barrie with an I-E," Arledge would say disdainfully. It all added up to a package that Arledge did not want to see every night on his air.

Charles Gibson was another talented journalist who was unable to impress Arledge. A hard worker and a gifted writer, Gibson was not deemed star material by Arledge because he came across as bland on screen. "I don't want him anchoring on this network," Arledge once said. Nevertheless, Washington producers used Gibson as a substitute anchor on the morning news and "Nightline," and he later became an anchor of "Good Morning America." By then, Arledge had come around, even implying that it had been his idea to make Gibson an anchor. But Gibson said, "Roone never would have pushed me along. Never."

Still, Arledge's taste in correspondents was sufficiently varied to allow some odd-looking people to flourish. Bob Zelnick, a former producer who wanted to become a correspondent, got an opportunity even though he was a squat, lock-jawed man who lacked warmth on and off the air. Arledge also put political analyst Hal Bruno on the air and hired correspondent Jeff Greenfield from CBS, although neither was telegenic. "As somebody who certainly doesn't look like your conventional television person, I can say these folks haven't been bothered by that," Greenfield said. ABC frequently arranged for people hired from print to take lessons from a New York image consultant named Lilyan Wilder, who helped them with their speech and appearance.

Not surprisingly, those correspondents whose careers flourished were those who combined journalism with cosmetic appeal. The so-called A-Team was an all-white, all-boys club that included Sam Donaldson, Brit Hume, Jim Wooten, John Martin, and John McWethy. All were solid reporters, and beyond that, they all had gravitas — they adopted a mildly cynical, we've-seen-it-all-before stance that struck Arledge as just right. They got the best stories and the most-sought-after assignments. Women found it hard to break into the starting lineup.

While Arledge devoted a great deal of time to the look of the show, he also pushed to improve the journalism on "World News Tonight." His point man was Jeff Gralnick, who took over as executive producer when Westin left for "20/20." Gralnick was Arledge favorite's producer, so much so that even after taking command of "World News," Gralnick remained in charge of special events and convention and election coverage — a back-breaking workload.

A native New Yorker, Gralnick, then thirty-nine, had trained at CBS News, where he'd worked for more than a decade as a writer, a deskman, a bureau manager, and a producer. He was schooled on the Cronkite show, and his news judgments were solid and respectable. His instincts, when it came to breaking stories, were terrific.

At heart, though, Gralnick was a rebel. He had modish long hair, wore open shirts and boots, and had a blunt, profane manner, all of which endeared him to Arledge. More important, he belonged to a new generation of producers who had been reared on television. Print, which had shaped the early practitioners of network news, had little influence on them. "We know nothing but television," Gralnick said, "and we grew up with all the machines. What we want to do is use the machines to help us be better."

His laboratory, for a time, was the Saturday night news. After Arledge removed producer Phil Bergman and Koppel, Gralnick took over with anchors Tom Jarriel and Sylvia Chase; weekend news was a place where ideas could be tested without fear of embarrassing failures, since few were watching. One night, they tried a split-screen technique, with the reporter on one side and the news story on the other. Another Saturday, they ran a long story about the powerhouse Moeller, Ohio, high school football team, using no reporter at all — just natural sound and narration by the coach. "Creative messing around" was what Gralnick called it. "We were a very, very young news division, and there was a whole maturing process going on. We were making it up as we went along," he said.

At "World News Tonight" Gralnick was a decisive leader — too decisive, some charged. The job was really several jobs in one — the broadcast had to be shaped and formatted, individual stories had to be edited, producers and correspondents needed supervision, and there were three anchors to manage. Gralnick was strong enough to take control of the program, and, unlike Westin, he tended to rule by fiat.

Gralnick attacked the news each day. He'd be up at 5:30 A.M., get some exercise, and check in with the assignment desk. During his morning commute, he listened to the "CBS World News Roundup," talked on his car phone with bureaus and correspondents, and decided what to cover. By the time he got in around 9 A.M., he had scoped out a lineup. "You could argue with him," said Mike Stein, a producer, "but he turned off a lot of people who heard the bark and never got beyond it." For the rest of the day, Gralnick would rarely leave the rim — a group of desks arranged in a semicircle, where the show was formatted and pieces were edited. His head was always in the show, even as he munched on the greasy grilled-cheese sandwich and a milkshake he'd have sent up for lunch.

He kept track of every second on the broadcast. While stories typically were formatted for ninety seconds or two minutes on the old "ABC Evening News," Gralnick liked to order pieces to run 1:20 or 1:40, or even 1:12 or 1:17. This was partly designed to pick up the pace of the show and cram in more news, but it was also a way to let correspondents know who was in charge. "It's like calling a meeting for ten minutes before the hour," explained a producer. "He likes screwing around with people's heads like that." Every day, it seemed, Gralnick would land on someone whose piece had run long. "Nobody believes two or three seconds is a very long time," he explained, "until you say, 'Light a match and hold your hand over the match and I'll tell you when three seconds is up. Then you'll know how long three seconds is.' "

Still, the best correspondents respected his skills. Gralnick talked about pieces as if they were living organisms, whose desires were revealed only to him. "This graf wants to be shortened," he'd say, or "This bite wants to be in there." Such veterans as Sander Vanocur and Jim Wooten, who'd worked at the *New York Times*, thought Gralnick was a great editor. "He can't open a charm school, but I've rarely worked with anybody who's got a better sense of the English language," Vanocur said.

Gralnick was at his least charming when dealing with producers or correspondents who failed to meet his standards — an important part of his job. Mornings at ten, he'd preside over a conference call with all the bureaus; he'd praise or critique, sometimes harshly, work done the night before. He also used his deputy, Rick Kaplan, a hard-driving, high-energy bear of a man, to police the weaker people. Kaplan, another CBS alumnus, relished the task; he admired ABC's frontline people, like Koppel and Donaldson, but he was stunned at the incompetence of the second string.

"There was no bench," Kaplan complained. "We had Babe Ruth at the White House and Lou Gehrig at the State Department and numb nuts at the Pentagon. They had some of the worst correspondents I've ever seen in my life at this network." Even ABC loyalists agreed that, beyond the Beltway, the news division's weaknesses were glaring.

At six feet seven inches and 220 pounds, Kaplan was an effective enforcer. "A lot of people weren't used to either getting yelled at by me or getting terrorized by Jeff, but if we hadn't done it, the show wouldn't have worked," he said. "We had some people who'd had the union save their jobs for them, and they had this mentality, like, 'Fuck you, I'm gonna be here forever.' The only way to get through to those people was to make their lives that day miserable." The worst of the correspondents were forced out, to be replaced by smarter, more aggressive newcomers.

Gralnick and Kaplan made few friends, but "World News Tonight" was sharper, as even rivals acknowledged. "You misjudge ABC if you think of them as just flashy and playing for a young audience," said William Small, the president of NBC News. "They have a very solid newscast, and I don't underestimate them for a moment."

Arledge told a reporter, "We've finally arrived at a point where when we say something, it's noticed and taken seriously. I think it's clear now that we've overcome our old credibility problem." This was true enough — but his three-anchor format was showing signs of strain.

The growth in the ratings of "World News Tonight" brought some satisfaction to Frank Reynolds, Peter Jennings, and Max Robinson — some, but not much. The twenty-two-minute pie simply was not big enough to feed three egos. Charlie Heinz, who directed the show, said that tensions sometimes ran so high that "each of the anchors ran a watch on their segments" — carrying on an ABC tradition established by Reasoner and Walters.

Each anchor had his own set of grievances. Reynolds never liked the three-anchor format, but he accepted it after he was permitted to open the show each night. That ratified what he viewed as his rightful status as the first among equals. "Frank was never happy unless he could have a piece of the big story, even if it was an overseas story," said Jennings.

Reynolds also complained that Washington stories were given short shrift by "World News." "Frank was absolutely convinced that the world wrapped around Washington and that his stuff was the most important of the day," said producer Mike Stein. This was a common complaint from Washington reporters, who felt that New York paid too little heed to news from the capital.

And Reynolds, more than anyone else, was wary of anything he saw as pandering for ratings. "He took the responsibility of what he was doing, broadcasting to the country, in the most serious manner," said Mike Clemente, his newswriter. Reynolds had an expression that some found pretentious — "Now, what shall we say to the nation about this tonight?" he would ask — but he felt an obligation to the viewers.

"Frank could be difficult in the extreme," Gralnick said. But he added, "There was an incredible moral center to Frank."

Reynolds's gripes were not with Gralnick, but with Arledge. His first, negative impression had never changed. "Frank considered Roone to be P. T. Barnum," said producer Tom Capra. "Contemptuous is a strong word, but there was some of that." Reynolds was a purist who saw himself as guarding the temple of broadcast news against barbarians like Arledge.

They fought, most famously, over suits. Reynolds liked to wear light-colored suits, especially on summer days in Washington, where, on the street, he cut a fine figure with his white hair, reddish face, and erect gait. On the air, though, the suits faded into the background, so Arledge pushed to have Reynolds wear dark grays or midnight blues, which looked authoritative. More than once, Arledge had George Watson, the Washington bureau chief, buy dark suits and sports jackets for Reynolds, and, one time, he had Reynolds model them on a videotape, which was sent to New York for his approval. Reynolds hated the whole business.

"Frank felt it was almost indecent to pay attention to any of the things that didn't have to do with pure news," Arledge said. "And I told him I agreed with him, in theory. But I said to him, 'You're a person who prides himself on succinct sentences and clear thoughts, but by the time that picture gets to half of America, you're a blur.' You can call that show business or you can call it the tools of the trade."

Reynolds was unconvinced. He felt that Arledge cared about style, not substance, and it was easy to see how he reached that conclusion. Arledge felt secure speaking out about graphics, clothing, lighting, or sets, all of which he'd dealt with in Sports, but in the early days at News he hesitated to intervene in editorial matters for fear of being challenged. Initially, Arledge also tended to overlook those people who, like Reynolds, were better journalists than they were performers. One ABC veteran said of Reynolds, "He did not have the kinds of qualities that appealed to Roone, which are flash, dash, and an ability to sell it. That was anathema to Frank."

Reynolds also did not like to see his old friends and colleagues cast aside by Arledge. The issue, to Reynolds, was loyalty — and few things mattered more to him. He believed in the old ABC, its people and traditions, and Arledge did not. Loyalty was so important to Reynolds that for years he went to lunch every day with pals — Sam Donaldson, Charlie Gibson, Brit Hume, and several producers — at Duke Zeibert's, a watering hole favored by establishment Washington. After Duke retired and shut the place down, they shifted their allegiance to Mel Krupin's, a place run by Duke's former maître d'. When Zeibert then came out of retirement to compete with Krupin, Reynolds was outraged. His lunch bunch stayed at Mel's. "Frank never set foot again in Duke's, and he let it be known that it was an act of betrayal to do so," said Donaldson.

Just as Reynolds believed in the old ABC, the old ABC believed in him. "The loyalties to Frank were very, very strong," Gibson said. "We wanted him to be the centerpeice of the department, the personification of ABC News." Curiously, the fact that Reynolds was so widely admired did not help his standing with Arledge. Indeed, it hurt. Reynolds was a strong leader, but Arledge wanted to be the only leader. The result was that neither man trusted the other.

The chill between them would take a toll on ABC News.

For all its artificiality and built-in conflict, the three-anchor format turned out to have one clear journalistic benefit. Locating an anchor in London worked well for Peter Jennings, for ABC News, and for viewers who cared about stories from overseas.

For starters, there was the speed with which Jennings could get to major events. When rebel soldiers shot Egyptian president Anwar Sadat in 1981, Jennings immediately took off for Cairo. That night, he anchored from Egypt while Cronkite sat at Kennedy Airport, waiting for a plane. Arledge had his public relations people call that bit of news around to the TV critics.

Having an anchor overseas also led ABC to stories that might otherwise have gone unreported. With time set aside for a foreign news block every day, if only to get Jennings on the air, demand for foreign stories grew. Jennings said, "I became the fighter, the voice out there for the other foreign correspondents, because I had the loudest voice and I could plug New York around the ears and they'd pay attention."

Best of all, Jennings and the producers at ABC's ever-expanding London bureau saw the world from a different vantage point. Instead of waking up to the *New York Times* or "Today," they read British newspapers and listened to the BBC. "It helped us look at the world from a global perspective," said Bob Frye, a London-based producer.

On the Iran story, for example, Jennings was the first American television reporter to interview the Ayatollah Khomeini, back in 1978 when he was an obscure Iranian cleric living in exile near Paris. There had been stirrings of trouble in Iran, and Jennings sensed that the Shah's regime might be cracking. The following year, when Khomeini returned to Tehran in triumph after the fundamentalist revolution, Jennings accompanied him on the flight. This was the kind of reporting Jennings loved, and his work impressed everyone in New York.

In his private life, too, Jennings was finally settling down. He had divorced his second wife, Annie Malouf, and, at age forty-one, married Kati Marton, a bright, cultured, and attractive woman who was an ABC correspondent based in Bonn. She relocated to London, and they had a daughter, Elizabeth, and a son, Christopher. Domestic life suited Jennings, although he still flew off to cover every big story.

What frustrations he felt grew out of the everyday constraints of the broadcast. He always wanted more time for himself and for other foreign stories. And when he did battle with New York, he felt disconnected. "It's a rule of thumb," sighed Gralnick. "The farther away you are, the more insecure you're going to be."

Jennings would tape his portion of the broadcast at 8 or 9 P.M., London time, and then feed it to New York, where it was mid to late afternoon. If he ran long, as he often did, Gralnick would simply send the taped segment into an editing room to be cut. This invariably provoked further protests from Jennings, who listened to "World News Tonight" by dialing an ABC number in New York. Gralnick sometimes spent much of his hour-long commute home to Connecticut on his car phone, arguing with Jennings.

One reason Jennings's segments were cut was that he tended to overwrite. He had a habit of backing into stories. "His writing is stilted, a little 'up-the-hill-went-the-horse' kind of copy," said a New York producer. Later, as the sole anchor of "World News," Jennings would open the show by saying "We begin tonight," a stylistic flourish that seemed pretentious to those at ABC who preferred the straight-ahead, wire-service style of getting right to the news.

While Jennings and Gralnick respected each other, they didn't get along well. Both were perfectionists — smart, strong-willed men with their own ideas about the broadcast. The result was what a producer called "terrible relations between Peter and Jeff."

"Peter and I fought like cats and dogs," Gralnick said, "but it was always professional, it never became personal. We'd yell and we'd scream and we'd hang up on each other and the next day it would be over. I love him but, boy, it's a good thing there was an ocean between us on a number of occasions." Jennings concurred, saying, "As much as I like Jeff, I wanted to kill him sometimes."

At least they were fighting about the news. Jennings would make the case, based on the merits, for more coverage of Poland or the Middle East; such debates made the broadcast better. From Chicago, Max Robinson lobbied too, but he was seen mostly as an irritant. Robinson's claims on airtime grew out of a dubious premise — that a third of the broadcast belonged to him, and so whatever story he had, regardless of its value, deserved equal time on the show. This was an argument that was greeted with scorn in New York, where Robinson was seen as the third wheel on the bicycle. And he knew it.

It was not entirely his fault — Robinson was only taking his press releases literally. Arledge had justified his plan to put an anchor in Chicago by saying that Robinson would be an advocate for the heartland, arriving each day to convey his middle American perspective to ABC producers in New York. "And by God, he did it," one recalled. "And everybody wanted to say, 'Max, shut up. It doesn't happen that way.' " Untrained at the network, Robinson pushed for stories of limited national significance — murders or fires — and bristled when they were cut to voice-overs. Rick Kaplan said, "Sometimes the only time you'd see Max would be for a ten-second lead, so he'd go home crazed."

Robinson tended to blame Reynolds, who he thought hogged the spotlight and who, he knew, had little respect for him. On the day a DC-10 plane crashed in Chicago, Robinson erupted minutes before airtime when he realized that the show was going to be opened by Reynolds. "They each cordially hated each other," said a producer. "Between Frank and Max it was the third fucking world war." Joked Gralnick, "The only thing that kept us all alive was that it was three anchors in a four-city operation."

But Robinson's problems went deeper than anchor rivalries. The trouble was that he was not up to the job he was being asked to do.

It was not that he lacked talent. As a pure newsreader, he was the best of the three anchors. He had a dignified presence and a deep voice he could skillfully modulate; he sounded as if he knew what he was talking about even when he read copy for the first time. As an interviewer, too, Robinson was effective; he empathized with ordinary people, black or white, and they opened up to him. Robinson also had the brains to be a network anchor, others felt. Betsy West, Robinson's writer, said, "He had a good mind and he really could have grown into the job."

The sad fact was he did not. His deficiencies, especially as a field reporter, were apparent, and he grew so defensive that he would not or could not make a sustained effort to overcome them. Early on, Arledge thought the difficulty was that Robinson did not have a strong producer alongside him. Phil Bergman, an experienced producer and a decent man, was sent to Chicago, where the first thing he did was take Robinson to lunch to hear what he had to say. Robinson complained that he was not getting the respect — or the perks — to which he was entitled.

"I should be consulted about what's going on in the show," he said. "And, if Barbara can have a limousine and Frank can have a limousine, I expect to have a limousine."

Bergman was taken aback. "Look, Max," he told him, "let's be realistic about this. If you want an equal say here, you're going to have to earn it. No way are they just going to give it to you."

One of Bergman's first outings with Robinson took them to Los Angeles to cover a forest fire — in a limousine reluctantly hired by Bergman, who hoped it would help the anchor feel more secure. As they toured the area, Bergman got out of the car at each stop to scout out the story, tape interviews, and arrange for the satellite feed to New York; there was plenty of work to do. But Robinson sat in the car even after Bergman urged him to get out and talk to people to get a sense of the story. Worse yet, when the time came for his stand-up, Robinson had not written his copy. Bergman was stunned. "That never would have happened with a guy like Frank Reynolds or Peter Jennings or Ted Koppel," he said. "They would have said, 'Hey, you're not writing my copy.' They would tell you what to say and where to go."

First those in Chicago, then Gralnick, then David Burke, and finally Arledge came to the realization that Robinson just did not want to go into the field. "His instinct was always not to do it," said West. "He'd never been a network correspondent and, in a way, it was unfair to him. Somebody would have to get a crowbar to get him out of there." Once persuaded to go, he could not be relied on; when Robinson and a production team from Chicago were assigned to cover a space mission in Houston, everyone else was on the plane, ready to take off, when word came that Robinson had taken ill at the last minute.

One problem was that Robinson, with his anchoring duties, had little time to develop his reporting skills. But he also lacked the curiosity that drives good reporters. Given his high-profile job, he could have gone to see anyone in Chicago or Illinois, but the mayor and the governor never heard from him. Even major events didn't get his juices going. "We used him election night in 1978, from Chicago, doing the midwestern races, and it was marginal," recalled Gralnick. "Then we used him on the convention floor in 1980, and that was marginal at best. There was no natural desire, no natural ability. You really had to work hard to get him on the air."

Deeper troubles held him back. His colleagues thought that he was nagged by doubts, unsure of his talent, and uneasy about his rapid rise to fame. Bergman, among others, came to believe that Robinson had "one of these combined giant ego and inferiority complexes." He said, "Max was not a stupid man. He had a lot going for him. So his failures were either an unwillingness to work or a terrible fear stemming from an inferiority complex. Most people at the time didn't see it, but that's what I always believed about Max: that he was just frightened to death."

Years later, Robinson was candid about his self-doubt in a *Washington Post* interview. "I think one of my basic flaws has been a lack of esteem, not really feeling great about myself, always feeling like I had to do more," he said. "I never could do enough or be good enough. And that was the real problem." He added, "In fact, it was probably the essential problem I had throughout my career, throughout my life."

His drinking again became a problem. "There are one or two days when I am convinced that we put him on the air drunk," a producer said. "But we got away with it." Flying to Texas to cover a tornado, Robinson drank so much that he fell asleep and could barely rouse himself to work. He fell back into his old habits of coming to work late or not showing up at all. Around the Chicago bureau, his frequent illnesses became known as "the vapors."

Gralnick and Kaplan found it hard to get through to Robinson. "With Max, you always got close, but you were never there," said Gralnick. "It was a real strange dance." Over time, David Burke assumed the role of Robinson's keeper; he'd call or visit him and take his anguished late-night calls. "I liked Max a great deal," he said. "I had high hopes for him, and I thought he would be an extraordinary role model — what a major breakthrough to have a national anchor who's black."

Burke could be blunt with Robinson. "Stop trying to b.s. your way through life," Burke would say, when the anchor blamed his woes on others. Late one night at Robinson's apartment in Chicago, the two of them got into an argument that led to name-calling and so angered Robinson that he challenged Burke to arm wrestle. Robinson went into the bathroom, presumably to prepare for combat, but he didn't come out or respond when Burke called his name. When Burke gently pushed the door open, he saw that his anchorman had passed out. Burke dragged him over to bed, tucked him in, and went home.

When Robinson chafed at his lack of clout within ABC, more than his ego was on the line. Always, he was dogged by the worry that he was not doing enough for blacks. He feared that he was a token, an empty symbol of black achievement. In a 1980 interview, he conceded that his role in shaping "World News Tonight" was minimal and said, "I'd be less than truthful if I said I was happy with the present situation. I'm always fighting for more influence." He came to believe that racism was holding him back.

His feelings exploded into view at Smith College in Northampton, Massachusetts, on a snowy Sunday in February 1981. Several weeks earlier, he had ruffled feathers by telling an audience in Los Angeles that the election of Ronald Reagan "was not a good day" for blacks. Now he turned his anger against his bosses at ABC.

Remembering the day the hostages were released, the biggest news day of his career, Robinson charged that he had been excluded from ABC's coverage because he was black.

"When Ronald Reagan was crowned and our hostages came home, there was an orgy of patriotism the likes of which I have never seen in my young life, and I'm forty-one. . . . And I must tell you that I watched from the sidelines because ABC elected not to include me in the coverage of either event, even though I'm the national desk anchor responsible for a good deal of the ratings at ABC. They have admitted it publicly, and they have admitted it to me. So I had to ask the question: Why am I being excluded?"

He answered his own question. "In this patriotic fervor, black people would interfere with the process."

The story made its way into newspapers across America — and it infuriated Arledge and Burke.

Arledge took the attack personally. He could not believe that one of his anchors would publicly accuse him of racism. Besides, Robinson had his facts wrong; black reporters had been part of ABC's inauguration coverage.

Arledge summoned Robinson to his office at ABC Sports. There, the anchor claimed, wrongly, that he'd been misquoted; the quotes, as it turned out, had come from a tape recording of the speech made by a student. Arledge ignored Robinson's denial, but he told his anchorman that he had no business criticizing ABC in public. "You can't drop a phrase like 'your company is racist' and not expect people to notice," Arledge said. After a long discussion, Robinson was persuaded to issue a statement in which he expressed concern about "unconscious racism in many individuals and institutions" but absolved ABC. He said, "I did not single out ABC News for criticism, nor did I intend to leave the impression that decisions at ABC News are based on racial considerations."

But the damage was done, not so much to ABC News as to the career of Max Robinson. He and Arledge, never close, had become permanently estranged. Arledge thought he'd been betrayed by someone who had squandered a great opportunity. And now, when Robinson spoke of his troubles, he was contemptuous not only of Reynolds but also of Arledge and Jennings, whom he referred to as "Roone Arledge's favorite child." He was a bitterly unhappy man, and it showed.

By this time, Arledge knew the three-anchor format would not be a long-term solution for "World News Tonight." The format had been an interesting experiment, which gave him time to build up the infrastructure of ABC News, but his three anchors were clearly no match for Walter Cronkite. The best he could do, Arledge thought, was to put a respectable program on the air until he could find a star who was big enough to hold down the anchor job alone.

Chapter Eight

STAR SEARCH

GEORGE WATSON, ABC's Washington bureau chief, was puzzled. He had never been close to Dick Wald, and now, after a luncheon with a delegation from China at ABC's headquarters in New York, Wald had drawn him aside for a private chat. They repaired to the bar of the Dorset Hotel, near ABC.

Wald, it turned out, was carrying a message from Roone Arledge. He got right to the point.

"Roone wants to make Carl Bernstein the Washington bureau chief," he said.

Watson was stunned. "That's the craziest thing I've ever heard in my life," he said.

"Don't let me ever hear you say that again," Wald replied.

"Well," Watson said, in his most sarcastic manner, "well, that's the most brilliant idea I think I've ever heard."

Wald was quick to assure Watson that he was not being fired. That was reassuring, Watson thought. He had worked for ABC News since 1962, after Harvard, Columbia Journalism School, and the *Washington Post,* serving as a correspondent and bureau chief in Vietnam, Moscow, and London. Soft-spoken and unassuming, a solid journalist and a likable man, Watson was respected in Washington, especially by the old-timers.

But Watson lacked flash or style. "It's fair to say that Roone has never regarded me as a spark plug," he said, years later. When Arledge thought about how he wanted ABC represented in Washington, the image that came to mind was that of his friend Ben Bradlee of the

Washington Post, a brilliant, hard-charging editor, a handsome and sought-after guest at Georgetown parties, and a confidant of the Kennedys. Jason Robards was never going to play George Watson in a movie.

But Carl Bernstein — now, he was going to attract attention. Bernstein, thirty-five, was high profile, and not merely because he had helped crack open the Watergate scandal; even when he wasn't writing, which was often, his social life kept him in the gossip columns. Indeed, Bernstein would be brought to life by Hollywood not once but twice — first by Dustin Hoffman in *All the President's Men* and then by Jack Nicholson in *Heartburn*, the movie inspired by his ex-wife Nora Ephron's account of their divorce. Carl Bernstein had flash and style. As one ABC producer said, "He was trendy before trendy was trendy."

By Arledge's account, Bernstein's hiring was almost accidental. Arledge had met the Watergate hero in the Hamptons, and they had talked about working together on a documentary profile of Henry Kissinger for ABC. "You could see him starting to get cold feet, that he wasn't so sure that could top toppling a president," said Arledge. Later, Arledge — prompted, he recalled, by Wald — raised the possibility of putting Bernstein in charge of the Washington bureau. "His eyes lit up and his hair stood on end," Arledge said. "That he liked a lot." Arledge claimed that he had instant regrets. "We wanted Carl Bernstein for investigative reporting," he said. "And in order to get him to ABC News we found ourselves offering him something that he had no clue how to do."

Reaction from ABC Washington was overwhelmingly negative. Watson was a popular figure, and the Bernstein hire was seen as another example of Arledge's star-fucking. "If you are a certified star — no matter what your field — Roone is just in awe of you and loves to be around you," said a correspondent, who spoke for many of his colleagues. "If you're just a good solid journeyman workman who gets the job done, but no social trappings, no star quality, Roone's always looking for someone to replace you. And that's what happened to George Watson."

Those who knew Bernstein were shocked. He was an endearing man, with a boyish enthusiasm about him, but by the time he arrived at ABC in 1980, the Watergate luster had begun to dim. "By that time, everybody was on to Carl," said Sam Donaldson. "Nice guy, hit the right moment, hit the right story, had great sources, did a great job, but that was it. The reputation was sliding." Ann Compton, an ABC correspondent who'd known Bernstein when they were young reporters in Richmond, had an indelible memory of a night when they'd gone out with friends; when Bernstein opened the glove compartment of his car, out fell dozens of unpaid parking tickets. To Compton, the idea of Bernstein running a complex operation with five hundred employees was ludicrous. "Carl couldn't manage his way out of a paper bag," she said.

At the meeting to introduce Bernstein to the bureau, he made a few remarks about how much he had to learn, but "the asides were already loud about what a buffoon this guy is," a correspondent said. Watson was supposed to train him, but he quit to run the Washington bureau of the brand-new Cable News Network. His deputy bureau chief also left. This left Bernstein, who'd never worked in television, to find his own way. "It wasn't fair to Carl," said Robert Murphy, a deskman who got a battlefield promotion to become his second-in-command. "Carl was lost."

But Bernstein did not help himself. He was slow to learn the business, had no appetite for the details of administration, and built few bridges to the old-timers. Reynolds, the bureau's spiritual leader, took an instant dislike to him. "Carl would storm in, in the middle of the afternoon, he'd have his clothes on all backwards like he just got up, and he'd have come back from New York where he stayed someplace, dancing with Bianca Jagger, and he's full of show-biz stories and name drops," said John Armstrong, a Washington producer. "This would just send Frank through the roof because in his sedate, ordered kingdom nothing like that could ever happen."

Bernstein became a joke. "He tried to bluff his way through the job, and people would ignore him," said Charles Gibson. "He spent more and more time in that office, with nobody going in there and nobody talking to him." When Bernstein requested a public display of support from Arledge, he was told to solve his own problems. "I cannot give you the loyalty or respect of the people who work for you. You have to earn that," Arledge told him. He couldn't, and after fourteen months as bureau chief, Bernstein was removed and made a correspondent.

Arledge said, "It's more our fault than his that he didn't succeed as bureau chief, because he never should have been in that position."

Bernstein went on to do some excellent reporting, mostly for "Nightline." Ted Koppel became his protector, partly, cynics said, because Koppel calculated that it would help his own relationship with Arledge. That was not inconceivable, but the truth was that

Koppel liked and respected Bernstein. "Carl Bernstein didn't become one of the best-known reporters in this country by being a dope," Koppel said.

But Bernstein was erratic — he'd do a strong piece, then spend months on another that never made air. He was nervous on camera. And he was irresponsible, a perpetual child, even according to friends; he once borrowed five hundred British pounds from a producer and lost it gambling at Claridge's, the black-tie London club. (The producer recouped the money in his expenses.) Bernstein's stock tumbled so low that, without telling him, higher-ups in the bureau assigned associate producers to check his facts before his pieces went on the air.

Bernstein left ABC in 1984. No one felt ill will toward him, but his hiring and subsequent failure reinforced the perception that Arledge was temperamentally inclined to recruit outsiders with marquee names, regardless of their talents, while undervaluing the people he had working for him at ABC. For years, the ABC veterans thought that Arledge's propensity to hire outsiders reflected his mistrust of the old-timers, as well as his resentment at the way he'd been treated by the old guard. But as time passed, a few Arledge-watchers came to believe that Arledge's tendency to go after established stars actually reflected his own insecurities and a lack of faith in his own judgment.

The theory went like this. If Arledge plucked, say, a Ted Koppel or a Charles Gibson from the ranks at ABC, gave him a prominent position, and it did not work out, Arledge could later be faulted for making a poor choice. But if Arledge hired an anchor or a reporter from elsewhere who was already a star, he was less likely to be second-guessed. After all, who could fault him for recruiting Sander Vanocur or Hughes Rudd or Carl Bernstein? They looked to be as close to risk-free hires as you could get.

Roone Arledge's reputation as the man who loved stars — and the man who was willing to pay them huge sums to come to ABC — went back to his earliest days in News when he'd hired Cassie Mackin from NBC for $100,000 a year. Her salary had set the business buzzing; top correspondents then earned $50,000 to $75,000. In those days, the news business was gentlemanly; when their contracts expired, correspondents customarily accepted modest raises and stayed with their employers. The networks, as a rule, avoided bidding wars.

One of those buzzing about Mackin — bellowing was more like it — was Sam Donaldson. Donaldson wrote Arledge a note saying he was glad Mackin had joined ABC and that he thought she was worth the money. "But," he went on, "if your White House correspondent isn't worth that much also, you ought to replace him with someone who is." Arledge called Donaldson to say that he agreed. Donaldson, who was earning $62,000 a year, got a raise that put his pay into the six-figure range.

Numerous ABC correspondents had similar experiences. Brit Hume, who covered Capitol Hill, got a call from Irwin Weiner, Arledge's moneyman, to say that Roone had decided he liked Hume's work and wanted to give him a raise — would Hume call back in a few days to work out details? Hume thought somebody might be putting him on, so when he called Weiner, he began by saying, "Did you call me last week?" Weiner burst out laughing, told him he had, and to expect a raise of $5,000 or $10,000, as Hume remembered it. "I was just shocked," Hume said. "We'd never seen anything like this before."

Arledge had only just begun. Especially when raiding the other networks, his generosity knew no bounds. When Arledge got the idea that he could make a star out of radio broadcaster Charles Osgood, who was earning $120,000 at CBS, he tried to lure him to ABC with a package worth close to $500,000. Osgood turned him down but wangled $400,000 from CBS, much to his amazement and delight.

Producers, too, enjoyed the bounty. Under Bill Sheehan's regime, Jeff Gralnick had earned $39,900 a year and was told he could not have $40,000; his pay was lifted to $70,000 by Arledge. CBS producers Rick Kaplan and John Armstrong had their salaries almost doubled when they defected to ABC. By 1980, top ABC producers, like top correspondents, earned six-figure salaries.

No longer was the business genteel. Agents for producers and correspondents shopped their people around. The networks had no choice but to pay everyone more.

Linda Ellerbee, then an NBC correspondent, said, "All of us who worked as correspondents owe Roone a great deal because he single-handedly upped salary levels at all three networks. Simply by bidding across the board."

The talent raids cemented Arledge's image as a big spender. His reputation was richly deserved, but critics often ignored the reasons why he was willing to part with ABC's money. The view that Arledge spent money recklessly first took hold at ABC Sports, when he paid ever-increasing rights fees for such events as the Olympics and NFL football to build the division. Arledge and his top aides also traveled first-class and stayed in the finest hotels. But the big events made money, and if people at ABC Sports lived well, they also worked harder and longer than anyone else in the company.

Besides, everyone at ABC was spending money in the late 1970s and early 1980s — extravagance had become a way of life, thanks to the enormous profits generated in prime time and daytime by such hits as "Three's Company" and "General Hospital." Like a poor man who wins the lottery, ABC was flush after years of scrimping and saving and feeling underprivileged. "The advertising revenue was flowing in," said Fred Pierce. "And the profits were growing at an incredible rate." The time had come, finally, to enjoy the perks that went with being a network — limousines, fine dining, meetings in Acapulco, and a suite at the Plaza Hotel, where executives entertained clients, friends, or celebrity guests in an eye-popping seventeen-room triplex that included a sixty-foot-long living room, dining room, billiard room, and bedrooms.

Arledge enjoyed the good life — it was at about this time that he hired a chauffeur to drive him around Manhattan in a Jaguar — but he was not a mindless spender, as critics charged. Because the news operation he inherited was woefully underfunded, Arledge had to invest in people, equipment, and technology, as well as coverage.

Inevitably, money was wasted, but Arledge believed that creative people, to operate at their peak, could not afford to worry about budgets. By all accounts, they didn't — the budget for ABC News grew from roughly $65 million in 1977 to about $150 million in 1980, which put it on a par with CBS and NBC.

While ABC News still lost money, Arledge's goal was to drive the division toward profitability. This, at the time, was a radical idea. Indeed, the news divisions for years were structured to lose money — they were supposed to function as the consciences of the networks, proof that the networks were public-spirited and deserved favorable treatment from regulators in Washington. At ABC, Bill Sheehan recalled, the company's general counsel once chided him for suggesting that the network expand its schedule of profitable prime-time news briefs. "I was forbidden to make money," Sheehan said. CBS, for its part, initially accounted for the profits from "60 Minutes" in its entertainment division so CBS News could continue to lose money.

Only gradually did news emerge as a potential money-maker for the networks. "Huntley-Brinkley" raised the stakes in the evening news competition, while "60 Minutes" demonstrated that news could generate huge profits in prime time. More than anything else, though, the expansion of local news programming changed the way news was regarded by the networks. Throughout the 1970s, local stations transformed news into a major profit center by packaging their newscasts to attract larger audiences. Network managers began to wonder why their news operations could not make money too.

Arledge was the first network news executive to openly embrace the goal of profitability. In this sense, despite his spending, he was a shrewder business executive than his counterparts at CBS and NBC. "I said we should be able to make a profit, and it was an alien concept," Arledge said. "People used to brag about how much money they lost on news." Arledge took the unsentimental position that he could best guard the independence of ABC News by making the news division a contributor to, not a drain on, the network. Arledge also figured that a profitable ABC News would enhance his own standing within the company.

Profits, he thought, would buy him autonomy.

"If you are a supplicant all the time, and you have to go ask for money, remember that a lot of the things you want to do are not going to have any commercial value," Arledge said. "But if we could demonstrate to people that we make money on most of the programs, and we are a strong profit center, it would give us the ability to function the way we want to function, as opposed to having to go clear everything."

The model, again, was ABC Sports. Leonard Goldenson had tolerated Arledge's eccentric management style — more than that, he had given him the News presidency — because of all the money that Arledge had made for ABC. As Irwin Weiner said, "The culture we came out of was the ABC Sports culture, where our profit-and-loss statement always showed a profit. A lot of Roone's power fell off that P and L statement." Arledge himself said, "The reason that I held on to the Sports job so long was because I wanted the clout that came from having a successful operation."

Money, to Arledge, was also a weapon to be deployed against competitors. He used ABC's money skillfully in the pursuit of a star anchor for "World News Tonight" during 1980 and 1981. While he didn't get one, he did set into motion events that determined who would sit at all the network anchor desks for the decade ahead.

Dan Rather was tempted to sign with ABC News. How could he resist? Roone Arledge was telling him he could do anything he wanted at ABC, and he would be paid potfuls of money to do it.

An anchor job at "World News Tonight" was just one piece of the package. Rather could anchor convention and election coverage. He could be an anchor for "20/20." He could do documentaries. There was even talk of "Nightline." In Arledge's words, Rather would be "the centerpiece of ABC News."

And just in case he worried that ABC did not have the troops to support him, Rather was told that he could name the producers he liked at CBS and they would be hired too.

"You tell me what you want to do and how you want to do it," Arledge would tell him. "I will consider it to be my job to see that you get to do it and do it right away."

It was a potent appeal — so alluring that there were times Rather could not believe his own ears.

"Does Roone know what he's saying here?" he once asked David Burke.

Burke replied, "He knows exactly what he's saying. And you can bank it."

That was not all Rather could take to the bank. The money ABC had put on the table was staggering. Rather, who was earning about $280,000 a year at "60 Minutes," initially dismissed as hyperbole his agent's suggestion that they might be able to get a million-dollar contract from ABC. After all, Walter Cronkite, the most trusted man in America, was then making about $650,000.

But Rather's agent, Richard Leibner, was too conservative. Arledge's pursuit of Rather set off a bidding war that drove anchor salaries to unimagined heights. William S. Paley, the CBS chairman, eventually authorized his people to offer Rather a ten-year contract worth about $22 million. Arledge was willing to pay more — "whatever it takes to make you feel good" was how he put it to a stunned Rather.

To Arledge, Dan Rather was the exceedingly rare newsman whose star appeal would put money in the pockets of ABC's stockholders. "Dan Rather had been on '60 Minutes,' he had a very high profile, he was coming off Nixon and Watergate and all of that — he was a hot personality," Arledge said. "We had the feeling somebody could build a news division around Dan Rather."

What's more, Arledge felt that he could work with Rather. "What I liked was his intensity," Arledge said. "If there was any problem we had with Frank Reynolds, it was caused by culture differences. He was the old guard, we were the young turks trying to change things. And you really need somebody whom you can conspire with." He told Rather that he wanted an anchor whom he could call in the middle of the night and put on a plane to wherever news was happening. "You couldn't do that with Frank," he said.

Arledge and Rather were already conspiring, meeting in hotel suites and out-of-the-way Chinese restaurants. One night, Arledge felt comfortable enough to bring up the name of Don Hewitt, the legendary creator of "60 Minutes" and Rather's boss. "Don's a great producer of news," said Arledge. "Maybe the greatest producer of news there has ever been." He paused for effect and said, "But let me tell you something — I'm better."

Rather wasn't sure about that. But the more time they spent together, the more he came to admire Arledge. "He has this mixture of intelligence, burning with a white-hot desire to win," Rather said. Arledge, he thought, was driven to excel in a classy way at the highest levels. "Roone doesn't just want to start," he said. "Roone doesn't want to be just all-league. He doesn't want to be in the Hall of Fame. He wants to be on the all-forever team."

Their dalliance lasted months. "It became almost the only thing on my agenda for a while," Arledge said. Once, when Rather was leaning toward ABC but felt he didn't know the company's top management, he found himself seated next to Leonard Goldenson at dinner in ABC's suite at the Plaza Hotel. The remarkable thing, to Rather, was that he had not expressed his doubts about ABC management but that Arledge had sensed them.

By this time, Arledge knew that the courtship of Dan Rather had become a no-lose proposition. To keep Rather, CBS had to give him the anchor job on the "CBS Evening News" — a job that, until then, everyone at CBS assumed would go to Roger Mudd, Cronkite's longtime substitute. What's more, CBS also had to persuade Cronkite to step down six months earlier than planned.

"It's a no-brainer," said David Burke. "If we got him, we would hurt CBS. And the only way CBS could keep him would be to get rid of Walter Cronkite." As they grasped the mischievous possibilities of such recruiting, Arledge and Burke approached Mudd. They didn't really want him for an anchor job, but they thought that if CBS made a strong offer to Mudd, CBS might lose Rather. "We really wanted Roger to go over and upset the applecart," Arledge said.

In the end, ABC got neither man. Rather decided to stay with CBS. He saw the dangers ahead — whoever replaced Cronkite ran the risk of getting blown out of the water — but his CBS loyalties ran deep. Mudd, meanwhile, was so infuriated when the anchor job went to Rather that he quit on the spot and joined NBC.

Arledge was disappointed. "My first choice would have been to get Rather," he said, "but I figured we came out of it better than we went into it." The only downside for Arledge was that the press got word of his efforts to hire Rather, which further displeased Frank Reynolds.

Nevertheless, Arledge remained in the hunt for a new anchor. Next he set his sights on Tom Brokaw, the former White House correspondent for NBC News who had become anchor of "Today."

Arledge and Brokaw were already friends. They were regulars on the Manhattan celebrity party scene, and they were both pals with Bob Beattie, the former Olympic skier who had become a commentator for ABC Sports. Brokaw's wife, Meredith, was fond of Arledge.

But Arledge did not put Brokaw in quite the same category as Rather. "Tom was terrific," Arledge said, "but nobody looked at Tom the same way they looked at Dan. And so there was not the intensity that there was with Dan."

Still, Arledge put together an attractive offer. He promised Brokaw an anchor slot on "World News Tonight," the freedom to roam the world in search of big stories, and, possibly, a chance to do a program about the outdoors, one of Brokaw's passions. When Brokaw expressed some concern about how he'd be accepted at ABC, Arledge had Frank Reynolds and Ted Koppel call to assure him that he would be welcome. Arledge also brought his own persuasive powers to bear.

"Roone's got style," Brokaw recalled. "It's out to a steak house, with a few drinks in the car and a lot of laughs about sports and news." Once, Brokaw and his father, who was visiting New York from South Dakota, were invited to watch a Leonard-Duran fight at ABC's suite at the Plaza. Another time, Arledge arranged for lunch at the suite only to find it locked; the two men wound up eating tuna fish sandwiches in the kitchen of Brokaw's apartment.

Brokaw was charmed. "There have been very few professional experiences that I've enjoyed more than just the time I talked to Roone about what we ought to be doing, about the news, about how to move into the future," he said.

If Arledge, with Rather, had stressed his seriousness of purpose and competitive instincts, he put forward his more easygoing, fun-loving side with Brokaw, who sometimes felt as if NBC people were deadly serious about the news, and deadly dull too. Brokaw and Arledge talked television as much as they talked journalism.

"A television genius" was the way Brokaw described Arledge. "He is a creature of the medium," Brokaw said. "I love this medium, and so does he. Yes, we've got to be good at what we do, and we've got to be serious. But at the same time, it's television. Let's make it exciting. How do we do that? How do we bring in the audience?"

To keep Brokaw, NBC first persuaded John Chancellor, the anchor of NBC's "Nightly News," to step down six months earlier than planned. Then Roger Mudd, whose NBC contract guaranteed him the anchor job, graciously agreed to share anchor duties with Brokaw. Finally, Brokaw was offered a seven-year, $18 million contract granting him veto power over major changes in the "Nightly News." Like Rather, Brokaw found it difficult to leave the network he'd called home for so long.

Arledge wasn't deterred. When Brokaw told him he'd decided to stay at NBC, Arledge scrawled a final contract proposal on a sheet of yellow paper and sent it by messenger to Brokaw's apartment on Saturday morning. The offer amazed Brokaw — it was for even more money than he'd been given by NBC — but he was on his way to play softball in Central Park, so he folded the paper, stuck it in his pocket, and rode to the park on his bicycle. He was so preoccupied, he recalled, that he played terribly in the game; he then rode over to see Thornton Bradshaw, the chairman of RCA, which owned NBC, at his suite at the Dorset Hotel. Bradshaw told him that Grant Tinker, a strong supporter of news, was about to be named chairman of NBC. That cinched Brokaw's NBC deal.

Once again, Arledge had come away empty-handed from a high-profile talent raid. But he had again shaken up a rival. Arledge had forced CBS and NBC to guarantee anchor jobs to Rather and Brokaw or face the certainty of losing them. Both times, ABC had gained. "We had to get rid of Cronkite to even the field," David Burke said. "Now we'd done the same thing at NBC with Chancellor." What's more, Brokaw and Mudd did not mesh, dashing the faint hope that they might rekindle some of the Huntley-Brinkley magic.

As Arledge told a reporter, "You'll never again see CBS with the kind of lead it's had in the past. It will no longer be Snow White with the dwarfs behind. It's going to be a whole new game."

With CBS and NBC losing viewers, "World News Tonight" won the weekly Nielsens for the first time ever in July 1981. Arledge had champagne shipped to Ottawa, Canada, where Reynolds, Jennings, and "World News" staff members had gone to cover an economic summit.

After the broadcast, Reynolds, who was not usually a demonstrative man, climbed up on an equipment case so he could addresss the troops. He beamed with pride.

"It's working," he said, toasting the staff. "It's just one week, and we'll probably go back to second or third. But it's a sign of what's to come."

While Arledge was seeking star power for "World News Tonight," his biggest star was bringing him both glory and grief. Geraldo Rivera had become a huge draw for "20/20." He had also become an unmanageable force inside ABC News.

Rivera was Arledge's best-paid reporter by a long shot. His friend and agent, Jon Peters, who was then living with Barbra Streisand and managing her career, negotiated Rivera's first "20/20" contract, which paid him $750,000 a year. In 1980, Rivera was bumped up to $1 million a year, after Ted Turner tried to lure him to the Cable News Network.

At "20/20" Rivera formed his own unit of producers and support staff, which his third wife, Sheri, ran like an independent company. She handled his ABC finances and expenses, attended meetings for him, traveled with him, and evaluated his staff. Unlike the other correspondents, Rivera held the title of senior producer, which meant that he was accountable only to "20/20" executive producer Av Westin. His contract, his title, his value as a ratings getter, and his pipeline to Arledge combined to give Rivera extraordinary power at "20/20."

Occasionally, this was to everyone's benefit. Rivera's clout led a "20/20" producer named Joe Lovett to approach him early in 1983 to ask that he approve a story about a new disease called AIDS. Lovett, who was openly gay, had heard about AIDS from his Greenwich Village friends, including playwright Larry Kramer, and after researching the story, he concluded that the epidemic was major news — especially because the government had been slow to respond. No network had looked closely at AIDS, and the disease had not yet made its way onto the front page of the *New York Times*. In part because no one else had done the story, Lovett was unable to sell it to Westin. He then pitched the story to Rivera, telling him that neglected victims of AIDS needed a champion.

His strategy worked. Rivera agreed to do a story about AIDS and gays, along with a companion piece about the spread of the AIDS virus into the blood supply. Rivera and Lovett threw themselves into the story, interviewing victims, medical experts, and activists until they had an emotional yet factual story about a community at risk. Lovett was elated; national publicity, he thought, would compel the federal government to act. The story meant so much him that, as airtime approached, tears rolled down his cheeks.

The AIDS story was Rivera at his best — using his influence on behalf of the underdog, harnessing his energy to produce compelling television. He brought his usual theatrical flourish to the task — "We are at Ground Zero for this frightening medical mystery," he declaimed — but, to his credit, he stayed with the AIDS story for years. Some of his pieces were better than others — the blood-supply piece, as it happened, had a hysterical tone — but Rivera and "20/20" devoted sustained attention to AIDS while others ignored the disease.

With nearly unlimited access to airtime, Rivera also tackled subjects too big to be covered in a fifteen-minute segment. He did an hour on the manufacture and trafficking of heroin and another on the politics of cancer research. With producers Charlie Thompson and Don Thrasher, Rivera delivered hard-hitting investigations into defense contracting and Pentagon waste. Westin, who collected toy soldiers as a hobby, loved military stories, as did Arledge, and "20/20" helped make such symbols as the $642 toilet seat famous.

But Rivera's unfettered freedom also got him in trouble. With his penchant for melodrama, he recklessly embraced the techniques of investigative reporting that came into vogue in the early 1980s — ambush interviews, hidden cameras, and confrontational questions designed not to elicit answers but to provoke hostility. One of his most public missteps came in February 1980, when a producer named Peter Lance used a hidden camera to tape a group of Chicago businessmen who were allegedly running an arson-for-profit ring; the use of hidden cameras constituted eavesdropping, a violation of state law. A few weeks later, Rivera was accused of plagiarizing a story about infant formula he did with a producer, John Fager, who, Rivera admitted, had "borrowed generously" from work done by an NBC station in Washington, D.C. At about the same time, Rivera and ABC News were sued by Kaiser Aluminum over a "20/20" story exposing the dangers of aluminum wiring in residential homes. Kaiser also filed an FCC complaint. "Geraldo kept a lot of lawyers in business," said Dick Wald.

ABC News won most of the suits, but the network was forced to settle a big one — a slander suit brought by a Justice Department official named Howard Safir who ran the government's witness protection program. In 1980, Rivera charged on "20/20" that too many federally protected witnesses were being killed by mobsters and that others resumed their criminal ways while under government protection. Some of the charges had merit, but Safir claimed that his "20/20" interview had been manipulated by Rivera to make him look like "a liar and an incompetent." He was right — one of his comments had been distorted in the editing, leaving some qualifying remarks on the cutting-room floor. Typically, Rivera didn't back down, saying, "These phony lawsuits aren't going to stop us." But Safir's lawyers eventually won a six-figure settlement from ABC. "I felt vindicated," Safir said. "It was a step in holding accountable someone who was totally irresponsible."

Initially, Arledge had been reluctant to curb Rivera. He thought that Geraldo, like Howard Cosell and Sam Donaldson, attracted more than his share of unfair criticism because of his larger-than-life personality. Besides, Rivera worked hard and was popular with viewers; if he discomfited the news establishment, so had Arledge. Speaking for Arledge as well as himself, David Burke once said to a producer who turned down a job in Rivera's unit, "Geraldo is the only guy with any balls at this network."

But the fact that Peter Lance and Rivera broke the law in Chicago embarrassed ABC News. A CBS-owned station in Chicago produced a program called "Watching the Watchdog" about "20/20," charging that ABC had been overzealous and unfair. Safir's lawsuit brought more unwelcome publicity. In response, Arledge issued a staff memo about investigative reporting, reminding people that "news gathering does not include a license to violate the law or the policies of ABC News."

Worried that his own credibility was threatened, Arledge named George Watson to a new position with the title of vice president, news practices. Informally, Watson was dubbed "vice president for Geraldo" — one of his primary duties was to bring Rivera and his unit under control. Along with ABC lawyers, Watson was assigned to screen all investigative stories in advance.

The more Watson learned about Rivera's "20/20" unit, the more disturbed he grew. "I was surprised to find that there were reporters or producers who felt little or no obligation to report other points of view," Watson said. "The producers were convinced that the other side is bullshit, and so why did they have to put it on?" This was Rivera's influence — he couched his work in moral terms, casting himself as a crusader against injustice. "Being right morally was more important to him than getting the facts," said a producer who worked with Rivera before asking to be moved off his unit. She said, "He doesn't put blatant falsehoods on the air. It's a question of a twist or an emphasis."

The way Rivera's sense of moral certainty came into play was best seen in an hour-long "20/20" called "The Unholy War," about the Lebanese civil war. Rivera unselfconsciously described the story to Westin as "another 'Geraldo Goes to War' piece," but the problems went well beyond the fact that he took center stage.

The story had been proposed by Barbara Newman, a "20/20" producer with contacts in the Mossad, the Israeli intelligence agency. Rivera permitted his reporting to be guided by the Israelis, who found him the hero he needed — Bashir Gemayel, the charismatic leader of a Lebanese Christian militia, who was cast as the savior of Lebanon. In truth, Gemayel was a complex figure, admired by many but seen by his enemies as a puppet of the Israelis. Rivera was captivated by him, as was Newman, who later became his lover. For "20/20" they produced an ode to Gemayel, ignoring contradictory evidence — they showed, for example, a car explosion that killed his daughter without saying that the bomb was set off to retaliate for an earlier killing by his allies.

Inside "20/20" several producers warned Westin that the story was slanted. When the report was broadcast anyway, Arab-American groups objected vehemently. Even Rivera was chastened after hearing them out. "I was embarrassed into rethinking my position on the Palestinians," he said.

Arledge was embarrassed too. This time, the problems created by Rivera spurred him to act on a program idea he'd been mulling for a while. Television, critics often said, had no equivalent of an op-ed page or letters column, no forum for viewers to talk back to a network and be heard. What's more, Arledge thought, no one had devised a way for the networks to explain themselves to the audience, to correct misconceptions about how they operated — the notions, for example, that networks would do anything for ratings and that bias was permitted to infect news stories. Arledge hated being misunderstood. He recalled that David Burke had once told him that "my idea of hell must be that I'm trying to explain something to somebody and they don't understand me and walk away." Arledge wanted to explain himself and ABC News to the audience.

To that end, Arledge created "Viewpoint.'" He made George Watson the executive producer, designated Ted Koppel as anchor, and scheduled the program to run occasionally in the "Nightline" time slot. On the ninety-minute show, which was broadcast live, media insiders and critics debated issues such as fairness and privacy and then took questions from a studio audience.

The first "Viewpoint," which aired in prime time, dealt with two Rivera stories — his exposé of aluminum wiring and the hour about Lebanon. Rivera felt second-guessed and resented it. But Arledge's willingness to provide a platform to ABC's critics was justly praised.

Still, Rivera continued to flout the rules of journalism — and he was permitted to do so by Arledge. In 1983, he commandeered another "20/20" hour, this time for a fawning profile of Barbra Streisand and Jon Peters, promoting her movie *Yentl*. Streisand, to be sure, did few interviews, so getting the "20/20" cameras into her Malibu estate was a minor coup. But Streisand knew she'd be treated kindly by Rivera, who, with his wife, Sheri, had bought a home nearby; the two couples were friends as well as neighbors.

Rivera was simply beyond control, as Marion Goldin, a "20/20" senior producer, learned after she changed the title of one of his segments.

"If you ever do that again, I'm going to Roone Arledge," he told her.

"Why stop there? Let's go to Leonard Goldenson," she shot back sarcastically.

Goldin was surprised that Arledge, as a producer, had permitted one of his stars to amass such power.

"The star system is so necessary because it gets people into the tent," she said, years later. "Yet it's so hurtful because it makes monsters out of mediocrity."

In spite of Rivera's appeal, "20/20" suffered a falloff in the ratings in the early 1980s. The biggest dip came during the 1981–82 TV season, when audience levels dropped by nearly 15 percent. That was the year NBC introduced "Hill Street Blues," an innovative police drama that siphoned Thursday night viewers away from ABC.

Av Westin felt the heat. Arledge, he thought, refused to recognize the impact of "Hill Street" and blamed him for the decline. He cast about for ways to pump up the numbers.

Good journalism alone would not do it. Already, "20/20" was doing strong reporting — the investigations into military spending, stories about missing and abused children before those issues became front-page news, and dispatches from trouble spots like Northern Ireland, Guatemala, and Libya — but these topics were not ratings grabbers.

Westin studied his audience; he paid close attention to the mail, to the ratings, and to ABC's research, which sought to discover what stories viewers wanted to see.

Such research was a delicate matter at all the network news divisions. While Hollywood entertainment programmers routinely tested concepts for new sitcoms and dramas, as well as the appeal of prime-time stars, Arledge and his executive producers did not want to admit that they used research to help shape the content of news programming; they preferred to have people think that they relied solely on their journalistic and creative judgments. Testing the market's reaction to story ideas, after all, was inconsistent with the idea of news broadcasting as a public service. But Westin felt that he needed research to compete in prime time. "It was useful because it would tell me what wasn't working," he said. The numbers told him, for example, that "domestic politics was a total zero." Most foreign stories also tested badly.

Finding out which stories would touch viewers was tougher. When research showed that "Hill Street" appealed to urban, upscale viewers, "20/20" countered with profiles of country and western stars to reach the rural audience. Similarly, because "Hill Street" had a lock on the young, "20/20" turned away from rock music and did stories about retirement and recreational vehicles, hoping to capture the fifty-plus crowd. These were the kinds of calculations that drove prime-time television — the producers of "Dynasty" or "Who's the Boss?" would add cast members to reach key demographic groups — but they were not, until then, applied to network news.

When Westin discovered a formula that worked, he milked it shamelessly. Producer Ene Riisna, for example, did a ground-breaking story on depression, exploring its chemical and psychological causes and telling viewers how to get help. Westin didn't like the piece — it struck him as a downer — but the story, narrated by a soothing Hugh Downs, brought a huge response. "20/20" went on to present "coping" pieces about anxiety, shyness, loneliness, anger, and jealousy.

To salvage a profile of Alexander Godunov, a splashy but inarticulate Soviet ballet dancer, Westin happened upon what became known as "process" pieces. "Let's explain what it's like to be a ballet dancer every day," he said. "You have to practice so many hours. The muscles hurt. And so forth." These "process" stories became the province of correspondent Bob Brown, who used celebrated artists to explain musical composition, choreography, and painting.

Foreign stories were also tough to sell without a convenient entry point for viewers. Janice Tomlin, a producer who covered several overseas tragedies, could not persuade Westin to send her to Ethiopia to cover a famine until she found a group of New York City school-children who were raising money to help. The American kids — or doctors or Red Cross volunteers, in other pieces — provided an identifiable window into the story, a way to "convey the horror, the death and destruction without overwhelming people," Tomlin said. This angle of vision ran the risk of turning the foreigners into passive victims, props used for visual impact to make heroes of the American characters who drove her stories. But Tomlin's pieces invariably generated numerous offers of help for the helpless, whether they were starving Ethiopians or young victims of civil war in Mozambique.

All "20/20" pieces benefited from Westin's editing. He had an amazing visual memory, as if a VCR ran in his head — he would remember the lady in the red dress, the bearded guy, the shot with the church in the background — and he knew instinctively how to arrange the elements in a story for maximum impact. "You move them around so the energy levels and emotional levels peak and valley, peak and valley," he would say. "And that's show biz. But I'm using show-business techniques to present information."

Westin was also a great motivator. He spent so much time prowling the corridors of ABC News, talking to people, that his "20/20" operation became known as Hallway Productions. Westin wanted a happy staff — after a veteran producer named Nola Safro grumbled that the show wasn't as much fun anymore, he convened a staff meeting and began by saying, "Maybe we're getting a little too square here. What should we be doing?" Westin became a revered figure at "20/20," although his detractors said that he surrounded himself with sycophants. "The cult of Av was second only to Chairman Mao and Kim Il-Sung in North Korea," griped one critic.

Westin's efforts, however, were not enough to drive the "20/20" ratings back up to pre–"Hill Street" levels. Frustrated, Arledge decided that he needed another star — Rivera alone could not carry the show, and no one was tuning in to watch Tom Jarriel or Sylvia Chase. To bring the show more sizzle, Arledge gently but persistently began to nudge his most underused star — Barbara Walters — toward "20/20."

Walters had already turned down one opportunity to anchor "20/20." Arledge had offered her the job in 1978, just as she was coming off the evening news, but she had felt that her career was too fragile to risk another failure. "I couldn't take the chance on another flop," she said. "It would have been my flop."

So she drifted. Walters did occasional high-profile interviews and assignments for "World News Tonight," but the kinds of stories that got her excited did not come along often. Arledge suggested that she try doing a video gossip column for "World News," but her heart wasn't in it. "She had to live as a correspondent rather than as an anchor," said Victor Neufeld, her producer. "It was very difficult for her." Along with her public image, her self-confidence had been shaken when she lost the anchor job.

"I had really been damaged by the way it was handled," Walters said. "I literally had to start all over again. I would do these stories that were very big and very important. Still, I had no place. I felt for a long time that I needed a home, and it wasn't on the news."

Her entertainment specials were her only showcase, and they initially proved to be a mixed blessing. On her maiden special, Walters was ridiculed for ending her interview with Jimmy Carter by telling him, "Be good to us, Mr. President, be kind." (Walters not only said it but chose to leave it in the show, since she did all her own editing.) Later, she was lampooned when she asked Katharine Hepburn what kind of tree she wanted to be, although the fact was that Hepburn brought up the tree business first. Talking to movie stars about their marriages, drug problems, and interior design — not to mention riding a motorcycle with Sylvester Stallone — did nothing for Walters's efforts to be taken seriously as a journalist.

But the specials, over the years, proved valuable to Walters and immensely profitable to ABC. She interviewed the biggest stars — Hepburn, Jimmy Stewart, John Wayne, Bing Crosby, Paul Newman, Clint Eastwood, and Bette Davis, to name a few — and, more remarkably, she usually got them to reveal something of themselves. Perhaps because she was a star, she empathized with celebrities and never pushed too far. But Walters could and did ask Richard Pryor if he had stopped using drugs, Don Johnson about losing his virginity, and Boy George about his sexual orientation. "She invented intimacy on television," said producer Ene Riisna. "No one else had done it before she came along."

She also accentuated the personal when she did occasional "20/20" interviews with people who did not fit on her celebrity specials — former First Lady Mamie Eisenhower, Richard Nixon, and President Reagan, among others. Even when talking to government leaders,

Walters said, "I care about what makes them tick." She did half a dozen to a dozen "20/20" stories a year in the early 1980s.

But Walters was reluctant to commit herself to "20/20." She wanted to work on her terms, with producers she trusted and on stories that fit her persona. "We'd try to get Barbara to do pieces," said a producer, "but all she wanted to do was interviews." She was managing her career shrewdly; if she did pieces like everyone else's, the cachet associated with a Barbara Walters interview would disappear. She felt, probably rightly, that she could not afford to become just another "20/20" correspondent.

Unsurprisingly, with that attitude, Walters was not immediately welcomed at "20/20." The surprise was that Hugh Downs, her former couchmate on "Today," led the resistance. It was nothing personal. Downs simply knew Walters well enough to realize that she would settle for nothing less than an anchor job at "20/20." And as far as he was concerned, the show had no need for another anchor. "I had no objection to Barbara," Downs said, "but co-anchoring is inherently awkward."

To avoid conflict, a compromise was worked out. Downs retained the anchor position, literally; seated at his desk, he was the only person directly facing the cameras. He also took the show on and off the air — saying good evening and good night. Walters was stationed in the wings, where she introduced her own pieces, debriefed correspondents, and chatted with Downs.

Even so, disagreements arose. Late in 1982, Walters arranged for a live interview with Nixon. Downs bristled, telling Westin, "She's not going to interview Nixon on my set." He had to be assured that the interview would be photographed so that it didn't look like Walters had taken his place.

No one liked the arrangement. Downs felt left out when Walters talked to the correspondents. Seated in the wings, Walters felt like a second-class citizen. "Neither of us was quite happy," he said. She agreed that "it was very awkward."

Ultimately, Downs accepted the inevitable. In September 1984, Walters was named co-anchor of "20/20." That required further negotiation. "One of the great debates," Westin recalled, "occurred over the line 'We're in touch so you be in touch.' Hugh was in his dressing room and Barbara was in hers and neither one was going to come on the air until it got resolved." Again, they compromised — Walters claimed the "be in touch" line, and Downs got the last goodnight. Later, they could all laugh about it.

Walters had found a home, albeit quietly. That was the best way, she thought, to shield herself from critics. "I kind of sneaked in," she said. "The last thing I wanted was to make a big splash."

Getting the "20/20" anchor job was satisfying, Walters said, because she felt that she had earned it. She had always doubted herself. Even after her success on "Today," she said, "You think maybe you were just lucky, maybe I was just doing the 'Today' show at the right time.

"In working my way back, I worked very hard," she said. "I finally felt that I deserved what I got. I got a kind of confidence that I wouldn't have gotten."

For that, she was forever grateful to Arledge. "Even though I don't think Roone knew quite what to do with me, I also knew he hadn't abandoned me," she said. "I was drowning, and there was no life preserver. The one who gave me the life preserver was Roone."

Chapter Nine

A SUNDAY MORNING
WAKE-UP CALL

His TIME on the evening news had passed, as had his sixtieth birthday, but David Brinkley had no plans to retire. If NBC News wanted to entrust its future to Tom Brokaw, that was fine, but he felt as sharp as ever. Surely there was a place for him on the network to which he had given his entire professional life.

Nor was Walter Cronkite prepared to fade out after vacating the CBS News anchor desk for Dan Rather. Cronkite even assured viewers of his final evening news broadcast that he would return, someplace, somehow, before long. "Old anchormen don't go away," he rumbled. "They keep coming back for more."

There were no precedents for the situations facing Brinkley and Cronkite — anchors emeritus, aging legends in a business that valued youth. Neither NBC nor CBS could figure out what to do with them, and the passing of the old guard created problems at those networks and opportunities for Roone Arledge and ABC.

At CBS, Cronkite's departure set off a sequence of events that did nothing less than bring an end to the old CBS News. The news division split into camps — Cronkite's men, a Rather faction, Don Hewitt's loyalists, and others. When Rather's evening news ratings slid late in 1981, CBS's top executives panicked; they lost faith in the traditional news managers and named Van Gordon Sauter, the president of CBS Sports, to run CBS News. Sauter, an iconoclast, rejected as stuffy and outdated the news values and no-frills production techniques that had given CBS News its special place in broadcast journalism since the days of Murrow.

Sauter was very much CBS's answer to Arledge, a measure of how the changes at ABC were reverberating through the other networks. He changed producers on the evening news, favored stories with popular appeal, jazzed up the visuals, and embraced the star system. "Give me a show without a star, and I'll give you a failed show," Sauter said.

But a correspondent who knew both men saw Sauter as a "$3.98 knockoff" of Arledge. "What Roone wants on the air is action and drama, so long as there's action and drama in the story," he said. "But Sauter went after raw emotion, divorced from real value or deeper meaning or intellectual context." What's more, CBS News traditions were so entrenched that Sauter met fierce and unyielding opposition.

Preoccupied with internal politics, CBS News frittered away its legacy and wasted opportunities. Cronkite, for example, had been promised after leaving the evening news that he could contribute occasional stories, interviews, and commentaries. But Sauter feared that Cronkite's presence would unnerve Rather. As a result, with the exception of a short-lived prime-time series called "Universe," Cronkite was virtually banished from CBS News. That was shameful, Arledge thought. "Why they wasted an asset like Walter Cronkite, I just never have understood," Arledge said. "You can't tell me that if you have the most trusted reporter in America, you can't find a role for him."

Arledge was getting help from instability at NBC, too. Lester Crystal, who replaced Dick Wald as NBC News president in 1977, was fired two years later and replaced by CBS veteran Bill Small. Small was a solid journalist but a blunt man who made plain his belief that NBC News was a second-rate outfit that needed an overhaul.

Small erred most grievously in his handling of Brinkley. In 1980, he muscled Brinkley into anchoring "NBC News Magazine with David Brinkley," one of NBC's many futile attempts to get a news program established in prime time. "I squirmed, fought and kicked, tried to get out of it, but they called in the chairman of the board of NBC, and everybody leaned on me hard, so I finally agreed to do it," Brinkley said.

NBC then neglected the show. By scheduling it opposite CBS's megahit "Dallas," the network ensured that Brinkley would have the humiliating experience of seeing his name at the bottom of the weekly Nielsens every Tuesday. Brinkley hated traveling to New York to do the show and took an intense dislike to Small. Years later, he could still get worked up into a lather over Small, saying, "In spite of his absolute ignorance and incompetence — you can quote this, please do — he insisted on dictating to me every week what to put on the air. And most of what he dictated was nonsense."

Over at ABC, Dick Wald got word that his old colleague was disgruntled. Wald heard a telling story about NBC's 1980 convention coverage — that after being operated on for a gallbladder condition, Brinkley had summoned the energy to go on the air and perform in pain because of his loyalty to NBC. Neither Small nor any other NBC executive expressed gratitude. Brinkley, who valued the social graces, could not stand being taken for granted.

The final blow came when Small replaced Brinkley's producer without talking to Brinkley, who was on vacation. Much as he would have liked to remain at NBC News, where he'd spent thirty-eight years, Brinkley could take no more.

When Wald approached him, Brinkley, as usual, was direct. "I'm leaving NBC," he said.

"Well, as it happens, I've got a coat that's just about your size," Wald replied. He thought it was insane for NBC to let go of Brinkley.

The timing was right for ABC. Arledge wanted to replace ABC's Sunday morning program, "Issues and Answers," which he described, accurately, as "an old, boring, typical Sunday ghetto program." After "20/20" and "Nightline" became established, Arledge began playing around with ideas for a new Sunday program. But he didn't see anyone at ABC News who could carry it.

Brinkley could. "David Brinkley gave us the serious, elder presence that ABC News didn't have," Arledge said. He could play the statesman role that Eric Sevareid had played for years at CBS. "You need a father, a grandfather, whatever," Arledge said, with his usual eye for casting. "David also gave us instant credibility with election coverage, convention coverage."

Brinkley was taken with the idea of a Sunday show; he had toyed briefly with the idea of starting his own program with a panel of print reporters and syndicating it to TV stations. In a few weeks — far less time than Arledge had spent pursuing Rather or Brokaw — Brinkley signed with ABC. For $800,000 a year, he agreed to anchor the weekly show as well as ABC's coverage of politics.

Several days later, Arledge unveiled his new acquisition at a Washington reception. "There is greatness in this room," Arledge declared, and he went on to introduce Brinkley as "one of the two or three gigantic figures in broadcasting history." This was only a slight exaggeration. In the history of network news, if not all of broadcasting, Brinkley was a giant. And although David Brinkley had just turned sixty-one, Arledge was sure that his best days lay ahead.

By hiring Brinkley, Arledge had finally brought a star to ABC News. Indeed, at his peak in the early 1960s, Brinkley had been among the biggest stars anywhere. One survey found that Brinkley and Chet Huntley, his NBC co-anchor, were recognized by more adult Americans than Cary Grant, John Wayne, or the Beatles.

Brinkley was initially discomfited by his celebrity. A shy man, he disliked being fussed over in public and found it hard to work in the field because his presence created such a stir. Gradually, though, Brinkley came to enjoy the benefits of fame. Without ever shedding the mantle of the outsider, which served him so well on the air, he became a friend to the powerful and a sought-after party guest in Washington. His social circle during the 1960s included Robert and Edward Kennedy, Senator Eugene McCarthy, LBJ aide Jack Valenti, and Robert McNamara, the secretary of defense. In a 1968 *New Yorker* profile of Brinkley, William Whitworth wrote: "Since he has close friends at all levels of government, from the Cabinet down, it is not unusual for him to find himself writing about someone he has dined with or played poker with the previous evening."

This was not the impression Brinkley left with viewers. "David Brinkley is the beneficiary of a myth," said an associate at ABC News. "That is that he has a sardonic and disrespectful view of power. That he is no respecter of persons. That he is vox populi, that he speaks for the people." The truth was the opposite — Brinkley, especially in his later years, became the quintessential Washington insider, who poked fun at politicians but did so in a bemused way that rarely angered anyone. If he was not exactly part of Washington's permanent government, he had come to reflect its view that democracy is a messy business, that the citizens are not to be trusted, and that decision making is best left to the elites. "Brinkley is a mossback," said the ABC insider. "It's a great trick."

To fairly claim outsider status, Brinkley would have to go back to his origins in Wilmington, North Carolina, where he was born in 1920, the youngest of five children in a working-class family. His father, a railroad clerk, died when he was eight, leaving him in the care of his mother, a strict and unemotional woman. By his own account, he had a lonely and unhappy childhood, which drove him to take refuge in books. He worked on the local newspaper after high school and made his way to NBC's Washington bureau in 1943.

Although he had a spare writing style that was well suited to radio, Brinkley adapted easily to television. He could explain complex subjects in simple declarative sentences; he cut through Washington's bureaucratese. Brinkley also learned never to tell viewers what they could see for themselves; he used narration to supplement the pictures. Reuven Frank, the NBC producer who paired Huntley and Brinkley, once said that Brinkley wrote silence better than anyone else in television.

Brinkley's other great asset was his delivery. Even when he had little to say, his habit of stressing odd words lent his statements an impressive certainty. Talking about election results, for example, he once observed, "Our figures show that message was one of generalized irritation and discontent, with inflation and a lot *more* . . . That and a lot of *other* messages arrived yesterday. It will be instructive to see if Washington listens to them or continues — as it has for a generation — listening *mainly* to *itself*." Later, Arledge would say that one of the great things about Brinkley and Howard Cosell was that they had to say only a few words and all America knew who was talking.

Network news changed forever when NBC put Huntley and Brinkley together in the anchor booth for the 1956 political conventions. Brinkley, then thirty-six, literally invented a new style of anchoring — rejecting the idea, which dated back to movie newsreels, that all news had to be treated as serious and weighty. The grave tone, Brinkley saw, did not fit the conventions; to the contrary, their pomp and pomposity called for a bit of irreverence. Brinkley had an eye for the absurd; a lady in a funny hat interested him as much as the party platform, and he poked fun at both in a conversational tone that came naturally. "The two platforms," he noted, "will fearlessly commit both parties to favor mother love and the protection of the whooping crane, and to oppose the man-eating shark and the more unpopular forms of sin." In 1956, this was refreshing, if not revolutionary.

Viewers took heed, as did critics, led by Jack Gould of the *New York Times,* who wrote that "the pontificating commentators of television . . . succumbed in the early hours of yesterday; they couldn't withstand the fresh breeze of David Brinkley's wit." That fall, Huntley and Brinkley were named the anchors of NBC's nightly news.

These were glory days at NBC News, thanks largely to Robert

Kintner, the network president. Kintner provided the money, airtime, and promotion and demanded that NBC News get on the air first and stay on longer than CBS. He was an unabashed salesman — the evening news always began with the boast that it was "assembled for television every weekday night by the world's largest and most comprehensive broadcast news organization — the news department of the National Broadcasting Company." Arledge worked for NBC at the time, albeit producing a puppet show, but he absorbed the lessons.

Arledge could also see how much television's first anchor stars meant to the success of NBC News. Their trademark sign-off — "Goodnight, David," "Goodnight, Chet" — entered the lexicon, and they became so famous that, at John F. Kennedy's inaugural, Milton Berle and Frank Sinatra toasted them with a duet, to the tune of "Love and Marriage," that went like this: "Huntley Brinkley/Huntley Brinkley/One is glum/And the other twinkly."

Twinkly he might seem, but off the air, Brinkley had few friends at NBC. His writing style reflected his personality; he did not like idle talk, he could not abide incompetence, and when provoked, he let loose with withering put-downs. To a viewer who sent him an article, he wrote, "In response to your note, no, I was not much interested in the piece you wrote in the UAW paper. I found it thin, shallow, and in general too sophomoric to be taken seriously."

Away from the office, Brinkley was good company. He enjoyed the Redskins, the horses, and poker; his circle included politicians Robert Dole and Robert Strauss, superlawyer Edward Bennett Williams, and Dwayne Andreas, a well-connected agribusinessman. He loved carpentry and taught himself architecture, designing a cabin in the Virginia woods and his home in Chevy Chase, Maryland. Brinkley's first marriage, to a reporter named Ann Fischer, lasted twenty-two years and produced three sons — Alan, a historian, and Joel and John, who became reporters. In 1971, he married a young woman named Susan Adolph; they had a daughter, Alexis.

He was never close to Huntley, but when his longtime partner chose to leave the air in 1970, Brinkley was cast adrift. For a time, he shared anchor duties with John Chancellor and Frank McGee, but the routine of the daily program bored him. Gradually, NBC executives came to view him as a retread, and a grumpy one at that. None of that mattered to Arledge. Brinkley was a legend, and he wanted him for ABC News.

*   *   *

Until Roone Arledge came along, Sunday mornings were a sleepy little outpost for the networks, a place to earn prestige and make friends by giving powerful men in Washington a national platform. The Sunday interview format had been virtually unchanged since 1947, when Lawrence Spivak took "Meet the Press," a program he had created for the Mutual Radio Network, to NBC television. A fixture in official Washington, "Meet the Press" was the place where the rest of America got its first close-up looks at such up-and-coming politicians as Richard Nixon and John F. Kennedy. CBS News created its own Sunday panel show, "Face the Nation," in 1953, and ABC arrived last, as usual, introducing "Issues and Answers" in 1960.

Although Spivak could be a pointed interrogator, a sedate mood prevailed on all the Sunday talk shows. To the extent that they competed at all, the Sunday programs gauged their success not by ratings but by whether their efforts registered in the next day's newspapers. Spivak once boasted that "Meet the Press" made the front page of the *New York Times* twenty-six times one year, an impressive feat, even given the paucity of news on weekends. This approach suited the guests, too, since their remarks were amplified by the print coverage.

Arledge was bored by the Sunday programs — and he hated being bored. He regarded Sunday morning, like late night, as uncharted territory waiting to be conquered. "The thinking about television news had stopped in a large part of the television news establishment," Arledge told a reporter. "Look at 'Meet the Press' and 'Face the Nation.' What you see are two dinosaurs from prehistoric times." He wanted to revive the genre by surrounding the newsmaker interview with new elements — a brief newscast, setup pieces to explain the issues at hand, a roundtable discussion, and a preview of the week ahead. None of his ideas were earth-shattering, but they were all driven by the idea that ABC's Sunday show would be produced for the viewing audience, not for the sake of a mention in Monday's paper.

Most of all, Arledge wanted a star, even before Brinkley appeared on the horizon. Bob Clark, the moderator of "Issues and Answers," was a solid reporter with excellent Washington sources, but he was dull. Of course, no one before Arledge ever demanded charisma on Sunday mornings. As Bill Monroe, who succeeded Spivak on "Meet the Press," once observed, "If you look at George Herman and Bob Clark and myself, all of us were veteran Washington correspondents and highly competent journalists, but we were journeymen. There was no glamour there." Clark was gradually eased off "Issues and Answers" so that Barbara Walters and Sam Donaldson, among others, could take a turn at the anchor desk.

In the meantime, Arledge asked Dorrance Smith, his producer of weekend news, to develop a new format for Sunday mornings. Smith worked up one prototype with a male-female anchor team and another that would originate live from wherever news was happening. But, he said, "It was never really a show you could put on the air, until you attached Brinkley's name to it. Then it fell into place." Once Brinkley came aboard, Arledge and David Burke persuaded the affiliates to give them a full hour on Sunday mornings. That was the only way Arledge could make room for all his new elements. And, with an hour, Arledge decided that the show could accommodate two or three guests each week, rather than one. Smith explained, "Roone's a very impatient person, and when you've lost him on a topic, you're not going to get him back, so you've got to be able to go someplace else."

Smith, thirty, was named executive producer of the Brinkley show. An Arledge protégé, Smith was a reserved but confident young man who had grown up in a well-to-do family in Houston; he'd played tennis and become friends with the sons of an up-and-coming Republican congressman named George Bush. As a student at Claremont College in California, Smith had paid his own way to sports events so he could work as a $25-a-day gofer for Arledge's ABC Sports.

His investment paid off. After graduating in 1973, Smith was rewarded with a full-time job as a production assistant at ABC Sports, where he traveled the country with the "Monday Night Football" trio of Howard Cosell, Don Meredith, and Frank Gifford. After a brief interlude as a White House press aide to President Ford, he was rehired by Arledge, this time in News.

Smith was sent to Washington, where the old-timers sometimes made him feel as if he was working behind enemy lines. "People saw me as Arledge's agent and regarded me with a healthy degree of suspicion," he said. After he hooked up with Sam Donaldson as his White House producer, however, Smith built bridges to the veterans. "Dorrance had been viewed as a lapdog or protégé of Roone's," said George Watson, the Washington bureau chief. "But after a period, Dorrance convinced most people that he deserved to be treated seriously as a news producer."

With Brinkley at center stage and Smith in charge, all that was left was to find a supporting cast. There, too, Brinkley proved valuable.

He persuaded his friend George Will, the syndicated columnist and occasional political analyst for ABC, to commit to weekly Sunday appearances, which Will had previously resisted. Getting Will was a coup — he was the leading journalistic voice of the new conservative establishment in Washington.

Will, forty, was both a serious thinker and a celebrity journalist. Oxford-educated, with a Princeton PhD, he liked to show off his knowledge of history and the classics, but he could also serve up delicious tidbits of gossip gleaned from his contacts with powerful Republicans. In the weeks before the 1981 inauguration, when Ronald and Nancy Reagan came east from California to attend three small dinner parties, Will and his wife, Madeline, were hosts for one and guests at the other two. More to the point, Will wrote engagingly not just about politics but about baseball, books, and pop culture. With his bow ties, wire-rimmed glasses, and puckish grin, Will looked like the smartest boy in the class. He spoke elegantly, in part because he'd collect his thoughts beforehand and jot down a phrase or quote that might come in handy. The Brinkley roundtable was not quite as spontaneous as it seemed.

Arledge decreed that the other contributors to the Brinkley show be drawn from a select group of journalists from outside ABC. They included, initially, his friend Ben Bradlee, Tom Wicker of the *New York Times*, Karen Elliot House of the *Wall Street Journal*, and Hodding Carter of PBS.

"This Week with David Brinkley" premiered inauspiciously on November 15, 1981. The show had booked David Stockman, the White House economics adviser, as its featured guest, a choice that seemed inspired when a controversial story published that week in *The Atlantic* revealed Stockman's deep doubts about Reaganomics. But Stockman "backed out at the last minute, which is unforgivable,'" recalled Brinkley. "And we frantically looked around for a replacement." The best his bookers could come up with were senators Fritz Hollings and William Armstrong and New York financier Felix Rohatyn, none of whom proved enthralling. The rest of the broadcast was cluttered with the day's news, two setup pieces, and previews of upcoming events from Capitol Hill, the White House, and Cairo. During a lifeless roundtable discussion, Karen Elliot House spoke in a monotone, and Bradlee was too much the Beltway insider. "We had nowhere to go but up from there," Arledge said.

In the next few weeks, Smith began to pare down the show, eliminating, for example, the previews of the week ahead. He consulted not with Arledge but with David Burke; that avoided interminable debate about how to proceed and gave Arledge the chance to do what he did best, which was react to the show on the air. He preferred the simpler version. "All of Roone's programs started off being too ambitious and then they kind of cooled down," Smith said.

Still, something was missing from "This Week." The interviews were not making news — not in the newspapers and, some weeks, not even on ABC's Sunday evening newscast, which was then anchored by Sam Donaldson. Brinkley was so polite and Will so philosophical, and they were both so deliberate in their questioning that they'd let guests off the hook. Donaldson would arrive later, griping because he didn't have a sound bite for his newscast; once or twice, he went out to interview the same guest again. It exposed a weakness of the Brinkley show. "Too often the guests were not being nailed down on the question of the day," Smith said.

The solution was blindingly obvious. No one was better at getting the sound bite of the day than Donaldson. That had been his stock-in-trade for years at the White House. Besides, Smith was hearing complaints from Arledge about the print reporters on the show; they lacked flair. So, again acting on his own, Smith put his friend Donaldson on the Brinkley panel one week and had him stay for the roundtable. He brought him back again and then told him to show up every Sunday until he heard otherwise.

Neither Brinkley nor Will welcomed him aboard. Donaldson had a reputation for antic behavior off the air, while, as a reporter, he was most famous for his brashness and leathery lungs, which enabled him to shout questions at Ronald Reagan over the racket of whirling helicopter blades. Such behavior might be acceptable at the White House, but Brinkley and Will were gentlemen journalists. They were not pleased to see this loudmouthed, pushy reporter elbow his way onto their Sunday morning program.

Sam Donaldson had to admit that the stories about the biting were true. Yes, he'd once bitten a stewardess in a hotel bar. And, yes, he'd once taken a nip at the arm of Bettina Gregory, his ABC colleague. Years later, though, long after he had kicked the habit, Donaldson grew tired of hearing about the biting. Wasn't there a statute of limitations that applied to past behavior? he wanted to know. Would he be forever remembered as the class clown? He felt burdened by his image. "I couldn't look at my name in the paper without an adjective," Donaldson said. "It wasn't Sam Donaldson or ABC correspondent Sam Donaldson. It was the abrasive or loudmouthed Sam Donaldson. People would write about the latest egregious act of aggressive behavior. The stuff I did on a daily basis — did I have the story and did I tell it? — very few people wrote about that."

Donaldson nearly always had the story, and he told it well. He was a serious journalist at heart, and that was what mattered most to him. But that was not why reporters came to write about him. They came not to see a White House correspondent at work but to review a performance. Donaldson knew it, of course, and he would oblige them by recalling his bad-boy exploits; a part of him cultivated his reputation as the obnoxious intruder on the dignified business of government, the newsman as pit bull. He recognized — and he knew that Roone Arledge recognized — that his style set him apart from the pack of staid, buttoned-down reporters who surrounded the President of the United States and respectfully documented his every movement.

Donaldson's showboating style became known as The Act. He had created the role for himself, and now he was stuck with it. "It is now so firmly embedded that, if I tried to remake myself in some other image, it would be a total failure," he said.

The Act, as it happened, was no act — aggressive behavior came naturally to Samuel Andrew Donaldson Jr., who was born in 1934 in El Paso, Texas, near his family's farm in Chamberino, New Mexico, and named after a father he never knew. Sam Sr. had died of a heart attack eight months before he was born, so Sam was raised by his mother, Chloe, a strict Baptist who dressed in black and had no use for frivolity. "I often thought as a young man that she believed the Lord had put her on earth to administer discipline to her sons in His name," he said. A conservative Republican, she asked him years later, "Why can't you be more like George Will?"

Young Sam was a trial to his mother. At age seven, caught up in the fighting spirit of World War II, he blew up the familiy truck by dropping a lighted match into the gas tank. Another time, he shot out the front tooth of a Mexican farm worker with a BB gun. He spent four years at a military school, which, he says, accounts for his stiff bearing, and he went on to study telecommunications at Texas Western College, where he got his first taste of radio, as a disc jockey and host of "Sam's Show."

Donaldson did not gravitate immediately to news. After military service, he worked as a stockbroker, a TV announcer, and, briefly, an actor. In 1961, he was hired by WTOP-TV in Washington as a reporter and producer. Six years later, he joined ABC News.

For a time, he was embarrassed by his limited experience in journalism. "Most of the top dogs in TV news were from print," he said. "They believed there was just one path to God. And if you hadn't been knighted through print, they looked down on you as some announcer buffoon." He made up for his lack of formal training with drive; one year, he worked seven days a week, covering Capitol Hill on weekdays, then flying to New York to anchor a fifteen-minute late-night newscast on Saturdays and Sundays. He was rewarded with high-profile assignments, among them the Watergate hearings and Jimmy Carter's presidential campaign, which carried him, with Carter, to the White House.

The White House beat suited him perfectly. He didn't mind the long hours or travel, and he thrived under daily deadline pressure. Most of all, he found ways to get the president to pay heed to him and respond to his questions. Donaldson would yell, or wave his arms, or call out a question after a ceremonial occasion; he would float a rumor or let loose with an unsubstantiated charge — whatever it took to get an answer. He had no fear of asking tough questions. "It has never bothered me that people think I'm rude and crude and should drop dead," Donaldson would say. "What bothers me is that there are lots of important questions that aren't getting answered."

All this required a certain talent, although not one that was widely recognized. Critics who praised Ted Koppel or Mike Wallace for their interviewing skills rarely noticed that Donaldson was equally adept in his chosen arena. Others, after all, had a half-hour broadcast or hours on videotape to draw out their subjects. Donaldson operated within a much tighter window. He explained, "If you're walking down a hall and you're the president of the United States and you're going to be there for about twenty-five seconds, I don't have time to be philosophical. I don't have time to be thoughtful. I don't have time to be polite. I need you to tell me something now. And I'm as good as they get on that." It was no idle boast.

His detractors said that Donaldson lacked depth, a charge to which he readily acceded. "I sometimes feel the old saying 'He's a mile wide but an inch deep' was coined for me," he once said. They also complained that his questions were designed to create sparks rather than elicit information; he was a "master provocateur," said Jody Powell, Carter's press secretary. There was some truth to this charge, too, but the sparks played well on the evening news. "Nine times out of ten, when the president says something that makes news, it was Sam who asked the question," Arledge would say. "What's really fun for me is watching the other two networks cut around him. Sometimes they're quite creative."

Despite his bark, Donaldson earned the respect of those he covered at the White House under both Carter and Reagan; they thought he was fair and dedicated to getting the story right, as well as a useful foil, especially for Reagan. He was also well liked by competitors. "It's funny how Carter and Reagan would light up when they saw Sam," said Lesley Stahl, who covered the White House for CBS. "He was like a life force, and we all came alive when he was around. Even when he was tired he had more energy than ten of us around here."

In fact, Donaldson sometimes acted like a hyperactive ten-year-old. He loved the spotlight — a colleague once said that "if there were no TV, Sam would go door to door" — and his insatiable need for attention occasionally got him in trouble. Once, at Lod Airport in Tel Aviv, as U.S. Defense Secretary Harold Brown bid a solemn farewell to his Israeli counterpart, Donaldson bellowed, "Tell him, NO MORE JETS, HAROLD! NO MORE JETS!" Administration officials were appalled. Another time, Donaldson was unable to contain himself when the president of Uruguay arrived at the White House on a wintry day, to be greeted by President Reagan on the South Lawn. First, to stay warm, Donaldson began conducting the military band with broad gestures as it played the Uruguayan national anthem. Then, as the visiting dignitary launched into a windy speech, Donaldson could be seen praying to the heavens for the end and giving an exaggerated "cut" sign by pulling his hand across his neck. Elliot Abrams, Reagan's deputy secretary of state, was so offended that he complained to Arledge, who relayed his concern to bureau chief George Watson in Washington.

"I've got a complaint from Roone," Watson said, after summoning Donaldson to his office the next day, "that you were making a horse's ass of yourself on the South Lawn."

"I plead guilty," Donaldson replied cheerfully.

"Okay," said Watson, and they went off to lunch.

The fact was that Donaldson was so much fun to be around and so big-hearted that most people forgave his excesses; he was loyal and generous and well liked by his colleagues. But Donaldson had a demanding and temperamental side. Traveling in Rome with Carter, he went ballistic when a technician inadvertently erased the videotape of his story just before airtime. "He was going to beat this guy's head. He was going to kill him," said producer Terry Ray, who had to physically restrain Donaldson. Even his close friend Dorrance Smith said, "He can make you feel small and unimportant and foolish in front of other people." To work with Donaldson, a producer needed a thick skin and immense reserves of energy.

Donaldson also developed a way of working that gave him near-total control over his pieces. He'd look at all the tape himself, a task some correspondents left to their producers, and then piece together his story sentence-by-sentence, carefully matching his words to the pictures. It was a painstaking process, done under pressure, which left no time for debate. "You may be a great collaborator," he would say, "but I want to do it my way."

He took the same tack with producers on the rim in New York, who reviewed scripts before broadcast. Donaldson alone escaped editing, by refusing to transmit his stories until just before airtime. He maintained, with some justification, that he waited as long as he did so that his stories would be up-to-date, but he also admitted that he wanted to avoid the rewrite men. The rim put up with him because he delivered. John Armstrong, a veteran producer, said, "Of all the people I've ever known in broadcasting, he gives more to it on a regular basis than anybody. He was always up, and he was there first, and he stayed later, and you couldn't mousetrap him on a story. He just never failed."

In personal terms, Donaldson paid a price for his commitment. Four days after the American hostages were taken in Iran in 1979, his second wife, Billy Kay, told him she wanted a divorce. They had been married for sixteen years and had three children. He also had a son from a brief early marriage. Donaldson blamed himself, saying, "I hadn't spent a lot of time at home. I just used it as a pit stop."

He took some consolation from the fact that, as an Arledge favorite, his star was ascending. He got more airtime than any other correspondent on "World News Tonight." He was named anchor of ABC's new Sunday evening half-hour newscast. And he was a candidate to host the new Sunday morning program before Brinkley came along.

His own feelings about Arledge were complicated. Donaldson was flattered when Arledge consulted him in the early days, and he welcomed the money and energy that the new regime brought to ABC. But Donaldson never felt entirely at ease with Arledge. He was pleased to get the Sunday night anchor job, for example, but he found it odd that he was not asked to do it until the last minute and then only by Av Westin, not by Arledge. That didn't feel like a vote of confidence to Donaldson.

Now a similar thing happened on Sunday mornings. In Arledge's original scheme, Donaldson had no place on the Brinkley show. And while Arledge had acquiesced when Donaldson was brought on by Smith, he never commented on his work or even told him face-to-face that he had earned a place on the show. To Donaldson, such things mattered. He was, after all, someone who liked to be noticed.

Donaldson was certainly noticed on the Brinkley show. He brought an edge to the questioning and a vitality to the roundtable. But credit for the first breakthrough for "This Week" belonged not to Donaldson or Brinkley or Smith but to Arledge, whose ever-present curiosity led to a most unusual booking.

The Brinkley show had been on the air for three weeks when Arledge returned to New York from an ABC meeting in Hawaii on Friday, December 10, 1981. He and his wife, Ann, watched "Nightline," where the topic was the sensational allegation that Col. Muammar Qaddafi of Libya had sent hit squads to the United States with instructions to assassinate President Reagan.

After "Nightline," Ann said she'd love to know what Qaddafi thought about the charge. Arledge told her that he might be able to find out.

He dialed Dorrance Smith at home. "Of course, you've got a bid in to get Qaddafi, don't you?" Arledge said.

Smith didn't. He had already gone to some trouble to book Ariel Sharon, the Israeli defense minister. And correspondent Jim Wooten had spent a week in the Middle East crafting a long setup piece.

Smith explained his plans to Arledge and said he didn't think that Qaddafi had ever done a television interview. Besides, he liked the idea of doing Sharon. That, by itself, was a departure from the norm, since the other Sunday shows nearly always stuck with studio interviews of Washington newsmakers.

"You mean you haven't even tried?" Arledge said. Qaddafi might say no, he said, but that was no reason not to ask.

The rest of the conversation was chilly. Do you really think Sharon would make a better interview than Qaddafi? Arledge asked. He noted that plenty of time remained to remake the show.

By the time they were done, Smith felt like slamming down the phone. Arledge, he thought, could be a royal pain. Instead, he picked it up to dial the desk in New York, to have Lou Cioffi, ABC's United Nations correspondent and a Mideast veteran, dispatched to Tripoli. Smith hired a charter plane, booked time for a live satellite feed, arranged for a translator, and commissioned a setup piece, all on the off chance that Qaddafi would agree to come on the program — which, to everyone's surprise, he did.

Before airtime, Smith and Brinkley sat, slightly stunned, in the Washington studio, watching via satellite as Qaddafi and a bevy of aides who buzzed around him prepared for the show. "He spent the entire time preening," recalled Brinkley. "He had a mirror brought on, he would adjust his hair, and it was quite disgusting. He did everything but check his lipstick." Once on the air, Qaddafi did not disappoint — he called Ronald Reagan "silly" and "ignorant" and "a liar" and called on the American people to topple him. The next morning, ABC's interview with Qaddafi was the lead story in the *Washington Post*. That time, making the newspaper meant something.

The Qaddafi interview was an exception that proved the rule. Few Sunday morning interviews were newsworthy or noteworthy; the only reason they made the papers was that news was scarce on Sundays. While the Brinkley show was the most adventurous Sunday program, its guests were practiced Washington insiders, familiar faces who could be counted on to say familiar things. As Will said, "On shows like ours, ninety percent of the interview is an experienced political person saying something he wants to get said. That's why he came on the show." Predictability was the norm.

The roundtable discussion, by contrast, was freewheeling. "It's part of the charm of the roundtable," Will said. "It is a semi-conversation. Remember that most people go through life, month after month, and never hear, let alone have, a conversation." The roundtable became everyone's favorite part of the show, although it did not start out that way.

Initially, the stars had no chemistry. Brinkley grumbled that Donaldson talked too much, while Donaldson thought that Brinkley was losing his touch. Will was smug. Some mornings they arrived at the studio primed for battle "like pit bulls, being held on the chain, ready to do what they do," an insider said.

This was where Smith's knack for diplomacy came into play. He had Donaldson's trust, and he won Brinkley and Will over. He would stroke their egos, but, more than that, he was fair-minded and a good listener. If Brinkley came up with a bad idea for a show, Smith could disabuse him of it gracefully, without bruising his feelings. And, despite his youth, Smith displayed maturity both on the job and away from the office. He was friends with the Kennedys, as well as the

Bushes, and it was not uncommon for a U.S. senator or cabinet member to show up at a barbecue at his home.

With Smith defusing tensions before they got out of hand, the stars gradually developed an easy rapport. Unlike so many anchor pairings, the roundtable worked because each man had a well-defined role. Although Brinkley rarely contributed anything of substance, he served as the courtly host, whose genteel manner brought a civility to the proceedings. Will, the house intellectual, displayed both the depth to put the day's political flap into a historical context and the television skills required to telescope his ideas down to sound-bite length. That left Donaldson to play the role of upstart, provocateur, and lightning rod, which he embraced with his usual verve. He'd get under Will's skin, even if it meant manufacturing disagreement, talking over him or misstating his case. "I am so much a better presenter of my position than you are, Sam," Will once told him haughtily, but Donaldson plowed ahead under the most adverse conditions and expressed even his outlandish opinions with total certainty. "The rule," he once explained, only half in jest, "must be to get the mouth in gear and hope that the mind will follow."

Donaldson's frankness incited viewers who were unused to hearing a reporter who covered the White House express his opinions in public; tradition held that news reporters should try to remain objective or at least keep their beliefs to themselves. But this was another departure from the norm that Arledge was willing to accept. Donaldson was another hot personality who, like Barbara Walters, Geraldo Rivera, or Howard Cosell, aroused strong reactions, as his mail showed every day. (The post office once delivered to him a letter addressed only to "Sandinista Sam, Washington, D.C.") But Donaldson's detractors kept tuning in, as Arledge hoped they would. Smith, who'd worked on "Monday Night Football," once described Donaldson, Will, and Brinkley as "a troika not unlike Cosell, Meredith, and Gifford."

While the analogy was imprecise — George Will had little in common with "Dandy" Don Meredith — it was clear that, just as ABC's "Monday Night Football" transformed the way football was shown on television, "This Week" made the other Sunday morning talk shows obsolete. Within a year, the Brinkley show overtook the venerable "Meet the Press" in the ratings. While Sunday morning audiences were relatively small, "This Week" attracted wealthy, well-educated viewers and became a prestige vehicle for corporations that wanted to reach opinion-makers. The TV critics also became Brinkley fans, and they derided "Meet the Press" and "Face the Nation" as stodgy and outmoded.

The rules of the Sunday morning game had changed, forcing CBS and NBC to react. George Herman, who had anchored "Face the Nation" since 1969, was replaced in 1983 by Lesley Stahl, a rising star. NBC, typically, was slower to move, but the network eventually dumped Bill Monroe and installed former CBS stars Marvin Kalb and Roger Mudd on "Meet the Press." Neither lasted long, and for the rest of the decade, "Meet the Press" struggled to find a voice. Sunday mornings belonged to ABC.

Arledge had again proved his brilliance not only as a producer but also as a network programmer. The creation of "This Week with David Brinkley" was neither as significant nor as dramatic as the launch of "Nightline," but it reflected the same modus operandi. Arledge spotted opportunities in fringe time periods that others neglected. He experimented with formats and talent until they clicked. And like all creative, ambitious people, he would not settle for the status quo.

"That's the difference between those who are very good and those who are mediocre," Arledge once said. "First, to be curious, and second, to say, what if I tried this?" Arledge was a relentless innovator, whether he was thinking about new equipment, a new way of telling a story, or a new program.

By the spring of 1982, after five years on the job, Arledge had laid the foundations for a strong ABC News. He had assembled a capable management team, especially his trusted second-in-command, David Burke, who at last had won the respect of the ABC veterans. Burke had fallen in love with the news business; he thrived on the competition, the excitement, the rush of events, as well as the sense that by doing his job well he could contribute to a greater good. At the next level, Arledge had a group of strong executive producers, including Av Westin, Bill Lord, and Jeff Gralnick; they had been tested under fire and had proved their mettle. Below them were a slew of talented younger producers.

The ABC correspondent corps was also vastly improved, to the point where Arledge's troops were superior to NBC's people and the equal of those at CBS. Not all his recruits succeeded — many never rose above the level they had achieved elsewhere, and a few flamed out — but in contrast to the old days when the bench was thin, now even capable correspondents at ABC had to fight their way onto the air. Arledge's hires included Sylvia Chase, Ray Gandolf, Barry Serafin, and Richard Threlkeld from CBS; Brinkley and Carole Simpson from NBC; Lynn Sherr and Bob Zelnick from public TV; John Quinones, Judd Rose, and George Strait from local stations; and Sander Vanocur, John McWethy, Jim Wooten, and Stephen Aug from print. Still, many of the famous faces on the new ABC News — Jennings, Koppel, Walters, Reynolds, Donaldson, Jarriel, Gibson, and Hume — had come from the old ABC News. They just weren't quite as famous until Arledge came along.

For himself, Arledge had overcome some, but not all, of the hostility that had greeted his arrival at ABC News. He remained too remote, too demanding, and too stingy with praise to be popular with his troops. He had never gone out of his way to win people over, and some resented it. Except when he ventured into the control room for big events, Arledge worked through Burke and his executive producers. He was likened to the Wizard of Oz; none of his underlings really knew the man behind the curtain, and so they never warmed up to him.

Still, even his critics and competitors had come to respect Arledge for what he had wrought. He had created "Nightline" and "This Week" and "20/20" and "World News Tonight." He had brought money and energy and creativity to ABC News. Just as significantly, he had transformed, slowly and almost imperceptibly, the traditional thinking about network news. As Reuven Frank, the president of NBC News, told a reporter, "He made everyone else look at what they were doing. He kind of shook things up, and that's a very good thing."

Following Arledge's lead, all the networks now packaged and sold the news with graphics and music and promotion. They all looked for stories with drama and impact not just in prime time but also for their newscasts. And the idea that the evening newscast should deliver only the most important news of the day, and not the merely interesting, had gradually been abandoned. Arledge brought about a quiet revolution — his approach to the news, once deemed heretical, had become mainstream.

On the night of March 9, 1983, the broadcasting industry, including the news establishment, bestowed its seal of approval on Arledge. A group called the International Radio and Television Society awarded its Gold Medal to Arledge at a gala dinner at the Waldorf-Astoria that glittered with news and sports stars: Walter Cronkite, Dan Rather, and Tom Brokaw joined ABC's best and brightest to pay tribute. In Arledgian fashion, nothing about the affair was understated. Entertainment was provided by actress Ann Jillian, an unknown comic named Arsenio Hall, singers flown in from Mexico, and the West Point Band and Glee Club. Spotlights that criss-crossed the room focused on celebrities from Hollywood, New York, and Washington, and ABC's Washington bureau managed to obtain salutes from all four living presidents, on videotape or by telegram. President Reagan, who presented the IRTS award, said, "Roone, your contributions have been significant enough. I want you to know that I consider Sam Donaldson a small price to pay." The fete lasted five hours, and it was covered not only by "World News Tonight" but by *People* magazine.

Roone Arledge was an outsider no more.

Chapter Ten

A DEATH IN THE FAMILY

WHAT WAS WRONG with Frank Reynolds? Roone Arledge desperately wanted to know. He'd been told that Reynolds was suffering from a bad case of hepatitis, but he needed to know more. This was his lead anchorman, who had been off the air for months. Without him, "World News Tonight" was crumbling. When would he be back? What doctors was he seeing? What treatment was he getting? Arledge had lots of questions but no answers.

An intensely private man, Reynolds had revealed almost nothing about his illness to the network. David Burke had flown to Washington and driven to Reynolds's home in Chevy Chase, only to be turned away at the door by his wife, Henrietta. She had informed him politely that Frank was not seeing anybody just then.

Much as he wanted to press further, Arledge felt he could not. "We had spent all our time with Frank trying to build up his trust and we wanted him to understand how nice we were and how we wouldn't interfere, and so we never, never bothered him about coming back," he said. "We were trying to respect his privacy."

What was known was this: Reynolds, fifty-nine, had hurt his leg during a Florida vacation in January 1983, then reinjured it in Washington when he slipped on a patch of ice. At first, he ignored the pain, thinking he had merely aggravated his World War II wound. But he soon learned that he needed surgery, which was performed in March. A month later, his doctors told him that he had contracted viral hepatitis from infected blood he had been given during the operation.

They prescribed rest, so Reynolds anchored "World News" on Wednesday, April 20, 1983, and went home to recuperate.

Arledge began to worry when Reynolds's recuperation period stretched through the spring and into the early summer. The fear that his condition might be more serious than first suspected grew as Reynolds pushed back the date of his expected return — first to July and then to late summer. "We started hearing rumors about Frank, but nobody could really pin them down," Arledge said. "He wouldn't talk to anybody."

In the meantime, ratings for "World News Tonight" were sliding. The ABC audience had grown attached to Reynolds, who had become the dominant figure on the broadcast. David Brinkley filled in for a while, but his laconic style did not fit the crisp three-man format. As viewers continued to defect, Arledge summoned Peter Jennings from London. On July 4, Jennings took over as lead anchor.

One morning the next week, as Jennings was settling into his new routine in Washington, he was told that Reynolds was on the telephone and wanted to speak with him. The two anchors had never become close — there was too much rivalry for that — but as time passed and Reynolds was securely installed as the lead anchor, they developed a mutual respect and a telephone friendship.

That morning, out of the blue, Reynolds invited Jennings to lunch. Slightly startled, Jennings accepted and offered to pick up some food on his way out. But Reynolds had something else in mind.

"Bring me a tape recorder," he said. "I want to practice."

When Jennings arrived, his first impression was that Reynolds had aged terribly. He seemed frail and walked with the aid of a stick. But as they settled down to lunch, Reynolds ate with gusto and his spirits lifted. They traded ABC gossip, discussed the news, and laughed quite a bit. "If I have to be sick," Reynolds said at one point, "now is a good time, because there's not much news going on." Generously, he praised Jennings's work on the show.

He'd said the same thing in a note to his friend George Watson, who was then an ABC vice president in New York. "I think the broadcast has perked up since Peter moved into the slot in Washington," Reynolds wrote. "Watching the broadcast makes me more anxious than ever to get back to work and, as the pro football players say, 'make a contribution to the team.' "

When Jennings returned to the bureau, he was besieged. "My phone was ringing off the hook," he said. "Every executive called. How is he? What's he look like? When's he coming back?" Jennings told them all the same thing — that Reynolds looked reasonably well, that they'd enjoyed getting together, and that Frank was very much looking forward to coming back.

A week later, Frank Reynolds was dead.

He had died in the middle of the night at Sibley Hospital in Washington. The viral hepatitis was one cause of death. Another was multiple myeloma — a form of bone marrow cancer.

Reynolds had lived with cancer for four years. He'd told only his immediate family, his longtime producer David Newman, and George Watson.

A part of him had wanted to be more open about his malady. In the fall of 1979, Watson had visited Reynolds at Sibley after he'd been diagnosed. They had talked for a long time about what to do, about whether to make a public announcement or keep mum.

This was Reynolds at his most serious — weighing his desire for privacy against his obligations to the public, which, he felt, was entitled to the truth, and his responsibility to the network. He had, after all, been entrusted with the evening news, which he believed to be the most important program at ABC.

"I suppose I'd better tell Roone," Reynolds said grudgingly at one point. "There's no reason why I should have to conceal it," he said. "Maybe I just say I have cancer."

Watson thought that was a terrible idea. Speaking not as an ABC executive but as a friend, as a man who had chosen Reynolds as the godfather to his son, he advised caution.

"This is a dread disease," Watson said. "Do people want to look at an anchorman who may be dying of cancer? Do you want to be known as the cancerous anchorman?"

Reynolds did not. He was not comfortable sharing himself with strangers under the best of circumstances; he could not bear the thought that he might have to discuss his health with people who approached him at airports or stopped him on the street.

Still, there remained the possibility of disclosing the truth, in confidence, to Arledge or Burke. That came down to a question of trust. Reynolds trusted them to keep the illness secret, but he did not trust them to keep him on the job. He decided he had little to gain and much to lose by letting the news get out.

After Reynolds died, Burke thought he understood the message the anchorman's silence had conveyed.

Overcoming their initial mistrust, Burke and Reynolds had grown to like each other. But, Burke felt, it was "not to the extent that I would have liked. I was very hurt when I did not know of his terminal illness. If I had really made it with Frank, and he had seen me as a human being, worthy of trust, he would have shared.

"It's sad," he went on, "because there were things about Frank I liked a lot. The extraordinary decency of his private life. His family. I wanted very much to be his friend."

When it came to Arledge, friendship was never in the cards. The two men had little in common. And Reynolds was forever suspicious of Arledge's attempts to marry journalism and show business.

"He always looked upon us as the enemy," Arledge said.

Frank Reynolds would have been discomfited by the fuss made by ABC News over his death. As he once said, "I don't want to become more important than the message that I'm bearing. It's not the messenger who's important."

But Reynolds's death was treated as a major story by ABC. "Good Morning America," "World News Tonight," and "Nightline" broadcast tributes. Portions of his funeral at Arlington National Cemetery were shown in prime time.

A few critics called it excessive, but the desire to pay homage to Reynolds was, above all, a human response; he had been beloved as a gentle, decent man of quiet dignity. His loss was deeply felt, as was the sense that his death marked the end of an era, that he was one of the last pure journalists in network news.

In one of the televised tributes, Koppel put those sentiments into words. "Ours is not a business that promotes privacy, nor is it an industry that normally favors substance over style," he said. "So how was it that a painfully shy — and he was that — intensely private journalist of great substance like Frank Reynolds, a man who eschewed the fast lane and the high life, how was it that he was such a success?" He left the question hanging.

Arledge had a more pressing question on his mind: Who was going to anchor "World News Tonight"? With Cronkite gone, Arledge thought ABC was finally ready to go head-to-head with Rather and Brokaw. He had felt for a time that either Jennings or Koppel could probably carry "World News."

Koppel, as a proven success, was perhaps the safer choice. But Arledge had to worry about whether "Nightline" could survive his departure. "I felt that if Ted did 'World News Tonight' we would ultimately lose 'Nightline,' " Arledge said. "And 'Nightline' was the defining program for ABC News. It was a franchise that no one else

had." Still, he thought that Koppel had earned a shot at the job —
if he wanted it.

In the midst of a phone conversation on another topic, Arledge
approached the matter gingerly.

"I just want to double-check something with you," he said. "You've
said many times that you really don't want to do the evening news."

Koppel saw what was coming, so he broke in.

"Roone, let me make it easy for you," he said. "I think Peter will
be a terrific anchor for 'World News Tonight' and I think you ought
to go sign him up."

Koppel had no desire to give up "Nightline," where he enjoyed
his freedom and influence, for the uncertainties and pressures of the
evening news. The trouble was, Jennings felt the same way — he had
grown so attached to his overseas duties that he had even resisted
spending the summer in Washington as a substitute for Reynolds.

His London job was ideal, Jennings felt, because it combined anchoring with the freedom to cover major stories. Unlike other anchors,
Jennings was also able to preserve his privacy by living overseas. He
and his wife, Kati Marton, who had left ABC to write books, had
fixed up a Victorian house in Hampstead, and they had no desire to
uproot themselves and their children.

Jennings hesitated for another reason too. He remembered the
trauma of his first go-round on the anchor desk, and the prospect of
a second failure frightened him. As he began to woo Jennings, Arledge
saw that those fears were the biggest obstacle he had to overcome.
Later, Jennings remembered their initial discussions as a "terrible,
terrible time of great tension between me and my boss."

Arledge decided to enlist Marton as an ally. Over dinner on a
Saturday in the Hamptons at a restaurant called "1776," Arledge
expressed his absolute faith that Jennings would succeed as an anchor
and praised his talents, especially his ability to perform live, which
Arledge said would be increasingly important as ABC covered more
live events. "He did his Arledgian dance rite," Jennings recalled. "I
was smart enough even then to know that Roone was one of the great
seducers of all time." This time, though, Marton had to agree with
Arledge. She had total confidence in her husband. "I knew it would
not be easy for us," she said, "but, down deep, I knew he would
succeed."

Late that night and the next morning, Jennings and Marton agonized over the decision.

So many things about the job gave them pause. Jennings worried that he would miss reporting and hate being confined to the anchor desk. Marton was already getting calls from people she hardly knew who, she thought, "just wanted a piece of us because suddenly we were the hot couple in New York. Peter suddenly became a movie-star-caliber celebrity. It was very unsettling."

The more they talked, the more reasons they found not to make the move. "I do not want to do this," Jennings would say. "We've got such a good life."

But Marton, in the end, urged him to accept.

"You know, the brass ring will not come around again," she said. "You have to take it." For all its drawbacks, the anchor job would bring Jennings the recognition he had always sought for his work, as well as the opportunity to shape "World News Tonight."

They also recognized the cold, hard fact that Jennings had no real alternative. Because Arledge had decided to ditch the three-anchor format, the London anchor job was no longer an option. Nor was becoming a correspondent again. Besides, they knew, Arledge tended to personalize rejection. "Had we said no," Marton said, "Peter's life at ABC would have been very short-term and very unhappy. Frankly, I didn't think Peter had another option."

Without much enthusiasm, he agreed.

When Arledge learned that Jennings would take the job, he, too, was more relieved than happy. Why, he groused, couldn't Peter approach the job with more enthusiasm? And while he had faith in Jennings, Arledge was worried that Jennings's self-doubts ran so deep. Jennings, he knew, would need all the self-confidence he could muster for his first major assignment, covering the 1984 elections, after spending so many years out of the country.

Arledge had other worries too. He had to deal with Max Robinson, which he knew would not be pleasant. Robinson had embarrassed himself by failing to show up for Reynolds's funeral, where he'd been assigned the seat next to Nancy Reagan. All Arledge could offer him was a job anchoring the Sunday night news and prime-time news briefs. (Robinson left ABC a year later and died of AIDS in 1988.)

Meanwhile, Arledge had to remake "World News." After Reynolds's death, "World News" had fallen to third place in the ratings, behind NBC. That was partly because ABC's prime-time lineup, which had fueled the growth of ABC News since Arledge's arrival, was faltering; the network had failed to develop hits to replace aging favorites like "Three's Company" and "Laverne and Shirley."

Clockwise from right: (1) Roone Arledge, in the control room, as president of ABC Sports in March 1977. His appointment that spring as president of ABC News outraged the traditionalists. (*AP/Wide World Photos*)

(2) Producer Av Westin was a vital contributor to ABC News until he quit after feuding with Arledge. (*ABC Photo*)

(3) Roone Arledge announced his new anchor team for "World News Tonight" in 1978: Max Robinson, Frank Reynolds, and Peter Jennings. (*AP/Wide World Photos*)

(4) Geraldo Rivera was Arledge's favorite reporter in the late 1970s. He provided the spark that kept "20/20" alive. (*AP/Wide World Photos*)

Max Robinson, the first black to anchor a daily network newscast, had an unhappy career at ABC News. (*Donna Svennevik/ABC*)

Above: Roone Arledge with his "World News" production team in the late 1970s. *Left to right:* producers Walter Porges, Jeff Gralnick, Arledge, Rick Kaplan, and Mike Stein. (*ABC Photo*)

Producer Jeff Gralnick and director Roger Goodman shaped ABC's outstanding special events coverage. (*Steve Fenn/ABC*)

Clockwise from above: (1) As ABC's Hong Kong bureau chief in the late 1960s, Ted Koppel made frequent trips into Vietnam. (*ABC Photo*)

(2) ABC's "Nightline" was the most significant addition to television news since the creation of "60 Minutes." Ted Koppel's guests on the first broadcast, on March 24, 1980, were Ali Agah, the Iranian chargé d'affaires, and Dorothea Morefield, wife of hostage Richard Morefield. (*ABC Photo*)

(3) Foreign affairs coverage was a hallmark of "Nightline," which helped Ted Koppel obtain the first extended television inteview with Nelson Mandela in South Africa. (*Alan Tannenbaum/ABC*)

(4) Ted Koppel and candidate Ross Perot during the 1992 presidential campaign. (*Tony Ashe/ABC*)

In 1981, David Brinkley became the first big star lured to ABC News by Arledge. (*ABC Photo*)

Boy anchorman Peter Jennings covered the midyear elections in 1966. His early failure as an anchor left Jennings reluctant to try again in the 1980s. (*ABC Photo*)

Peter Jennings, foreign correspondent, reported from Vietnam in the late 1960s. (*Capital Cities/ABC Photo*)

Left: On Election Night in 1988, Henry Kissinger visited with Peter Jennings and David Brinkley. (*Steve Fenn/ABC*)

Below left: Peter Jennings and wife Kati Marton. (*ABC Photo*)

Below: By the mid-1980s, Roone Arledge had shed his safari jackets and joined the establishment. (*ABC Photo*)

Above: After struggling as an evening news anchor and special correspondent for ABC, Barbara Walters found a home as co-anchor of "20/20" with Hugh Downs (*Steve Fenn/ABC*).

Above right: On her first prime-time special for ABC, Barbara Walters was ridiculed for ending her interview with Jimmy Carter by telling him, "Be good to us, Mr. President, be kind." (*ABC Photo*)

Barbara Walters with Egyptian president Anwar Sadat. (*ABC Photo*)

When actress Robin Givens described life with heavyweight boxing champ Mike Tyson as "torture" and "pure hell" in 1987, "20/20" devoted a full hour to their interview with Barbara Walters. (*Robert Maass/ABC*)

Barbara Walters interviewed Muammar al-Qaddafi from his tent in Tripoli, Libya, in 1989, for "20/20." (*ABC Photo*)

Barbara Walters with former president Ronald Reagan in 1989. (*Steve Fenn/ABC*)

Barbara Walters was the first reporter to interview General Norman Schwarzkopf after the Persian Gulf War. (*Laurent Chamussey/ABC*)

Barbara Walters with President Bush in June 1992. When Bush offered to sit down with her again just before Election Day, she declined. (*Steve Fenn/ABC*)

Diane Sawyer's interview with Patricia Bowman, who accused William Kennedy Smith of rape, brought "PrimeTime Live" its highest ratings ever. (*Craig Blankenham/ABC*)

Sam Donaldson's coverage of the Persian Gulf War gave "PrimeTime" a much-needed ratings boost in 1991. (*Brent Peterson/ABC*)

In September 1991, three presidents met at the Kremlin: Mikhail Gorbachev, president of the Soviet Union; Boris Yeltsin, president of the Russian Republic; and Roone Arledge, president of ABC News. (*Anthony Suau/ABC*)

Roone Arledge with candidate Bill Clinton before a presidential debate in 1992. (*Shelly Katz/ABC*)

Diane Sawyer interviewed President-elect Clinton in January 1993 for "PrimeTime Live." (*Steve Fenn/ABC*)

The Magnificent Seven: Donaldson, Sawyer, Brinkley, Jennings, Koppel, Walters, and Downs. The first time they were photographed, there were squabbles over who would stand where. (*Timothy White/ABC*)

Left: After Dan Burke and Tom Murphy of Capital Cities took over ABC, they struggled to take control of Roone Arledge. (*Hans Neleman*)

Below left: Joanna Bistany, Arledge's most trusted aide in the late 1980s and early 1990s, became a controversial figure within ABC News. (*ABC Photo*)

Below: As executive producer of "World News Tonight," Paul Friedman helped make the program the top-rated evening newscast. He became Arledge's second-in-command and heir apparent in 1993. (*ABC Photo*)

And Arledge had to rebuild "World News" with a new executive producer because, a month before Reynolds died, Jeff Gralnick had quit.

Gralnick, who had run the show since 1979, was simply worn out. While producing a network evening newscast under any circumstances is a taxing job, wrestling ABC's three-headed monster onto the air every day was especially grueling. Gralnick's hands-on approach, as well as his competitive nature, meant that there was never a day when he coasted. " 'World News Tonight' was a seven-day-a-week, twenty-four-hour-a-day job for anyone who cared about where the news division was going," he said. Gralnick was also in charge of the political unit and special events, which meant long days in the control room during such events as the Falklands War. "After four years, he was burnt toast," said Charlie Heinz, the "World News" director. With another election year approaching, Gralnick gave plenty of notice that he wanted off of the evening news.

Arledge was unsympathetic. He thought that Gralnick was a chronic complainer, and, in fact, Gralnick often did walk the halls of ABC with a pained expression suggesting he was on the verge of collapse. "Jeff is always burned out," Arledge would tell his aides, when they'd report that he wanted off the show. When Arledge refused to give him a date when he could leave the show, Gralnick simply told everyone that he was leaving the newscast in June. That infuriated Arledge. He felt abandoned in the midst of crisis.

With no natural successor to Gralnick — his second-in-command, Rick Kaplan, had never produced his own show — Arledge turned to Robert Frye, forty-three, a thoughtful, intelligent producer who had worked for ABC News since the late 1960s. Frye's strength, in Arledge's eyes, was that he got along with everyone. "We thought he had the people skills that, at that point in our history, seemed to be very very important," Arledge said. "The biggest problem we had was making this troika work." Unlike Gralnick, who barked out orders, Frye favored a low-key, collegial approach.

Frye was also experienced. He had worked in New York, Washington, and London, distinguishing himself as executive producer of "The Secret Negotiations" documentary with Salinger. In 1982, Frye had created and produced an hour-long morning newscast, anchored by veteran Steve Bell and newcomer Kathleen Sullivan, that was an instant success.

But Frye was unprepared for the evening news pressure cooker. Technically and editorially, the morning program was challenging, but, politically, all that was required was to get the broadcast onto the air without causing problems. Compared to the evening news, mornings were a backwater; for one thing, Arledge usually wasn't watching.

What's more, while Frye had worked for years with Jennings, the two men no longer got along well. The source of the tension was unclear — some insiders thought it dated back to Frye's dealings with Kati Marton when she was an ABC correspondent in Bonn — but their relationship became crucial when it turned out that Frye would be producing not a three-anchor show but a broadcast centered around Jennings.

The result was that, with the ratings slipping, "World News Tonight" was entrusted to an insecure new anchorman from London and a new executive producer whom he didn't especially like.

No wonder Arledge fretted.

"We lost all our momentum," he said. "People don't realize it, but we had to start all over again from scratch."

The word was soon out on Bob Frye — he was not going to make it as executive producer of "World News Tonight." His supporters said that he was too thoughtful, too caring, and not tough enough to take command of the machinery required to get on the air each day. "He was a very smart man and a good judge of news in the broad sense, but he didn't seem quite in touch with the reality of doing a broadcast," said Dennis Dunlavey, a producer who worked with Frye. Others, perhaps the majority, saw him as indecisive, as a wandering soul in a deadline-driven world. Jennings likened him to a brooding Hamlet. "It was Zen news," grumbled director Charlie Heinz.

The unfortunate thing about Frye's failure was that he was, in some ways, a man ahead of his time. By 1983, when he took over "World News," the landscape of television was shifting. While ABC's ratings were down, so were ratings for CBS and NBC — in an ominous development, the nightly news shows together had lost 10 percent of their viewers since 1980. That was the year Ted Turner had launched the Cable News Network, which, while still small, enabled news viewers to stay informed even when they missed their dinner-hour appointments with the networks. Turner never tired of saying that "people want to see news when they want it, not when the networks tell them that it's news time." Damage was also being inflicted on the networks by their affiliates, whose expanded local newscasts increasingly reported on national news. By the time ABC, CBS, and

NBC came on with their evening newscasts, many viewers felt they'd seen enough.

Frye wanted ABC to respond by producing a more serious newscast. He thought that "World News Tonight," with its rat-tat-tat pace, too closely resembled the local news programs, and he wanted to set ABC apart by putting on stories that went beyond the headlines to offer perspective. One of his first moves was to order the removal of a wire-service machine from the executive producer's position on the rim. He didn't want to be bothered with the twists and turns of every story. "I wanted to have some thinking time," he said.

Some correspondents embraced his approach. When a Korean Air Lines plane was shot down over the Soviet Union, Pentagon correspondent John McWethy opened the broadcast with an eight-minute story recreating the event and analyzing the implications. Capitol Hill correspondent Charles Gibson, who liked covering social issues as well as the bureaucracy, did a piece on divorce in which he wrote, "When you look at the divorce rate in America, you know that it is the land of the free. And yet when you look at the remarriage rate, you also know that it is the home of the brave." Even Frye's critics admired the ambitious, award-winning ten-part series about U.S.-Soviet relations that he'd commissioned. "I wanted to do that every night," Frye said.

But for Frye's approach to work, the entire news division had to shift gears. "We had an organization set up to respond to breaking news," he said. His pleas for analytical and textured coverage were resisted by some correspondents. "He wanted to write poetry," said one. He had few allies on the assignment desk, which deployed the network's troops, and he even encountered opposition from some producers who worked for him on the rim. Support from Arledge would have helped, but he was unwilling to commit himself to Frye or his ideas. As always in television, there was fear that change could drive away viewers who were satisfied with the program they were getting. An insider said of Arledge, "He wants a new broadcast, but he wants the same broadcast."

Frye also struggled to translate his philosophy into specifics. An aide to Frye said, "He was trying to solve the great dilemmas of the age and not coming to terms with what you had to do to get the broadcast on that day." At times, Frye seemed incapable of settling on a lineup, although he insisted that what looked like indecision was an attempt to stay flexible. He also commissioned more stories than he could use, a sure way to alienate people in the field.

The broadcast suffered. "We were floundering," Jennings said, "and yet Bob was really trying." When Jennings tried to make more decisions on his own, Frye felt that his authority was being challenged. The two men argued, first in private, then publicly. "There's always give-and-take between your anchor and your executive producer over the placement of stories and how long they are and how to approach them," said Cherie Simon, a "World News" producer. "But this was a real power struggle."

The view around the rim was that Jennings was trying to assert himself, to let everyone know that he was no longer a neophyte news-reader and had better be taken seriously. This was fine with all, but Jennings was often clumsy about the ways he inserted himself into the process, particularly when he waited until the last minute to make changes to a story or demand a rewrite. He either didn't know or didn't care when he threw the production process into disarray. "His attitude seemed to be 'I am the anchorman and I have to put my imprint on this,' " said a producer.

But Jennings didn't know any better than Frye how to produce "World News Tonight." While experienced in the field, Jennings had spent no time around the rim since his first tour of duty as an anchor, as he admitted. "I was sharing the chair, sharing the space, sharing the anxiety, and it was aimless," he recalled. "It was incredibly aimless. And management came to me a couple of times and talked about making a change, and I couldn't. It's funny. In the case of Bob Frye, it was hard to abandon ship."

These weren't happy times for the anchorman. "Peter was terribly nervous," said his friend Tom Yellin, an ABC producer. "He had had the job before and failed, and that's a scar that will never go away." Jennings encountered all the problems he'd anticipated and a few he had not. He felt cooped up in the newsroom; he felt ill-prepared for the upcoming elections; and he felt overwhelmed by the sense that he had become the property of ABC News, which placed constant demands on him. Affiliates wanted him to do promotion. Media people wanted him for interviews. Charitable groups wanted his support. Businessmen and political leaders wanted to meet him. And viewers wanted to shake his hand, or get an autograph, or tell him what they thought of his work. Meanwhile, there was a show to do every night. For his part, Jennings made matters worse by wanting to be involved in everything, partly because he found it hard to turn down a request from a worthwhile cause or pass up the opportunity to meet someone new and interesting. The result was that he felt besieged. What was worse, from his standpoint, was that many of the claims on him had little to do with journalism.

It was no wonder that Jennings felt terribly conflicted about the anchor job — the fame and the money and the power came at a steep price. He had spent fifteen years traveling the world as a correspondent to prove that he was a serious reporter, and he had succeeded spectacularly. Now success meant that he had less time to practice journalism because he had to perform as a newsreader and serve as a promoter and goodwill ambassador for ABC. As Elizabeth Kaye wrote in a profile of Jennings for *Esquire*, "Sometimes he'll think how ironic it is that his reward for establishing himself as more than a face and a voice is a job that makes so much of both."

Even on days when he did not have to tape a promo, sit for an interview, or make a public appearance, Jennings was reminded that he was part entertainer when he went into makeup. Arledge understood his discomfort, saying, "It's tough for anybody who becomes an anchor, because it is a nuisance. There's lights and there's makeup and there's what color background should there be? And all this stuff has absolutely nothing to do with journalism at all, any more than setting type has to do with journalism at the *New York Times*." But Arledge aggravated the problem when he would call Jennings after the show to tell him that his lapels were too wide, his tie was too busy, or his pocket handkerchief was a distracting flourish.

Jennings's ambivalence about stardom surfaced in other ways. For a while, he fussed about doing promotion; when ABC's press people approached him, he would lecture them to the effect that a news organization should not need a press department. Eventually, he relented and did a few interviews. Then he did more — he embarked on a whirlwind tour of the United States, anchoring from ABC stations in a dozen locales. It was Jennings's way of seeing America, where he had spent almost no time since the 1960s, as well as ABC's chance to introduce its new anchor to affiliates, community groups, and TV critics in the hinterlands. David Burke managed the effort like a political campaign, dispatching Jennings to cities where ABC needed a ratings boost. Jennings found it liberating to get out of the newsroom and talk to people outside New York.

Still, he had reached the pinnacle of *commercial* television, whose values his father, who believed in broadcasting as public service, had fought against so hard. Jennings experienced his success as a mixed blessing; he was determined not to abandon the principles that were his father's legacy. "I still — to a very great measure — want to impress my father," he would say.

This determination, as well as his lingering embarrassment over his lack of formal education, helped drive him. Richard Threlkeld, who as a correspondent worked for Jennings at ABC and Rather at CBS, thought that both men forever tried to compensate for what they perceived as deficiencies in their schooling. "Peter Jennings is one of the best educated men on the face of the earth," Threlkeld said. "So is Dan Rather, but they'll never believe that." Jennings loved to immerse himself in his ABC briefing books, tearing out some pages, marking others with his orange highlighter, quizzing those around him when he wanted to know more, until he was satisfied that he had soaked up as much knowledge as he could.

Like any anchor, Jennings often felt exposed. His mistakes on the air were noticed, and he was a target for television critics and advocacy groups. Some Jewish groups, for example, advanced the canard that Jennings was pro-Palestinian, which had no basis in fact. When Jennings felt vulnerable, he wanted to know that he could rely on the support and protection of his boss, but here, too, he was disappointed. Arledge was disinclined to stroke or reassure his people, and even when he tried to compliment Jennings, he didn't always succeed. Arledge had a habit, for example, of describing Jennings as "the anchor for the nineties," which Jennings took to mean that he was not yet the best of the anchors. "Hey, hold it, Roone, this is the eighties," he'd once said. Arledge also identified himself so strongly with ABC News that Jennings sometimes thought his boss saw the contest among the network newscasts as "Brokaw versus Rather versus Arledge." Their relationship was complex. It was hard to say whether Arledge's reluctance to praise was management technique, similar to the "creative tension" his friend Ben Bradlee sowed at the *Washington Post*, or simply an outgrowth of his personality. And there was no way to know whether Jennings's emotional needs could have been satisfied by a more supportive boss. Whatever the underlying forces, they created a dynamic that both unnerved Jennings and drove him to work harder to please Arledge.

While Arledge insisted that his commitment to Jennings never wavered, he was also frustrated by him. For a time, Arledge thought that Jennings's anchor style was too detached and aristocratic, and he told him so. "Peter had been in England so long that he sounded and looked like a BBC newsreader," Arledge said. The pocket square, he thought, was another unwelcome reminder to the audience that ABC's anchor was not a product of America's heartland.

Under the same heading — the desire to Americanize Jennings — came the delicate question of citzenship. Jennings was a Canadian, of course, and he'd kept his Canadian passport during his nineteen years at ABC. It had come in handy when ABC needed someone to travel to a country that did not welcome Americans; Jennings's first exposure to Arledge had come in the late 1960s when he'd gone to Cuba to cover a volleyball tournament for ABC Sports. Now, though, Arledge had decided that he did not want a Canadian as his principal anchor, especially after a few TV critics made it an issue. "At the time," Arledge said, "we were all still pretty well traumatized by all the press reaction to everything we did." Initially, Jennings agreed to Arledge's request that he become an American citizen. But he soon felt a countervailing pressure from his mother, who wrote him a passionate letter urging him not to sever his ties to Canada. When Arledge raised the issue once too often, Jennings bristled, saying, "Did it ever occur to you that this is a personal choice, not a business decision? And I'll come to this in my own due time." The matter was dropped.

Most of the time, though, Jennings could not afford to ignore Arledge. His standing was too precarious. Viewers who had deserted "World News" had not come back. CBS and Dan Rather had regained the momentum. "The ratings come out every Tuesday. And they cast a bit of a pall, to be perfectly honest," Jennings said, a few months after taking over.

Publicly, Arledge downplayed the ratings. He told a reporter, "Obviously, I wish we were always first, but it's all very close and very tight and I think it's utterly meaningless." But he could not ignore the weekly Nielsen report card. Ratings translated directly into revenues, and even a small decline in audience size had significant dollar impact. In 1984, when CBS averaged a 12.3 rating for the "CBS Evening News with Dan Rather," the network could sell a thirty-second spot for about $50,000. With its 10.3 rating, ABC could attract only about $35,000 for a spot on "World News." With the networks selling twelve spots a night, five nights a week, a single rating point was worth upward of $25 million a year. No network executive could dismiss numbers of that magnitude, and, indeed, when the ratings climbed, Arledge would post a congratulatory memo or send champagne. Everyone got the message.

Now, with the ratings down, Arledge fired Bob Frye. The decision was only partly driven by the Nielsens. Frye had unwisely alienated

David Burke as well as Jennings. Arledge had concluded that he was a "master chef" in a job that required a "short-order cook."

Bill Lord was named to replace him. Lord, the executive producer of "Nightline," had lobbied hard for the job, courting Jennings and Arledge. He was an experienced producer with a hard-news bent who promised to end what some called the "era of mush" under Frye. Ted Koppel was not happy about losing Lord, but his objections were set aside. The problems at "World News" had grown too severe. If Lord was the man to solve them, "Nightline" would have to manage without him.

Going into 1984, Arledge faced an awesome set of challenges. As president of ABC Sports, he was responsible for coverage of the Winter Olympics in Sarajevo, Yugoslavia, and the Los Angeles Summer Olympics. In his case, that meant not only planning the production and programming, choosing the anchors and commentators, and working with the Olympic bureaucracy, but also taking command of the control room during the Games, to produce ABC's prime-time programming. As president of ABC News, Arledge would supervise coverage of the presidential campaign, the political conventions, and election night — all important tests for his new political anchor team of Jennings and Brinkley. His year would climax in January 1985, when he would produce ABC's first-ever Super Bowl telecast in Palo Alto, California, then fly overnight to Washington to produce coverage of the inauguration the next morning.

No further proof was needed of Arledge's stature. But just to make sure that people understood that he now traveled in the most elevated of circles, Arledge provided a list of his phone messages to reporter Harry F. Waters, who was profiling him for *Newsweek*. The story began with an impressive list of names:

> Henry Kissinger called to chat about world events and how television should deal with them. Frank Sinatra called to protest an anti-Sinatra remark made by a local ABC newscaster. The Rev. Jesse Jackson called to set up a meeting with the network's executives about his presidential campaign. Israeli Defense Minister Moshe Arens called to arrange a similar get-together about his nation's position on Lebanon. Woody Allen called to wangle a seat at a VIP screening of a closed-circuit boxing bout. John Denver called to propose that he serve as a singing troubadour during ABC's telecast of the Winter Olympics. Pete Rozelle called to complain about something someone said on

"Monday Night Football." The U.S. ambassador to Chile called to discuss Latin American affairs, and the Yugoslavian ambassador to the United States called to report that he was leaving his post. Mollie Parnis, Swifty Lazar and Helen Gurley Brown all called to issue invitations to their dinner parties. Sen. Howard Baker called to line up a lunch . . . as did Bill Moyers . . . Reggie Jackson . . . Pierre Salinger . . . Jeane Kirkpatrick . . . Pete Dawkins . . . Barbara Walters.

No wonder mere unknowns who called the president of ABC News found their messages ignored. They were not alone: Jody Powell, when he was press secretary in the Carter White House, complained to an ABC correspondent that Arledge did not return his calls. And even Arledge's home phone was answered by a service, whether or not he was there. Peter Jennings and Ted Koppel sometimes waited for days to get their calls returned.

It was also easy to see how Arledge could feel overwhelmed by his job. Indeed, while ordinarily he might have relished the excitement of an Olympic-and-election year, he approached 1984 with trepidation. His worries were both professional and personal.

To begin with, the sheer scope of his duties weighed on Arledge. Since 1977, he had been consumed by News, but he had refused to cut his ties to ABC Sports or delegate authority to his second-in-command, Jim Spence. Instead, Arledge undercut Spence by dealing directly with the Sports producers and stars — when they could get through to him. Spence, who turned against Arledge when he was passed over for the Sports presidency, later said, "His system was to pit one executive against another, one production person against another, one announcer against another. That way, no individual within the organization could achieve a level of success or prominence beyond that ordained by Roone Arledge." Even Jim McKay and Howard Cosell, both of whom had been close to Arledge, thought that he neglected Sports. But as much as he preferred News, Arledge would not let go of ABC Sports. The profits he made there remained an important source of his power inside the network.

Arledge had reason to worry about his corporate clout. For the first time in News, he had come under pressure to curb his big-spending ways. His flagship programs, "Nightline" and "World News Tonight," were spared cutbacks, but jobs were eliminated from news bureaus and from Pam Hill's documentary unit, and a prime-time magazine show in development never got off the ground. All ABC operations faced critical scrutiny by Wall Street and the business press; the company had incurred heavy losses in cable, and the network's prime-time ratings were tumbling. The company's stock price was depressed.

Nevertheless, what nagged most at Arledge, at least at the office, was the sense that, after five years of extraordinary progress, the growth of ABC News had stalled. The ratings for "World News" and "20/20" were slipping, and an expanded hour-long version of "Nightline" had failed.

The pressures were getting to him, he conceded in a rare interview with Nancy Collins of *New York* magazine. Personal happiness, he said, had been more elusive than success as a television executive. She had asked him, "What makes you insecure?"

"I guess I'm insecure about my own life," Arledge replied. "This is a business that takes a lot of your energy. When I first took over this job, I was in pretty good shape. I played golf, I went hunting, fishing. Then I got out of shape. I said, 'This is ridiculous. What's the point of accomplishing something if I'm losing the person I am?'

"Things that give other people pleasure are my work. It is not recreational for me to go to a professional football game on Sunday. Yet, so much of my life is a fairyland, anybody would want to be doing it — going to Henry Kissinger's birthday party, election night in London. Still, I find I had more fun as a producer when I could just take off and go on a safari for a month. Now if I did that, there'd be 400 calls and they'd be sending cassettes in on elephants' backs.

"It's important not to let the fun go out of our lives. I was at a dinner one night with Secretary of State Shultz, and I asked him if he was having any fun. He said, 'I didn't take this job to have fun.' I said, 'I know, but do you go home at night feeling enjoyment from what you're doing, feeling that you did something unique and important?' He said, yeah, he guessed that he did. Well, for me, it's very important to feel that a lot."

It was a revealing response. Arledge was not enjoying life as much as he once had. Nor was he as much fun to be around. He had been more relaxed in the old days, more willing to let down his guard to enjoy the company of ABC colleagues or friends. Now he was nearly always on duty, whether in News or in Sports or even, at least in his mind, at a Giants game on a Sunday. His idea of "fairyland" had become Kissinger's birthday party or election night in London — events that helped him feel that he was doing something "unique and important," that he belonged in the company of Kissinger and Shultz. Longtime colleagues noticed that Arledge was more prone than ever to name-dropping. Said one, "I never remember sitting with him in the old days when he would start giving me a litany of people that he just had dinner with."

By the time he entered his fifties, Arledge had paid a heavy price for his devotion to his work. "You sacrifice a lot of home time in this job," he said. His four children had suffered from his not being around, he said, as had his first marriage. His relationship with his kids was awkward; sometimes he hesitated while trying to decide whether to take a phone call from one of his daughters. He felt guilty for having been an absent father for so long.

To relax, Arledge turned to such longtime friends as Frank Gifford and author Larry Collins, as well as to his second wife, Ann. "Ann is maybe my best friend," he said. "Somebody whose opinion I value, someone whom I share things with and judge things by. She is my top priority." Friends said that they seemed to enjoy each other and that their marriage represented a sanctuary for Arledge. "She was very good for him," said his longtime aide Jeff Ruhe.

Their marriage, nevertheless, was disintegrating. Ann had married young, and now she wanted more from life than to be the wife of a famous television executive. "She just went through a period where she decided she wanted to be her own person," said Arledge. He set out to save the marriage, and when he could not, he was devastated. "It was something that I had never, ever expected," he said. "I always had this feeling that I would ultimately be able to talk to her, and reason would prevail, and things would work out. We went from going to see counselors and psychologists to lawyers. It just was awful. Just terrible. It really had a major impact on my psyche that year."

Inside ABC, Arledge was more elusive than ever. He sometimes disappeared for days at a time, and he found it hard to keep his personal problems from affecting him. "I figure if I fall apart, everybody's going to fall apart, so you can't do that," he said. "But it was really depressing. The divorce was particularly depressing because I knew it was a waste. There was no reason for it." He was still in love with Ann, and she claimed still to love him, but as he explained later, she needed to find her own way. An ABC colleague said, "He loved her, but he didn't know how to keep her. She wanted a husband who was home, and she wanted a family, and he was not willing or able to give her either of those things." It was the most difficult period of his life. Arledge, who feared failure, felt that he had abandoned Joan and his four children as they had grown up, and now he felt that he had failed in his second marriage. He was burdened by his guilt,

friends said, and lonely. More than ever, he needed emotional sustenance from his work.

Then, on the eve of the political conventions and the Summer
Olympics, Arledge came down with a bad sore throat. Doctors found
a tumor on his thyroid gland that required surgery. Because the pro-
cedure could not be delayed, Arledge checked into a hospital to be
operated on the next morning. The tumor turned out to be benign,
but ABC chairman Leonard Goldenson was so worried about Arledge — and about ABC's $225 million investment in the Olympics —
that he stopped by the hospital, seeking reassurance that his Sports
chief would be able to take his place in the control room.

Arledge recovered in time to deliver a gold-medal performance in
Los Angeles, at least in commercial terms. For seventeen star-spangled
days, America was enthralled by ABC's 180-hour video epic, a real-
life miniseries with a huge cast, as spectacular as anything ever seen
on television. The ratings and profits exceeded expectations, as ABC
averaged a 23.5 rating in prime time and made about $75 million.
Arledge's Olympic coverage did nothing less than lift the spirits of a
nation.

One of the winners was Peter Jennings, who, given his druthers,
would not have gone to Los Angeles at all. But Arledge persuaded
his news anchor to join host Jim McKay for the opening ceremonies
and to conduct a ceremonial interview with President Reagan. The
interview, Jennings knew, was a no-win proposition: ask tough questions and he'd be seen as a spoilsport, but go easy on the president
and he'd be accused of playing into Reagan's hands. Jennings recalled,
"My wife and I sat outside our hotel in Los Angeles for about two
hours trying to devise a set of questions that would be both political
and benign. And it was awful!"

The interview *was* awful. Jennings began with an old standby:
"How do you feel today?" He went on, lamely, "Did I hear a rumor
earlier that you said you had never seen the spirit of America expressed
so well as down there on the field?" And he asked, "Do you think
these Games can add to international peace?" He hated every minute
of it.

And yet, for the rest of the evening, Jennings was the ideal host.
Thanks to his assiduous preparation, he delivered impromptu remarks
about many of the 140 countries represented at the Games — recalling
his experiences overseas, serving up little-known facts, and providing
viewers with a vivid sense of the world's diversity. Jennings's boyish
enthusiasm, perhaps his most likable trait, came through. More people

saw Jennings that night than ever before — no one knew better than Arledge the value of marketing during an Olympics.

Another winner was Ronald Reagan. Arledge's Olympics became a red-white-and-blue love fest, the perfect lead-in for Reagan and his "Morning in America" reelection campaign. Their messages complemented one another: America is back. And Arledge's eighteen-day orgy of patriotism was all the more powerful because it did not arrive in homes as a paid political announcement. Just as the nightly drumbeat of Arledge's "America Held Hostage" had solidified the image of a helpless Jimmy Carter and helped to elect Reagan in 1980, ABC's Olympics helped return Reagan to office in 1984.

This is not to imply that Arledge was a Reagan fan. His politics, as best as anyone knew, were independent; he had been raised a Democrat, but he had edged to the right with the rest of the country in the 1980s. Besides, Arledge's political views were irrelevant; they did not come into play when he was operating as a producer. His goals were not partisan but commercial — whether he was creating "America Held Hostage" or broadcasting the Olympics, suggesting stories to "20/20" or recruiting stars, Arledge's preeminent desire was to attract an audience: the impact of his programs, as well as his own career, depended on it. In this sense, he was, above all, pragmatic. Certainly he cared about informing the viewers, but he knew that first he had to engage them, by telling stories, touching their emotions, or speaking to what was on their minds. His gut instincts told him how to tap into the national mood, to capture that mood in news or sports programming, and to broadcast it back to his audience.

This was not the traditional function of news. To the contrary, the notion of playing to the public mood was antithetical to good journalism, which ought to upset or surprise people, or contradict what they think they know or feel. But success in television means being in sync with the public; programs as disparate as "All in the Family" and "Hill Street Blues" spoke to what was on America's mind. So did Arledge: like the great programmers, the William Paleys and Fred Silvermans and Brandon Tartikoffs, he had an uncanny ability to discern what viewers wanted, sometimes before they knew it themselves. "It's a sense," he once said, "of what people are interested in, being not too far ahead and not too far behind the public." Having this sense did not make him a great newsman, but it helped him to produce great television.

Chapter Eleven

BLIND SPOTS

ROONE ARLEDGE was trying to be nice — maybe too nice, thought some of the women who worked for ABC News.

Arledge had invited all sixteen of ABC's female correspondents to a luncheon on May 9, 1985, in New York. That night, Barbara Walters was to be honored by a group called American Women in Radio and Television. This lunch would mark the occasion and give the women a chance to mingle with the ABC News brass over cocktails and an elegant meal.

But the women didn't want cocktails or lunch. They didn't want to mingle. And they surely didn't want to be bought off by what one of them called "Roone's effort to make nice-nice to the ladies."

What they wanted was equality.

After the plates were cleared and Arledge and Walters had said a few words, Carole Simpson, a handsome woman with a deep voice and a commanding presence, rose from her place at the table.

"I just want to say that we're all delighted to be here," she began, turning toward Walters, "and we'd like to congratulate you before you go." Everyone clapped politely as Walters left; she had a piece to edit for that night's "20/20."

Simpson remained standing.

"While I have the floor, gentlemen," she went on, "we would like to talk to you about some of our concerns. Barbara has done a lot, and we're proud of Barbara. But we've got some serious problems that you need to hear about."

Her speech had been carefully rehearsed and cleared with the other correspondents in the room — Rita Flynn, Betsy Aaron, Sheilah Kast, Bettina Gregory, and others — most of whom felt that their careers had stalled at ABC. For the occasion, Simpson had even bought an expensive dark blue silk dress, subtly decorated with medallions featuring women's faces.

Without a trace of rancor in her voice, Simpson informed Arledge and his aides that women producers and correspondents who worked for ABC News had been meeting informally for more than a year. They had gathered information on the status of women in the division. For months, she said, they had sought a meeting with Arledge — to no avail. Now the time had come to deal with the problem of what she called "institutionalized sex discrimination" at ABC News.

At this point, Simpson passed out evidence. By feeding the daily rundowns of all the programs broadcast by ABC News into a computer, she had generated charts proving that the women lagged far behind the men in terms of airtime on ABC's important programs. Women made up 18 percent of the correspondents — sixteen of ninety — but contributed just 9 percent of the spots on "World News Tonight." The so-called A-Team remained an all-male club.

Off the air, the problems were just as bad.

"We don't have women making any of the news decisions," Simpson said. "We don't have women who are overseas. We have no bureau chiefs who are female. We have no senior producers — much less executive producers — who are women.

"In a world in which half the population is female," she went on, "it seems wrong to us that all of the news we present to our viewers is determined and decided by upper-class, middle-aged white men. Something's wrong. That's not the world."

Simpson had struck just the right tone. She spoke forcefully and from the heart, but not in a threatening way; in fact, she smiled through most of her speech. She knew, as she spoke, that she was taking a risk, but Simpson was determined to step forward, if only on behalf of her sixteen-year-old daughter, who would soon enter the workplace. One listener thought that Simpson had a "wonderful ability to be warm and charming while telling you that you have really fucked up."

Arledge, who had stared at her the whole time, thanked her for her presentation. He seemed more bewildered than anything. The women's issue had not yet registered on his radar screen.

"To tell you the truth," he said, "I really haven't given this much thought."

"That may be true," Simpson replied. "And that's why we're here. To help you think about it."

What followed was a free-flowing, sometimes heated discussion. Some of the men were defensive, noting, for example, that Pam Hill ran the documentary unit and that female producers handled much of the work at "20/20." The complaints about airtime, Dick Wald said, were not peculiar to women. "All reporters — men and women — feel they don't get on the air enough," he said. And Rick Kaplan drew nods of agreement when he said that the issue was talent, not sex or race. "I don't care whether you're man or woman, green, purple, or blue," Kaplan said. "We just want the best." The men grew fidgety; they had shows to get on the air.

But Arledge was in no hurry. His style when confronted was to try to win over his critics, and so, although he said little, he took everything in. The luncheon had begun at noon, but not until 4:30 did the talk wind down.

Wrapping things up, Arledge said that he was delighted that the women had come forward. These issues were important to ABC, important to him, he said, and changes would be made. He promised to look into the problems that had been raised, to come up with a response, and to meet again with the women.

Simpson was pleased. She thought the women could turn Arledge into an ally.

Others were not as sure.

While Carole Simpson always remained calm when she spoke on behalf of the ABC News women's group, she had been slighted enough over the years to be angry. Simpson was bright and well educated, but after twenty years in the business, she had been unable to break into the front ranks of correspondents. In Washington, that meant getting a major beat — the White House, Capitol Hill, the State Department, the Pentagon, or the Supreme Court, all of which guaranteed regular airtime. "No one ever told me that there's a problem with your voice or your writing or your reporting," Simpson said. She believed that she had been pigeonholed as a general-assignment reporter because she was black and a woman.

The evidence was mostly anecdotal. Executives, including Arledge, frequently praised Simpson as "articulate," a word that suggested to her that they had minimal expectations of the black reporters at ABC News. "I was hired by this man to communicate," Simpson would say. "Why then is he surprised that I can do it?" She also recalled a time when, after she remarked lightheartedly at a news division lunch that all the network could afford to serve was sandwiches, someone had joked back at her, "What do you want? Barbecued ribs and fried chicken?" Another time, a network manager greeted her at a going-away party for another correspondent by saying, "Where's your cap and apron? Aren't you going to serve?" After all the years of working at her profession, this man still saw her as the maid. Simpson thought, If people feel comfortable saying things like that, what kind of place is this?

The ABC women's movement had emerged out of a series of social get-togethers shortly after Simpson had come to ABC in 1981. "After a few glasses of wine and our chicken walnut casseroles, they turned into real gripe sessions," she recalled. "Many of us had the experience where we would cover a story and they would call a man in to come do the 'World News' spot after you'd been there all day long. We started hearing about women who had been here for long periods of time and training men to do their jobs, and these men then sailed by them."

The complaints were not unique to ABC News, of course. While pressure from the Federal Communications Commission led all the networks to hire more women in the early 1970s, industry attitudes were slow to change. Linda Ellerbee, the NBC correspondent, was once invited to appear on a panel about women in TV news at a broadcasters' convention; she was pleased until she learned that her panel was scheduled to talk not to the broadcasters but to their wives. "We came between the clinic on floral arrangement and makeup," she said.

But the women at ABC News lagged behind even their counterparts at the other networks. NBC News had been forced to hire and promote women in the mid-1970s after female employees there won a class-action suit, while Richard Salant, at CBS News, had made a commitment to provide opportunity to women. "Things were worse here," Simpson said. "ABC had not dealt with this issue." By the mid-1980s, CBS and NBC had Diane Sawyer, Connie Chung, Jane Pauley, Lesley Stahl, and Andrea Mitchell in prominent roles, as well as female producers and executives who were making gains. ABC had only Barbara Walters and Kathleen Sullivan, Arledge's newest star, whose ascent, as it happened, helped spur the other ABC News women to organize.

Sullivan was a twinkie, to use the industry parlance — a woman whose career had been driven by her looks. Arledge hired her to anchor

"World News This Morning" in 1982, and not because of her reporting experience; she had almost none. Just twenty-eight, Sullivan
had worked in television for three and a half years, at a station in
Salt Lake City and as a CNN anchor. What set her apart was her
charisma, which made her a favorite not only of Arledge but of male
viewers. "She lights up the dawn with a thousand kilowatt smile,
enormous doe eyes and a mellow alto voice just on the wholesome
side of sexy," gushed a writer for *People*. Arledge was more restrained,
although he did tell one reporter that "she has a presence that jumps
out of the screen, especially her eyes."

The other women were offended. Sullivan's looks and charm made
her the golden girl — "Roone's doll-baby," one producer said —
while their efforts went mostly unnoticed. "Kathleen's hiring and
prominence seemed to underscore the idea of women as pretty rather
than women as newspeople," said correspondent Sheilah Kast. Nor
was hers an isolated case — while Arledge and his aides had hired
some experienced women, they hired others who were young and
pretty but unqualified. The Los Angeles bureau, in particular, went
through a series of young female correspondents who had on-air appeal but could not do network-quality work. "The women we hired
in the LA bureau certainly did not have the rigorous scrutiny that a
man would have had," said a Los Angeles–based male producer.
"And then when they got there and needed help, there seemed to be
less inclination to help them than men."

All the female correspondents got the message that their looks
mattered to the men in charge. Anne Garrels, who was assigned to
cover the civil war in El Salvador, remembered that "the only telex
I ever got from New York was 'Don't ever wear a T-shirt again and
who cut your hair?' They were right — the haircut was horrible. But
it was all I could get in Salvador." And if a T-shirt was deemed too
casual for battle, Garrels wasn't sure what was appropriate dress.
Worse, some producers in New York — men with the power to de-
termine who got on the air — made cruel jokes about women's looks;
one referred to a woman as "dogface," and "World News" executive
producer Bill Lord once said he'd use a certain correspondent on his
show only if she put a bag over her head. Clearly, a double standard
was at work: women were expected to be physically appealing, while
men like Bob Zelnick and Jim Wooten were left alone. "Television is
run by guys," said ABC correspondent Hilary Brown, "and middle-
aged men like young girls."

Arledge was no exception. None of the women activists knew him firsthand, of course, but everything they had heard left them suspicious. Arledge had come from ABC Sports, a bastion of macho swagger, where he had invented "honey shots," those glimpses of scantily clad women designed to grab the attention of viewers when the action slowed on "Monday Night Football." After his first divorce, he had married Ann, his secretary and a former beauty queen. And now that she was gone, there were rumors that he was involved with Kathleen Sullivan. Arledge had sent her flowers, but they said their friendship was platonic and there was no reliable evidence to the contrary.

After the women's group formed, a few women wanted to take ABC to court. Kathy Bonk, an organizer with the National Organization for Women, told the group she thought they had a strong case of sex discrimination. But most of the women preferred to work within channels — frustrating as that could be. Arledge and Joanna Bistany, an aide he had assigned to work with the women, kept putting off their requests for a second meeting. Not until January 1986, eight months after the lunch honoring Walters, did Arledge meet with the women, this time at a Washington hotel.

Once again, the women came prepared. Simpson took the floor, after distributing new charts showing that women had made little progress in their efforts to get on the air. In the months since their first meeting, women accounted for 11.8 percent of the spots on "World News," 7.4 percent of the spots on "Nightline," and no appearances on "This Week with David Brinkley" until Simpson was invited on during Christmas week. The best times for women to get on the air, she noted acidly, were in July and December, when the men on the A-Team were on vacation.

She concluded with a pointed comment for Arledge.

"There is another issue," she said, ". . . sensitivity to women's concerns. And Roone, I must tell you that women correspondents were very disappointed in your comments in the December issue of *Broadcasting*. In it, you're quoted as saying that ABC has the best corps of correspondents of any of the networks. And if you're quoted correctly, you ticked off ten to twelve names of whom you consider the best people, and there was not one woman included. . . . It left the impression that you just don't consider any of us to be as good as the men you listed."

"Didn't I include Lynn?" Arledge said, a bit sheepishly. "I usually list Lynn Sherr. But I know it's dangerous to list, and I know I should avoid doing it. I think I even forgot to list Jack McWethy in that one."

Arledge's deputies were even more defensive. When Simpson complained that no women correspondents worked in foreign bureaus, Bob Murphy, who ran the assignment desk, claimed that he had "polled all the women correspondents on an overseas assignment and all said no." With that, Simpson, Kast, Jeanne Meserve, and Betsy Aaron all rose to say they'd never been asked. But the most heated exchanges were set off after producer Rhoda Lipton charged that male producers were paid, on average, 30 percent more than women.

Dick Wald challenged the claim. "Where did you get your figures?" Wald asked.

Lipton said she could not divulge her sources. The women had allies in clerical jobs who had given them a salary breakdown, by sex but without names.

The claim of pay inequity scared ABC News executives. They could smell a lawsuit coming.

Before the meeting ended, the women presented a set of specific proposals. They wanted ABC News to hire a full-time recruiter, to post job openings, and to institute employee evaluations; no one at ABC News had ever been formally evaluated, which suited Arledge just fine, since it gave him the freedom to move people around as he wished, without explanation. The women also asked Arledge to support their efforts to form a women's advisory board, to serve as a formal body to deal with women's issues.

Arledge ended the meeting as he had begun — by thanking the women for their ideas and by asking that the discussion not leave the room. Nevertheless, an account of the meeting appeared the next morning in John Carmody's column in the *Washington Post,* and over the next few weeks, other publications covered the story. Kathy Bonk of NOW said that a lawsuit was under consideration. Some women had come to believe that public pressure was their best weapon, especially as they felt increasing resistance from Joanna Bistany.

Bistany had become a controversial figure within ABC News. She had been hired to run the press department in 1983, at age thirty-five, after working for David Gergen in the Reagan White House; the news division often hired publicity people from politics, on the theory that they were news junkies accustomed to long hours and able to work under pressure. Bistany also had a master's degree in child psychology which, she joked, qualified her to deal with the egos in network news. A dark-haired, high-strung woman, she was intensely loyal to Arledge but not intimidated by him, as some were. She'd recently been named director of special news projects, but she functioned as a special assistant to Arledge.

While Bistany's promotion was sometimes cited as evidence that women were making gains at ABC, few women in the rank and file saw her as an ally. "She's a barrier, not a bridge," said one producer, in a comment echoed by others. Their suspicions were confirmed when Bistany said publicly that she disagreed strongly with some of the women's complaints.

Distrust of Bistany intensified because she was thought to be having an affair with Arledge. Rumors about them circulated for years, and there was no denying that they had a close friendship that extended beyond the office. Bistany, at one point, was bold enough to tell the assignment desk that she could be reached over the weekend at a phone number that the desk people knew to be Arledge's place in Sagaponack. This was disheartening to other women — the message, as they saw it, was that the only way for a woman to advance within ABC News was to sleep her way to the top. How, they thought, could they complain to Bistany about sexism at ABC News?

What made matters worse was that Bistany, at this stage, was not well regarded inside ABC News. She had no experience in journalism or production. And while she was smart, the rap on her was that she did little more than parrot Arledge's ideas and shield him from bad news. Reflecting a widely held view, a female producer said, "The highest-ranking woman in the news division isn't good, has no résumé, and is sleeping with the boss. What signal does that send to the women who were working in the trenches for years?"

Still, it was Bistany who eventually delivered some good news to the women. In June 1986, she told the leaders of the women's group that ABC had completed a salary study that confirmed their charges about inequities in pay. Sex discrimination, the network insisted, had not caused the inequities; other factors, such as job tenure, were at work. But that was the rhetoric. What mattered was the remedy. Within weeks, forty-five female producers — and a few men who, for various reasons, were paid below-average wages — got raises, ranging from $4,000 a year to as much as $11,000 a year. (Correspondents, whose contracts were negotiated by agents, were not affected.) The pay hikes, while generous, were a defensive response to the threat of a lawsuit. ABC's lawyers had warned that the newswomen could have gone to court and won.

Arledge granted several other demands made by the women's

group. Amy Entelis, a "World News" producer, was given an executive-level job as a recruiter, and a handful of women were named bureau chiefs or senior producers. Arledge and Bistany also agreed to establish a women's advisory board, with elected members, to deal with affirmative action, sexual harassment, and maternity leave, among other issues. With that, the women's group declared victory. The pay raises, promotions, and advisory board were all steps in the right direction.

But their celebration was muted, in part because their other proposals were turned down. Not all job openings would be posted. And there would be no formal evaluation of employees. Arledge and his aides did not want to be required to explain, on paper, why some correspondents were doing well and others were not; those judgments were art, not science.

What's more, Arledge and his producers showed no inclination to provide more airtime for female correspondents — the issue that had first led Simpson to organize. Turnover on the top beats was rare, and in the years that followed, when frontline jobs did open up, they were usually filled by men. Even Simpson was snubbed: she had covered George Bush's campaigns in 1980 and 1984 and did so again in 1988 until he became the Republican presidential nominee; she was then replaced by Brit Hume, who went on to become White House correspondent. While Simpson was made a weekend news anchor, she could not help thinking that ABC's powers-that-be had been unwilling to give the White House job to a woman. Not until Cokie Roberts was hired from National Public Radio to cover Congress was a woman given a high-visibility reporting beat. "You look at us on the air," Simpson said, "and it's worse than ever."

Behind the scenes, though, women gradually made significant gains. By 1993, several women had advanced to the rank of executive producer — Shelley Lewis was running an overnight news program called "World News Now," Phyllis McGrady was developing a prime-time program called "Turning Point," and, most important, Emily Rooney, the news director of an ABC affiliate in Boston, was hired to take charge of "World News Tonight." Several of Rooney's top producers around the rim were women, and they helped open up opportunities for female correspondents. Better yet, on the prime-time news programs, women were prominently featured as anchors and correspondents, and they made up nearly half of the production staffs. Still, with the exception of Joanna Bistany, the senior executives closest to Arledge were all men. And the changes had come at a slow pace.

The costs, to ABC news and its viewers, had been mostly intangible. A few talented women quit, frustrated because their careers had stalled. Others never had the opportunity to prove themselves. And the paucity of female voices at decision-making levels affected story selection and tone. Programs like "This Week" and "Nightline" tended to book the same white male guests. The female producers at "World News" often found it hard to sell stories on women's health, birth control, or sex discrimination to the men on the rim. "It was infuriating some days to see things passed over that should have been on the air," said Cherie Simon, a "World News" producer.

In the end, the problem was that the women's concerns had never registered with Arledge. He was, at heart, a man's man, a product of the 1950s, who liked sports and pretty girls, drank hard liquor, and kept his feelings to himself. He meant well when dealing with the ABC women's group, but once they disappeared, he worried about other things. Only when he felt threatened by bad publicity or a lawsuit did he act, and even then his response was pragmatic. Arledge was willing to buy off the women with money and promotions, but he would not give ground when it came to airtime or power over programming. To put more women on the air because they were women would be a mistake, he felt — the public face of ABC News was too important. That had to remain his sole domain.

Av Westin could not believe his ears. "20/20" had latched on to a great story, an explosive story, about the death of Marilyn Monroe, her ties to the Kennedys, and the threat of blackmail by organized crime, and Roone Arledge was telling him that he did not think the story should go on the air. That made no sense, Westin thought — the reporting was solid, and the story was a surefire ratings grabber.

Besides, Arledge had known for months that "20/20" was working on a piece about Monroe. Why had he waited so long to react? They had already spent more than $100,000 on the story, money that would be wasted if the piece was spiked.

Westin had smelled trouble when he had been summoned to meet with Arledge; the two men rarely saw each other alone. Even so, Arledge was being cagey. Deliberately, he did not order Westin to kill the piece. That, he said later, was a decision he wanted to leave to his executive producer. "I didn't want to overrule him in front of all his staff. I wanted him to save face," Arledge said. Westin saw things differently — he thought he was being asked to do the dirty work so that Arledge's fingerprints would not be all over an unpopular and controversial move.

What actually transpired between them has been lost in the fog that, years later, still shrouds the "20/20" story about Marilyn Monroe; the truth about how and why Arledge killed the segment remains elusive. But there is no question that Arledge's decision sparked a public furor and distanced him from two people — Westin and Geraldo Rivera — who had been extremely important during the years of building ABC News.

Westin already felt distanced from Arledge — literally. He remarked on the way that Arledge's office, which once opened directly onto a hallway, had been set back, so that even those who walked the halls of the executive floor could not see in. Two secretaries guarded the entrance. And while David Burke, Dick Wald, and Joanna Bistany could drop by unannounced, others, including his anchors and executive producers, found him less accessible. Mere producers or correspondents might not set eyes on him for months. "He withdrew further and further," Westin said. "You had to make an appointment. Or you'd be told, 'He'll get back to you,' and the call would never be returned."

Westin turned that situation to his own advantage. At "20/20," he fostered an "us-vs.-them" mentality that allowed him to remove himself from unpopular decisions made by Arledge. He'd tell the staff that Arledge ignored the show and that he alone recognized their value. There was some truth to this — Arledge left "20/20" alone after a while, permitting Westin to run his shop almost as if it were an independent production company within ABC News.

The result was that, as word spread that Arledge was pressing him to kill the Monroe story, Westin figured he was in a no-lose situation. If the story ran, he'd be a hero for saving it; if it didn't, everyone would blame Arledge. That would embarrass Arledge and conceivably help Westin realize his own ambition, which was to become president of ABC News. From the time he'd returned to ABC in 1977, Westin had seen himself as Arledge's heir apparent. By this time, he was growing impatient.

So production of the Monroe piece went ahead. Producers Ene Riisna and Stanhope Gould had hooked up with Anthony Summers, the author of an upcoming book called *Goddess: The Secret Lives of Marilyn Monroe*. With correspondent Sylvia Chase, they had developed compelling new evidence of Monroe's affairs with President John F.

Kennedy and his brother Robert; they had eyewitnesses who said that Monroe's home had been wiretapped by Jimmy Hoffa, the union leader with ties to organized crime; and they had an on-camera interview with Fred Otash, a private detective, who told them that he had arranged for wiretaps on Monroe and listened to tapes of her with the Kennedys. Their hypothesis was that Hoffa planned to use the tapes to get Robert Kennedy's Justice Department to ease up on organized crime.

Gould said, "It was the documentation, coupled with the mob angle, that made it a major story — the fact that the president and attorney general of the United States had put themselves in a position to have the nation's most powerful criminals eavesdrop on their affairs with the nation's most famous actress and were exposed to blackmail. That's one hell of a story."

Ignoring the warnings from Arledge, Westin scheduled a twenty-six-minute version of the story for the "20/20" season premiere on September 26, 1985. He was sure they had a blockbuster.

The first ABC News executive to review the segment was Bob Siegenthaler, a traditionalist who had replaced George Watson as vice president of news practices. His charge was a narrow one — to decide whether the story met ABC's standards for fairness and accuracy — and he judged that it did. But he was unhappy about the implication that Kennedy was being blackmailed by Hoffa, which went beyond the facts in the piece. As Siegenthaler put it later, he approved the piece even though he didn't approve of it.

Under other circumstances, David Burke, as Arledge's second-in-command, might then have vetted the piece, but he excused himself; as Ted Kennedy's former chief of staff, he felt too close to the family to render an impartial judgment.

That left matters up to Arledge, who had his own set of Kennedy connections. There were not only his friendships with Ethel Kennedy and Stephen Smith, a Kennedy brother-in-law, but other ties, too — Ethel's daughter Courtney Kennedy had married Arledge's longtime assistant Jeff Ruhe, while her son Michael Kennedy had married Vicki Gifford, the daughter of Frank Gifford, one of Arledge's best pals. Arledge insisted that his friendships played no role in his decision, saying, "I've already offended half the friends I have."

After screening the Monroe story, Arledge had two objections. The first was broad — he thought it was unseemly to dredge up dirt about a former president and his brother, neither of whom could defend themselves. His other complaint was specific — he wanted proof that the mob had taped the encounters between Monroe and the Kennedys. "I want to hear the tape," he said.

Here again, recollections differ. Westin believes he was given the go-ahead to take a final crack at the story. Arledge says he made it clear that the piece should be killed. People at "20/20" say they were told that they could get the piece on the air if they cut it down, which they did, to about thirteen minutes.

Word that Arledge wanted the piece spiked, once and for all, did not come down until about 5:30 P.M. on Thursday, October 3, the new air date. By then, Sylvia Chase was in makeup for the taping; the staff gathered on the set with Hugh Downs and Barbara Walters. "We were astounded," Downs said.

Geraldo Rivera was more than astounded; he was incensed. Impulsively, without having seen the piece, he took sides — he would stand by his "20/20" colleagues and against Arledge. "This is a fucking outrage," he said. "Arledge should resign." Rivera said later, "I looked on '20/20' as my show and I did not like anyone, even Roone, tampering with it. We were a news program, and this was news. We were not in the business of shielding friends and relations from the harsh light of press scrutiny."

That night, Rivera unloaded to syndicated columnist Liz Smith, who had been following the story.

"We were appalled that the head of this network would suddenly show such an interest in this particular story when he hasn't shown interest in so many others we've done," Rivera said.

Twisting the knife, he went on, "We were appalled that Roone would overturn a respected, honorable, great newsman like Av."

Arledge shot back in the same column, saying, "Television's impact is so great, so much greater than print, that if we devote two-thirds of '20/20' to a premise, we'd better be able to prove it. My objection to the piece as it stands is that it's a piece of sleazy journalism. Just not good enough for us."

This was misleading — the scaled-down version of the story was thirteen minutes, not two-thirds of the program — as well as insulting to the "20/20" producers. Arledge denied using the word sleazy, but Smith wrote the next day, "I believe he did." Besides, Arledge expressed a similar opinion to the *New York Times,* calling the story "gossip-column stuff" that did "not live up to its billing."

Arledge was desperate to preserve his own reputation even if that required putting down his own employees in the press.

By this time, reporters were noting the ties between Arledge and the Kennedys. And Rivera's defense of the story was buttressed by Hugh Downs. Downs praised the producers, Gould and Riisna, and said that the piece was "more carefully researched than most of the reports I had seen on Watergate."

That, too, was a stretch, but the story was certainly as well documented as others on "20/20." As for Arledge's claim that the Monroe segment was "gossip-column stuff," that did not disqualify literally dozens of other stories broadcast by "20/20," which ran such segments as "TV's Wicked Women" ("Bad and beautiful women we love to hate") and "Behind the Royal Doors" ("The prince's valet serves up the facts"). Even at its most serious, "20/20" never ran the risk of being called highbrow.

At best, Arledge's decision reflected his concern about his reputation and the reputation of ABC News. Circumstances had changed from the days of the Son of Sam and Elvis exposés. By 1985, "20/20" was on solid footing — the Monroe exposé wasn't needed to juice the ratings — while Arledge valued his standing as a serious player in the world of broadcast news. A peek into Marilyn Monroe's bedroom was not going to help.

The only other plausible explanation for his decision was that Arledge's feelings about the Kennedys had, in fact, come into play. Arledge loved to associate himself with the famous, and no family in America was more star-studded than the Kennedys. Still, if Arledge did kill the piece to protect his friends, this was an isolated case — no one at ABC News can cite another instance where he spiked or significantly altered a story for personal reasons.

Public controversy over the Monroe story soon faded.

Its repercussions within ABC News, however, were long-lasting.

Within months, Sylvia Chase left "20/20" to become an anchor at KRON-TV in San Francisco. Stanhope Gould, her producer, went along. While Av Westin remained, his relationship with Arledge was damaged beyond repair.

So were relations between Arledge and Geraldo Rivera. They had been comrades, ready to shake up the network news traditions; now they were on a collision course.

Rivera had long simmered with resentment at Arledge. He griped that Arledge, once the rebel outsider, had abandoned him. In a sense, he was right — Arledge was unhappy about all the lawsuits and wearied by Geraldo's refusal to play by the network rules. Said Arledge, "He'd become a very difficult person to deal with."

In Arledge's eyes, Rivera had become a public relations problem.

"Geraldo had become a symbol in so many people's mind of how the line had been blurred between news and entertainment," he said. Rivera, he felt, singlehandedly dragged down ABC's reputation to the point where some people said, "Yeah, they're good, but they're not really serious or they wouldn't have Geraldo on."

Even before the Monroe controversy, Irwin Weiner had informed Rivera that there would be no raise when his contract came up for renewal in September 1985. Rivera was making $1 million a year, but he was upset by his inability to wangle even a symbolic raise out of Arledge. He settled, grudgingly, for a renewal of his existing deal. On a flight to Manila to do a "20/20" piece, Rivera vented his feelings in a letter he wrote but never mailed.

"Dear Roone," he wrote. "So now we are to be contractually associated for three more years. I wonder if you will have the guts to call me during that time. I doubt it. Tom Shales & Peter Jennings would not approve. Regards, Geraldo."

The Monroe brouhaha was Rivera's chance to strike back. He wanted, he said, "to make Roone pay publicly for his refusal to deal with me on other, more personal matters. I actually enjoyed trashing Roone to the press. It felt right, and good." As Barbara Walters put it, "Geraldo was like a child trying to get attention, and he got it."

That he did. First, Rivera was upbraided by Bob Siegenthaler, in his role as vice president for news practices, for making a $200 contribution to a local political campaign. This was a trifling lapse when compared, for example, to George Will's coaching of candidate Ronald Reagan in 1980, which had been condoned by ABC, so the fact that Siegenthaler had brought him in for a scolding told Rivera that he was in trouble. Rivera ranted at Siegenthaler, telling him there was no way ABC was going to get rid of him. "You tell Roone that if he tries to breach our contract, I'll drag him into court," Rivera said, storming out of the office.

A few days later, Rivera's girlfriend, C. C. Dyer, gave ABC another reason to move against him. She sent an ABC messenger to pick up what was reported to be a small amount of marijuana from a friend — an action that was discovered by the network and made the papers, to Rivera's chagrin.

The next day, Arledge called him at home.

In clipped, cold tones, Arledge said, "I want you to quit."

"Bullshit," replied Rivera. "I'm not quitting."

"You can't continue," Arledge said, "not after this."

Rivera had never been sent a new contract, but he had made a verbal agreement with Irwin Weiner. He insisted that ABC News was obligated to keep him.

Arledge did not want to argue. He hated conflict. He just wanted to hang up the phone.

"Show me the contract, Geraldo," Arledge said. "We have no contract. Show me the contract."

"Are you saying I'm fired?" Rivera asked.

"Well," replied Arledge, "you can use whatever words you want, but I don't think you're going to work here anymore." A few days later, ABC offered Rivera $250,000 in severance to go away quietly. His agent, William Griffin, talked the network up to $500,000. In exchange, Rivera agreed not to speak publicly for two years about his departure from ABC.

ABC News issued a statement that papered over the conflict — to say the least. Arledge was quoted as saying, "After fifteen years of hard, honorable work with ABC, Geraldo Rivera has told us that he wishes to leave to pursue other opportunities. Although we sincerely regret this decision, ABC does not wish to stand in the way of his future plans."

The truth was that Rivera stood in the way of Arledge's future plans.

"Like so many things," Arledge said, "you look at it as you grow, and you say, he was terrific for a while, but he's now doing more damage than he is helping us."

Rivera hadn't changed, but Arledge had. Ratings still mattered to him, but so, increasingly, did the approval of elites. He wanted to be taken seriously, to be known as the man who socialized with Henry Kissinger and George Shultz, not as the man who employed Geraldo Rivera.

"Geraldo did two interesting things for ABC News," Arledge concluded. "He helped us tremendously, up to a point, in our early growth. And he helped ABC News immensely by leaving."

Chapter Twelve

THE PARTY'S OVER

WHILE HE RODE FIRST-CLASS, as always, Roone Arledge could not fall asleep on the eighteen-hour flight from Johannesburg to New York. He had left South Africa on Sunday to get to New York early on Monday, spend the day in meetings, and then fly back to Johannesburg. This was not a trip he had planned to make, but he had no choice — his company, ABC, had just been sold.

Fred Pierce had called him in South Africa to deliver the news. Pierce hadn't said much — no public announcement had been made — but he had described the deal as a friendly merger. Otherwise, Leonard Goldenson would never have agreed to give up ABC. Pierce said he was pleased that the new owner, Capital Cities Communications, was a broadcasting company, which owned ABC affiliates in Philadelphia and Houston. The Capital Cities people knew the business.

Still, Arledge thought, Fred must be upset. Pierce had dreamed of running the company when Goldenson retired. His mind raced with questions: Would the new owners understand his importance? Would they recognize his contributions? For twenty-five years, Arledge had poured his energies into ABC — he had, with Fred and Leonard, turned the network from an also-ran into a force. The new owners might be great people, but Arledge knew the place would never be the same.

He also could not get South Africa out of his head. Arledge had been there for only a day, but he had been energized as "Nightline" prepared for a week of what he hoped would be high-impact programs about apartheid. He loved to travel to foreign locations and to hobnob with world leaders — that was the only way to get a real feel for a story, he thought. Arledge also felt needed in South Africa because Ted Koppel and Rick Kaplan, his new executive producer at "Nightline," were not getting along. Now they would have to do their first program without him.

He was already eager to go back.

That morning — Monday, March 18, 1985 — the merger was announced. Capital Cities had agreed to pay $3.5 billion for ABC, making the deal the largest ever outside the oil industry. Thanks in part to President Reagan's deregulation-minded FCC, this was the first time a broadcast network had been sold since Goldenson's United Paramount Theaters merged with ABC in 1953.

Fred Pierce convened a morning meeting of his senior aides to go over what he was still calling a merger.

From Arledge's standpoint, the message was mixed. Pierce had been told he would continue to run all of ABC, including the network news, sports, and entertainment divisions, the owned TV stations, and the cable-programming ventures, such as ESPN. His title would be vice chairman. That was encouraging. "We were all comfortable with Fred," Arledge said.

But Arledge worried that, despite his title, Pierce would be only the number three executive in the new company, which would be called Capital Cities/ABC Inc. Tom Murphy, the fifty-nine-year-old chairman of Capital Cities, would remain chairman, while Dan Burke, fifty-six, his second-in-command, would be president and chief operating officer.

Pierce assured everyone that he had the support of Murphy and Burke. "I don't think there will be any less autonomy," he said optimistically. "The reporting mechanism is just something on a chart."

No one knew how to react. The merger had made very rich men out of dozens of ABC veterans, including Arledge. ABC stock had traded in the 60s, so Goldenson had nearly doubled its worth by selling for $118 a share — and the company's generous stock plan meant that senior ABC executives owned thousands of shares. "Leonard had done well by everybody," said one executive.

But as Pierce spoke, the mood was tense. A few men fought back tears. Capital Cities was an unknown. Murphy and Burke were said to be straight shooters, but they were also notoriously frugal. Goldenson himself had indicated that they might try to wring more profit out of ABC by cutting costs. One Cap Cities anecdote made the rounds quickly, about how, in the company's early days, when its Albany station badly needed repainting, Murphy had ordered that only the sides of the building facing the main road be spruced up. "Everyone was worried," recalled Barbara Walters. "Leonard Goldenson was a warm grandfather. Suddenly we had these cold businessmen. At least that's what we heard."

Later, Goldenson and Pierce, with Murphy and Burke, held a news conference. When a reporter approached Arledge, he tried to sound upbeat. "I don't see anything dramatically different," he said. "I would think that I am one of the major assets at ABC, and I would think that they merged, not because of me, but in looking over the assets they are getting, I imagine I am part of this deal." That evening, Peter Jennings began "World News Tonight" by saying, "To paraphrase Pogo, we have seen the news and it is us."

After he got back to South Africa, Arledge did his best to explain to everyone "how a company as big as ABC could be taken over by a company they had never heard of." He did not, however, describe the deal as a marriage or a merger of equals — which remained the party line in New York. Cap Cities, he said, would run the show.

"They seemed like nice guys," Arledge said, "but this was no merger. It was a takeover. This little company just took us over."

While Arledge pondered his suddenly unpredictable future at ABC, Ted Koppel faced a more immediate concern. Would "Nightline" be able to pull off an audacious series of broadcasts in South Africa? "Nightline" staff members had never seen Koppel so nervous; he'd started smoking again, five years after kicking the habit. A few minutes before the first show, Koppel ran into Rick Kaplan, his executive producer, in a stairwell leading to the control room.

"Do you feel like barfing in the trash can?" Kaplan asked.

"You bet," Koppel replied.

"Me too," Kaplan said.

"Nightline" had never tried anything so ambitious. That was Kaplan's doing. Since taking over ten months earlier, Kaplan had set out to lift the show to new heights — to make it more compelling, more exciting, even "greater than great," to pick one of his favorite superlatives.

The push to focus on South Africa had come from Koppel and other staff members, notably black producer Lionel Chapman. While South Africa was not then front-page news, Koppel had watched the anti-apartheid protests at the South African Embassy in Washington, and he believed the story would get bigger. "We were seeking to create public appetite for a story that deserved more attention," he said.

The idea of traveling to South Africa for a week was Kaplan's. While "Nightline" had broadcast from remote sites before, the program had never gone overseas. Kaplan loved the idea of taking the show on the road, relocating a staff of thirty to Johannesburg, and promoting the venture in an effort to boost ratings and persuade more ABC stations to clear "Nightline" live. It was the kind of big-event television that got his juices going.

The pitfalls were many — a major story could break elsewhere, the South African government could censor the programs, the state-owned broadcasting facilities could prove inadequate, and whites or blacks could refuse to sit down with each other — but Kaplan managed to convince Arledge that the risks were worth taking.

Perhaps the biggest risk was that Kaplan and Koppel were not getting along. Everyone knew that Kaplan, who had never worked at "Nightline," had not been Koppel's choice to replace Bill Lord. "Rick was like a stepfather," Koppel said. "Dad was gone, and here's this new guy." Other staff members agreed. "It was like our family had been invaded," said producer Susan Mercandetti.

Overrun was more like it. With a build like a defensive lineman, a booming voice, and an outsize personality, Kaplan had barged into his new assignment. "Rick is big. His ring looks like a bracelet. His watch looks like a belt," Mercandetti said. "Rick thinks big. Rick does nothing small. There's not a subtle bone in his body. Rick is the most undiplomatic, unsubtle person in the world."

Kaplan, then thirty-seven, had been with ABC News since 1979, mostly as Jeff Gralnick's deputy on "World News." Growing up in a middle-class family in Chicago, Kaplan was a child of television — he loved to watch sitcoms and dramas, as well as news, and he began working at CBS-owned WBBM-TV while still in college. He moved to CBS News in New York and worked as a producer on the Cronkite show, where, as he put it, "I was totally happy, plus I was rich. I was making $39,000, which was $12,000 more than I am years old — you know, your goal is $1,000 for every year of life, right? So hey, Rolls-Royce is right around the corner." Arledge made him richer, doubling his pay to bring him to ABC. For that alone, Kaplan became an unabashed Arledge fan, admiring, as well, Arledge's creativity, showmanship, and attention to detail. Kaplan's hard-driving approach led to a job as executive producer of "World News This Morning," from which he was plucked to take over "Nightline."

Koppel was unimpressed with that résumé. Unlike Bill Lord, Kaplan had not toiled for years at ABC News. He'd never worked in Washington or overseas, nor had he shown much devotion to the issue-oriented coverage favored by Koppel. "This is a difficult thing to say about someone who is six foot seven and weighs two hundred and fifty pounds, but I thought Rick was a lightweight," Koppel said. "I thought he was too inclined to emphasize production values over substance." It didn't help when Kaplan declared, early on, that what "Nightline" really needed was a new opening and new graphics. The show, he said, had to shed its State Department look — a comment that irritated Koppel.

But Kaplan's instincts were on target. He'd seen ABC research saying that many viewers would check "Nightline" to see what was on and then tune out. So he went with a "cold open" that put his most eye-catching pictures and sound bites ahead of the theme music, to build excitement. "I learned that from Roone," Kaplan explained. "Look, what's the most important minute of the show? The first minute. Then what's the second most important? The second minute. Followed by the third minute, and so on. Because they can tune out any minute."

Some of Kaplan's other ideas also struck Koppel as wrongheaded. To mark the fortieth anniversary of the D-Day invasion, Kaplan produced an hour-long "Nightline" as if it were June 6, 1944. After setting the scene, Koppel introduced reports using archival footage from John McWethy at the War Department, Sam Donaldson at the Roosevelt White House, and Pierre Salinger in Paris, and then debriefed the reporters with scripted questions. It was acting, and Koppel worried that it could undermine the credibility of "Nightline." Kaplan loved it — he felt as if he were producing a movie.

Their disagreements flared on the conference calls, held each morning at eleven, with Kaplan in New York, Koppel in Washington, and staff members gathered around each of them. Everyone could listen as Kaplan's efforts to push the program toward more popular topics were resisted by Koppel. "It was for-the-people Rick versus erudite Ted," recalled producer Deborah Leff.

One time, Kaplan responded enthusiastically when a producer suggested doing a "Nightline" about reincarnation. He launched into a monologue about how you would approach the subject and who might be booked as guests while staffers in Koppel's office in Washington studied his face for a reaction.

Koppel waited for Kaplan to lose steam, then spoke up quietly.

"Rick," he said, "I don't think that's a news story."

Kaplan came back at full bore. Millions of people believe in reincarnation, he said, some of the world's great religions are built around the idea, and, besides, they could find scientific experts to debunk it if that would make Ted feel better.

"Rick," Koppel said again, "I don't want to do this."

Seeing that he could not persuade his anchor, Kaplan decided to bully him. He came from the school that said the executive producer was in charge.

"You know, Ted, I don't care," he said firmly. "We're doing it."

"That's fine," replied Koppel, seemingly resigned to the new reality. "I'm starting to believe in reincarnation. In a prior life, I was a journalist."

His punch line defused the tension, and the idea was eventually dropped.

Other disputes were not as easily resolved. "They'd argue and argue and argue in front of us," recalled Susan Mercandetti. "It created a bad atmosphere." After one battle, a frustrated Koppel told Kaplan, "As long as they want us to work together, we'll work together. But I'm not sure we'll ever be a team."

Their chemistry just wasn't right. "When you don't bond," Kaplan said, "you sit there and you can find fourteen hundred things the other person does that irritate you." One woman who knew both men was reminded of the cultural gaps that once divided New York's German Jewish aristocrats and the newly arrived Russian Jews: "Ted is a German Jew and Rick is an Eastern European. It was almost like Ted looking down and going, 'Oh my God, this boorish guy with a big gold watch and so noisy, so loud' . . . Ted is haughty, elegant . . . it's perfect," she said — except, perhaps, for the fact that Koppel's swimming pool was garishly decorated with the "Nightline" silhouette.

Preparing for South Africa eased some of the tension, as the effort drew out the best qualities in each man. To Koppel, the story was an opportunity to educate. In time-honored "Nightline" fashion, he thought, they could bring together people who had literally never spoken to each other. Kaplan also cared about the story, but what really got him excited was the chance to put five "greater than great" shows on the air. "He brought an almost fraternal, let's-put-on-a-show feeling," said producer Kyle Gibson. "It could be exhausting, and it could be frustrating, but you had that fire under you to produce in an unusual, creative way." Kaplan was also incredibly well organized — he tracked stories, interviews, meetings, and schedules in spiral notebooks, using blue highlighter to denote ABC business, pink for "Nightline" activities, and yellow for personal matters. "Rick is one of the original anal compulsives," Koppel said — but he was impressed.

All their combined skills, energies, and persuasive powers were needed to pull off the South Africa trip. They began at the South African Embassy in Washington, arguing that the apartheid regime had been getting such uniformly bad publicity that the government ought to take the opportunity to get its story out. "It was going to be live, and it was not going to be edited out of context, so at least they had an even chance of getting something across," Koppel said. One South African official was impressed when he was told that a thirty-second spot on "Nightline" cost $25,000 — he calculated that South Africa could get millions of rands of publicity.

In South Africa, though, "Nightline" producers Betsy West and Tara Sonenshine ran into a wall as they tried to set up the shows. Their first meeting with government officials ended when their proposal for a joint appearance featuring R. F. "Pik" Botha, the government's minister of foreign affairs, and Bishop Desmond Tutu, the 1984 Nobel Peace Prize winner, was rejected out of hand. The two men had never talked in public — indeed, to that point, the government had no dealings with Bishop Tutu.

When West and Sonenshine returned to their hotel to deliver the bad news to Koppel and Kaplan, they expected sympathy. Instead, they got a tirade. We will not have apartheid on television, Koppel insisted, and if this is the government's attitude, we will drop the whole project and report what has happened. Kaplan sounded outraged too, telling the women to come home if they couldn't make immediate progress. West and Sonenshine were distraught. In the heat of the moment, they had not realized that the indignation was aimed not at them but at government officials — who Koppel figured had bugged the hotel phone. He'd warned the women beforehand that he might use their calls to send messages to the South Africans.

Whatever the explanation, Sonenshine recalled later that "the South Africans' attitude had changed dramatically by the next meeting." She never knew whether the phones were tapped, but the government promised to cooperate. West and Sonenshine then had to labor nearly as hard to win over black leaders, some of whom refused to participate because they did not want to grant legitimacy to the apartheid regime.

On Monday, the day of the first "Nightline" from South Africa, Koppel and Kaplan were summoned to lunch in Cape Town with Pik Botha, the foreign minister. Botha and Bishop Tutu had agreed, through aides, to be the guests that night.

Botha sat at the head of a long table, with his aides on one side, and Koppel, Kaplan, and Sonenshine on the other. The foreign minister tapped his glass, said grace, and inquired about the plans for that evening's program.

Koppel described the format, talked about setup pieces being prepared by correspondents Jeff Greenfield and Kenneth Walker, and thanked Botha for his cooperation.

"As you know, Foreign Minister," Koppel said, "we're very excited because this is going to be the first time that we will have you and Bishop Tutu on the program together."

"What?" Botha interrupted. "No one had told me about this."

Koppel and Kaplan glanced at one another, horrified.

"This is not possible," Botha said.

"Look, Minister," Koppel replied coolly, "I've spent years traveling around the world with Henry Kissinger, and that's exactly the kind of gambit he would use. I have to assume that, at this point, if no one had told you about this, you would fire everyone sitting on the other side of the table."

Botha grunted and then grinned. He told them he would appear. But, he warned, cooperation would be withdrawn if ABC News did anything to embarrass him or the South African government.

That night, Kaplan took his place in the control room and Koppel settled into the studio in Johannesburg. Both were still nervous, as was director Roger Goodman, who had been working feverishly to teach modern television techniques to the crew from the South African Broadcasting Co. They had hooked up remotes to Botha in Cape Town and Bishop Tutu at his church in Johannesburg.

Kaplan opened the microphones one at a time.

"Bishop Tutu," said Koppel.

"Yes," came the reply.

"Mr. Botha?" Koppel asked.

"Yes, Mr. Koppel," he said.

"Can you hear each other?" asked Koppel.

"Good evening, Mr. Minister," said Tutu.

Then came a long pause.

Fuck, thought Kaplan, they're not going to talk to each other. At one point, Botha's people had said the minister would talk to Koppel but not directly to Tutu.

Finally, Botha's voice was heard. "Yes, Bishop Tutu, how are you?" he said.

A moment later, when the first split-screen picture of the two men was shown, Kaplan could no longer contain himself. "Do you believe it!" he shouted.

The pictures alone were momentous — the two men appeared side by side as equals, the split-screen image bestowing on Tutu the parity he had been denied by his government. Political debate in South Africa is lively, Koppel noted, but opponents usually talk about each other, not to each other. This face-to-face confrontation was extraordinary, and never more so than when Tutu made a personal plea for justice.

"I'm a bishop in the church of God," Tutu said. "I'm fifty-three years of age. You would, I suppose, say that I'm reasonably responsible. In my own country, I do not vote. According to this government, I am not a South African. My travel document says of my nationality that it is undeterminable at present. So blacks have been turned into aliens in the land of the oppressed."

Koppel was moved. "I was getting goosebumps," he said. "It was just one of those truly electric moments."

It was an unforgettable week for everyone at "Nightline." Jeff Greenfield, a veteran political reporter, was threatened during a meeting of an angry neo-Nazi group and stumbled onto a near-riot in Soweto. This isn't exactly the Iowa caucuses, he thought. Lionel Chapman, the black producer who had pushed for the coverage, was invited into the home of an affable Afrikaner who, unaware that the light-skinned Chapman was black, proceeded to explain why blacks were inferior to whites. Arledge returned to Johannesburg in time to supervise coverage of riots that broke out midweek in Port Elizabeth. Each night after the broadcast, Arledge would preside over a late-night dinner with Koppel, Kaplan, and Bistany in his hotel suite, where they would talk about the show, plan for the next night — and wonder about the future under Cap Cities.

The "Nightline" series earned raves in the United States and in South Africa, where the SABC rebroadcast the interviews — without the taped pieces, which the government complained were slanted. The *Pretoria News* wrote, "South Africans who have been watching television for the past two evenings are for the first time getting an inkling of what they should have been served by SABC-TV in the nine years since its inception: penetrating, no-holds-barred debates between our politicians and their critics." The *Rand Daily Mail* agreed, saying, "It is an indictment of our rulers and the TV service they have created that a programme of such vital importance to us all should have been created by an American team."

The ultimate compliment came from an SABC director, who worked side by side with Roger Goodman and was married to a conservative Afrikaner. Fighting back tears, she told Goodman and Kaplan that, after watching the programs, her husband had told her for the first time that apartheid was wrong, that change was inevitable. When we leave, Kaplan thought, this place won't be the same.

By then, Koppel and Kaplan had bonded. Koppel had orchestrated the interviews brilliantly, but that had become expected of him. The surprise, for those at "Nightline," was Kaplan's performance: the way he had organized the complex undertaking, cheered on the staff, produced each show from the control room, and resisted the unrelenting pressures from the South African government. "What Rick did was nothing short of heroic," said Jeff Greenfield. "He showed some real guts."

At one point, Koppel approached Kaplan.

"You know, you're a great producer," Koppel said.

"I know," said Kaplan, grinning. He was like a giant child, who wanted nothing more than for everyone to like him. He told Koppel, "But you ought to know that I also think you're a great anchor."

Producer Betsy West said later, "That was when they got married. They realized that Ted had the ability to carry out Rick's grand schemes and ideas. They were a perfect team."

The triumph belonged to Arledge too. It was not just that he had created and supported "Nightline," but that he was never fully satisfied with it. "Nightline" had been a good program under Bill Lord, Arledge thought, but he knew it could be bolder and better. Koppel said, "Roone would be the one who will always say, 'Yeah, sure, so you've run twenty-five miles, I don't care, run another mile,' and you need that. It's more than being a slave driver. It is a product of the fact that he is smart, he is creative, the man is incredibly well informed. His instincts are just terrific. I cannot imagine working for anyone that I would enjoy working for more."

The South Africa week fulfilled Arledge's desire to find ways to set ABC News apart from the competition. "Nightline" in South Africa became an event that was literally created and produced by ABC

News. Certainly it was a legitimate news story, but it was also a dramatic, compelling, made-for-television miniseries that was exclusive to ABC. That satisfied Arledge's competitive drives.

Arledge was also proud of the South Africa programs because they mattered. Like Kaplan, he thought that the programs could help some South Africans see that blacks were entitled to a more just society. Arledge had become fascinated by South Africa, and he liked the idea that his news division had played a part in its history. Since his early days in Sports, he'd thought about television in global terms; he'd been proud when, at the height of the cold war, "Wide World" broadcast U.S.-Soviet track meets that showed that the two nations could compete peacefully on the playing field. Now he felt good again, about linking black and white South Africa and broadcasting the results into millions of living rooms. This was Arledge's altruistic side, which few saw, but which drove him to do important stories. This was also the side of him that liked being a player; he could come home and discuss South Africa with Henry Kissinger or the Kennedys. No one could fail to be impressed, he thought. He hoped the men from Cap Cities had been watching.

It had always been one of Arledge's peeves: the people he worked for didn't watch enough television. They were never home to see "World News Tonight." And few stayed up for "Nightline," as he did. "People should know you're watching," he said. "It's a criticism I have of a lot of the top management." He couldn't understand it. How could people running a network measure success if not by watching the programs on the air? How could they judge him if they didn't watch ABC News? That was the bottom line for Arledge — programming. Put on successful programs, and from there all good things would flow — prestige, ratings, and profits.

The Capital Cities people, as it happened, did watch news when they could. Occasionally, they stayed up for "Nightline," and they would call to praise a show they liked. But Murphy and Burke were fundamentally managers, not programmers. They knew how to run companies; they knew how to do deals; and they especially knew how to control costs. Their bottom line was performance for the shareholders, which, over the years, they delivered: a share of Capital Cities stock bought in 1974 for $18 was worth $183 at the time of the ABC takeover. Wall Street loved Cap Cities — the company's stock traded at 18 to 20 times earnings, well above the industry average.

The corporate philosophy at Capital Cities was simple. Murphy and Burke believed in rigorous budgeting and decentralized control. Each year, they required the executives who managed their TV stations and newspapers to justify every nickel they planned to spend. Then the general managers and publishers were left alone to run their enterprises. Larry Pollock, who ran Cap Cities' TV station in Philadelphia, said of Murphy and Burke, "They haven't been here in two or three years, but they know exactly what's going on." They could afford to take a hands-off approach because WPVI-TV, their station, had a staff of just 196, versus 284 at the CBS affiliate in Philadelphia and 290 at the station owned by NBC. What's more, WPVI's news dominated the market.

The contrast between Capital Cities and the networks was even more dramatic at the top levels. Cap Cities ran its empire of seven TV stations, twelve radio stations, fifty-four cable TV systems, ten daily newspapers, thirty-six weekly newspapers, and thirty-six trade publications with a corporate staff of about thirty people. Murphy boasted that the corporate office had no legal department, personnel office, or public relations staff. "The New York office doesn't make money. We just spend money," he would say. ABC had about four hundred people on its corporate staff, thanks largely to Pierce, who had added layers of bureaucracy over the years.

While Murphy and Burke could be close-fisted and tough — Cap Cities was known in the newspaper industry not for the quality of its papers but for its hardheaded attitude toward unions — they were also decent, public-spirited men, who gave generously of their time and money to charities. Both were strict Catholics, and they approached their jobs with a moralistic sense of right and wrong. They valued honesty, loyalty, modesty, and family, as well as frugality. And they had zero tolerance for deceit. Writing in the trade magazine *Channels of Communication*, reporter L. J. Davis observed, "They had a hard Catholic edge beneath the easy geniality — the ruler in the hand of the nun."

Tall, balding, and gregarious, the Brooklyn-born Murphy was the son of a New York State supreme court judge who had inherited the family gift for politicking. His style was informal — "Hi pal" was the way he greeted business associates — but he was a shrewd judge of character and a savvy negotiator equipped with common sense and a Harvard MBA. Murphy's television career had begun modestly, as the first employee of Cap Cities' tiny UHF station in Albany. "What I learned," he said, "was how few people you really needed to keep things running." He moved to headquarters in New York in 1960 and patiently built the company into a media giant, albeit one with a low public profile.

If Murphy was "Mr. Outside," the deal-maker who concentrated on acquisitions and strategy, Dan Burke was "Mr. Inside," the stickler for detail who ran the company — and would oversee ABC News — with an evangelical commitment to eliminating waste. He grew up in a small town outside Albany, in a family of high achievers; his mother, an extremely intelligent and demanding woman, assigned her kids stories to read each day in the *New York Times,* which were discussed over dinner. Burke went to the University of Vermont, then served as a Marine officer in Korea, an experience that matured him before he followed his older brother, James, to Harvard Business School. James, who would go on to become CEO of Johnson & Johnson, was a friend and classmate of Tom Murphy. In 1960, Murphy hired Dan Burke, then a rising young executive at General Foods, to run the Albany station.

That began a collaboration and friendship that would span more than thirty years. Of the pair, Burke was the more reserved, the more focused, and the more analytical. There was no pretense about either man; nor did they care about getting credit for themselves. "Dan is so secure and self-confident that he can be the caretaker of other people's ego needs," said an admirer. Their pictures did not appear until the last page of the Cap Cities annual report.

Cap Cities' TV stations were known for their hefty profit margins and their commitment to news. "We've always recognized that the station that was number one in local news was number one in town," Murphy said. He liked to remind people that Lowell Thomas, the longtime CBS newsman, had been a founder of Cap Cities.

This heartened Arledge. He realized that ABC News could benefit from fresh ideas and perhaps even from some belt tightening. But his primary instinct was to find ways to cement his hold over the division. To that end, Arledge appointed a five-member commission to study the operations of ABC News. With Cap Cities on the horizon, the study commission would help ensure that he, and not the new owners, would decide how the operation would be run.

"Nobody is going to come in here and tell us what to do with this news organization," Arledge told his staff at a management retreat after the merger announcement. "But we can control our own destiny only if we are a well-run, well-managed organization." Bob Siegenthaler, the veteran producer who had become vice president for news practices, was named to chair the commission. "We looked at the entire division from the ground up, bureau by bureau, show by show. It was pretty thorough," Siegenthaler said.

They found a culture spawned by affluence — one that Arledge had fostered. His first commandment was to cover the story at any cost. Bob Murphy, the executive who ran the assignment desk, which deployed correspondents and crews around the world, said, "If there was any pressure, it was to stay on the air as long as was necessary, with as much information as possible, and do whatever you have to do to be the best. There was never any second-guessing when you did too much. When we got criticism, it was always, why didn't you do more." Budgets were honored more in the breach than in the observance. "Everybody understood that the budget was just a piece of paper," an executive producer said. During the years of expansion, the ABC News budget had mushroomed from $55 million in 1977 to $300 million in 1985.

Excesses abounded. A "Nightline" producer doing a story about college sports flew with a crew to Alaska to interview author James Michener, who had written about the subject. "That's five thousand dollars for one sound bite — literally a fifteen-second clip in a spot," the producer said. Another time, "Nightline" sent producers, engineers, and crews to Nepal to follow a Canadian expedition to the top of Mount Everest, renting helicopters from the Royal Nepalese Air Force and setting up microwave links using portable generators to get a live shot — all at enormous cost, tens of thousands of dollars, had anyone been counting. Petty abuses were tolerated. One executive producer accounted for unexpected spending by citing the Fingerman Poll in his budget reports; he'd called a neighbor named Fingerman to get her reaction to his show. Filling out an expense form, correspondent Hughes Rudd once wrote that he'd traveled to interview "an E. Braun about her rumored marriage to an A. Hitler."

The Siegenthaler Commission delivered the message that ABC News could no longer spend money recklessly. "For the first time, there were clearly going to be limits to what we could do," Siegenthaler said. The commission found some relatively painless cost-control measures, such as ordering fewer hours of satellite time, which were put into effect. The panel also recommended staff reductions, which Arledge promised to review.

But commission members had wanted to go further. One proposal, to consolidate the staffs of the weekday and weekend "World News" operations, was nixed by Arledge, although it would have saved at least $500,000 a year. Arledge thought the money was worth spending so that the weekend newscasts could maintain their own identity. "I wanted the weekend to remain a place where you could develop people and fresh approaches to things," he said.

The commission also called for the individual shows to give up staff and autonomy to the assignment desk, which could deploy people to stories as needed. Siegenthaler thought that ABC News had become balkanized, with people thinking of themselves as working for "World News" or "Nightline" rather than for ABC News; even their sign-offs — "This is James Walker for 'Nightline' " — reinforced the idea that each show was an independent duchy. Sometimes two or three programs competed, assigning producers and crews to the same event. This was wasteful.

But Siegenthaler's plan to enlarge the pool of people who could move freely among shows "was greeted like a skunk at the wedding reception," he said. Executive producers like Av Westin and Rick Kaplan refused to give up staff, saying they wanted their shows to retain their own casts and styles. Arledge backed them up — he was a producer at heart, and he was reluctant to do anything that might blur the distinctions between programs, endanger quality, or upset his executive producers or anchors.

In retrospect, Siegenthaler and other commission members thought their work should have had more impact. "It started the thinking, but it was ineffective," Siegenthaler said. Some felt stymied by Arledge. "We made an honest attempt to look at what was going on," said an insider. "I don't think in the final analysis that he made an honest attempt to make changes." The report itself was interred. Cap Cities never saw it, and after a time Siegenthaler could not even locate his own copy; he joked that he felt like Dan Ellsberg's psychiatrist.

In the meantime, the rest of ABC bustled with preparations for the merger, which would take effect in January 1986. Like Arledge, Fred Pierce tried to recast himself as a cost-conscious executive; he cut the workforce and made speeches about fiscal responsibility.

But Pierce's problems went well beyond the bloated payroll. ABC's prime-time lineup was collapsing, and all the broadcast networks were losing viewers to cable and independent stations. By 1985, the three-network share of the audience — the percentage of viewers watching ABC, CBS, and NBC on any given night — had slid to 77 percent, from 92 percent a decade earlier. For the first time since 1971, the year tobacco advertising was banned on television, commercial revenues for the Big Three fell from the year before. As the network mired in third place, ABC took the worst hit.

In the meantime, Pierce had made huge programming commitments for the years ahead: $650 million for five years of "Monday Night Football," $309 million for the 1988 Winter Olympics in Calgary, $90 million for the miniseries "War and Remembrance." All were based on the assumption that the demand for network advertising would grow, as it always had. That was now demonstrably false.

ABC was caught in a terrible squeeze — its costs were rising as its revenues fell.

No one was more troubled by the numbers than Dan Burke. As he went over the books, he figured that ABC — which was earning about $100 million in profits in 1985 — stood to lose up to $150 million in 1986. "It was frightening," Burke recalled. What bothered him, as much as anything, was his sense that there were no alarm bells ringing inside the old ABC.

Murphy and Burke decided to sound their own alarm. Just before Christmas, they stopped Arledge and Pierce from buying the rights to yet another sports property, the NBA. The deal looked too risky to Cap Cities, although not to Arledge. "We would have made a considerable profit, and they absolutely would not go for it," he complained.

But Cap Cities had lost faith in Fred Pierce. They didn't think he realized how tough the road ahead was going to be. Murphy and Burke scaled back his authority, removing ABC's cable interests and TV stations from his control so that he could focus on the network and its woes. "They wanted to change the ground rules," Pierce said. He took a skiing vacation, pondered his options, and quit.

Roone Arledge had lost his most valuable ally at ABC.

Next he lost the presidency of ABC Sports.

Cap Cities broke the news to him on a Friday, the day corporate executives often deliver bad tidings. Murphy and Burke were there, with John Sias, a veteran Cap Cities executive they had named to replace Fred Pierce as head of the network. They couched their edict in the most favorable terms — News was so important, they said, that it needed Arledge's full-time attention. "News is absolutely vital," Burke keep saying. The meeting lasted three hours, and afterward, Murphy described it as "pretty tough."

It was more than tough for Arledge. He had run ABC Sports for nearly twenty-five years. It was his creation, his organization, his pride. ABC Sports had been a part of his life — "Wide World," "Monday Night Football," the thrill of the Olympics, the trips to the Super

Bowl, and when he could get away, the British Open. Some of his best memories of life at the network were tied up with Sports, and now it was gone, in a flash, taken away by people who hardly knew him.

The Cap Cities men were unsentimental about Sports. They saw a division that was bleeding buckets of red ink and sorely in need of more attention than it was getting from Arledge. Sports was no longer the cash cow; so much sports was being broadcast in so many places that the advertising market for sports had crashed, even as rights fees grew. "I was thunderstruck to find the size of the fiscal problems we were confronting in Sports," said Dan Burke. "It just was going to be a nightmare. And I had no idea it was possible to lose money on 'Monday Night Football.' " Those were valid concerns, Arledge thought, but he felt harshly and prematurely judged. He wasn't to blame for the losses, he insisted. "If I had any quarrel with Cap Cities," Arledge said, "it's that there's always a history to these things — unless you assume that the people just had no clue what they were doing." The Cap Cities people never even talked to him about the losses in Sports.

That was what really hurt — the snub. Arledge had been willing to give up day-to-day management of ABC Sports — he'd offered the job to Peter Ueberroth after the Olympics, and then to his deputy, David Burke — but he'd wanted to pick his successor and to keep a hand in Sports. Now Murphy and Burke had stripped him of his authority, named their own man, and, to rub salt in the wound, they asked him to cut his salary, which had climbed to $2 million.

Arledge refused. It was left to his agent, Ron Konecky, to come up with a face-saving deal that preserved Arledge's pay package and his role as executive producer of the 1988 Olympics in Calgary. Cap Cities also gave Arledge a title — group president, ABC News and Sports — that made it sound as if he retained some influence over Sports.

Just the reverse was true. Dennis Swanson, the Sports president installed by Cap Cities, disdained Arledge. Swanson was a gruff, no-nonsense ex-Marine, a Big Ten guy who had made money for ABC by doing the unglamorous work of running TV stations — just like the men from Cap Cities. Swanson thought that Arledge and his Ivy League crew in Sports did not know the value of a dollar or the meaning of an honest day's work, and he said so at his first meeting with the Sports staff. "If Roone were Jimmy Carter's adviser," Swanson said, in a line that did not sound spontaneous, "the U.S. would surely have gotten all its hostages out of Iran, because Roone always travels with two or three too many helicopters." His point was made: the Arledge era in Sports was over.

Arledge was starting to understand what it felt like to be on the receiving end of an unfriendly takeover. Unlike in 1977, when he'd shaken up ABC News, he was now the one being viewed with suspicion by newcomers; he was being held accountable for all the failures of the past; he was being made to feel like an outsider in his own company. Tensions rose as the Cap Cities and ABC people struggled to adapt to new roles. "Cap Cities was horribly insecure. And we were insecure in this new setting," recalled David Burke. "The question being asked on both sides was: Who are these assholes?" Arledge felt even more edgy after his first extended encounter with Cap Cities, at a retreat in Phoenix soon after the takeover.

About 160 senior managers of the two companies were invited to the three days of meetings, which opened with a twenty-minute film about the merger produced by a Cap Cities executive and narrated by Peter Jennings. The intent was humorous — a sound bite from Vice President George Bush, Dan Burke's friend and neighbor in Maine, predicting success for the two companies, was followed by a clip of two trains racing into a head-on collision. But Arledge found it hard to laugh when, after Jennings noted that "ABC over the years has attracted executives of talent and uncommon modesty," Arledge appeared on-screen saying, "I can certainly go along with that!" At another point, a Carnac-the-Magnificent look-alike said, "The answer is: St. Thomas Aquinas, Abraham Lincoln, and Roone Arledge. The question is: Who are three people who never return your phone calls?" While the film poked fun at Cap Cities' executives too, Arledge took his reputation so seriously that the barbs stung. He didn't want to be known as the executive with the big ego who did not return phone calls.

Back in New York, there was more unpleasant news. Cap Cities shut the executive dining rooms, eliminated first-class travel, trimmed mail deliveries, and gave up the luxury penthouse at the Plaza, the place where Arledge had wooed Rather and Brokaw. "Limousine rentals will not be reimbursed unless approval is obtained from John B. Sias, President, ABC," read one internal memo, although Arledge was spared the indignity of taxicabs — he retained his Jaguar and his longtime chauffeur, an easygoing Chilean-American named Orlando Castillo. Orlando had worked for him since a night in the late 1970s when he'd waited outside Yankee Stadium for Arledge long after all the other chauffeurs had gone home, driven away by neighborhood hoodlums. Arledge, who had stayed late to socialize with George Steinbrenner and Governor Hugh Carey, was appreciative. "From now on," Arledge had said, on their way downtown, "whenever I go anywhere, I want you to take me." He didn't care what Cap Cities thought — he was not going to give up Orlando.

But Arledge was willing, albeit reluctantly, to reduce the size of ABC News. Guided by the findings of the Siegenthaler Commission, he decreed the elimination of about 75 positions from the 1,100-person news division. The "Close-Up" unit was hit hardest, losing about a dozen people and cutting back production of documentaries from twelve to fifteen hours a year to half that much. The layoffs were accomplished humanely and created none of the controversy that was produced by layoffs at CBS and NBC.

Instead, Arledge tried to turn the layoffs to his advantage, to show that he had shed his extravagant ways. "A lot of people at all three networks have grown up expecting the golden ring to always be there, and that's not a fact in this economy," he told a reporter. In the *New York Times,* Arledge's supposed metamorphosis was reported under the headline "The Spendthrift Turns Miser at ABC."

It wasn't that simple. Publicly, Arledge put the best face on things. "It's painful to make cuts. It's painful to go through the process we've all been through. And it's very, very time-consuming," he would say. "But it's like any kind of surgery. Clearly you come out of it stronger than when you went in." Privately, Arledge saw the Cap Cities people as intruders, and he resented their presence, but he and his top aides could not agree on a strategy for dealing with Murphy, Burke, and Sias.

David Burke, Arledge's closest aide, took a hard-line approach. The Cap Cities people were arrogant, he thought, and they had to be disabused of the idea that they were going to straighten out ABC News. "They had an opinion about everything," Burke said. "There had to be something to stop that train, because they were coming at us at a hundred miles an hour." Burke threw himself in the way. "It's an Irish trait," he said. "If you're new to my neighborhood, the first thing I'll do is scare the shit out of you. Then we'll become friends."

By contrast, Arledge was a Fabian — like the Roman general Fabius Maximus, he fought by using the tactics of delay or harassment, in order to avoid a pitched battle. His style was to do business as usual, to charm the Cap Cities people when they came around, and to ignore what they had to say. His hope was that, once they could be made to understand what he had built at ABC News, they would leave him alone to do as he pleased.

As David Burke explained it, "Roone's first reaction when he is threatened is to try to become your friend. Then he'll screw you. First, I'll screw you. Then I'll become your friend."

The Cap Cities men did little to reassure Arledge. The one who most got under his skin was Sias, fifty-eight, a former publishing executive who, by his own admission, knew little about television. He was, however, absolutely loyal to Murphy and Burke, a zealous cost cutter, and a practical jokester. One morning at 8:30, well before Arledge's usual arrival time, Sias had climbed on a desk in the newsroom and bellowed, "Where's Roone?" Arledge hated it.

In the meantime, Arledge's most concrete response to the new regime was a characteristic one — rather than shrink ABC News, he would produce more programs. He was willing, and even eager, to generate more profits for Cap Cities, but he wanted to do so his way, by driving up revenues, rather than by holding down costs. A news division, in that sense, operates like a factory: it can become more productive by increasing output as well as by trimming costs.

Arledge's first project was a nostalgia-driven program called "Our World." Cap Cities had requested the show after Dan Burke had learned that an hour-long news program could be produced for about $400,000 a week, roughly half of what ABC paid to license an hour of entertainment programming from Hollywood. The network needed a low-cost, low-risk vehicle for Thursdays at eight, a time period dominated by NBC's blockbuster "Cosby" show.

Av Westin was put in charge of developing the show. With "20/20" producer Pete Simmons, Westin had produced a popular documentary history of postwar America called "45/85," which used archival footage, music, and eyewitness accounts to tell the story of the postwar era in a lively three-hour news special. Now Westin and Simmons went to work on individual hour-long shows pegged to recent events — the fall of 1956, say, when the Soviet Union crushed an uprising in Hungary, or 1962, the year of the Cuban missile crisis. They hired a pair of literate anchors, Linda Ellerbee, who happened to be Simmons's ex-girlfriend, and sports reporter Ray Gandolf, both of whom brought a touch of class to the effort. "Our World" premiered in September 1986 and was greeted with favorable reviews and predictably low ratings.

Arledge never much cared for the show. His role was limited — he screened the premiere, which was about the summer of 1969 and, in a typical reaction, wanted to know why the producers had failed to obtain an interview with astronaut Neil Armstrong, who had not talked publicly in years. It was hard for Arledge to get excited about a program that, unlike "20/20," was envisioned as a stopgap measure, not a long-term prime-time performer. Beyond that, he didn't like the way Cap Cities had positioned the show. "John Sias announced to the affiliates and everyone else, before it even got on the air, that it was just filler, and so it was treated that way by everybody," Arledge said. Telling people a show was cheap was no way to sell it, he complained. Nor did he like competing against "Cosby" — he told TV critics that launching "Our World" felt "like a Japanese kamikaze pilot taking off on a mission."

After "Our World," Arledge created two more new programs: "Business World," a half-hour Sunday morning show anchored by Sander Vanocur, and "The Health Show," a half hour with Kathleen Sullivan as host, targeted for Saturday or Sunday. Both programs struggled to get cleared because local affiliates did not want to displace money-making syndicated or religious programs to make room for them. With its audience of upscale men, "Business World" made a modest profit. But "The Health Show" never won the stations over, and it was canceled after Sullivan left ABC.

Arledge soon realized that there was no way the new shows would make enough money to shield ABC News from the scrutiny of Cap Cities. While Cap Cities preached decentralization, the new owners also demanded accountability — so Dan Burke, as president of the corporation, joined John Sias for the first Cap Cities review of the ABC News budget in September 1986. This came after the layoffs imposed by Arledge, after the closing of control rooms, and after a host of small but symbolic measures — "20/20" staffers, for example, were told that ABC would no longer pay for everyone to go to dinner at a Chinese restaurant on Thursdays before taping, an inexpensive, morale-boosting tradition known as the "Shun Lee Shuffle." In terms of budget cutting, Arledge had gone as far as he wanted to go.

The ABC News people, led by Irwin Weiner, had prepared for the sessions, arriving with loose-leaf books detailing the division's costs. They weren't sure what to expect, but they thought they had nothing to apologize for — they put on good programming and they were a profit center for the corporation. By its own accounting, ABC News had made $55 million in 1985, a fact in which Arledge took great pride.

That was not enough to satisfy Dan Burke. Burke was responsible for all of ABC, which was projected to lose $100 million in 1986. And while seventy-five people had been let go by ABC News, roughly two thousand jobs had been eliminated by the rest of the company since the takeover.

Dan Burke devoted three full days to the ABC News budget review, subjecting Arledge and his aides to an intense grilling. The Cap Cities people let nothing go unchallenged. Do you really have to have bureaus in Chicago *and* St. Louis? Why do you need magazine subscriptions in Dallas? Aren't 110 correspondents excessive, since so few get on the air each night?

They uncovered oddities — a chef in the Paris bureau. The fact was that a woman laid out bread, cheese, and fruit for lunch and occasionally served a hot meal; she was soon let go.

The Cap Cities people also couldn't believe the salaries — up to $300,000 for executive producers, up to $125,000 for producers, and wildly varying amounts for the correspondents. Those at the top of the scale, like Donaldson and Salinger, earned more than $500,000 a year, a lot more than Cap Cities paid most of its executives. Even more bothersome was that second-rank people, who rarely appeared on "World News," were paid more than $100,000. Surely competent reporters could be found who would work for less.

Why, Sias would remark, CNN puts on news twenty-four hours a day for half of what it cost to run ABC News. It didn't make sense.

Grudgingly, Arledge cut deeper. He agreed to spend less money on sets. Fewer people traveled to special events. And when reporters Richard Threlkeld and his wife, Betsy Aaron, produced a three-hour documentary called "After the Sexual Revolution," they did most of their interviews around New York, to save money.

The budget sessions left everyone disheartened.

Arledge felt that he had been put through a wringer — it wasn't his job, he thought, to keep track of subscriptions in Dallas or to worry about whether "20/20" could do without a producer or a tape editor. The Cap Cities people, he believed, paid far too much attention to costs and not enough to programs and profits. They failed to see that a successful program such as "Nightline" could generate more profits than any cost-cutting campaign. Arledge felt that his accomplishments had not been recognized and that he was being penalized because of his reputation as a big spender.

"For ABC, first in sports and then in news, to become what we have become, it was necessary for us to be almost ostentatiously competitive," Arledge explained. "In doing that, you create an image of yourself.

"That image can work two ways," he said. "It can work in a way where a major personality from another network or, in the case of sports, a U.S. Open or the Kentucky Derby is willing to take a chance on coming to a sub-par network because they believe in you personally, and you get a reputation for being willing to spend top dollar. That's the good part.

"The bad part," he went on, "is that the reputation stays with you and even when you are saving money, when you're operating twice as efficiently as anybody else, when you're the first news division ever to make a profit, you still have that image. Once you get a certain reputation, any rumor, any gossip is taken with more credibility than it is if your reputation is as the penny-pincher who is in third place all the time — but pinching pennies."

Dan Burke did not buy it. It seemed to him that Arledge was terribly defensive. The ABC News executives may have thought they were ready for the budget review, but Burke was unimpressed. "They didn't radiate a sense of control of their circumstances," he said. "This had not been part of their culture."

That was understandable. No one at the old ABC had been taught to manage costs. But Dan Burke was troubled because Arledge did not seem committed to change, while Burke believed that radical change was needed. With audiences and advertisers turning away, Cap Cities wanted to cut $150 million from the ABC network budget; this was a tall order, requiring a revolution in the corporate culture from top to bottom. To his dismay, Burke sensed resistance from Arledge. And it was true that he was affected by Arledge's history; he'd spent time in sports, and he'd come to believe that ABC Sports had overpaid for events and then lost money on them because the budgeting had been cynical. "Sometimes when they bought major sports, the projections of revenues were doctored to make them look good," Burke said. This was a serious matter, he thought, a question of trust.

"We spent eighteen months at ABC, with very little confidence in any of the numbers," Burke said. "Predictably, some people from ABC bought in faster than others. News bought in quite slowly." Burke didn't care that CBS News and NBC News were losing money, and he rejected the idea that ABC News should be exempt from close scrutiny because it was profitable. "That violates every tenet and principle that I believe in, in a business sense," he said. Even in good times, Burke refused to tolerate waste. "Those are the times to be most vigilant, most alert about it," he would say. Burke saw himself, above all, as the representative of the stockholders, the owners of the company. No one had the right to waste their money.

In theory, Arledge agreed. In practice, the problem was that no one could define waste. Was it waste to maintain a news bureau in Rome, which might contribute only a few stories each month to "World News Tonight"? Was it waste to buy a state-of-the-art graphics generator, to enliven news stories on the economy? Was it waste to pay people more than they might command on the market, to show they were appreciated? These were difficult, subjective judgments that Arledge felt were best left to him. Dan Burke believed that, at least, the questions needed to be asked.

And there were some things that, in Burke's eyes, were simply indefensible. He told a story he'd heard from Peter Ueberroth, about how at an organizational meeting for the Los Angeles Olympics, three ABC executives, among them Arledge and Pierce, arrived in three stretch limousines, two gray and one white. Ueberroth, the story went, found it peculiar, but he thought it even more ridiculous when he realized that they'd come from the same hotel. "That's how you expressed yourself, in some cases, here," Burke said. "Don't you think that's wasteful? It's not criminal, but it comes pretty close." The counterargument, of course, was that ABC Sports made a vast profit on the 1984 Olympics; whatever the outlay for limousines, the Games were a creative and commercial triumph. When Arledge heard the three-limousine story, he denied it but said, "The fact of the matter is the Los Angeles Olympics were probably the single most successful event, along with 'Roots,' that ABC has ever done."

But Burke was adamant. "If they made seventy-five million dollars, and the cars cost three hundred a day each, I would argue that one car was okay and they could have squeezed in, and they would have made seventy-five million, six hundred dollars, instead of seventy-five million," he declared.

"There's no defense for it," he concluded.

Chapter Thirteen

POWER PLAYS

Peter JENNINGS could not smoke, so he chewed gum — furiously. Here he was, stuck on the runway at La Guardia in a snowstorm, waiting for the shuttle to get him to Washington. He had a meeting with Vice President Bush, and he was going to be late if the plane didn't take off soon. Being late for important appointments made him crazy. Sitting beside him, his assistant, Gretchen Barbarovic, could feel his tension.

It was January 28, 1986.

Jennings let out a sigh of relief as the plane climbed into the sky. An hour or so later, he arrived at the White House just in time to see Bush and attend a briefing by Donald Regan, the White House chief of staff, about the State of the Union address to be given that night by President Reagan. The speech was routine — by this point, midway through his second term, Reagan was not going to surprise anyone — but Jennings had looked forward to his trip. He liked to get away from the anchor desk, liked to get out of New York, liked to talk to people — not only famous people, like Bush or Regan, but ordinary people, like the driver who'd picked him up at the airport. This was one of Jennings's endearing qualities; after twenty-five years of reporting, he still retained his curiosity and boyish enthusiasm for the news. As Jennings made small talk while awaiting the president, an aide entered the room and handed a note to Don Regan. He read it out loud: "The space shuttle *Challenger* has exploded — details to follow."

Only CNN had been on the air when the *Challenger* exploded at

11:39 A.M. This was the twenty-fifth shuttle flight, and everyone thought the launches had become routine. Still, producer Jeff Gralnick and director Roger Goodman, who were in ABC's Washington bureau for the State of the Union speech, had interrupted their preparations for long enough to watch the lift-off on CNN. "That's really strange looking," someone said, as the shuttle sliced through the bright blue sky. An instant later, Gralnick exclaimed, "Holy shit — it blew up!" Steve Bell, the morning news anchor, was rushed to the anchor desk, while Gralnick commandeered a control room. The speech was forgotten. Now they had a real story to cover.

ABC's coverage began inauspiciously. With nothing to go on but the pictures of the shuttle disappearing into a plume of smoke, Bell suggested that an escape system might have been activated. He was wrong, of course; he had to be wrong, because this shuttle had no ejection seats. But hope had put the words in his mouth. That was the problem with live broadcasting — you had to say something.

Jennings knew enough to be more cautious. "Don't get excited," he would remind himself, when big stories broke. "Be careful — be certain," he'd say. Gralnick, an experienced special events man, was also prudent; he had never forgotten the awful moment when, during ABC's coverage of the assassination attempt on Reagan, Frank Reynolds had reported the death of presidential press secretary James Brady. Afterward, when doubts arose during live coverage, Gralnick would think, We don't want to kill James Brady again.

Strange as it seemed, though, since special events often meant tragedies and disasters, Jennings and Gralnick and Goodman lived for these moments. "The live crisis work for someone who is, by natural instincts, a reporter is the most gratifying aspect of being an anchor," Jennings would say. Gralnick agreed, saying, "Next to sex, there is nothing better than producing live television." Jennings, Gralnick, and Goodman had worked as a unit since 1983 — at the political conventions, on election night, at summit meetings, and through all kinds of crises — and they had become a smooth-functioning team.

As executive producer, Gralnick deployed the troops in the field and presented a menu of choices to Jennings: a correspondent with news, a taped backgrounder, an expert waiting to be interviewed, or the latest developments from the wires. Seated nearby, Goodman directed the cameras and orchestrated pictures and graphics. "We constantly talk to each other, like pilot and co-pilot," Goodman said. On the air, Jennings managed the flow of information; like all good anchors, he had an uncanny ability to deliver the news or conduct an interview while listening to a producer through his earpiece or reading a note passed to him by a researcher crouching nearby, out of camera range. It was Jennings who set the tone and shaped the story. "The newspaper equivalent of live broadcasting is writing roughly ten thousand words or more directly onto the front page," Jennings said. "It is a unique skill. It requires a measure of confidence that when you turn left, right, center, up, down, wherever, that your system is going to work."

The day the *Challenger* exploded, the system worked without a hitch. Gralnick arranged for interviews with the best-informed experts, while Goodman's crew generated graphics at a feverish pace. While Jennings had never covered the space program, it so happened that his producer, Mike Clemente, was the son of a NASA executive and a space buff. For five uninterrupted hours, Jennings skillfully and, it seemed, effortlessly wove the news, interviews, and background information into a coherent narrative with pace and drama — a story line, in Arledge's phrase.

After anchoring an hour-long prime-time special, Jennings prepared to sign off for the night.

"The flags are at half-staff tonight, here in the nation's capital and across the country, and here's why," he said. "The picture is now etched in our minds, but still horrifying: the disastrous end of the twenty-fifth shuttle mission, the sudden death of seven astronauts, America once again reaching for the stars and this time, for the first time, not making it."

He went on to summarize the day's events, providing not only facts but context. He speculated about the role of manned versus unmanned spaceflights. Finally, looking straight at the camera, slowing the pace for emphasis, he wrapped up:

"We invested a large part of our national psyche in the space program. This is a catastrophe, and it will surely set the program back. But America will stay in space. That's where America belongs. I'm Peter Jennings. Thank you for joining us."

The critics approved, as did the viewers. More than six hundred wrote to ABC to praise Jennings. "I felt as if he was consoling each viewer personally," said one. Once again, television had led a nation in mourning — in such times are reputations made.

The *Challenger* disaster helped cement ABC's reputation as the network that best covered breaking news. Jennings, who could be counted on to perform at the top of his game when the pressure was on, was a big reason why. He conveyed authority and sophistication and a low-key sense of urgency — unlike Dan Rather, he never over-heated — and, best of all, he provided understanding. No matter how fast a story unfolded, he remembered the basic questions of journal-ism — who, what, when, where, and how — and so he'd locate events, identify characters, and offer perspective. This was enormously val-uable, and satisfying, to the viewers.

It also pleased Arledge. His own compulsion to explain things meshed with Jennings's approach, as did his love of live television. Invariably, Arledge pushed to get ABC News on the air first and to keep it on longer than anyone else during special events. When TWA Flight 847 was hijacked in June 1985, setting off a sixteen-day hostage crisis during which thirty-nine Americans were held in Beirut, ABC News dominated. Most memorably, correspondent Charles Glass se-cured a tarmac interview with the TWA pilot, John Testrake, who spoke while a hijacker pointed a gun at his head — an image that made the covers of *Time* and *Newsweek*. The following year, viewers watched Jennings, Barbara Walters, and David Brinkley anchor the spectacular Liberty Weekend celebration — an event literally owned by ABC, which bought the broadcast rights from the group that restored the Statue of Liberty.

Taken together, these events — along with such milestones as the Iranian hostage crisis — established ABC News as the place to turn to in a crisis. The television critics said so, and when big news broke, viewers tended to migrate toward ABC News. This, of course, had been one of Arledge's first goals, going back to Son of Sam and Sadat-Begin in 1977. Reaching that goal was a major accomplishment, one that in the history of network news often presaged a shift of deeper loyalties. First NBC and then CBS established itself as the network that best covered big stories; dominance of the evening news com-petition followed.

That didn't happen at ABC — not for a while. The reason was that, unhappily for Arledge and his news division, the teamwork that was so crucial to ABC's success in special events never became part of the everyday culture of ABC News. While, in a crisis, everyone pulled together — Arledge, Jennings, Gralnick, Goodman, and the entire corps of ABC producers and correspondents — under normal circumstances, the sense of shared mission was not nearly as strong.

This was partly because Arledge was so removed from the rank and file that people's loyalties flowed to an executive producer, to an anchor, or to a program, not to Arledge or to ABC News. More important, Arledge did little to promote cooperation; he thought that pitting his shows, his executives, and his anchors against one another would make everyone work harder. It probably did, but the culture of every man for himself also brought about a series of power struggles inside ABC News, which only intensified after the arrival of Capital Cities. Arledge himself fought with Cap Cities, even as one of his senior executives schemed to unseat him. All the while, an ugly battle for control was being fought around the rim of "World News Tonight."

Back when Bill Lord was installed as the executive producer of "World News Tonight" in 1984, replacing the ineffectual Bob Frye, there was ample reason to believe that he was the right man for the job. His record at "Nightline" was exemplary, and he was a strong, decisive producer — the perfect antidote to Frye. He was ready to take command of the broadcast.

That turned out to be exactly the problem with Bill Lord. Lord believed that he had been handed a failing broadcast that needed an overhaul. He thought that the responsibility for the mushiness of "World News" belonged not just to Frye but also to Jennings. And his mission, he thought, was not only to remake the show but to rein in his anchorman — a view that he communicated bluntly to all, including Jennings. While others advised Lord that it was foolhardy to take on his anchorman, he would not, or could not, stop himself.

To some extent, Lord's own insecurities drove him to assert control. Patiently, he'd climbed the career ladder at the old ABC News to become a vice president, only to be exiled by Arledge; then he'd been forced to work his way up all over again. "When that happens, there's a defensiveness associated with that, like you never know when you're going to be unmasked," said one of Lord's allies. "You are never comfortable with your authority or with your standing. Bill's guard was up as soon as he came here."

Lord also did not think much of Jennings. While Lord had labored for all he had accomplished at ABC News, he thought Jennings had coasted — the onetime boy anchor, Lord felt, had been blessed with good looks and a sophisticated on-air persona that hid his defects. Jennings, he thought, was indecisive. He was not a good writer and his news judgment was suspect.

"Bill Lord perceived Peter as a prissy outsider, a little bit arrogant, and overintellectual," said a "World News" producer. "He perceived that Peter looked down on the rest of the world and on Bill Lord in particular." Jennings, as it happened, had begun with high hopes that

Lord was the answer for "World News," but he was soon disappointed.

At first, they argued about the news. Lord was a hard-news man; Jennings preferred issues and trends. Lord favored stories from Washington, where he'd worked; Jennings's head was still overseas. Lord was always conscious of pictures; Jennings thought that if a story was worth telling, they should find a way to tell it. Such arguments are common between anchors and executive producers, and ordinarily, compromises are worked out.

Between Lord and Jennings, however, the arguments brought only more arguments — about who was in charge of the show.

"God, he and I were just wrestling for the agenda all the time," Jennings recalled. "It's sad. It was sad for both of us, and much more for the people around us. I don't think I was mature enough to know how widespread the impact was."

Lord was of the old school. He believed that the institution vested its authority in the executive producer, not the anchorman, particularly a failing anchorman. But Jennings saw himself as equal partner in the broadcast. His own ego needs meant that he had to prove his value as a journalist; nothing bothered him more than to be treated as a newsreader, which was how he was treated by Lord.

Lord could be cold, abrupt, and nasty. A prominent correspondent thought he was "a snake . . . who took some delight in hurting people." His mean side had not surfaced much at "Nightline," but at "World News" he directed his venom at Jennings. In the control room during the newscast, Lord would refer to Jennings as a pretty boy or as a jerk. "Bill became a mutterer. That was a very uncomfortable time," said Charlie Heinz, the "World News" director.

Lord could not pass up a chance to put down Jennings. When six-year-old Elizabeth Jennings would call her father late in the day, as everyone rushed to get the show on the air, Jennings would take the call, if only to say, "Daddy's got to go now, he's going to be on TV." Lord would snicker or shake his head in disgust.

All this raised the temperature around the rim. The "World News" staff split into camps, Lord's people and Peter's people, and a few who tried to work both sides of the fence. Correspondents played one off against the other or, if they were unlucky, got caught in the crossfire. "It got pretty ugly at the end," said producer Stu Schutzman. "You can't have an executive producer and an anchor at each other's throats."

Jennings suffered with everyone else. "It utterly unnerved Peter after a while," said correspondent John Martin. "What could be worse for a show than to have an anchor be uneasy?" Jennings, after all, had to perform every night on camera, and frequently he arrived on the set distracted or agitated. He'd calm himself to do the show, but afterward an unkind word from Lord could unravel him. "God knows I went home like that a lot at night," Jennings said. "I hated it. I hated it. I hated it."

He did not, however, do much about it. Once, hoping to hash out their differences, Jennings arranged a lunch with Lord, and they talked about the need for mutual respect and loyalty. Lord made all the right noises, and Jennings naively figured that things would get better; they did not.

But Jennings would not go the next step and push to get rid of Lord. "I'm very self-conscious about power," he said later. "Maybe I was always afraid to test it." What if Arledge stood by Lord? What if there was a plan to replace him with Koppel? With "World News" running third in the ratings, Jennings did not feel secure enough to deliver a him-or-me ultimatum to Arledge. "I would never say that because they might say, 'Fine, it's you, goodbye,' " he said.

They also might have fired Lord, which, ironically, would also have upset Jennings. It was important to Jennings to remain pure, to remain a journalist, and not become the proverbial eight-hundred-pound gorilla who can sit anywhere he wants. His father, the idealist whose career had been destroyed by commercial television, remained a model, and Jennings often said he preferred being an employee to being the boss. In those days, he didn't want to be seen throwing his weight around.

So Jennings did nothing, although he was bothered not only by Lord but by Arledge's indifference. "It would have been nice if someone had rescued us all from that," Jennings said years later. At the time, he'd wondered — why had Roone let it go on for so long?

To some degree, Arledge was out of touch. He rarely left his office and barely knew the staff people who were most affected by the battles between Lord and Jennings. So he had no firsthand information about the tensions at "World News." Arledge recalled, "You'd hear these stories that they didn't get along, and I never really believed them. I still have a blind spot on that."

On another level, Arledge did not want to admit failure. Jennings was a gifted anchor. Lord was a good producer. They could work it out, he thought. Never did he consider replacing Jennings, and his instinct was to support his producers. An ABC correspondent said,

"In their heart of hearts, all producers stand together against all correspondents. Roone's a producer. Correspondents belong in the kindergarten, in the sandbox. They're infantile. They're not really serious. And they get paid all that goddamn money and they are the ones who have the glory." Arledge was especially hesitant to remove Lord, whom he'd demoted before. He never forgot that he'd taken Lord's office when he'd come to News. "I always felt a little guilty about Bill Lord," Arledge said. "I used to think to myself every time he comes to see me, I must remember that this was his office, and there's got to be some lingering feeling there. I think I tended to go overboard in excusing some of his behavior."

This, however, did not fully explain Arledge's behavior toward Jennings. Even knowing that his top anchor was getting no help from Lord, Arledge did not step up to offer support; he was disinclined to stroke or reassure people. To the contrary, Arledge tended to exploit the vulnerability of his anchors and executive producers, to prod them to do better. Inside ABC, his critics felt that this was the dynamic at work while Jennings suffered under Lord — that, at some level, Arledge did not mind seeing his anchor and executive producer at odds. Insecurity, he thought, made everyone work harder — and the struggles around him cemented his own position as the ultimate authority at ABC News.

Besides, while Lord and Jennings and the rest of the staff at "World News" were unhappy, the program was not in crisis. Rather and Brokaw had better household ratings, but Jennings was making gains in the big-city markets and among upscale viewers. Among the top twenty-five markets, "World News" was the number one rated evening newscast.

Still, Arledge saw a need for change in the program, if not yet in the executive producer. Ever since ABC dropped the three-anchor format in 1983, all the network evening newscasts looked alike. Each had a middle-aged male anchor who introduced similar stories, which appeared in roughly the same order on any given day. What was worrisome, by the mid-1980s, was that many of the stories already had been shown on local stations or CNN. This was the problem that had driven Bob Frye to experiment with longer stories, offering depth and perspective, during his stint at "World News." Since then, Lord had returned to a more conventional hard-news format. Seeking new ideas, Arledge convened a daylong meeting of his senior staff and executive producers to reexamine "World News Tonight."

They met for five hours on January 13, 1987, at New York's posh

Lowell Hotel. Arledge began by challenging everyone to rethink the newscast, with no rule other than to exploit whatever advantages ABC had over other news outlets, particularly local stations. Quickly, they agreed on a few things that set them apart — they had a world-class anchor in Jennings, a corps of talented correspondents, and a world-wide news-gathering organization, all of which enabled ABC not only to report the news but to explain what it meant to viewers. That was fine, but it was not clear how to do that in twenty-two minutes and still tell the day's news.

Dorrance Smith, the "Brinkley" producer, came up with a radical proposal recommending that "World News," as the flagship broadcast, should draw on the talents of all the best people at ABC News. Smith wanted to make room on the broadcast for interviews by Barbara Walters, discussions moderated by Ted Koppel, and commentary by David Brinkley. By using all its stars, Smith said, ABC would set itself apart from the locals and the other networks.

Arledge agreed but saw an obvious problem. "It was a terrific idea," he said. "But it was vague, and Peter, who in those days was so insecure . . . No way did Peter want to preside over a program with all these people."

The other idea that impressed Arledge came from Paul Friedman, a former NBC executive who recently had been hired to run the bulk of ABC's overseas operations from London. Friedman had spent his six-hour plane ride to New York tinkering with the twenty-two-minute format, until he devised a way to use the time differently.

They could begin, Friedman proposed, with about five minutes devoted to the day's lead story and an analysis, emphasizing the analysis because so many viewers had heard the news on radio or local television. Into the second segment they could cram "all the rest of the news of the day in four and a half minutes" — headlines and newsbriefs read by the anchor and a wheel of thirty-second pieces by correspondents. Segment three, which could stretch for as long as seven minutes, would be the centerpiece, featuring an interview by Jennings, an investigative piece, or a story by a star reporter who could be debriefed on the set by Jennings. Segment four would be devoted to "news you can use," such as health or consumer tips. The final segment would be the traditional show closer.

This was nearly as radical as Smith's idea. In effect, Friedman wanted to cram the day's breaking news into the first two segments and then branch off in new directions. Arledge was impressed by Friedman's devotion to the task and by his self-confidence as he rattled off his ideas. Arledge also could not fail to notice how little had been offered by Bill Lord. All Lord had done was to dismiss some ideas raised by others as impractical.

As a result, Arledge asked Friedman to spend time in New York testing his scheme. Friedman could work with Jennings, put some segments on tape, and show them to Arledge. This sounded logical, but it proved to be difficult to get all three men together — Friedman was flying back and forth to London, Jennings was busy with the day's news, and Arledge was consumed by a myriad of other projects. He had to plan the programming for Liberty Weekend, negotiate new contracts with Jennings, Koppel, and Kathleen Sullivan, deal with an unexpected crisis at "20/20," and fend off Cap Cities. For most of 1987, he did nothing about "World News."

This was not unusual. Arledge was a master of delay; he felt, sometimes rightly, that problems would resolve themselves if left alone. But Arledge also had a terrible habit of ducking tough decisions. Getting rid of Bill Lord would require a confrontation, which he hated. And revamping the evening news format was a risky move, one that might fail. The result was that the problems on "World News Tonight" festered for much longer than they should have. In the end, Jennings — not Arledge — would have to rescue himself and the show.

While Roone Arledge and David Burke were threatened by the arrival of Cap Cities, one executive at ABC News saw the arrival of new owners as a godsend. Partly that was because Av Westin knew Tom Murphy and Dan Burke. In the mid-1970s, after he had been fired by Bill Sheehan, Westin had worked as a consultant for Murphy and Burke, helping develop news programs for Cap Cities.

Westin fervently hoped that the new owners would make him president of ABC News. He knew they viewed him as an ally. The Cap Cities executives liked the profits made by Westin's shows, "20/20" and "Our World," and they thought he was more open and less rigid than Arledge. One Cap Cities executive told Westin that Arledge was driving them crazy by resisting their efforts to cut costs and stonewalling their requests for information.

That was all Westin needed to hear. At the Lowell Hotel meetings about "World News," he'd been reminded of the way he'd produced the ABC evening news in the old days, with far fewer people and a much smaller budget. The key, he thought, was planning — exercising judgment about what to cover, commissioning fewer stories, putting pieces into a "bank" for use on slow days. He called Les Brown, who edited the stylish trade magazine *Channels of Communication,* and proposed an article about producing the news in an era of austerity. With Brown's encouragement, Westin set to work on what amounted to his job application to become president of ABC News.

He produced a bold eighteen-page document titled "Days of Penury, Days of Affluence." The days of penury were 1969, he wrote, when ABC News employed just thirty correspondents and a dozen field producers around the world. Because the network relied on local stations to cover some stories, viewers were sometimes shortchanged on spot news, he admitted. But ABC "managed to cover the news, and fill each night with information, stylishly presented and competitive," he wrote. In Westin's memory, these were the good old days — the days when he ran the show.

The days of affluence, by his reckoning, began in the late 1970s — when Arledge came to ABC News. Affluence brought "more correspondents, more field producers, more videotape editors; it also built up the bureaus' substructure: researchers, secretaries, cars and drivers, local 'fixers' . . . more rent, more phones, more wire service machines and, ironically, even more business office personnel to keep track of it." Attitudes had changed as well: "Executive producers are no longer laying out an editorial direction other than 'don't miss anything.' The result has been the mass assignment of men and women to stories that really do not have a chance of making the day's line-up." Westin compared the news division to an "expensive, oversized, gas-guzzling automobile" and recommended a "redesign" to create a new ABC News, streamlined and efficient and governed by prudent judgment. He concluded, "The network's salvation may actually lie in a downsizing in 1987."

Westin did not submit the article to *Channels.* When he'd mentioned to Arledge that he was putting some ideas down on paper, Arledge had warned him not to publish anything. So Westin ran off copies and sent them to Murphy, Burke, and Sias, as well as to Arledge. Tom Murphy called him to arrange for a lunch. "Thank God somebody is listening to us," Murphy said.

They never had lunch. Arledge exploded when he saw the memo, then erupted again when copies were leaked to the papers. He saw the Westin memo for what it was: an assault on his leadership of ABC News. "For him to go out like Sir Galahad and distribute this document all over the world — it's just unforgivable," Arledge said. He wished he'd rid himself of Westin after the debacle over the Marilyn

Monroe story on "20/20." "He was trying to make me look as bad as he possibly could, and I should have fired him right then," Arledge said.

Still, Arledge hesitated. Westin was a pain in the ass and not to be trusted, he knew, but he was a talented producer. Besides, Arledge hated firing people. Arledge talked to Sias, who told him that it was his call, but advised him not to fire Westin.

On Thursday afternoon, February 26, 1987, Westin was summoned to Arledge's office, where he was greeted coldly by Arledge and David Burke.

"You know what this is?" Burke said, holding the memo aloft. "This is a palm piece."

"What's a palm piece?" Westin asked.

"It's what politicians used to hand out, presenting their credentials," said Burke.

Westin protested that he had meant no harm, that he had only wanted to stimulate debate, but this was unlikely. With Arledge and Cap Cities at loggerheads, he knew that sending the memo to Murphy and Dan Burke would undercut his boss.

Arledge knew it too. "For the good of the division, I can't have you around," Arledge said.

But Westin got off almost scot-free. He was suspended from ABC News, which was humiliating, but he would be paid his annual salary of about $400,000 while he stayed home. Not only that, he'd been assured by Murphy and Burke that he could return once the storm passed. "I recognized as an adult that somebody had to fall on a sword," Westin said later. "I also knew the sword wasn't going to penetrate very deeply." Cap Cities wasn't about to punish him for recommending that the news division cut its costs.

That night, Westin got "20/20" onto the air, then gathered his staff at Shun Lee, where there were hugs and kisses and tears all around for their departing leader. A few people wondered defiantly how they could get back at Arledge, but Westin advised them that protesting his suspension would only make matters worse.

A few days later, Arledge called the "20/20" staff together. It was their first meeting with Arledge since 1978, when he'd come to their offices after the premiere to announce that he was dumping the original anchors. This time, he wanted to explain why he had suspended Westin; he also wanted to put an end to the newspaper stories about their feud. He hated negative publicity.

He began by praising Westin. "He is responsible for some of the greatest things we have on our air," Arledge said. "Nobody wanted this to happen." But, he said, he had no choice. "Suddenly, I was faced with someone who is subordinate to me, going over my head and leaking things to the press." This was insubordination, Arledge said, and it could not be tolerated. "I'd like anybody in this room to put themselves in the position of a manager or someone who is running a company who is faced with this. I think you would agree that I had to take some action," he said.

Arledge wanted to make another point, too, about leaks. ABC News, he said, is a bit like family. "We have family fights, we disagree, people argue, people yell, and almost always we make up. And like family, when we go out, we put our good face on for the outside world. Our dirty linen has almost never been aired in public. This has helped us enormously." Arledge was right about that. He had watched warring factions tear apart CBS News, each using the press as a weapon.

Arledge brushed off questions about Westin's future. While his suspension was described as temporary, it was not clear when or if he would return. Arledge put Victor Neufeld, Westin's second-in-command, in charge of "20/20" on an interim basis and assigned Peter Kunhardt, a senior producer, to run "Our World." Neufeld's appointment, even on a temporary basis, worried some producers and correspondents, who held him in low regard, but few expected him to remain at the helm for long.

Arledge patiently responded to all other questions, staying more than an hour. "I'm sorry it took this to have us all get together," he said, as the discussion wound down. He added politely, "I hope we'll have more of these meetings."

With that, Av Westin's career at "20/20" was over. "20/20" had in every sense become his program — his sensibilities shaped every broadcast. He had reason to be proud. Like Don Hewitt at CBS's "60 Minutes," Westin had mastered the art of balancing the competitive demands of prime time with the requirements of journalism, so that when possible both commerce and the public interest were served. At its best, "20/20" presented newsmaking interviews, hard-edged investigations, lively coverage of pop culture, and useful self-help pieces. At other times, however, the program was shallow or sensationalistic. This, too, reflected Westin. His biggest flaw as a producer was that, when forced to choose between grabbing the audience and producing journalism that mattered, he opted to entertain. In this respect, he was an ideal executive producer for Arledge — his journalistic credentials were impeccable, but he was at heart a showman.

Three months later, Westin was brought back to ABC News to take over the "longform" unit, a term he coined because he thought that the word "documentary" had taken on a negative cast. He was right; the documentary had come upon hard times at all the networks, including ABC, where cost-cutting pressures had shrunk a once-lively documentary factory and left a small, dispirited crew. Westin's last assignment was to preside over the demise of the "Close-Up" unit he'd created fifteen years earlier. He decided to leave ABC when his contract expired in 1989.

Once he'd announced his plans, Westin wanted to say a proper good-bye to Arledge. While they had never been friends, and their relationship had ended sourly, the two men had worked side by side for more than a decade. As an executive producer, Westin had managed the final days of Harry Reasoner and Barbara Walters; he had introduced the three-anchor format on "World News Tonight"; he had put "20/20" onto solid footing; and he had created "Our World." But by the end of his tenure at ABC, Westin could not get in to see Arledge.

On his last day of work, Westin walked uninvited into Arledge's office and told him he had come to say good-bye.

"You're not really doing this, are you?" Arledge said.

"Yes, I am," Westin replied.

An awkward silence followed.

Arledge seemed terribly uncomfortable, so much so that, for a moment, Westin felt bad for him. Then it struck him — was that all Arledge was going to say? He had wanted more, at the least some sign that his contributions had been appreciated. He wondered if he should bring up the old days but thought better of it.

Arledge wished him good luck and said that he would be missed.

"Good luck to you, too," Westin replied. "You'll do just fine."

"Yes, I guess we will," Arledge said.

Westin left the office and went home. This was not how he had envisioned the end of his career at ABC News.

Some years later, though, Westin expressed guarded admiration for Arledge and all he had accomplished.

"Roone created a seedbed in which individuals like me could flower," Westin said. "He rode in the sedan chair, which all the rest of us were carrying. And he would move us, and point in a certain direction, and create the concepts which others could implement. The result of that effort was to bring greatness to himself and to ABC News.

"The sad thing about it," Westin said, "was that Roone couldn't acknowledge what everybody else was doing."

If Av Westin engaged in insubordination when he circulated a memo criticizing Arledge's management, Arledge was guilty of nothing less when he lambasted Cap Cities a few months later. He not only attacked the programming savvy of Tom Murphy and Dan Burke after they decided to move "20/20" from Thursday to Friday nights — a shift some thought would doom the show — he also questioned their sanity. What's more, he did so publicly, allowing his frustrations with Cap Cities to spill out during an interview with Harry F. Waters of *Newsweek*. "The idea that they would move one of their few successful shows strikes me as almost insane," Arledge said. "But to move it to a night on which very few people want to see a serious news program is just beyond rational judgment." These were strong words, but everyone, including Murphy and Burke, understood how Arledge felt. He had been dealt his worst setback since losing Sports.

The simplest explanation for the "20/20" move was that Barbara Walters had lost out to Dolly Parton. After ABC finished last in the prime-time Nielsens for the 1986–87 TV season, for the third year in a row, the solution to the network's woes was deemed to be an hourlong variety show called "Dolly," starring the flamboyant singer and actress. Brandon Stoddard, ABC's West Coast programming chief, signed Parton to a three-year contract worth $34 million and scheduled her show for 9 P.M. on Sundays, the night of the week when television viewing peaked.

This required some juggling, as Stoddard explained to about forty ABC executives gathered in New York in May 1987 to preview the fall schedule. Arledge and David Burke had been told to be prepared to defend their two prime-time shows, "20/20" and "Our World." They soon learned why.

To make room for "Dolly" on Sundays, Stoddard said, he wanted to move ABC's movie-of-the-week to Thursdays at 9 P.M. That would mean canceling "Our World" and moving "20/20" to 8 P.M., where it would compete against the number one show on television, NBC's "Cosby."

Arledge was appalled. Scheduling "20/20" against "Cosby" would kill the show — it was unthinkable. Stoddard, he thought, had no idea of the struggles required to create a franchise like "20/20." This was an insult to Walters, an insult to Arledge, a declaration that all he had built at ABC News could be pushed aside at the whim of the entertainment division. This was the ultimate snub, if Cap Cities allowed it to stand.

David Burke agreed — and said so.

"Why don't you run Dolly Parton at eight P.M. on Thursday?" Burke asked.

"What, are you crazy? You tell Dolly!" said Stoddard.

"You tell Barbara!" Burke shot back.

Arledge grew so angry that he threatened to halt production of "20/20" if the show was moved to Thursdays at eight.

The argument raged on not just at that meeting, which had to be adjourned when tempers flared, but for days. Underlying the debate was an assumption that Arledge refused to accept — that the prime-time hours on the network belonged to the entertainment division, as a matter of right, and that the news division filled time only when called on to do so. Even after prime-time news shows such as "60 Minutes" and "20/20" generated more profits than all but the most popular entertainment shows, the conventional wisdom remained unchanged — prime-time news hours were to be used to shore up weak time periods or as inexpensive sacrifices against hit shows on the competition. To Arledge's dismay, this mind-set prevailed at all three networks. "Where is the logic that says when you build these prime-time news hours you make it as impossible as it can be for them to succeed?" he would say.

Arledge won a small victory when Murphy and Burke agreed not to send "20/20" on a suicide mission against "Cosby," but in the end the Cap Cities men backed Stoddard, their entertainment chief. They canceled "Our World" and moved "20/20" to Fridays. Arledge and ABC News had lost. Fridays would never work for news, he thought — too few people stayed home, and those who watched television wanted to ease into the weekend by relaxing, not by tuning in to news. At a final, uncomfortable session with Murphy and Dan Burke, Arledge, David Burke, and Irwin Weiner voiced their unhappiness. "I don't understand something," said Weiner. "You tell us how great we are, but we never win a decision from you."

Arledge was stung by the defeat. He didn't mind losing "Our World." That was a Westin creation and, against "Cosby," it had been the lowest-rated show in prime time.

But "20/20" and Barbara Walters mattered. Arledge had spent

years trying to find a showcase for Walters. She had been loyal to him and ABC; she deserved better than to be shoved aside for Dolly Parton. Arledge did his best to assure her that he would not let "20/20" die on Fridays.

Losing a network power struggle mattered too. On Thursdays, "20/20" had generated more than $20 million in profits for ABC News, money that could be used to pay for news-gathering costs or turned back to the corporation. If, as Arledge expected, the move to Friday hurt the show, the pressures on him to generate profits would intensify. Arledge had no interest in the broader picture — what was good for all of ABC or the possibility that "Dolly" could become a hit. He could not look at things that way. All he saw was another loss for ABC News.

He took it personally. This was more than Dolly versus Barbara and entertainment versus news — it was Brandon Stoddard versus Roone Arledge. In Arledge's eyes, that should have been an easy call. Stoddard was a respected programmer who had helped bring "Roots" and "The Day After" to ABC, but his accomplishments were dwarfed by Arledge's. In fact, Stoddard had just steered the entertainment division to its third-place finish, Arledge thought, and now his failure was being rewarded. That seemed unjust.

So when Arledge announced the move of "20/20" in a memo to the news division, he could not resist taking a sharp dig at Stoddard. ABC News management, he said, had strongly opposed the move and had fought it for three days. "In the end," Arledge wrote, "we did not succeed primarily because of the enormous pressure placed on the decision makers by the extraordinarily poor performance of ABC's prime-time programming, and the resultant economic loss facing the network." Some ABC executives who read the memo were appalled that Arledge would be so publicly critical of a colleague.

But Murphy and Burke understood. "I can understand why News was upset," Murphy said. "We made that move for Brandon Stoddard. It looked like they were playing second fiddle to the entertainment division." Later, after "Dolly" flopped, Dan Burke called the decision "probably the dumbest thing we ever imposed on any element of the company. We'd never repeat it." But Burke also noted that, just as Stoddard had misjudged "Dolly," Arledge had underestimated the appeal of "20/20." Burke was right about that — "20/20" survived the move to Fridays, and over time its audience grew.

Nevertheless, Arledge came away from the experience feeling both unappreciated and embattled — feelings he was having more often than ever. He was acutely sensitive to the way he was treated by the Cap Cities people, who he thought did not trust him to run ABC News.

"I did not build ABC News from nothing to what it is today to preside over its destruction," Arledge said after losing the "20/20" fight. "I will not allow it to be picked to death. If that time ever came, that would be the time for me to consider doing something else."

This was, in truth, unlikely. Arledge's power and prestige, both of which meant a great deal to him, flowed from his position at the top of ABC News. Twice now, he had lost important battles to Cap Cities — over ABC Sports and over "20/20" — and twice he had accepted defeat. Dan Burke was beginning to think that Arledge had come to need ABC News as much as ABC News needed him.

Chapter Fourteen

STAR POWER

TED KOPPEL could not believe his ears. Al Campanis, the vice president of the Los Angeles Dodgers, who had been invited onto "Nightline" to reminisce about his old roommate Jackie Robinson, was ruining himself, right there on live television. The more Koppel tried to help him dig himself out, the worse things got. There was no escaping it: Campanis, who had been brought onto the program to deliver a lesson in racial tolerance, sounded like a bigot. Blacks, he said, in the sound bite that was replayed for days, "may not have some of the necessities" to be managers or general managers in the big leagues.

That Campanis landed on "Nightline" on April 6, 1987, the opening day of the baseball season, was for him an unhappy accident. The idea for the program came, not from anyone at "Nightline," but from baseball buff George Will, who had persuaded Koppel to do a show pegged to the fortieth anniversary of the season when Jackie Robinson broke the color barrier in the major leagues. "We thought it was going to be a sweet tribute to Jackie Robinson," said Richard Harris, the producer who booked Campanis.

Normally, Koppel paid little attention to sports. "He's a moron about baseball," said reporter Jeff Greenfield. But Koppel knew he was onto a big story when he asked Campanis why baseball had no black managers or general managers and his guest replied that few blacks succeeded as baseball pitchers or football quarterbacks — positions that require brains as well as athletic ability.

Politely, but firmly, Koppel said, "I gotta tell you — that really sounds like garbage, if you'll forgive me for saying so."

Campanis tried earnestly to explain. "No, it's not — it's not garbage, Mr. Koppel," he said. "It just might be — why are black men, or black people, not good swimmers? Because they don't have the buoyancy."

By this time, people in the control room were stunned. "For all Campanis's faults, he really was speaking genuinely," said Harris. This was true — the program only made news because Campanis, unlike the vast majority of "Nightline" guests, was untutored. He was not editing himself as he went along.

His frankness cost him dearly. Campanis was forced to resign from the Dodger organization. Civil rights groups pressed baseball to bring more blacks into its executive ranks. Commissioner Peter Ueberroth instituted reforms and went on "Nightline" to defend the game. Later, Koppel said that the Campanis interview had become "a major program by inadvertence. It certainly wasn't anything we had planned," he said.

Perhaps not, but Koppel was having the kind of year in 1987 where every pitch he hit became a home run. Hardly a month went by when his "Nightline" interviews did not make headlines or break news that other reporters had to chase. Covering the Iran/Contra affair, for example, "Nightline" guided its viewers through the tangled arms-for-hostages deal and secured the first interviews with Robert McFarlane and Richard Secord, key figures in the scandal; the story was tailor-made for Koppel, with his foreign policy expertise and willingness to tackle complexity. "Nightline" was every bit as aggressive in its pursuit of fallen evangelists Jim and Tammy Bakker. "There was absolutely no disagreement about that story, none at all," Koppel said. "It was a legitimate story, *and* it involved religion, money, sex, and a couple of enormously well known people." The Bakkers hid out for months until they agreed to do "Nightline," bringing the show its highest ratings ever. "I guess we had invitations to just about every program to come on," Bakker explained to Koppel, "but I felt that you're not only tough, but I felt that you would be fair and give us a chance to share with people all over the country." Presidential candidate Gary Hart chose to appear on "Nightline" for much the same reason, as he tried to end the media frenzy over his dalliance with model Donna Rice.

As usual, Koppel's timing was just about perfect. He had become the most celebrated star in television news just as his contract with ABC News was about to expire. But his celebrity created new problems for "Nightline," for ABC News, and eventually for Koppel himself. Stardom changed him — he became more powerful, wealthier, more self-assured, and more difficult to manage. This was a dynamic that would play itself out across ABC News, as all the anchors and their programs became well established. For Roone Arledge, the challenge of building an organization, which had occupied him for so long, would be replaced by the new and equally complex problems of running a successful operation. The star system that he had done so much to foster was coming back to haunt him.

Personally, Koppel remained the most down-to-earth of anchors. He still lived in the suburban Maryland home he'd bought when he was State Department correspondent, and his wife and children were what mattered most to him. He eschewed the Georgetown party scene and turned down an invitation to the Bohemian Grove, an exclusive retreat for the power elite. "Our function as journalists really is not to be buddies," Koppel said.

Around "Nightline" Koppel was admired as a man of compassion and principle. One wintry night after the show, a producer came upon Koppel on his hands and knees cradling the head of a homeless man who had fallen outside the bureau. His strong convictions also drew him to stories others ignored. "Nightline," for example, explored the morality of executing a man for a crime committed as a juvenile — an issue that engaged Koppel, who believed so strongly in the sanctity of human life that he opposed not only the death penalty but abortion, according to associates. Koppel denied that he had ever discussed his private views with colleagues, but he did say, "The importance of a program like this is fundamentally in two areas, educational and moral."

Koppel was also generous about sharing credit with his staff, led by executive producer Rick Kaplan, who brought energy and creativity to "Nightline." Gil Pimentel, a booker, said of Kaplan, "He excites you and scares you at the same time, so you achieve things you thought you were not capable of." The South Africa trip, for example, inspired further overseas adventures, including a dramatic series of programs from Manila in February 1987, when Ferdinand Marcos was driven into exile. Kaplan also came up with a town-meeting format that enabled "Nightline" to convene open-ended, late-night talkfests on such topics as AIDS, the stock market crash, and drugs. "Nightline" and Koppel also profited immensely from the contributions of such talented correspondents as political analyst Jeff Greenfield and the intrepid James Walker.

Still, over time, "Nightline" in the eyes of viewers had become The Ted Koppel Show. More than any other news show on television, "Nightline" was built around the singular talents of its anchor; when he was away, the program sagged, and there was always doubt about whether the show could survive without him.

All this gave him enviable leverage as he reached the end of his contract with ABC late in 1987. "He was as close to irreplaceable as you can get," said David Burke, who had to negotiate Koppel's new deal. "And he was red-hot at the time — just red-hot. That is a very valuable asset." Because "World News" and Jennings were still struggling, Koppel and the "Nightline" franchise were vital to ABC News. Burke knew he was in for trouble when he read an admiring cover story about Koppel in *Newsweek*. There Koppel said he was thinking about leaving "Nightline."

This was no negotiating ploy. In the aftermath of the Cap Cities takeover, Koppel was concerned about his future. While he had faith in Arledge and David Burke, he worried, with reason, that the cost-control pressures might diminish the quality of news programs. He had been appalled to learn, for example, that plans were afoot to erase much of the ABC News videotape library so that tapes could be reused, to save money. "I thought it was outrageous that we would erase our patrimony," he said, "and I also thought it was a stupid move from a business point of view." To his credit, Koppel offered to buy the ABC News library himself, to preserve the old footage. This was also a time when tabloid television shows were gaining in popularity, and Koppel was not sure whether ABC's new owners would resist pressures to take the low road.

David Burke, as it happened, shared Koppel's concerns about Cap Cities, but he did his best to persuade Koppel that ABC News was in good hands. At Burke's suggestion, Tom Murphy visited Koppel at his home for lunch, as did the billionaire investor Warren Buffett, who owned a big stake of Cap Cities stock. They assured Koppel that they cared about news and "Nightline." "We never talked about my contract," Koppel said. "They are much too sophisticated and much too subtle for that." Just the same, he came away feeling that Tom Murphy was a good man who would protect ABC News.

Even so, Koppel wanted to protect himself. He proposed that the network help him form his own production company, which would be given commitments to produce programs for ABC News. "If I felt, as I feared at the time, that Cap Cities was going to take us off in the wrong direction, I was going to jump ship and get on my lifeboat and sail off into the sunset," Koppel said.

This was an audacious idea, unprecedented in network news, if common in the entertainment world. Prime-time stars like Roseanne Arnold and Ted Danson often extract production commitments from the networks, guaranteeing them production money and time slots. The closest thing to such a deal in news was ABC's agreement with Barbara Walters, who produced and owned her celebrity specials. But Koppel's proposal went further. He wanted ABC News to buy programs from him and allow him to produce programs for cable, public television, and private industry.

David Burke tried to dissuade him. "You shouldn't be in this business," Burke said. "You shouldn't be into personnel problems and hiring people and running your own company." Arledge, too, opposed the idea; he worried that Koppel would neglect "Nightline" if he committed his time and energy to the new company. "I thought it would be bad for him and bad for the show," Arledge said.

But Koppel could not be swayed, and eventually Arledge and Burke came to believe that Koppel would not sign a new contract without a production deal. "Ted is very secure in his own right," Burke said. "He would go and stand on his own two legs." The contract they signed in March 1988 committed ABC News to buy four programs a year from Koppel and left him free to produce for other outlets.

Arledge was displeased. All his instincts told him that it was a mistake to grant that much power and freedom to any anchor, even to one he liked and admired as much as Koppel. But "Nightline" needed Koppel, and Arledge needed "Nightline." It was not only the signature program of ABC News; it was Arledge's creation. If starting a company for Ted Koppel was the price of keeping him, Arledge decided he had to pay it.

Soon after signing his new contract, Ted Koppel traveled to Israel for a series of broadcasts called "Nightline in the Holy Land." This was another Rick Kaplan extravaganza, a road show that he vowed to make even bigger and better than "Nightline" in South Africa or the Philippines. For a full week, Koppel and "Nightline" broadcast live from the divided city of Jerusalem; they explained the issues, the tensions, the passions, and the history that divided Israelis and Arabs. Most memorably, they convened an open-ended town meeting that brought together Israelis and Palestinians, who were then locked in bitter combat over the uprising in the Israeli-occupied territories.

Actually, "Nightline" didn't bring the two sides together — the antagonists were divided by a four-foot-high wooden wall, constructed on the stage at the last minute in response to a demand from the Palestinians that they be separated from the Israelis by a physical barrier. That the Israelis and Palestinians agreed to talk at all was testimony to the valiant efforts of Gil Pimentel, the twenty-nine-year-old "Nightline" booker who had labored for six weeks to persuade them to share a platform. Even so, on the morning of the show, Arledge was so worried about the risk of violence that he suggested to Kaplan, in all seriousness, that they call the whole thing off. Security was tight even by Israeli standards.

As the broadcast began, Koppel literally straddled the fence. It was both a casual and a deliberate gesture, a visual metaphor for the divisions in the Middle East — much as, in South Africa, the side-by-side pictures of Botha and Tutu had asserted a claim about the equality of the two men. "You may have noticed this little fence I'm sitting on here," Koppel said. "I must tell you that it has been so difficult to arrange this broadcast, that was one small price that we were prepared to pay, so here it is. I will try and spend as much time on one side as on the other."

That he did — from his perch he balanced issues and arguments, prodded and stroked the panelists, and nimbly orchestrated a three-hour-and-ten-minute discussion that shed both heat and light on the Arab-Israeli conflict. This was Koppel and "Nightline" at their best, and the rest of the week was nearly as exciting; one night, "Nightline" ran long back-to-back pieces looking at the Holy Land through Israeli and Palestinian eyes. Back home, the critics reached for their superlatives. It was, wrote Howard Rosenberg of the *Los Angeles Times,* "the bravest, most important, most needed television."

Although no one could have known it then, "Nightline in the Holy Land" turned out to be the last hurrah of the Koppel-Kaplan team at "Nightline." By then, the two men were friends as well as collaborators. "Ted was like a brother," Kaplan would say. "We shared a lot of personal stuff, everything." But their interests diverged after Israel, and "Nightline" suffered from a series of problems spawned by their success.

Koppel's celebrity, for starters, was not an unalloyed benefit to "Nightline." Gradually, Koppel's interviews took center stage on the broadcast, so that less time and money were spent on reporting the taped pieces that opened the show. Now the setup pieces were literally designed to set up the debates to follow, rather than to tell stories, as they once had. As Kaplan put it to a "Nightline" correspondent, "You are the foreplay. The interview's the real thing."

Off the air, the democratic spirit that had animated the staff in the early days gave way to a more conventional top-down style of decision making. Betsy West, a senior producer, noticed the change after she returned to Washington from a tour of duty in London; the morning conference calls had come to be dominated by Koppel and Kaplan. "Fewer and fewer people piped up," West said. "There was a little bit of reluctance to go mano a mano with Ted." Those who did take Koppel on found the going tough, and they read him carefully — if he interrupted with a "forgive me" or an "I gotta tell you," it was time to quit. One producer said, "I've been on conference calls when Ted has been absolutely dead wrong, and yet you'll never convince him of that because he can argue rings around just about anybody."

Koppel recognized the problem, but he had less patience with long, free-flowing debate than he'd had early on. "I try very hard not to be arrogant and pompous, but clearly I fail more than I should," he once said, and, as usual, his perception was accurate. He did try — his office door was plastered with news clippings and viewer mail that exhibited his self-deprecating side; he posted letters addressed to Chet Koppel, Red Koppel, and Tex Koppel and a supermarket tabloid headline that read "Ted Koppel Taught Me How To Kiss." The point was that Koppel, while a star, could still laugh at himself. After all, he once balanced a dog biscuit on his nose on NBC's "Late Night with David Letterman"; another time, he donned a white glove and sunglasses to dance the moonwalk before a "Nightline" about Michael Jackson.

But on an ordinary day at the office, Koppel tended to act, if not like a star, like the smartest guy in the room. He was less open-minded and quicker to dismiss story ideas that, early on, he might have helped reshape or redefine. Nor did he push himself to tackle issues that fell outside his comfort zone. One glaring weakness was economics, as he candidly admitted. "Financial stories really bore me," he said. "It's a function of my own ignorance." It was a function of his arrogance, though, that he did not make more effort to learn — of 1,850 "Nightline" programs during the Reagan years, a period during which the national debt grew by $1.6 trillion, Koppel devoted exactly six shows to the deficit, according to the *Washington Monthly*. Another 25 shows were devoted to the economy, compared to 70 programs on Central America and Africa, more than 100 on East-West relations, and 180 on the Middle East. Those who relied on "Nightline" for their news learned almost nothing about corporate takeovers, the trade deficit, or the rise of Japan as an economic power. Few other news programs would have permitted an anchor's tastes to similarly shape news judgments.

As Koppel grew more powerful, "Nightline" also focused more narrowly on Washington elites. So, at least, said a left-leaning media watchdog group called Fairness and Accuracy in Reporting, or FAIR, which issued a critical report in 1989 charging that the "Nightline" guest list was dominated by white males from the government, military, and corporate establishments. This by itself was unsurprising, since "Nightline" set out to book government officials and other newsmakers. But the FAIR numbers, compiled over a four-year period, were nevertheless striking — 92 percent of guests were white, 89 percent were men, 80 percent were professionals from government or business. The most frequent guests were conservative policymakers like Henry Kissinger, Alexander Haig, and Elliot Abrams, who, no matter how sharply challenged by Koppel, tended to frame issues in ways that fit the thinking of official Washington. Peace and public-interest groups, labor leaders, and minorities, all of whom could have offered fresh points of view, were rarely heard.

Koppel's public response to FAIR was dismissive. "We're a news program that likes to have newsmakers on," he said. "For the past eight years, we have had a conservative, Republican, white male–dominated administration in power." But, as Jeff Cohen, FAIR's executive director, argued, "This excuse for conservative domination of a TV program could have been uttered by a Soviet news broadcaster — pre-glasnost. In the U.S., television news is not supposed to be a forum for representatives of the state." More than one "Nightline" staffer thought that the FAIR study had some validity, and Koppel later conceded that the program would benefit from a broader array of guests.

The more serious problem for "Nightline" was that Koppel's time, energy, and attention were divided between the program and his new company, called Koppel Communications Inc. Typically, he began work at about noon at KCI, which rented space two blocks from ABC's Washington bureau, then put in a full day at "Nightline" from mid-afternoon until midnight. It was a grueling regimen, one that put stress on Koppel and "Nightline."

Koppel got off on the wrong foot by asking some of the best people at "Nightline" to work for him at KCI, which to some indicated that the new company had become his priority. Kaplan and Betsy West, among others, turned him down, but Koppel hired two "Nightline" producers and borrowed other ABC News staff members, including Kaplan, for his first few KCI specials. "The lines were totally blurred, to the point where it was 'Nightline' staff that put the specials on," Kaplan said. Those left behind at "Nightline" felt overburdened; the feeling developed that what they were doing mattered less than the prime-time specials. A field producer said, "All we knew was that we'd been working hard for ten years, and all of a sudden there was something more important than what he was doing at ABC. That was a slap in the face."

Staffers felt conflicting emotions about Koppel. He'd been beloved at "Nightline" for his talent, principles, and humanity. His loyalty to some people forged long-lasting bonds; Koppel had provided help to the wife and children of a "Nightline" director who had died, and he'd come to the aid of a producer who needed medical care when his stepson got thyroid cancer. Koppel also kept a couple of old-timers on the payroll, although their contributions were limited, because they had stood by him over the years. But these kindnesses, ironically, made it harder for people to accept Koppel's commitment to KCI; they felt abandoned. Some also complained that Koppel neglected to make the small gestures — throwing a holiday party or giving gifts — that would have conveyed his appreciation to the staff. People felt they were giving their lives to "Nightline," and they wanted more back.

Koppel tried to empathize. "There was no one who had spent more time on the program than I. Most of them had been here maybe half the time," he said. "So yes, I appreciated their problems, but in my own head I was saying, 'Am I going to be doing this for the rest of my life?' The answer was no."

Still, Koppel felt torn by his dual allegiances. His KCI people wanted more of him, as did those at "Nightline." And he was too much the professional to coast through a day. "Ted was tired. Just exhausted. And you can't blame him," said Betsy West. "What he does is phenomenal. The concentration he has and the intensity he puts into that half an hour every night." Kaplan said, "He ended up doing five jobs at once, and it was driving him into the ground." Later, Koppel conceded, "I was working twelve-, fourteen-, sixteen-hour days, and I was trying to divide the day, so that I wasn't spending a full day in either place, and that could not be sustained in the long run."

Compounding the strain was that Kaplan, too, was looking beyond "Nightline." Worn down by the long hours, he contemplated leaving ABC News to produce movies. Personal crises, including the death of his father, sapped his strength. Around "Nightline," Kaplan was no longer as gung-ho. "Normally, Rick had a lot of energy, but that last year he just wasn't there," a producer said. He'd get charged up for big events but otherwise he glided.

Taken together, these pressures transformed the old culture of "Nightline." Until the late 1980s, "Nightline" had been seen by those who worked there as a calling; staff members were driven by an ethic of public service, and they were proud to be contributing to one of the rare programs on commercial television that valued ideas and sought to enlighten the viewers. This was critical because "Nightline" demanded a nearly total commitment, a willingness to put the needs of the show ahead of friends and family. "I never had one plant in the house, and the reason I never had one plant in the house is because it would have been dead," joked senior producer Deborah Leff. Staffers were thrilled when Koppel had mentioned during his contract talks that he was trying to work out a deal to cut back "Nightline" to four days a week during the football season, to give everyone a break. As it happened, Koppel alone won the right to take off Mondays, when the show was delayed until 12:30 A.M. by "Monday Night Football"; everyone else still worked the full week.

Morale sank at "Nightline," once deemed the best place to work in television. More important, the program stagnated. It grew less adventurous and more predictable, and viewers turned away. Ratings for "Nightline" fell by more than 15 percent between 1986 and 1989.

A "Nightline" insider said, "Ted's production company was in full flower. He was disinterested and disengaged. And Rick wasn't paying attention. The show reflected it. Everyone was burned out and walking around exhausted and zombie-like."

"Ted changed," said a veteran producer. "Ted became enamored with his own publicity, and he became more arrogant, less patient, more dismissive of the people who were working for him. He was less appreciative of the commitment that people made to him."

The frustrations boiled over when Washington and New York staffers gathered for the first-ever "Nightline" retreat, at the Warwick Hotel in Philadelphia on a Saturday in January 1989. Two topics were on people's minds: the impact of KCI on "Nightline" and the future of Rick Kaplan.

Koppel had not wanted to discuss KCI, but after listening to complaints, he promised that in the future he would bring in substitutes or freelancers to replace any "Nightline" people who were detailed to his company.

The Kaplan problem was thornier. Arledge's newest project was a prime-time program that would star Sam Donaldson and Diane Sawyer, if he could steal her from CBS. This was where the action would be at ABC News. Kaplan, everyone knew, loved the action, and he was thought to be eager to run the new show.

Herb O'Connor, an outspoken producer, put the issue on the table.

"Ladies and gentlemen of the jury, and fellow shriners," O'Connor said, trying to strike a light tone, "here's the word on the grapevine. Rick, you're bored with 'Nightline.' You want to leave . . . If you leave, what does this meeting accomplish?"

"I have no plans to go to the new program," Kaplan replied, carefully leaving himself some wiggle room. He admitted to feeling some boredom and fatigue but said, "I have a wonderful job. And this is a great program."

"Well," said Koppel, "the only question I wanted to ask has been asked."

Everyone realized then that Kaplan had one foot out the door. He was still dreaming big dreams, but they were not about "Nightline." Others also wanted out and began to drift away, to work on the new prime-time show or "World News Tonight." It became clear, even to those who remained, that "Nightline" was no longer the best place to be at ABC News.

This was inevitable — television programs pass through stages, from vibrant youth to seasoned maturity, and the sense of fun and discovery and idealism that powered "Nightline" for so long could not be sustained forever. As Koppel observed wryly, "You can only be a virgin once."

A producer who worked there for a decade said, " 'Nightline' didn't seem to be part of the real world of television in the beginning. It was just this wonderful sort of creative family. Ultimately, when it became a product of television — and Ted became a product of television — it was disillusioning."

What was truly remarkable, though, was how long "Nightline" had thrived in its own rarefied world, apart from the egos and power plays and commercial pressures so prevalent elsewhere in network news.

*   *   *

Peter Jennings was having the worst summer of his life.

His executive producer, Bill Lord, remained hostile. His wife, Kati Marton, was leaving him. And an ABC colleague, Charles Glass, was being held hostage by Iranian-backed terrorists in Beirut.

Charlie Glass was more than a colleague. Jennings had been his mentor and the best man at his wedding, and he had watched with pride when Glass had brought glory to ABC News by standing on the tarmac at the Beirut airport, shouting questions at the pilot of hijacked TWA Flight 847 back in 1985. More recently, Jennings had cautioned his friend against returning to Lebanon. "He is the kind of guy who believes that because he loves other people so much, things will be okay," Jennings said.

On the afternoon of July 7, 1987, as he anchored live coverage of the Iran/Contra hearings in Congress, Jennings was told that Glass's captors had released a videotape. Jeff Gralnick, who was producing, interrupted the hearing to broadcast the tape of Glass.

Jennings watched with everyone else.

Glass looked as if he hadn't slept in weeks. He seemed affectless, disconnected from the words he spoke in a slow drawl.

"Many of you only know me as a journalist," he said, "but few know the truth. I used the press as a cover for my main job with the CIA." Glass went on to accuse the United States of having imperialist designs on the Middle East, before concluding, "I want to send my love to all my family. I love you." He had a wife and five children in London.

Back on camera, Jennings could not speak. Tears trickled down his cheek.

Correspondent John McWethy, standing by, heard Gralnick's voice in his ear — "Peter's hurting. Help him." McWethy filled in for a minute or so, until Jennings regained his composure.

On the air again, Jennings apologized. "I'm sorry for my hesitation," he said. "He's a colleague and a close friend." He had never before lost control during a broadcast.

The pressures on Jennings were becoming too much to bear.

His workload was overwhelming. He'd traveled to the Persian Gulf after the USS *Stark* was hit by an Iraqi missile. He was hard at work on a prime-time special with Ted Koppel. And he had dutifully immersed himself in the details of Iran/Contra, in order to guide viewers through the hearings.

When Glass disappeared, Jennings threw himself into efforts to secure his release. Although Glass had left ABC News to write a book, Arledge put David Burke in charge of a campaign to free him. Jennings spent hours on the phone working his diplomatic contacts and more hours trying to comfort Glass's wife and children, at a time when Jennings, too, needed comforting.

After eight years together, Kati Marton had told him that she was leaving him for another man. Their marriage, she said later, had gone "on automatic pilot," largely because of the demands of his job. Apart from that, Marton wanted to develop an identity that went beyond being Mrs. Peter Jennings. Since coming back to the United States, she had written a novel and become very much a part of the literary scene in New York. In early July, Marton left for their home in the Hamptons with their children in tow.

Jennings begged her to stay, but it was no use. He was upset, angry, and humiliated — more so when their marital difficulties became fodder for the gossip columns, which reported that Marton was having an affair with *Washington Post* columnist Richard Cohen. A few colleagues who remembered Jennings as a cad thought he had it coming, but his friends knew he was deeply in love with Marton. They offered sympathy and support, as he struggled to keep his family together. He set everything else aside, and after a few weeks, Marton agreed to come home and try to patch things up. Gradually they were reconciled.

In his moment of crisis, though, Jennings got no support from Bill Lord. To the contrary — Lord discouraged others from helping the anchorman. To an ABC News publicist who fielded some press calls about Jennings's marriage, Lord said, "You are nuts to do this for him. You're not the personal p.r. person for Peter Jennings." Later, when writer David Blum spent time at "World News" preparing a *New York* magazine profile of Jennings, Lord did little to hide the scorn he felt for his anchor.

Lord was destroying not his anchorman but himself. Even Arledge, who had turned a deaf ear for so long to the tensions at "World News," began to suspect that Lord, in a perverse way, did not want Jennings to succeed. He thought about replacing Lord.

Then Jennings forced his hand. His contract expired in August 1987, and CBS had expressed interest. On a walk on the beach in the Hamptons, Howard Stringer, the president of CBS News, had talked about hiring Jennings as a roving anchor to complement Dan Rather. While Jennings wanted to stay at ABC, he wanted to do so on his terms. He wanted a substantial raise from his $850,000 annual salary,

which made him the lowest paid of the three evening news anchors.
He wanted the title of managing editor that Rather and Brokaw had.
He wanted the right to veto any co-anchor, and most of all, he wanted
Bill Lord replaced with an executive producer to his liking.

Arledge demurred. He was fearful of granting too much power to
his anchorman. It was at about this time that Rather, in a dispute
over a tennis match that ran long, walked off the set of the "CBS
Evening News" and left the network with six minutes of dead air.
Arledge thought that Rather's executive producer should have ordered
him to stay put. "When it comes time to go on the air and decisions
have to be made at the last second, that cannot be done by an anchor,"
Arledge said. "The ultimate authority on any news broadcast should
be the executive producer, just like the editor of a newspaper."

In practice, though, the demands of network anchors were hard to
resist. Rather and Brokaw had amassed considerable power at CBS
and NBC. And Arledge did not want to lose Jennings. So even as
Capital Cities looked for ways to reduce costs at ABC News, Jennings
was given a contract that doubled his salary to $1.8 million a year.
He was given the title of senior editor. And, he was told, "World
News" would get a new executive producer.

Two candidates emerged. Dorrance Smith, who yearned for a
change after five years of producing "Brinkley" and weekend news,
had the support of David Burke. The other candidate was Paul Friedman, the London-based executive who had devised a new format for
"World News" but had not produced any programs at ABC. Seeking
a consensus before making his choice, Arledge arranged for a series
of lunches — Jennings and Smith, Jennings and Friedman, Burke and
Friedman, and, finally, Arledge and Jennings, at the Cafe des Artistes,
across from ABC. There, Jennings threw his support to Friedman,
whom he regarded as the better candidate — more intelligent, more
experienced, more worldly and self-assured. That cinched the deal.
On Christmas Eve, after months of delay, Arledge called Friedman
at home in London, offered him the job, and told him to be in New
York to start work the following Monday.

Like David Brinkley, Paul Friedman was a gift to ABC from NBC
News, courtesy of Bill Small. The son of a Brooklyn high school
principal, Friedman had gone to work for NBC after Princeton and
the Columbia Journalism School. As a young reporter, he'd made a
name for himself covering the New York City school strike in 1969,
where he beat the competition by calling school officials who knew
his father and introducing himself as "Bill Friedman's son." "NBC

thought I was a genius," Friedman said, "and I never disabused them of that notion."

He abandoned on-air work to become a producer for "Huntley-Brinkley," an executive producer of local news at WNBC in New York, and then, at age thirty-one, executive producer of "Today." When he tired of the morning grind, Friedman tried his hand at producing prime-time news programs for NBC, with less success. He didn't get along with Small, and so he was receptive when Dick Wald, who had known him at NBC, offered him a posting in London, overseeing ABC's coverage of Europe, Africa, and the Middle East.

While Friedman, at forty-two, was coming home to New York to run "World News," the combination of his Princeton education, his years in London, and his British wife, Gillian, had by this time erased all traces of Brooklyn from his speech and manner. If anything, the lean, mustachioed Friedman had a refined, almost European way of comporting himself, a casual self-confidence that lent a welcome air of calm to "World News" after the tempestuous reign of Bill Lord. For his part, Lord was put in charge of a new ABC News unit that created programming for new technologies such as laser discs. Later, Jennings told a colleague, "Bill Lord is now doing what he should be doing — working with machines."

Friedman pledged his support to Jennings. He had been around long enough to know that he needed to win his anchorman's trust. "Peter came to know relatively quickly that I would never, ever do anything to make him look bad," Friedman said. At Friedman's suggestion, they agreed not to "fight in front of the children," meaning the rest of the "World News" staff, and they agreed to present a united front to Arledge. The message was that "it's you and me against the world," an insider said. That was just what Jennings needed to hear.

His mood lifted visibly. No longer did Jennings worry about what was being said behind his back. "I've heard from people that I seem happier and more fulfilled on the broadcast," he said, "and I think that's perfectly true." The two men argued about the lineup, about stories, or about which correspondents to use, but they never argued about who was in charge. They were true partners.

Their first major assignment was the 1988 elections. Jennings approached the campaign with his usual verve, but ABC News did not serve its viewers well. Its coverage, like that on the other networks, suffered from an excess of polls, an undue emphasis on campaign strategy, and, most of all, an overreliance on the words and pictures supplied each day by campaign image-makers. "The networks," said one critic, "were gulled by visual manipulation."

Arledge was among those disappointed by the coverage. "If you see how we were being led around by the nose, and how our access was restricted, and how commercials took the place of thoughtful interviews, it's a very serious problem," he said. But he added, "It's very hard to cover substance when there's no substance there." This was only half true — if George Bush and Michael Dukakis weren't talking substance on the campaign trail, both had public records that could have been examined in greater depth.

What Arledge didn't say — or see — was that he, as much as anyone else, had unleashed the forces that left the networks so vulnerable to the media manipulators. It was Arledge, after all, who drove his producers to illustrate their stories with vivid pictures; he was not alone, but he was always reminding people that television is a visual medium. By 1988, all the networks had become obsessed with visuals, to the point where field producers consulted with campaign managers about camera angles. Nor could the networks resist a punchy sound bite, substantive or not. Knowing this, the campaigns came up with a line-of-the-day ("Read my lips") and a symbolic backdrop (the flag factories) and then awaited their evening news coverage. Usually, they got it, albeit with acidic commentary from network correspondents, some of whom complained over the air that they were being used. But the networks could not resist compelling footage, even if it was manufactured news.

ABC News fared better in 1988 with its own campaign to make Peter Jennings the nation's favorite anchor. Jennings was far more comfortable than he had been in 1984, when, just back from London, he'd felt obliged to defer to David Brinkley. "Peter had been on very shaky ground, and he was the first to admit it," said Stu Schutzman, his producer. "This time, he was totally in command. He was the standard-bearer of ABC News."

His finest moment came at the first presidential debate. For days, Jennings worked on his questions. "I enlisted everybody, including my mother," Jennings said. "I couldn't walk through the halls around here without asking, 'What's your question?' " He winnowed the list and then put Nancy Gabriner, his diligent researcher, to work checking the candidates' records and statements all weekend before the Sunday night debate. Friedman, who accompanied Jennings to the debate in Winston-Salem, North Carolina, was struck by his preparation. "The perfectionist in him is just unbelievable," Friedman said.

"This was obviously a very highly focused public demonstration of what he could do. And he was very, very nervous about it. We essentially locked ourselves up in a hotel room for thirty-six hours and just went over and over the questions." They tried to come up with questions that would be probing, revealing, buttressed by evidence, and likely to wean Bush and Dukakis away from programmed answers.

To Dukakis, Jennings observed that "the theme that keeps coming up about the way you govern is passionless, technocratic — the smartest clerk in the world." With Bush, Jennings noted that he'd said he was "haunted" by the lives of children in the inner cities and asked, "If it haunts you so, why over the eight years of the Reagan-Bush administration have so many programs to help the inner cities been eliminated or cut?" Jennings also pressed Dukakis to explain how he'd pay for new social programs, asked Bush what was wrong with Dukakis's support for the American Civil Liberties Union, and called on both candidates to say what they would do to secure the release of American hostages in the Middle East. His polished performance won praise from viewers and critics. A headline in *Newsweek* read, "One surprise winner: ABC's Peter Jennings."

Arledge was not as quick to applaud. He, too, went to Winston-Salem, but he felt slighted because Jennings and Friedman had not included him in their debate preparation. When they finally got together afterward, Jennings asked his boss what he thought. Arledge replied curtly, "You didn't want my opinion before."

Now Jennings was the one to feel hurt. He had always craved Arledge's approval, in part because he respected Arledge's judgment and in part because of his own self-doubt. "I don't think Roone ever says anything to me that doesn't stick, at least for a period of time," Jennings said.

But Arledge's opinions mattered less to Jennings as he grew closer to Paul Friedman. His new executive producer was thoughtful, composed under fire, and skilled at managing the ABC correspondent corps, all qualities that Jennings appreciated. What's more, "World News" had by 1988 pulled into a virtual ratings tie with CBS. After the election Friedman introduced a new segment called the "American Agenda" that further differentiated ABC from the competition. To Jennings, these were all welcome changes.

What pleased him most of all, though, was the way he could count on Friedman, in a way he'd never felt able to rely on Arledge. He trusted and liked Friedman and enjoyed spending time with him away from the office. They'd get together occasionally in the Hamptons on weekends, to play tennis or go to a horse show; both had young daughters who liked to ride. Their closeness meant that Jennings was no longer as dependent on Arledge as he had been; their success meant that together they had become a force to be reckoned with inside ABC, as Arledge gradually would discover.

Like most people at "20/20," Barbara Walters was unhappy when the ousted Av Westin was replaced as executive producer by Victor Neufeld, his longtime right-hand man. "All of us tried to save Av," Walters said. "Some people were quite verbal about it. It was very tough for Victor." But Walters, unlike others, saw that Westin's departure left a power vacuum at "20/20" — one that she was more than willing to fill.

Victor Neufeld was no Av Westin, as he well knew. "Av was such a great charismatic leader," Neufeld said, "and I was always in his shadow." Neufeld, forty-one, was a plodder, a modest, low-key, prematurely gray-haired manager, whose strength was not his leadership ability but his instinctive feeling for what the audience would watch. That was partly because Neufeld never lost touch with his own roots in Jersey City, New Jersey, where his father sold draperies and his mother raised the family. After college at Rutgers, Neufeld got a master's in communications from Brooklyn College because he was fascinated by television. "I was a TV news junkie," he said. "I watched everything."

His on-the-job training came at New York's WNEW-TV, Channel 5, where he rose to produce "The Ten O'Clock News," a gritty, street-smart local newscast. He joined ABC News in 1973, worked for Westin on "World News," and followed his mentor to "20/20" in 1979. By his own account, Neufeld served as a useful sounding board for Westin. "Av trusted me a lot with instinctive, gut things because Av was a very cultured person and I'm much more blue-collar," said Neufeld. Of all the pieces he did for "20/20," Neufeld's favorite was his 1980 profile of Rodney Dangerfield. That was fitting because, around ABC News, Neufeld got no respect.

As executive producer of "20/20," Neufeld ran into immediate opposition from Westin loyalists. They complained that their new boss was reluctant to take risks on offbeat ideas, new approaches, or costly investigations that might not pan out. Some producers rebelled; others quit. "You can't convince this guy to spend six months on a story," complained investigative producer Charlie Thompson, who left for "60 Minutes." Other staff members tried to embarrass Neufeld by leaking word of morale problems on "20/20" to the *New York Times*. "It was a pretty tortuous period for a year or two," said Neufeld, who knew his authority was being tested.

But Neufeld got rid of a few detractors, wore down others, and gradually set out to reshape "20/20." He was guided by his own instincts and by research that told him that the available audience on Friday nights was middle-aged and middle-of-the-road, more attuned to *Reader's Digest* than *Vanity Fair*. "We're not an urbane, hip, ultra-sophisticated program, and we don't want to be," Neufeld would say. If anything, he said, Friday nights demanded "more of a tabloid-type program," with promotable stories that would engage "the conservative, traditional American household."

To Neufeld, that meant fewer news stories and more features. In particular, he sensed that the self-help and medical stories that brought millions of viewers to "Oprah" and "Donahue" could be adapted to prime time. In Neufeld's first year in charge, "20/20" did stories about female sexuality, male plastic surgery, asthma, arthritis, headaches, hysterectomies, mastectomies, cancer phobia, people who fear flying, and child bullies, as well as a full hour about aging. Some hard-edged news stories also got done, among them a prescient warning about the dangers of silicone breast implants and a critical look at tobacco marketing in the third world. While both the news-you-can-use features and the harder-edged pieces were well produced, the tone of the show had changed. Unlike Westin, Neufeld had little desire to stretch the horizons of his viewers by exposing them to the unfamiliar. Neufeld's "20/20" was driven less by journalistic curiosity and more by marketing.

"Victor had an unerring sense of what would sell, what would be a gut wrencher, what would hit an emotional chord with the audience," said Danny Schechter, a "20/20" producer. "He knew what his mother-in-law or his mother would watch. He set up the organization so that everything had to go through the filter of, will it play in Jersey City?"

One person who played well everywhere was Barbara Walters. She was a "middle-American superstar," Neufeld said, and her influence over the show grew. During his stint on the evening news, Neufeld had worked for Walters as a field producer, and she still regarded him as an employee. "She treats Victor like the janitor," said a "20/20" insider. This was an exaggeration but not by much. Neufeld could stand up to her on little things — he'd insist that she retape her "cast chat" segments if they lacked energy — but Walters usually decided what she wanted to do and then informed Neufeld. So long as she delivered, she had her way.

And Walters did deliver, regularly securing interviews not only with celebrities and political leaders but with the most-sought-after people in the news. For "20/20" Walters virtually invented a new genre of television interview — the first look at a previously unknown person who is thrust into the headlines. She interviewed Jean Harris, the upper-class educator accused of murdering her lover; Claus Von Bulow, the socialite charged with trying to kill his wife; and Barbara Walker, the ex-wife of convicted spy John Walker Jr. These emotional true-crime sagas proved to be reliable ratings winners. And while Ted Koppel questioned Gary Hart on "Nightline" about his relationship with model Donna Rice, Walters went after — and got — Rice.

Few "20/20" stories had as much impact as Walters's interview with heavyweight boxing champion Mike Tyson on September 30, 1987, after reports surfaced that he was manic-depressive, suicidal, and abusive toward his wife, Robin Givens. As a boyish Tyson escorted Walters around his lavish New Jersey mansion, her first impression was favorable. "He was tender, touching, sweet, intelligent," she said. "I liked him enormously." Walters realized that she was onto a big story when, after taping the interview with Tyson, Givens pulled her aside to say that she was not getting the full truth. Then, with Tyson beside her, Givens proceeded to describe her new husband as violent and a manic-depressive. "It's been torture," Givens said. "It's been pure hell. It's been worse than anything I could possibly imagine. I'm not talking about once a week. I'm talking about every day it's been some kind of battle, some kind of fight." To Walters's amazement, Tyson replied calmly that he still loved his wife and was dealing with his illness. "I was stunned," Walters said. "I just shut up and let them talk." After the taping, he brought out a cake in honor of Walters's birthday. "They were huggy, kissy, and gave me this birthday cake," she said.

Walters told Neufeld that she needed the full hour of "20/20" for the story. Neufeld was skeptical, but he went along — and the interview scored high ratings. "This was a big breakthrough for Victor and me," Walters said, "because since then, when I've said, 'Trust me,' he does." By then, Walters had become a Neufeld fan. "I think he is greatly underestimated," she said, "but we have a strong and good and exciting show week in and week out and that's Victor. Victor has made this show an enormous success."

That, in the end, was Neufeld's best response to his critics. They could complain all they wanted about how he had narrowed the scope of "20/20," but his retooled version of the program was a resounding success in the way that mattered most in television — in the ratings. Despite the move to Friday, a night when fewer people stayed home, "20/20" lost only a fraction of its audience. By the 1988–89 TV season, "20/20" had become the highest-rated hour of news or entertainment on ABC. By then, the show was generating close to $50 million a year in revenues for ABC News.

Arledge was satisfied, even if "20/20" wasn't his favorite show. "Victor proved himself after a relatively short period of time," he said. "He did a hell of a job."

But although few saw it then, the locus of power was shifting at ABC News. Koppel at "Nightline," Jennings at "World News," and Walters at "20/20" had all taken greater control over their work for ABC — Koppel by forming his own company, Jennings by aligning himself with a strong producer, and Walters by settling for a malleable one. Arledge would have preferred to maintain control through a strong group of executive producers who answered only to him — his "knights of the round table," as one put it — but there was no way to hold back the stars he had helped create.

Dorrance Smith, the Brinkley show executive producer, said later, "One thing that's changed in Roone's tenure is that he used to have a strong core of managers and executive producers, and he would always be able to maintain a certain amount of control over the anchors. Now every show is driven by what the anchor wants, and every producer is a subject of the anchor as opposed to part of a centralized management team under Roone Arledge."

Arledge saw the danger. Even the stars who remained loyal to him — and not all did — had become difficult to control. "I'm like Gunther Goebbel Williams," he said. "He has to go into this cage every day with these seven huge tigers and have them all sit on the chairs and do what they're supposed to do, knowing any one of them can eat you up."

The peril to Arledge grew when David Burke, his most valuable ally at ABC News, quit to become president of CBS News.

Throughout his time at ABC News, Arledge profited from mistakes made by the competition. NBC News was chronically unstable, going through five news presidents — Lester Crystal, Bill Small, Reuven Frank, Larry Grossman, and Michael Gartner — while Arledge ran

ABC. Turmoil was also endemic at CBS News, which had been debilitated by factional struggles over power and news values. Like ABC, NBC and CBS were sold in the mid-1980s to new owners, but neither General Electric, which bought NBC, nor Laurence Tisch, who took over CBS, had any experience in broadcasting. Like Tom Murphy and Dan Burke, GE's Jack Welch and CBS's Tisch set out to eliminate waste at the networks, particularly in the news divisions, but the battles at CBS and NBC were noisier and bloodier than those at ABC.

The perpetual unrest at NBC News and CBS News, combined with Arledge's ability to keep most of his problems out of the public eye, benefited ABC News in countless ways. Negative press coverage harmed the images of CBS News and NBC News. Inside those networks, people were often distracted by internal politics, while those at ABC News were better able to focus on their jobs. The problems elsewhere also helped Arledge recruit people such as David Brinkley and Paul Friedman, who had been cast aside by NBC, and to persuade his own people not to defect. Ted Koppel, Peter Jennings, Barbara Walters, Sam Donaldson, and David Brinkley all had serious offers from the competing networks, but all were convinced to stay at ABC.

David Burke was arguably as important to ABC News as any anchor, but Arledge could not convince him to stay. After a decade as Arledge's right-hand man, Burke hungered for the opportunity to run his own shop. He was the first outsider ever hired to run CBS News, and, as Arledge noted, it was a sign of the new competitive order in broadcast news that he had come from ABC. "He richly deserves this recognition, which is a compliment both to him and to ABC News," Arledge said. "I'm going to miss him, of course. He's like a brother to me."

All of ABC News would miss Burke. On a day-to-day basis, Burke ran ABC News, dealing with the affiliates, other network divisions, and Cap Cities, and handling dozens of chores that bored Arledge. Burke, in fact, was a near-perfect complement to Arledge. He did not know much about production or programming, which were Arledge's strengths, but he had a host of qualities Arledge lacked: he was straightforward, decisive, accessible, and a hands-on executive. He was, in some ways, the glue that held together ABC News.

"David Burke knew how to manage people. He knew how to manage offices. He knew how to produce decisions," said executive producer Jeff Gralnick. "If you needed to get a message to Roone, and you couldn't get it through directly, you could give it to David." Burke listened for Arledge and spoke for him too.

Burke took on small jobs and big ones, such as the effort to free Charles Glass. "Burke was magnificent," said Peter Jennings. "I mean, I truly loved him after that." Burke stayed in touch with producers and correspondents he'd hired, as well as with the power players at ABC — Jennings, Koppel, and the executive producers, who respected him. Dorrance Smith, the "Brinkley" producer, said, "There are not a lot of people whom you admire in the network world. Fewer and fewer. And he was somebody I admired and looked up to."

Burke would stroll through the newsroom in the afternoon, cup of tea in hand, chatting with whoever was around. "It was the most important, subtle, inoffensive display of management at work that you can imagine," said Jennings. "He just walked the deck. He never came down carrying a bullwhip or beating a drum, but he could get very excited and very passionate about things." Later, Jennings tried to persuade Arledge to find a way to mingle with the troops, but he could not. Arledge remained isolated, in part because he simply wasn't comfortable in uncontrollable settings. As Burke explained, "Roone is horribly, terribly shy and insecure. He likes his office a lot."

Arledge was powerless to keep Burke, but he could have tried to replace him. He did not. His pride came into play — he knew that some people at ABC News thought Burke was indispensable, and he wanted to prove them wrong. He also was not sure that he wanted a strong second-in-command; it had bothered Arledge when Burke got involved with programming "Nightline" and "Brinkley." Fond as he was of his friend, Arledge set out to prove that he could beat CBS News and David Burke without replacing him.

To that end, for the first time, Tom Murphy and Dan Burke gave Arledge permission to raid CBS. The Cap Cities executives had tried until then to avoid costly bidding wars among the networks for talent. Murphy, in fact, felt that he and his friend Larry Tisch had an unspoken agreement that Tisch had violated by hiring David Burke. "Tom was upset," Arledge recalled, "because he had hoped that he and Larry Tisch were not going to raid each other's people or talent. This led to a change of heart."

It would soon lead to Diane Sawyer.

Chapter Fifteen

NOT READY FOR PRIME TIME

NOT SINCE THE COURTSHIP of Dan Rather had Roone Arledge pursued anyone as long and as hard as he pursued Diane Sawyer. He was, if not in love with Sawyer, in love with what she could do for ABC News. "She was the one person," he said, "who had the potential to really break through and become a superstar." If ABC News could get Sawyer, Arledge thought, people might finally see just how good his news division had become.

He had wanted to hire Sawyer when her last contract had expired in 1986. Her agent, Richard Leibner, had told him then that Sawyer would leave CBS only for a co-anchor position on the evening news, an idea that held no appeal for Peter Jennings. Besides, Tom Murphy and Dan Burke, who had just arrived at ABC, had not wanted to enter a bidding war for Sawyer. "They almost forbade it," Arledge said. Reluctantly, he concluded that there was no way to get Sawyer then for ABC. But he promised to stay in touch.

That he did — steadfastly. They met occasionally for lunch. More often, Arledge would call after she appeared on CBS. He was curious as always, once debriefing her at length after she traveled to the Soviet Union. A theme began to emerge: Sawyer was doing terrific work but not getting the support she deserved from CBS.

Arledge told her that "60 Minutes" had grown stale, that the program was no longer at the cutting edge of television news. He criticized the opening, which always showed Sawyer in the same yellow dress. And after the 1988 political conventions, where CBS used Sawyer as its podium correspondent, he called to say that he would not put Barbara Walters on the air with antennas growing out of her head. This was a telling remark, since all the reporters at the conventions wore headsets; the message was that Sawyer had become too big a star to wander the convention floor.

In the meantime, Arledge set out to create a fitting home for Sawyer at ABC. He began with Murphy and Burke, who had gradually come to recognize the profit potential of news in prime time; they regretted even the decision to cancel "Our World." Arledge, who did not want to repeat that unhappy experience, insisted on getting a long-term commitment from Cap Cities for his next creation. At a meeting with Murphy, Burke, and Sias, he cited the example of "Good Morning America," which ABC had launched against "Today" with the understanding that the new show would have at least a year to become established. "If we are going to do a serious magazine program, it has to have that same sort of commitment," Arledge said. "You don't go into a time period and announce after thirteen weeks that you're going to take it off like an entertainment program." This was a crucial insight. The networks had introduced at least a dozen prime-time news magazines since the mid-1970s, all of them failures except "60 Minutes" and "20/20." News programs needed time to find their audience, Arledge knew. He also knew that he needed an ironclad commitment to get Sawyer. To their credit, Murphy and Burke pledged to keep the program on the schedule for at least two years.

To develop a format, Arledge created an uneasy partnership between Dorrance Smith, the "Brinkley" executive producer, and Phyllis McGrady, a bright, engaging producer who had produced Barbara Walters's prime-time specials. They were asked to generate ideas for a new program, but their real job was to supply Arledge with the bait he needed to hook Sawyer. "Diane was the key," said McGrady, who assumed that without her there would be no show. As Smith composed formats for Arledge to pass along to Sawyer, he felt like Cyrano de Bergerac, the soldier-poet who wrote flowery love letters on behalf of a shy suitor.

All of it — Arledge's critiques of CBS, the commitment from Cap Cities, and the opportunity to launch a new show — made an impression on Sawyer. There was something else too. Arledge wanted to do his new program live, to recapture the excitement of live television that was missing from prime time. Even "20/20" was now taped most of the time, leaving Arledge's "Monday Night Football" as the only regularly scheduled live program in prime time. Sawyer was challenged by Arledge's vision. "If you were willing to go live, willing to get off the TelePrompTers, willing to take chances, willing to make mistakes — some of which will be mortifying — but if you're willing to do that, you can create something alive and exciting," she said. "That was the siren call."

Arledge himself was a lure. The more time they spent together, the more appealing Sawyer found him. "For all the talk about his beguiling qualities, his hypnotizing raptures that he leaves everyone in, it comes down really to one thing: he's smart, he's really smart," she said. "He really believes in the ability of serious broadcasts to be interesting to the public at large . . . And he dreams always of having the most intelligent broadcasts he can put on the air. I think that's the secret of him. It's not the rest. It's not flattery." Just as Arledge had appealed to Dan Rather's competitiveness and Tom Brokaw's sense of fun, he was perfectly attuned to Sawyer — what she desired, above all, was to be desired for her brains.

"Roone," she said admiringly, "dreams big dreams."

Arledge's dream included Sam Donaldson as co-anchor for Sawyer. Late in 1988, he approached Donaldson to tell him, in confidence, something he already knew — that ABC was trying to hire Sawyer so they could do a show together. That sounded terrific to Donaldson, who wanted out of the White House when Ronald Reagan's term, and his ABC contract, expired in January. Knowing as much, Arledge assumed, wrongly, that he'd have no trouble persuading Sam to sign on for the new show.

After New Year's, Arledge called Donaldson to say that the prospects for getting Sawyer looked good, although he added, offhandedly, "If we can get her, I think we'll go ahead with this program. If we can't get her, we probably won't." That gave Donaldson pause. Wait a second, he thought. I'm the caboose? He felt he deserved better than that.

So it was an apprehensive Donaldson who was summoned to New York in late January to meet with Arledge and have dinner with Sawyer. Before the dinner, Arledge informed him that he'd made two promises to Sawyer: "One is that her name will be first. The second is, she'll say good evening."

Donaldson was taken aback. He didn't care about top billing — someone's name had to come first — but he wasn't sure what was meant by saying good evening. "I'm not saying it's a problem," he said, "but I want to think about it." He had not even begun to negotiate, and Arledge had bargained away elements of the show.

Arledge tried to explain. Sawyer, he said, was walking away from

CBS and "60 Minutes." She needed reassurance. "She's leaving home," Arledge said. "This is your home, Sam. You're one of us."

Now Donaldson's alarm bells were clanging. He could not help feeling that "this is not a show that Roone is constructing to have co-anchors who are equal. And that's a problem. That is a problem." Striking a friendly tone, Donaldson said that, before he'd sign a new contract, he wanted a "level playing field" on the show and salary equality. "Not a penny more, but not a penny less" was the way he put it.

That night's dinner with Sawyer went well. They liked each other right away and shared a feeling of excitement about creating a live prime-time show. "It was a wonderful evening," Donaldson said. Sawyer recalled, "I very much wanted to work with Sam."

When Donaldson returned that night to Washington, he had a message waiting. David Burke, who as president of CBS News was fighting to keep Sawyer, had called Donaldson's lawyer, Bob Barnett, to say that he wanted to hire Donaldson whether CBS lost Sawyer or not. Burke said that he would take the CBS News magazine "West 57th" off the air and give Donaldson his own show. The CBS offer put Donaldson in a formidable position when he returned to New York to negotiate with Arledge.

The future of two of the biggest stars in television news hung in the balance on that evening of Monday, January 28, 1989. Arledge had arranged to have dinner with Donaldson, Bob Barnett, and Irwin Weiner at Nonni Il Valleto, a pricey East Side restaurant and a favorite Arledge hangout. A few blocks away at the Regency Hotel, Sawyer had dinner with Larry Tisch, who owned the hotel as well as CBS. Tisch was making a last-ditch effort to keep Sawyer, who had just finished gently explaining to her friend William S. Paley that she had all but decided to leave CBS, the company he had founded sixty years earlier.

Arledge had not anticipated trouble at his end. Here he was, offering Donaldson the chance to co-anchor a prime-time show with a guaranteed two-year run on ABC. He was giving him the escape from the White House grind he had wanted for years. And he was giving him a huge raise. "I thought it was the biggest break of Sam's career," Arledge said. "All he had to do was come along, and he was going to vault up to a level where he had not been before."

Arledge expected gratitude. Instead, he got a hard time.

Money was not the issue. Donaldson would be paid about $1.7 million to do the new program, which was fine with him. It was a mere $5,000 less than Sawyer, who, he assumed, had been promised that she would be the best-paid anchor on the show.

The sticking point remained airtime. Donaldson felt he was being asked to accept a subordinate role. Arledge tried to assure him that he would be Sawyer's equal, but Donaldson said he wanted the promises spelled out in writing.

Arledge seethed with anger. Donaldson, he felt, was being petty. "You are not willing to take my word," Arledge said. "Why would you even raise this issue? It's silly."

"Roone, it may be silly to you, but it's not silly to me," Donaldson replied.

They went back and forth. Arledge tried to convince Donaldson not to worry, that he'd succeeded at everything he'd done, that with his energy and personality, he was the one who would dominate. "You'll take over!" exclaimed Arledge. "Our problem will be trying to make her visible, next to you."

That was fine with Donaldson, but he wanted it written down.

If Arledge had reason to be upset — he didn't like having his integrity questioned — Donaldson had reason to be suspicious. He'd heard through the grapevine that Sawyer was telling people at CBS that the program would be structured around her, and he wondered whether Arledge had made other commitments to Sawyer.

As it happened, Arledge had promised Sawyer that she could work with Donaldson. "Diane unwittingly gave him incredible leverage," Arledge said. "By this time, Diane had talked herself into the fact that she and Sam would be wonderful together."

That was what really got under Arledge's skin. Sawyer was the prize he had coveted for years. And a very stubborn Sam Donaldson stood in his way.

Arledge decided he had no choice but to give in to Donaldson.

Arledge agreed — grudgingly — to write into Donaldson's contract the guarantees he wanted. The contract specified that the anchors would share screen time in close to equal measure. They'd have equal opportunity to do stories. And since Sawyer had been told she could open the show, Donaldson was assured that he could say good night, although that was not written down. He'd won, but his victory was bittersweet.

Afterward, Donaldson was unhappy that he'd been forced to negotiate for what he felt was his rightful place on the show, earned by his work for ABC over twenty years. The negotiations had only heightened his fear that if things went sour he would be thrown overboard first. In his heart, Donaldson knew that no contract would prevent Arledge from reshaping the program in any way he liked.

Arledge, too, came away displeased. He didn't like being forced to cede his authority over a program, although he'd been willing to do so for Sawyer. But what really infuriated him was hearing from Donaldson that he could not be trusted to keep his word. "I was so pissed off," Arledge said. "It caused a major rupture between Sam and me."

But Diane Sawyer was worth it. The proof came with the morning papers, where her decision to leave CBS was front-page news. Sawyer made the covers of *Time* and *New York* magazine, and her defection was seen as evidence of the ascendancy of ABC News, just as Arledge had hoped it would be. In *New York* magazine, Ed Klein wrote, "In a medium where symbols are as important as reality, Sawyer's choice of ABC over CBS signaled that a decisive shift had occurred in broadcast journalism. . . . It was no longer CBS but ABC that was the dominant network in news." Other critics struck a similar tone, which was understandable: Sawyer was the biggest star to leave CBS since Harry Reasoner quit in 1970. What's more, she was leaving a high-profile job as one of Don Hewitt's chosen few on "60 Minutes," the most popular show in television history, for a program still to be invented by Arledge.

Arledge had triumphed in more ways than one. By getting Diane Sawyer, he had bested CBS News, the organization he had once envied as the epitome of success in television. At last, he felt, people would understand that ABC News — led by Roone Arledge — was the standard-setter in broadcast journalism. Besides that, the fact that such great significance was attached to Sawyer's move was itself a triumph for Arledge and the star system that he had embraced and driven to new heights. Counting stars had become the way Arledge measured success in television, not because he didn't care about serious journalism, but because that was the way the press and the public had come to define success in an age of celebrity. The world had changed dramatically since ABC's hiring of Barbara Walters as an evening news anchor for $1 million a year had provoked outrage from the journalistic establishment; this time, there were only cheers for ABC News and Sawyer. It was striking: ABC News had piled up scores of points with its journalism over the years, but it took the arrival of Diane Sawyer to certify that the game was over.

Diane Sawyer had climbed to the top of the network news business with astonishing speed. What had driven her so far so fast? Why was she so fervently desired by the men who run the networks? Even television insiders had to wonder.

Sawyer, after all, had spent only a few years covering a beat, and she was not known as an especially gifted interviewer. Nor was she a proven audience draw; her work on the "CBS Morning News" had pleased critics, but the program's ratings had grown only slightly. On "60 Minutes," Sawyer had performed well but not exceptionally well. Her stories were carefully crafted but not as hard-edged as Mike Wallace's, or as elegantly written as Morley Safer's, or as humorous as Harry Reasoner's. Wallace himself had said, "She's got to find her own voice in the show." She never did.

But Sawyer's journalistic shortcomings mattered little. She was selling star quality, and Roone Arledge was an eager buyer. Diane Sawyer was one of those rare television personalities who, he was sure, possessed a presence so regal that, in the right setting, she could virtually command viewers to watch. It was not merely her beauty, although few women on television were as striking, but her cool and elegant manner, her rich silken voice, and her ease on camera. Not only that, Sawyer was smart: she was book-smart, occasionally ostentatiously so — slim volumes of poetry were prominently displayed in her office — and more to the point, she was TV-smart, able to speak off the cuff in a thoughtful and perceptive manner. "A thinking man's Angie Dickinson" was the way one critic summed up the package.

Her charisma was matched only by her drive. This was Sawyer's secret weapon, unseen by the viewers but evident to all around her. No one worked harder. No one paid closer attention to the details. No one cared more.

The fuel that powered her engine was not mere ambition, but a striving for perfection in all she did. She would pore over scripts for hours or days, seeking the right structure, tinkering with the language, exhausting producers, but never satisfying herself. A routine story in her hands could become an ordeal. One colleague said, only half joking, "Everything Diane does, Diane feels is the worst thing she's ever done. She's just that way. Very tough on herself. And she thinks that gives her the right to be tough on everyone around her."

That is not unlike the picture Sawyer paints of her mother, Jean Sawyer, who, she confesses, is the primary source of her "why-not-an-A-plus" approach to her work. "I'm a prisoner of my genes, literally, in every way," Sawyer said. When Sawyer brought her new husband, legendary film director Mike Nichols, home to visit, Jean

Sawyer sent him to the basement to scrub the bottoms of his shoes with an old toothbrush before he could tread on the carpet. "That's my mother," she sighed.

Born December 22, 1945, in Glasgow, Kentucky, a suburb of Louisville, Diane Sawyer was the second daughter of Jean and E. P. "Tom" Sawyer, a respected politician. Her mother was a small woman with coal black hair, but "a pistol, a ball of fire, just a very scrappy woman," Sawyer said. "She tells everybody what to do about everything, and everybody does it instantly because you don't dare not. And she gets you up in the morning, and gets you out the door, and criticizes your hair, and makes sure your ears are clean, and that's who she is — she just took care of all of us."

Her father, a Republican county judge, was a ramrod-straight man who also held himself and others to high standards. Sawyer said, "My father was very tall and very funny and very principled, scrupulously, agonizingly honest. He cared about the right thing as much as anyone I've ever met in my life. Everybody who knew him felt that he was an extraordinary and noble man." He died in an auto accident when Diane was twenty.

She had proved, by then, that she was an extraordinary young woman. Her mother had given her "every imaginable lesson on earth" — piano, guitar, acting, fencing, tap, ballet, and horseback riding — and encouraged her to compete in beauty pageants. She was chosen America's Junior Miss at age seventeen, and the summer before starting college at Wellesley, she embarked on a cross-country tour of pageants and civic events. "I gave two and three and four speeches a day, which I would write myself," Sawyer said, "because I had this sort of ridiculous sense that it mattered."

After earning her college degree in English, Sawyer returned home to Louisville to work as a TV reporter and weather girl. There, she sometimes enlivened the forecasts with a few lines of Emily Dickinson or Baudelaire. "The weather was extraordinarily boring," she said, "so I'd have a quote every now and then." This grew old in a hurry, so with the help of her late father's Republican friends, she secured a job in the press office of the Nixon White House and moved to Washington in 1970.

Sawyer first got the president's attention after she composed an article about Nixon's mother that ran under his byline in a women's magazine. Later, she became the press office's reigning expert on Watergate, mastering the details of the scandal through her sheer diligence. When Nixon resigned in 1974, Sawyer was one of a handful of aides on the plane that flew him home to San Clemente.

Unexpectedly, she stayed for four years, helping the disgraced president write a self-serving memoir. She did so, she said, out of duty and loyalty, as well as concern for Nixon and the sense that she was needed. "I fell into the most seductive trap that awaits every one of us," she once explained, "which is the fiction of one's indispensability . . . I was being loyal and noble. They're among my worst faults." Her personal life also came into play; Sawyer was dating Frank Gannon, a speechwriter who also worked on the memoirs.

The book completed, she left to work in television and nearly landed at ABC. Bob Zelnick, then deputy bureau chief in Washington, interviewed her — they'd met when Zelnick produced David Frost's interviews with Nixon — and recommended she be hired. But before Arledge made her an offer, she signed up at CBS News, where the Washington bureau chief was Bill Small, a Louisville native and Sawyer family friend.

Initially, she met resistance. Dan Rather, among others, didn't want a Nixon partisan working for CBS News. But Sawyer won over the doubters by her unstinting commitment to her work as well as her fairness and intelligence. After a couple of years at the State Department, she was named co-anchor of the "CBS Morning News," a long-troubled outpost at CBS. She found an empathetic co-anchor in Charles Kuralt, who, like Sawyer, cared a lot about writing and fought stubbornly to do a program that respected the audience; she also found that she loved doing two hours of live television every day. But the excitement wore off after Kuralt was coldly dumped from the show and the ratings slumped. In 1984, Sawyer was thrilled when, after only six years in the business, she was picked by Don Hewitt as the first woman to join the cast of "60 Minutes."

It was about this time that the whispering began about Diane Sawyer. She was a brilliant office politician, people said, an alluring woman whose meteoric rise was propelled by her ability to charm powerful men — Gannon, Hewitt, CBS chairman William Paley, and later, CBS owner Larry Tisch. This speculation was not unfounded — when she was summoned from a meeting by an aide who said that "Mr. Paley is on the phone," everyone took notice — but it was, at heart, unfair. Sawyer's friendships may have smoothed her climb, but she clearly had the talent to capitalize on every opportunity she got. As Sawyer said, "Yes, I've been taken to dinner by Larry Tisch and

Bill Paley, but to assume that that's how I made my career at CBS is ridiculous. I'm no radical feminist, but that charge is clearly sexist." The man who, more than anyone else, helped her rise was her longtime beau Richard Holbrooke, a brilliant Wall Street investment banker and former State Department official. Her relationship with Holbrooke meant that she was taken seriously by the establishment in New York and Washington; he talked endlessly with her about the news, critiqued her work, and even helped select her clothes.

Moreover, Sawyer's career had also suffered from CBS office politics, which turned bitter by the mid-1980s. Kuralt's demotion, for example, had stunned her, preceded as it was by press leaks suggesting that he was too fat and uncharismatic for morning television. A network capable of such cruelty to a man like Kuralt could do anything to anybody, she thought, and, indeed, the civil wars at CBS intensified in the years that followed. While Sawyer tried to avoid the feuding, she found CBS News an uncomfortable place to work, a place where people could not be trusted to keep their promises. In particular, Sawyer was frustrated when she tried to revive the Edward R. Murrow program "Person to Person" as an occasional prime-time series, an opportunity she'd been promised in her contract. In that effort, she was thwarted by Hewitt and got no support from Howard Stringer, who ran CBS News. "You can't dance at two weddings with one tukhas," said Hewitt, who was not as strict with Mike Wallace and Ed Bradley, who worked on other shows as well as "60 Minutes." Nor was Sawyer given the opportunity to substitute for Dan Rather on the "CBS Evening News." She felt that opposition to her efforts was further evidence that CBS had become a snakepit.

She no longer wanted to live among the snakes.

By February 1989, Roone Arledge had Diane Sawyer, Sam Donaldson, and six months to figure out what to do with them. The program he envisioned was characteristically audacious — an unscripted hour of television that would transport viewers, live, to wherever news was happening. Arledge wanted the show to be as spontaneous and exciting as the Olympics, where, as executive producer, he had sat before a wall of monitors and selected only the most dramatic events for broadcast. Now, he would have all the world from which to choose.

First, though, he had to choose an executive producer. After creating an awkward partnership between Dorrance Smith and Phyllis McGrady, Arledge could not decide who he wanted in charge. Smith, he thought, lacked the requisite flair, while McGrady had never run a show for ABC News. Arledge considered asking them to produce the show together, but that was impractical.

Instead, he turned to Rick Kaplan, who he knew was strong enough to muscle a new show onto the air. That, however, meant finding a replacement for Kaplan at "Nightline" who was acceptable to Ted Koppel. After McGrady turned the job down, Arledge told Kaplan he could take over the new prime-time show — provided he could convince Koppel to accept Dorrance Smith as the executive producer of "Nightline."

Kaplan refused. He disliked Smith and didn't think he would be good for Koppel. He also felt that Smith was getting "Nightline" only because he had been passed over for the evening news and the prime-time show. With some bitterness, Kaplan said, "The day 'Nightline' becomes somebody's booby prize, that's a great day for ABC News."

Arledge was back at square one.

Finally, on March 1 — a full month after Sawyer's signing — Arledge installed McGrady as executive producer of the new show. She won his confidence after getting the support of Sawyer and Joanna Bistany, who had emerged as Arledge's closest aide since David Burke.

McGrady faced a daunting task. The show had no staff, no set, no theme music, no name, not even offices to call home. "I was really really afraid that we couldn't get it on the air," McGrady said. Fortunately, the feeling had spread that the new show would be an exciting place — there would be money, the chance to innovate, and attention from Arledge — so McGrady was able to hire some of the best producers and correspondents in television. Judd Rose, a gifted writer, and Chris Wallace, the former NBC White House reporter who had joined ABC, were among the first to come aboard.

The staff plunged into long meetings to figure out how to bring Arledge's vision to the screen. Everyone wanted the new show to be different from "20/20" or "60 Minutes," but that didn't get the discussion very far, and Arledge's contributions, at this stage, were limited. Some thought this was to his credit, that he had the courage to let others develop their own ideas. But the prevailing view was that Arledge held back either because he did not want to be held accountable for any misjudgments, or because his grand vision lacked specificity — or both. "He would articulate a concept, but it had never been worked out in his mind," a key producer said. Sports remained a reference point, as did the notion of mixing live and taped coverage.

"What they wanted," said one producer, "was Super Bowl–quality excitement, NBA Final Four excitement, Indy 500–type events, each week."

A few fresh ideas emerged. One producer coined the term "WOW," which stood for wonders of the world and referred to attention-getting stories that would take viewers to places they had never been before. Producers tested the idea by mounting tiny cameras to a roller coaster at the Magic Mountain theme park in California; they hooked up sensors to monitor the speed of the coaster, the gravity forces, and a rider's heart rate and blood pressure. The high-tech approach required two production trucks and a forty-person crew, and it cost about $165,000, but it seemed to work, and there was talk about doing "WOWs" at the White House and the Taj Mahal.

Director Roger Goodman, meanwhile, urged everyone to devote close attention to the texture of stories, to create a look for the new show that was visually richer than that of "20/20" or "60 Minutes." To get eye-catching pictures, the producers were taught to adapt Hollywood filmmaking techniques to the news, using cranes, dollies, and steadicams. The idea was to come up with sensual, visceral stories.

At Arledge's suggestion, McGrady also decided to bring in a live audience to react to the news in the style made popular on daytime television by Phil Donahue. The studio audience, they hoped, would bring out Donaldson's warm and engaging side, which emerged when he spoke to groups but had not been seen on television.

Then McGrady was struck by an untimely blow. Her mother suffered a heart attack in North Carolina and needed someone to oversee her treatment and recovery. After talking the situation over at length with Arledge, McGrady decided to leave the show. "If we had been much further along, I think I could have juggled it," she said. But, more than anyone else, she saw how much remained to be done.

This time around, there was no question — Kaplan would take over. CBS had just made him an offer to do "exactly what I wanted to do, which was produce and write movies," he said, but the lure of his own prime-time show was irresistible. Arledge told him that no one else could save the show.

With just seven weeks left before the premiere, Kaplan threw himself into the job. Guided by Arledge and Goodman, he had an elaborate set constructed, the heart of which was a $400,000 video wall composed of sixteen television monitors stacked atop one another. Bill Conti, who scored *Rocky* and "Dynasty," composed majestic theme music. Names were tested — they included "Smoking Gun,"

"Scoop," "Day of Air," and "TV One" — until Arledge settled on "PrimeTime Live." It wasn't catchy, but everyone figured the show would live or die as "The Sam and Diane Show." They would be "like Astaire and Rogers," Arledge had said.

That spring, "PrimeTime Live" was billed as a blind date between Lady Di and the loudmouth from the White House lawn, as "a sonata for harp and jackhammer," in Sawyer's words. In interviews, Sawyer and Donaldson talked — no, gushed — about each other in pithy quotes designed to give listeners a taste of the over-the-air banter planned between them.

"We're like Emily Dickinson and the Terminator," Sawyer said. "We disagree on everything from psychological to philosophical to political issues. But he's one of the most gracious, generous, spirited, smart, lively people I've ever worked around."

Donaldson returned the favor and then some: "Let's not mince words. I think Diane Sawyer is *terrific!*" He went on, "Beneath that cool, elegant exterior, she is aggressive and a tough competitor."

The compliments were heartfelt. But behind the bonhomie were conflicting ideas about what the show would be — conflicts that had yet to be resolved by McGrady, Kaplan, or Arledge.

Donaldson had no interest in doing a traditional magazine show. He envisioned "PrimeTime Live" as a live, timely, newsy show tied to the week's events, a prime-time version of the Brinkley show or "Nightline," albeit slicker. Before the premiere, Donaldson walked into the office of Betsy West, Kaplan's deputy, brandishing a list of stories in the works, and demanded to know what was going on. "Why do we need this?" he intoned. "If we do these stories, they'll be in the bank. If they're in the bank, we're going to have to run them. And I don't want to run them. I want to react to the news."

Sawyer wanted to be live when events warranted, but from "60 Minutes" she understood the power of well-written and polished taped pieces. She talked about video essays, about investigations, and about finding new ways to do intellectually fulfilling stories. Once, she mused, "I think the next chic is going to be irreverent reflection, maybe even depth. Profundity chic."

No wonder Kaplan was confused. "I'd say to people, what is the show about, and everyone has a different answer. They'd want to know what I thought the show was about," he remembered. "I went home one night, and I had a terrible headache because I knew we were in deep shit."

Others shared his jitters. Sawyer expected stumbles, saying, "There are going to be times when we're going to be sitting there not with just eggs on our face but, I would say, omelettes." Some saw disaster ahead. "All of us had doubts," said one.

No such doubts were reflected in the publicity buildup for "PrimeTime Live." Sawyer's ABC debut got buckets of ink, as did Donaldson's boast that they would knock NBC's "L.A. Law" off the air. "Your world will never be the same," boasted the promotional campaign mounted by ABC News. As "PrimeTime Live" became the most-talked-about event of the 1989 TV season, even Arledge, who loved promotion, worried that he had gone too far. "Once you start a p.r. operation in motion, it's harder than an earthquake to stop," he said later.

About a week before the premiere, correspondent Judd Rose strolled back to work after lunch and was amazed to see how expectations for the show had spiraled out of control.

"Every newsstand I passed, I saw a different magazine with Sam, Diane, or both on the cover," Rose recalled. "It really struck fear in my heart. We weren't that good in any case, and to try to live up to this publicity was going to be fatal."

Roone Arledge and Rick Kaplan wanted a big splash for the premiere of "PrimeTime Live." Thanks to the charms of a booker named Maia Samuel, they got one.

Bookers are the unsung heroes and heroines of network news. They are often attractive women with an alluring phone manner, no fear of rejection, and a willingness to go to great lengths in pursuit of sought-after newsmakers. Samuel's particular weapon was her British accent, which, she found, made her sound important to some people and sexy to others — in this instance, the people surrounding a Washington lawyer named Thomas Root.

Root was a mystery man whose story, while inconsequential, captivated the news media for a few slow weeks during the summer of 1989. While flying his small Cessna, he had blacked out; the plane, wandering on autopilot, led U.S. military jets and helicopters on a four-hour, thousand-mile chase to the Bahamas, then ran out of fuel and crashed, whereupon Root was fished out of the sea with an unexplained bullet wound in his stomach. Every TV news show wanted him, but he did no interviews until Samuel persuaded his brother, his lawyer, his bodyguard, and finally Root himself that he ought to appear on "PrimeTime Live." On the morning of the premiere, Thursday, August 3, 1989, Samuel checked her prize catch into a hotel on Central Park West and stationed herself in the lobby as a precaution, in case a rival network tried to spirit him away.

A competitor arrived soon enough, but she wasn't from CBS or NBC. Lynn Murray, an associate producer on "20/20," went to the hotel to persuade Root to ditch "PrimeTime Live" and talk to her boss — Barbara Walters — the next night. This was a mind-boggling ploy that meant that someone at "20/20" was so hell-bent on getting Root that he or she was willing to disrupt the long-awaited premiere of ABC's new show.

Walters was the prime suspect. But Victor Neufeld, the "20/20" executive producer, said he had suggested that Murray pursue Root. "It was my fault," he said. Walters denied any role, insisting that she did not want to hurt "PrimeTime" — although she had put out the word that "20/20" should be more aggressive than ever about booking major interviews. With the arrival of Diane Sawyer, Walters was determined to protect her standing as the first lady of ABC News.

Even before getting Root, "PrimeTime" had lined up an impressive guest list for its debut. There was Roseanne Barr, the biggest star on television; Secretary of State James Baker, to talk about American hostages in Lebanon; and such supporting players as ABC's ex-hostage Charles Glass and former CIA chief Stansfield Turner.

But "PrimeTime" failed to generate any opening-night excitement. Instead, by the end of the hour, the program had neatly illustrated the pitfalls of live television.

The Root interview, for starters, went nowhere. Teaming up, Sawyer and Donaldson struck the pose of investigative reporters. "I'm going to ask you what you know a lot of people think, that you tried to kill yourself," Sawyer said. Donaldson demanded, "Do you use drugs?" Predictably, the questions produced a Kabuki-like ritual, which enabled the anchors to sound tough and invited easy denials from Root. With time for a longer interview that could have been edited, either anchor might have been able to poke holes in Root's unlikely tale. Better yet, "PrimeTime" could have done its own investigation.

No better were the segments on the hostages. Poor Chris Wallace had to fly all the way to Jerusalem to do a live, predawn, ninety-second update, while Donaldson was left to preside over a silly audience-participation segment in which viewers were invited to explain what they would do, as president, to bring the hostages home.

Sawyer's disjointed chat with Roseanne Barr was another letdown, partly because she failed to ask Barr about being snubbed when the Emmy nominations were announced earlier that day.

Mercifully, the show was nearly over by then — all that remained was some stagy Sam-and-Diane banter about whether men and women can be just friends, pegged to the movie *When Harry Met Sally*.

"It helps us to remember that '20/20' and 'Nightline' both had first nights too," Sawyer said before signing off. She neglected to say what happened to the hosts of "20/20" after their debut.

The next day's reviews were mixed, but the ratings brought a shock. After all the buildup, "PrimeTime Live" achieved only a 10 rating and an 18 share against summer reruns on CBS and NBC. Few people cared to watch a blind date between Emily Dickinson and the Terminator, let alone a sonata for harp and jackhammer.

Arledge stepped in after the premiere, albeit tentatively. He saw that "PrimeTime" needed more taped stories, and he began to say that they shouldn't be live for live's sake, that the viewers don't care — something no one had heard from him before. He was right, but shifting gears to get more stories on tape wasn't easy; magazine stories take weeks to do well, and many of the producers had been hired to do live television. When Arledge demanded taped pieces right away, Kaplan was annoyed. "It's like telling a farmer that you need corn, so he goes out and plants seeds, and then you come back a week later and say, 'Well, where's the corn?'" he grumbled.

Besides, Kaplan remained committed to doing a live, newsy show — even as the limits of live television began to impose themselves. A few weeks in, for example, Kaplan ordered a live segment about the outpouring of sympathy for the Treaty Oak, a five-hundred-year-old poisoned tree in Austin, Texas. An associate producer named Bob Wheelock rushed to Austin, spent $12,000 for spotlights needed to bathe the tree in a bright nighttime glow, and set up cameras to cover every angle — only to find there was little to show. In the control room, Kaplan bellowed, "What does this tree do? Make it do something!" Wheelock replied, "It's a dying tree. What's it supposed to do?" This was not what was meant by ABC's claim that "anything can happen on live television."

The fact was that not much happened at 10 P.M. on Thursdays. Kaplan and his producers covered a rock concert by Cher and the occasional breaking news story, but they soon found that the only way to guarantee compelling live segments each week was to create them. That first summer, "PrimeTime" commissioned a live drug test to measure cocaine's impact on a patient and convinced President Bush and the First Lady to take Sawyer and Donaldson on a live White House tour — which turned into a great show. But the producers soon ran out of ideas that matched the hype about how "PrimeTime Live" was going to revolutionize television. They'd tell each other, "This is a really good story, but it's not big enough for this show."

Virtually every attempt to differentiate the show from other magazines proved to be misguided. While Donaldson occasionally plunged into the studio audience, Donahue-style, to stir up controversy, Sawyer was hesitant and distracted by the crowd. "You'd be in the middle of an interview with someone, and they'd laugh at the wrong moment," she said. Kaplan agreed to get rid of the audience, which meant reconfiguring the expensive Roman arena–style set that had been built to accommodate the crowd.

The anchor banter also fell flat. Sawyer was too self-conscious to engage in robust debate, while Donaldson, when his competitive juices flowed, displayed an unseemly eagerness to score with a put-down. Lacking scripts, they fell back on clichés or mangled them. "If man wanted us to fly, he would have given us wings," Donaldson once declared with his customary certainty.

Astaire and Rogers they weren't. Indeed, Sawyer told herself, "If only I could be this spontaneous Kathie Lee to Sam's Regis, then our chemistry would work. But I couldn't, and it didn't." Both anchors were relieved when the chatter was eliminated.

This process of learning what didn't work was necessary but not sufficient to make "PrimeTime Live" a success. Arledge, as usual, found it easier to second-guess than to devise solutions. With his show slumping, Kaplan felt besieged. "I was getting picked at left and right," he said. "Everyone started offering advice, and everyone was negative."

The worst of it came the night the Berlin Wall came down, when "PrimeTime" put on a terrific show. They had live reports, a history of the wall, an interview with Secretary of State Baker, Donaldson with Ronald Reagan, and the recollections of Pierre Salinger, who had visited Berlin with President Kennedy in 1961 after the wall went up. Watching from home, Arledge was so enthused that he joined Kaplan, Sawyer, and Donaldson at the Ginger Man, their habitual gathering place after the show. Arledge went on about how proud he was of Diane and Sam and Rick, about how this was what the show should be, about how this was what ABC News was all about.

The next day, Nielsen reported that "PrimeTime" had its worst numbers ever, a 6.8 rating and an 11 share. Now when Arledge called Kaplan, he was unhappy. The opening segment, he said, was confusing. Donaldson's talk with Reagan had gone on too long. And, he wanted to know, what were they planning for next week? That Arledge felt the need to pick the show apart after the fact did not, by itself, bother Kaplan or the others. Arledge had to worry about ratings. But they were disconcerted by the way his views were so changeable. It was as if the previous night's celebration had never occurred, as if the problems with the show were all theirs. An insider complained, "When it's time for the team to get together to present the game ball, Roone Arledge is ready to be there and accept it. But after a loss, he's nowhere to be found."

The pressure was getting to Kaplan. Nothing in his experience had prepared him for failure. He'd succeeded everywhere, most spectacularly at "Nightline," and he was so competitive, a colleague said, that "if there was a race to come out of the womb, you know Rick came out first and won." Now he took every setback to heart, growing irritable. Kaplan hadn't taken time off in months, and he wasn't sleeping well. "I felt like I was letting everybody down," he said. "I was really wrung out."

When an earthquake rocked northern California on October 17, 1989, causing extensive damage and disrupting the World Series, Kaplan saw the chance to redeem himself and "PrimeTime." Here was a great live story — he dispatched Donaldson and Judd Rose to San Francisco, sent Chris Wallace to Armenia, where an earthquake had killed 25,000 people ten months earlier, put a crew in an AT&T phone center to explain how emergency calls were handled, and arranged live interviews with politicians, geologists, and survivors.

Most, but not all, of the show went well. The AT&T segment was lifeless, just people sitting around a computer room, despite the best efforts of associate producer Bob Wheelock to please his bosses. "They were expecting it to be crazed, people running around like a movie," Wheelock recalled. "But things don't happen like that, that's why they make movies, to create that illusion. I brought in people on overtime for AT&T. I picked up the tab, so there would be people in the room. These are journalistic things I'd never done before, but it shows how desperate I was for my career. I found myself that night trying to create an illusion, and I was really troubled." Kaplan got angry anyway — not because of the staging, but because the segment was dull. He told Wheelock that his ABC career was over, that he belonged in the lobby checking IDs with the security guard.

That, it turned out, was merely a tremor. As the show ended, Kaplan called David Doss, a respected producer who had run the operation in San Francisco, and began to chew him out because a piece was late. Kaplan, enraged, was yelling into the phone loud enough so that a group gathered around Doss could tell something was wrong. "What's he saying?" Donaldson asked. Doss held out the receiver so everyone could hear the rant, which went on and on. "Don't you know what you're doing?" Kaplan yelled. "You don't deserve to be on this show." He really lost it when he screamed, "Oh, David, just die!" Doss, whose wife had cancer, replied, "Nice thing to say to me."

When the tirade ended, everyone was spent. The San Francisco group knew they had put on a good show under trying conditions. It was left to Donaldson, who was himself dispirited, to try to lift the others up, so he took the entire crew to a restaurant that he persuaded the owner to open. Donaldson ordered wine and offered a spirited toast, praising Doss and everyone else for a job well done. "Never mind what that son of a bitch had to say," he declared. "You are all heroes in my eyes." It meant a lot to everyone — this was Donaldson at his best.

The next day, Kaplan was so consumed with guilt that he apologized to everyone for his outburst. "I was just totally out of line," he said. He felt a bit better when his friend David Burke, then president of CBS News, called to congratulate him on the show — although he never heard from Arledge.

The Berlin Wall and earthquake programs were, as it happened, among the journalistic high points of the first season of "PrimeTime." These were the best shows, and they caused trauma. The low point was the Thanksgiving show — which, because of Kaplan's desire to be live, served up such thin gruel as a visit to the home of a Dallas Cowboy after the traditional turkey-day football game. ABC News then transported its prime-time audience to the Truck Stop of America in Ontario, California, where free turkey dinners were being served to hungry truckers.

"Those are the trucks now," Donaldson explained helpfully, as a camera panned the parking lot. "That's a live shot of the trucks actually parked."

"It's kind of like grass growing," he added.

As the cameras found the truckers inside chowing down, Donaldson knew he was in the wrong place at the wrong time.

He had covered Congress and confronted presidents, but this was his first truck stop Thanksgiving. He fervently hoped it would be his last. But he set about to interview Barbara Hughes, the head cook, in the only way he knew how — with gusto.

"Tell us about the work that goes into those meals," he said.

"I was going to say, how late are you open tonight?" he asked.

"What do the truckers say when you give them the meals?" he wondered. "I guess they're appreciative."

A desperate Donaldson then reverted to the Sam of old. "How much does it cost, Barbara?" he demanded to know.

Even that stratagem fell flat. She declined to reveal how much the truck stop had budgeted for its Thanksgiving feast — not that anyone could have cared.

On a slow day at the White House, Donaldson liked to say, his job was to turn chicken shit into chicken salad. This Thanksgiving night, Donaldson could not produce even a turkey salad out of such meager pickings.

When the show ended, everyone was downcast.

Everyone but Arledge — who had deliberately tuned out. "I'm not going to get myself upset tonight watching that program," he'd told a colleague. "I know it's going to be awful."

That was no comfort to Kaplan. "It was the worst hour I've ever been associated with," he said. "It would have been a bad morning show.

"Sam Donaldson and Diane Sawyer are great names in broadcast journalism," he said, "and I'm using them to interview people at a bloody truck stop at Thanksgiving. I mean, that's hideous."

That first season, "PrimeTime Live" was seen by the broadcasting industry as a colossal flop, the television equivalent of the movie *Ishtar*, say, or *Heaven's Gate*. This was unfair — "PrimeTime" put on some programs that were as good as "60 Minutes" or "20/20" — but the show lacked consistency. What's more, Sawyer's pretensions and Donaldson's bombast made easy targets. "We were the punch line to every Jay Leno joke," said Judd Rose, "and to a degree deservedly so."

Morale sank. People weren't exactly ashamed to be associated with "PrimeTime," but they weren't proud either. Marc Burstein, a broadcast producer who had come from the Brinkley show, didn't replace his "This Week with David Brinkley" luggage tags with new ones from "PrimeTime" for a year. "You'd be hard-pressed to find someone who went around with 'PrimeTime' hats, sweatshirts, or anything," Burstein said. Even Kaplan kept an atypically low profile. When people asked what he did for a living, he'd say, "I used to be the executive producer of 'Nightline.' "

That "PrimeTime" struggled at first should have surprised no one. No network news magazine, not even "60 Minutes," had been an overnight success. And as Arledge never tired of pointing out, "PrimeTime" had been launched into the toughest time period in television, against "L.A. Law" and "Knots Landing" on a night when ABC was a virtual no-show in the Nielsens. He told reporters, "I'm not disappointed because I didn't expect it to do great."

In truth, Arledge was terribly disappointed — by the ratings, by the ridicule, and by the show itself. "There was one period there where I just tuned out, I was so disgusted," he later confessed. This was not "Our World" or even "20/20," whose creation he had left to others. Arledge cared about "PrimeTime," and he cared even more about Diane Sawyer. "I was determined that, even if the show was going to fail, she was not going to fail," Arledge said. He wanted to prove to her, to people at CBS News, and to everyone else that he could take a star from the Tiffany Network and make her an even more sparkling jewel. He wanted to prove that he was the master of path-breaking live television. And he wanted to prove that he could perform his magic not only at the edges of the stage, where he had won acclaim for "Nightline" and the Brinkley show, but in the bright lights of prime time.

He had failed on all counts: Sawyer floundered, the adventure in live television had proved disastrous, and the ratings were adequate at best. Arledge had no one to blame but himself. He would later seek scapegoats, but the concept, casting, and execution of "PrimeTime Live" all were driven by the impulses of Roone Arledge. Just as "Nightline" was a product of Arledge's best instincts — his vision, his creativity, and his determination to do television that mattered — "PrimeTime" reflected his worst tendencies.

The show was star-driven. It was live for live's sake. It was wildly overpromoted. And particularly in the weeks leading up to the debut, enormous energies were spent on the look and feel of the show — on the directing, the lighting, the staging, the interweaving of live and tape, the music, and the set — while scant attention was paid to content, to the fundamental question of what the show would be about.

Dorrance Smith, who had wanted to run "PrimeTime," said later, "He wanted dancing bears, he wanted glitz, he wanted eighty-five TV screens, you know, bombs bursting in air. That's what he wanted, and he got it, and it was a disaster."

Then Arledge provided little support, except to Sawyer, while his criticisms sapped the spirit of Kaplan and others who labored to get the show onto the air. Arledge was not to blame for the week-to-week chaos, for the way pieces were crashed onto the air instead of crafted, but he was slow to intervene and reluctant to accept any responsibility for his misjudgments.

And yet — to his credit — Arledge refused to accept failure. To give up on the show would mean admitting that he had been wrong about Sawyer. To give up would mean admitting to Cap Cities that he could not deliver what they wanted: an hour of reliably profitable prime-time programming. Arledge would not repeat the mistakes made by NBC and CBS, which had been too quick to abandon news magazines with such stars as Charles Kuralt and Roger Mudd and Bill Moyers. He told Kaplan and Donaldson and Sawyer to charge ahead. Through trial and error, they would find their bearings as millions watched.

It might not be pretty, and it surely wasn't going to be easy. But Arledge was determined to see "PrimeTime" become a hit.

Chapter Sixteen

ROONE AT THE TOP

ONE MORNING in June 1989, seven of television's biggest stars gathered for a picture-taking session in TV One, an ABC News studio on West 66th Street. Inside ABC, they were called the Magnificent Seven — Peter Jennings, Ted Koppel, Barbara Walters, Diane Sawyer, David Brinkley, Sam Donaldson, and Hugh Downs — and they were about to become part of the most lavish campaign ever created to promote network news. Soon a striking group portrait of these stars would be seen on bus shelters in New York, billboards in Los Angeles, and in newspapers everywhere — a picture postcard to the nation from the house that Roone built.

A decade earlier, Roone Arledge had virtually invented network news promotion. Before then, the networks had considered it unseemly to hype their news programs in the way TV movies and sitcoms were sold. News promotion was "very lame, no more than an afterthought," said Bruce Soloway, the promotion manager hired by Arledge in 1979. With Arledge's backing, Soloway built up a fourteen-person staff to sell ABC News.

The Magnificent Seven campaign was the Rolls-Royce of network ad campaigns. For the all-day photo shoot, Soloway had constructed a giant lazy Susan, which methodically rotated the anchors, one by one, into camera range, and he rented a special 300mm lens to keep everyone in focus. The still photographs were taken by Eddie Adams, the Pulitzer Prize–winning photographer. Laszlo Kovacs, a Hollywood cinematographer who worked on such movies as *Five Easy Pieces,* directed the television commercials. Production costs alone ran more than $250,000.

Near the end of the shoot, Arledge appeared. The Magnificent Seven were about to become the Magnificent Eight. This, in a sense, was Roone Arledge's ultimate accomplishment at ABC News: he had made himself into a star. He took his place at the head of the line for the picture that would launch the campaign when it appeared on the front page of *USA Today* on June 13, 1989, the very day that Arledge was to speak to ABC affiliates in Los Angeles. The station owners who awoke that morning to find the paper outside their hotel room doors had to be impressed. It was another reminder that Arledge had turned ABC News into the leader in network news.

But success spawned a thicket of new problems for Arledge. While he'd once bemoaned the absence of famous faces at ABC News, now he had so many stars that they were bumping up against each other and making competing demands on him.

The Magnificent Seven campaign exemplified the problem. When Barbara Walters saw the pictures, first in the papers and then on New York City buses and billboards, she was distressed by her place in the lineup — behind Diane Sawyer and apart from Jennings and Koppel, Arledge's favorites. She made her feelings known. "Barbara was unhappy," Soloway recalled. "She felt she should be closer to Peter." To mollify her, Soloway sent the photos back to the lab for a makeover to move Walters up front, ahead of Sawyer. ABC bought more billboard space to display the reshuffled lineup.

Such ruffled feelings were nearly impossible to avoid. While most of the ABC stars liked each other, their competitive urges were fierce. Arledge felt he could never satisfy them all.

"It's like having ten children," he said, "and trying to keep them all not feeling that you're preferring one over the other. It's very hard to do, particularly if they're all competing for the same lollipop."

The simile was telling. Like small children, television news anchors could be egotistical and self-involved. What Arledge did not see, however, was that he could be every bit as temperamental and needy as the stars he collected. One reason he understood stars so well was that he was driven by the combustible mix of insecurity and ego that was common among television performers. The result was that intense emotions swirled around him. And the success he had chased for so long, and had finally achieved, did not bring peace or satisfaction to him or to ABC News.

*   *   *

Roone Arledge was not only the president of ABC News. He was also the patriarch of an unruly brood of dependents who competed for his favor. While some sibling rivalry was unavoidable, Arledge fostered and exploited the vulnerability of his anchors by drawing them close to him and then pushing them away. His hold over people was an important source of his power.

The uncertainty people felt about where they stood with Arledge grew partly from his habit of focusing on one thing at a time, to the exclusion of all else. Never was Arledge's focus more directed than when he wanted something from someone — when he wanted Barbara Walters to gracefully exit the evening news, or Peter Jennings to return from London, or Diane Sawyer to join ABC. Said one anchor, "He doesn't tell you that he loves you and you're the center of the universe, but he makes you feel that way. It's only later that you realize that he isn't in love with you, he's in love with what you can do for him." His single-mindedness was "one of Roone's greatest problems and at the same time one of his greatest strengths," said Ted Koppel. He explained, "If you are inside that little cocoon, and Roone is focusing his entire attention on you, the fact that everyone from the president of the United States on down may be trying to reach him unsuccessfully is very flattering. If you happen to be on the outside, and it's essential that you reach Roone, and he's in with somebody else, it can be one of the great frustrations of your life." It was especially frustrating when those who had basked in Arledge's warm glow found themselves cast into the darkness.

But Arledge's fabled reluctance to return phone calls only began to explain the intense feelings that he provoked. Inside ABC News, he played the role of distant father — remote and demanding — with the result that his charges went to extraordinary lengths to excel. He expected his anchors, executive producers, and vice presidents to place the demands of the news division ahead of their families and private lives, as he himself had done for years. Arledge even begrudged people vacations, although he took his own. One aide said, "He runs a little slave labor camp around here" — although his slaves were well compensated for their sacrifices.

Every one of Arledge's stars and executive producers wanted to please him. "We always think about him when we do things," said Sawyer. But his aloofness worked best as a management tool with those who sought emotional sustenance, as well as professional satisfaction, from their work. Walters, Sawyer, Jennings, and Donaldson all invested a great deal of emotion in their relations with Arledge, and all were, from time to time, disappointed. These were the people who often lived through their jobs, at considerable cost to their personal lives — Walters, Donaldson, and Jennings all had marriages fall apart while they worked for ABC, and Sawyer was a notorious workaholic who skipped her husband Mike Nichols's sixtieth birthday party to edit a piece. Sometimes their efforts were recognized by Arledge, but often they were not. Walters, for instance, would await a call after an exceptionally well done interview or a high-rated "20/20," and if the call didn't come, she was wounded. "Every one of us has been hurt by him," Walters said, although she hastened to add that Arledge did not intend to cause harm. "There's nothing mean about Roone. But he can be cold."

While Arledge claimed that he tried to bring "a sense of family and caring and nurturing" to ABC, the fact was that Arledge and his stars fed off each other like a "dysfunctional family," an insider said. Ed Tivnan, a writer who worked briefly for ABC, once likened Arledge to a character from Aristophanes about whom it was said, "They love him, they hate him, they cannot live without him."

Just about everyone who dealt with Arledge had a sad story to tell. After Sawyer's hiring, Donaldson went to great lengths to organize a formal dinner party in her honor in Washington, renting a historic mansion and catering a black-tie affair. For the first time in his life, he invited the Washington A-list — James Baker, the secretary of state, and Dick Cheney, the secretary of defense, among others — because, he said, he wanted it known in Washington that he welcomed Diane Sawyer to ABC. Naturally, Donaldson invited Arledge and, to ensure that he felt special, asked him to give a toast. But at the last possible minute, Arledge called to cancel, citing a painful hand injury. Donaldson and Sawyer were amazed — they would have dragged themselves out of a sickbed for a dinner to honor a friend — until they deduced that Donaldson was being penalized for his unyielding position in their contract talks a few months before. Much as he liked Arledge and felt grateful to him for his past support, Donaldson was hurt. "Roone makes it so difficult to really embrace him and say, 'Boy, what a wonderful thing in life to have gotten to know this guy and call him my friend,' " said Donaldson.

Another story involved Dorrance Smith, who sought Arledge's support as they began to develop "PrimeTime Live." Arledge, Smith, and Bistany went to lunch at Cafe des Artistes, where Smith began by explaining that he could not devote sufficient attention to the primetime project while working on the Brinkley show and weekend news. Smith, an Arledge protégé, talked about his desire for a new opportunity and made clear that he was asking not only for professional support but personal advice. He ended his pitch and looked expectantly at Arledge, whose eyes were trained on the menu. Looking up, Arledge said, "Should I have the hot asparagus or the cold?" Seeing that there was no sense going on, Smith and Bistany ordered drinks. Arledge just didn't want to make a decision about "PrimeTime" or about Smith, and he ultimately let Smith and Phyllis McGrady compete over the show. After that, Smith said, "I think a lot of us decided that we would rather not be a part of this team."

Nor were lower-rank staff members spared. A trip to Moscow with Jennings began badly for Arledge when he was stuck at the airport because of visa problems. His mood darkened after the Soviets unexpectedly summoned Jennings to meet privately with Mikhail Gorbachev and did not include Arledge. Finally, Arledge was miffed when he handed an expensive gift to Gorbachev, who ungraciously turned it over to an aide. While Arledge was angry at Jennings for not bringing him into the meeting and angry at Gorbachev for the slight, he turned his wrath against Steve Coppen, ABC's new Moscow bureau chief, who had been working for days with little sleep and, most thought, had done an outstanding job. Arledge excoriated Coppen for failing to meet him at the airport, for not making any effort to tend to his needs, and for running a slovenly-looking bureau, where, to Arledge's irritation, no place had been reserved for him to sit. "You are on thin ice, mister," Arledge warned him. Onlookers were stunned, and the story spread through ABC News.

This insensitivity was not so much a management technique as it was a character trait. Arledge was self-centered and self-absorbed, so taken with his own sense of self-importance that he frequently ignored the needs and desires of other people. An ABC executive who knew and liked him felt that Arledge had only a limited ability to empathize. "There's something about his personality that doesn't connect at a deep level with people," the executive said. "His measure is always how things affect him." Another aide said that there was nothing calculated about the distance Arledge put between himself and others. "That's the way he deals with the world, and it's the only way he can deal with the world," the aide observed. His marriages had failed; his children had scattered; and he had drifted apart from old friends and longtime colleagues, even some who tried to keep lines of communication open. Some people who worked closely with Arledge were convinced that he was a narcissist — in a childlike way, he saw the world around him only as it related to him.

And yet those who glimpsed a less visible facet of Arledge's personality — his gnawing self-doubt — were sympathetic. Some people sensed a sadness about him, a restlessness exhibited by those who are not comfortable in their own skin. One friend from his early days at ABC News described Arledge as a "sweet, needy soul" and remembered being drawn to him but finding him hard to reach. "People would think, with my love, you shall be released," said the friend — but they came away disappointed. It was also true that Arledge had a kind and tender side, which emerged when others were most in need: Walters, when she felt cast adrift by ABC, or Jennings, when his marriage was troubled. "Roone can be, when he deems it essential, among the most supportive people around," Jennings said. When reporter Cassie Mackin was stricken with cancer, Arledge sat by her in the hospital and assured her she would be taken care of, financially and otherwise, by ABC. Another time, when the teenage child of a news executive attempted suicide, Arledge went immediately to the hospital to lend his support. He also stood by an aide who needed treatment for drug and alcohol abuse, returning him to his old job after he was rehabilitated. "It makes the relationship that much more complicated," said an ABC colleague who was grateful for Arledge's support during a personal crisis. "Because there are some times you just want to hate him. And you can't."

Not all of Arledge's dealings with people were so fraught with emotion. Ted Koppel, David Brinkley, and Hugh Downs, whose lives did not revolve around ABC, were not as wrapped up in their relationships with Arledge. Koppel's priority was his family, and so he used his clout to secure more time for himself away from "Nightline" and ABC; this, by itself, was unusual, since most anchors lobbied for more, not less, time on the air. Brinkley and Downs held what were effectively part-time jobs, and they liked it that way. They all appeared to be at peace with themselves, less needy, and therefore less dependent on Arledge.

Even Brinkley, however, could feel slighted. All he asked was that Arledge support his Sunday program and recognize his efforts now and then, but Arledge did neither. Brinkley, who felt taken for granted when he quit NBC, came to feel the same way about Arledge. To an old NBC colleague, Brinkley said, "How many times in the past year do you think Roone Arledge has called me up?" When the NBC man guessed that he spoke to Arledge about once a week, Brinkley shot back, "He called me once to trot me out for some cocktail party." When Brinkley's contract expired in 1990, he entered into serious negotiations with NBC News that he broke off only after Arledge reluctantly agreed to give him a five-year contract, guaranteed, even in the event of his death.

Later, Arledge conceded that he had lost touch with Brinkley. "This Week," he explained, was taped at 10:30 A.M. in Washington and broadcast an hour later in New York. By the time Arledge saw the show, everyone had left. "I probably should have called him at home," Arledge said, "but by that time it's Sunday afternoon."

Brinkley's near-defection to NBC cost Arledge more money than he'd wanted to spend, but the important thing was that he had kept Brinkley. His other anchors, too, stayed at ABC, despite their complaints. Over the years, Jennings, Koppel, and Donaldson all passed up opportunities elsewhere because they felt loyal to ABC and Arledge. This was testimony, more than anything else, to their belief in his gifts as a producer. He might neglect them off the air, but they trusted him to take care of them whenever they appeared on ABC. Even Jennings, who recognized Arledge's flaws, said, "This news operation could not run without Roone Arledge. I absolutely believe that. The place would begin to just come apart at the seams."

One night near the end of 1989, after the broadcast of "World News Tonight," Roone Arledge stood by the rim and read a list of names to people who had gathered for a celebration.

"John Dunn. Mary Laing. Walter Peters," Arledge said. No one had any idea who those people were.

"Bill McSherry. Syd Darion. Bill Seamans," he continued. Now a couple of old-timers got the message.

"Harry McCarthy. Walter Pfister. Syd Darion. Av Westin." In chronological order, Arledge was reading a roll call of the executive producers of ABC's evening news.

"Dick Richter. Ernest Leiser. Steve Skinner," he said. "Bob Siegenthaler. Av Westin. Jeff Gralnick. Bob Frye. Bill Lord."

None had done it. None had done what Paul Friedman, with Peter Jennings and everyone else at "World News Tonight," had just done — won the Nielsen ratings for an entire year. Coming six months after Arledge's hiring of Diane Sawyer, this proved that ABC News was number one. "Nightline" and "20/20" and "This Week with David Brinkley" were successful, but a network news division is measured, above all, by the reach of its evening newscast. It had taken Arledge a dozen years, but ABC had finally overtaken CBS News and become the dominant news organization in television.

In the grand scheme of things, the ratings victory meant little. The Nielsens were not a reliable indicator of journalistic quality, as Arledge had never failed to point out when "World News" was running second or third. And ABC News had already won the more significant competition for evening news revenues and profits. By reaching the young, urban, upscale viewers prized by advertisers, ABC had been able to command 20 to 30 percent higher rates than CBS for its commercials.

But the Nielsens mattered to Arledge and to everyone else at ABC. They were printed in the newspapers each week. They certified his triumph. He was in an unusually generous mood as he praised Jennings, Friedman, and the staff and uncorked a bottle of vintage champagne. Not even Dan Burke could object as the bubbly flowed freely.

Jennings stood to reply. "Roone," he said, "I can tell from your voice that this time you really mean it, and I thank you." It was a jarring response, reflecting as it did Jennings's sense that he did not always trust Arledge's praise. This evening, though, Jennings felt close to his boss. He was proud of ABC, where he'd worked for twenty-five years. He'd known what losing as an anchor felt like, and winning felt much better.

Several factors made the difference for "World News," not the least of which was the impact of afternoon talk-show host Oprah Winfrey. The ABC-owned stations all broadcast Winfrey's show, and many of her viewers flowed through local news and into "World News Tonight." Researchers estimated that Winfrey added a fraction of a rating point to the total for "World News," which bested the "CBS Evening News" for the year by less than a tenth of a point.

The broad strength of ABC News also helped, as did the decline of NBC News, under the penurious rule of General Electric, and a string of controversies that dogged CBS News anchor Dan Rather in the late 1980s. "We benefit from the destruction of NBC News, which, I believe, unfortunately, is now beyond redemption," Friedman said. "And we benefit from what I take to be a general uneasiness about Dan."

Most important, "World News Tonight" was better than ever. Friedman had lifted the evening newscast to a higher level, one that reflected both the journalistic maturity of network news and the competitive pressures created by local news and cable. His reformatting of the twenty-two-minute news hole accomplished two things at once:

he put more stories into the show, to provide greater variety, and he created a four-minute block of airtime, in the next-to-last of the program's five segments, to provide depth. "There's a little bit of conjuring involved," Friedman said, "but basically the idea is to reduce the stuff that everyone is going to do and expand the optional stuff."

Originally, Friedman had planned to set aside the day's long segment for a Jennings interview or an investigative piece, but he was also seeking ways to make the broadcast more useful to viewers. Viewers, he sensed, wanted stories that touched their lives, an idea that led to the creation of the daily segment known as the American Agenda. The American Agenda was designed to explore the nation's biggest problems and, just as important, to point to possible solutions; teams of producers and correspondents were assigned to education, health, the family, crime, and the environment. While Arledge had reservations, he approved the concept and agreed to finance it. The Agenda was expensive because reporters needed time to become experts, and stories took weeks to produce; pieces cost up to $15,000, twice the price of a typical evening news feature.

The money was well spent. American Agenda managed both to improve the quality of journalism on "World News" and to make the program more commercial. Correspondents thrived when given time to learn their beats, and by highlighting solutions, they responded to the complaint that the networks present only negative news. They would report, for example, how one community got started recycling or how another improved children's math scores. "There had been a 'pro-problems' bias," said Bill Blakemore, a former teacher who covered education. "We had been ignoring an entire half of reality." Best of all, American Agenda engaged the viewers by speaking to their deepest concerns — their family, their health, their safety, their kids' schools, and their environment. Friedman said, "To be crass about it, you could consider American Agenda a grown-up way of doing 'news you can use.' Because it deals with things that clearly affect people's everyday lives."

American Agenda also countered the feeling some viewers had that "World News" overemphasized foreign news and that Jennings was not as American as Rather or Brokaw. He was not, of course — despite Arledge's urgings, Jennings never gave up his Canadian passport — but his exposure during the political conventions, the Olympics, and Liberty Weekend overcame the perception that he was insufficiently American to anchor the evening news. That he was able to win middle America over, while maintaining the urbane, sophisticated image that made him a favorite of elite viewers, was no small tribute to his gifts as an anchor. "He's the best ever," said his colleague Brit Hume. "He can explain things clearly. He has this incomparable memory. And he's absolutely unflappable."

Their victory cemented the bond between Jennings and Friedman. As executive producer of the top-rated evening newscast, Friedman became a force within ABC, someone whose opinions counted not only inside the news division but with Dan Burke. Friedman would not be pushed around by anyone; he was a demanding editor, a harsh critic of the assignment desk when stories were missed, and a fierce defender of his program when his decisions were questioned. "When he believes someone has not done a good job, he's very hard on them," said correspondent John McWethy. "This is a very tough business. You've got to have high standards, and he has them."

Jennings, too, grew more assertive — too assertive, some said. Always a hands-on anchorman, Jennings was more involved than ever in assigning stories, editing copy, hiring staff, and deciding which correspondents would get on the air. This was perhaps inevitable; most network anchors recognize, sooner or later, that their success depends on the appeal of their broadcast and the strength of the organization, and so they demand a broader role. But Jennings, many thought, was overinvolved, and he clashed with people in the field.

Correspondents complained that they were needlessly relegated to minor roles when Jennings was in the anchor chair. They felt that Jennings, more than Frank Reynolds or Ted Koppel, guarded his airtime, particularly during live coverage. The way he asked questions revealed his attitude: he'd say, "Let's go very briefly now" to a correspondent and then ask a long, windy question of his own that seemed intended to display his mastery of a subject.

"Peter to this very day won't pose a question which does not (a) disclose his superior knowledge of the subject in the most arcane sense and (b) demonstrate that he is the ringmaster who will call the shots," a senior correspondent said. "Peter doesn't want the audience ever to forget not only who's in charge but who really is the star, who really has the knowledge." Another correspondent believed that Jennings was more generous with airtime when talking to outside experts, the academics or ex-government officials hired by ABC, than he was when dealing with his own people. Even Brit Hume, a Jennings admirer, said, "Peter can be competitive with his correspondents."

Jennings's "incredible drive for perfection" also meant that he could be "hard on other people, just as he is hard on himself," said

Friedman, who counseled his anchorman to ease up sometimes. His style rubbed some people the wrong way. "Peter calls everybody mate. Drives me crazy," said a Washington reporter. "We're not mates, and he's not the captain. It's a little thing, but it always grates a little bit." Women felt that, while fancying himself a liberated man, Jennings was a sexist; he made unsolicited comments about their dress or hair and, when told by one woman that she was having a baby, replied, "Does that mean you'll be leaving us?" The result was that the troops, especially holdovers from the Reynolds years, had mixed feelings about him. An old-timer said, "There's respect for Peter. There is admiration for his success. But is he beloved in the same way Frank was? No."

As the top-rated anchor, Jennings also came under increasing pressure not to stray from the anchor chair. This was flattering, on the one hand, but it exacerbated long-standing tensions with Arledge over his vacations and his desire to get into the field. In 1989, Arledge approved a prime-time documentary series featuring Jennings, called "Peter Jennings Reporting," but the two men clashed when Jennings set out to take the title of the programs literally — he wanted to get out of New York to report on topics he cared about, among them the return of the Khmer Rouge to Cambodia, the spread of guns in America, and the impact of the abortion debate on electoral politics. "Roone hated the Cambodia idea," Jennings recalled. "Didn't want me to go. Didn't think anybody cared, thought I'd be out of pocket." But when Jennings went anyway and returned with an important story, critical of United States policy, Arledge applauded. "When the show was very successful and very influential, Roone thought it was a brilliant idea," said Jennings. "But we all know that's Roone. The boss is entitled to credit."

His abortion program did not lead to as happy an ending. While the broadcast explored the politics of abortion in Louisiana, Pennsylvania, Florida, and Minnesota, Jennings confined his work to New York, largely to assuage Arledge. As a result, the fieldwork was done by producers while key politicians, such as Louisiana governor Buddy Roemer, were flown to New York for interviews with Jennings at ABC locations that were gussied up to look like their offices back home. What seemed to viewers to be the Louisiana governor's office, for example, was a conference room at Capital Cities. This was not the way Jennings wanted to work, but it was a minor problem compared to the difficulty of scheduling the show.

Arledge wanted the documentary, along with a live, late-night panel discussion anchored by Jennings, to be broadcast in August, but Tom Yellin, the executive producer, did not want the show to air during the summer, when viewing levels are low. And Jennings would not postpone a long-planned vacation, making the August airdate impossible. For weeks, Arledge refused to set a new air date, even after Jennings and Yellin pressed him to do so. It became clear to everyone that, because of fall premieres, sports events, and the elections, the show would have to run on November 1. But Arledge did not approve that date until a few days before — too late to get the program previewed in *TV Guide* or sent to most TV critics for review. Although they had no proof, Jennings and Yellin were convinced that they had been punished for not agreeing to the August date.

Arledge denied it. "There would be no real reason for me to do that," he said. But it was revealing that both Jennings and Yellin believed that the president of ABC News would sacrifice a program on his network in an effort to show his anchorman who was in charge. Arledge viewed ABC News as his creation, his kingdom, and no challenges to his rule were to be tolerated — not even from the anchor of the top-rated newscast in television. He had to remind Jennings who was the real number one at ABC News.

By the end of the 1980s, everything at ABC News was successful except "PrimeTime Live." Looking back on the struggle to turn the show around, Arledge later said that he'd known all along that the live format would never work. It was Dorrance Smith, he said, who wanted the show to be driven by news events, and Sam Donaldson who compared it to "Wide World of Sports." "You never heard me say that," Arledge insisted. "Sam said that once, and I almost wanted to kill him." What's more, Arledge said, he'd always known that hardhitting reporting was what "PrimeTime" needed. Back when he recruited Sawyer, he recalled, "I kept telling Diane the basis has got to be investigative journalism."

Once again, Arledge was rewriting history. Several "PrimeTime" staff members remember that he compared the show to "Wide World," albeit in a casual way. More important, his instincts and impulses had shaped the original format. The notion that Dorrance Smith or Sam Donaldson could bulldoze their concept onto the air over his objections wasn't credible. While Arledge had allowed everyone leeway as they developed "PrimeTime Live," responsibility for the program was his, and the fact that he had trouble accepting it was evidence of how frail his self-image could be. Even after all his victories, Arledge still found it painful to admit to his defeats.

Arledge did, however, deserve credit for seeing almost immediately that the original "PrimeTime Live" was misguided. He knew that gimmicks had to be replaced by polished pieces and meatier stories — proving, as he had with "20/20" and "Nightline," that, whatever his limits as a show creator, his producer's eye told him what worked and what did not. Reluctant as he was to admit to his mistakes, Arledge was swift to correct them. "I knew early on it was the wrong program," he said. "You have to have pieces. You have to have a bank." Others, however — notably Rick Kaplan and Sam Donaldson — were slow to discard their original vision. As a result, the show's turnaround proved painful for all.

For Diane Sawyer, whose supposed power to attract an audience had been at the heart of the program, the show's early failure was personal. Her former CBS News colleagues, led by Don Hewitt, spread the word that she'd made a dreadful mistake by leaving "60 Minutes." "I was getting clubbed to death, day in and day out, by my old network," Sawyer recalled. "The CBS people would call people who knew me to send word that I had really made a mess of my life." Sawyer's friends also fed her a steady stream of criticism and advice.

For months, Sawyer struggled to find her role on the show. For a time, she was showcased in gorgeously produced pieces that took her to remote or exotic locales. She ventured into the Peruvian jungle with DEA agents and visited Cambodia with photojournalist Dith Pran, whose life inspired the movie *The Killing Fields*. In Kenya, Sawyer profiled Dr. Richard Leakey, the paleontologist and protector of wildlife, and, in Paris, she strolled past the Eiffel Tower with Mikhail Baryshnikov. When she wasn't globe-trotting, Sawyer did high-minded profiles of the novelist William Styron; Dr. Oliver Sacks, the neurologist and writer; and Dr. Robert Coles, the author and child psychiatrist.

Some of these efforts paid off. The Styron profile, for example, was an unlikely television story — others thought Sawyer foolhardy to attempt a piece about a depressed author of literary novels — but she produced a highly watchable drama about a man's struggle with his demons. Her travels in Peru and Cambodia also made for good television. More than anyone else at "PrimeTime," Sawyer knew how to produce a compelling magazine piece — how to introduce characters, create drama, vary the pace of storytelling, and deliver a satisfying payoff. She'd learned from Hewitt at "60 Minutes."

And yet, perhaps because she knew so well what effects she wanted, Sawyer's early pieces had a stagy quality. Visiting Leakey in Kenya, for example, Sawyer went airborne in a balloon with a crew so that her producer, Rudy Bednar, could film her against the backdrop of the African landscape. For a shot at dusk, they had Masai tribesmen light torches because, Bednar explained later, he did not want to rig up a noisy generator to power lights and "it just felt more romantic to do it by candlelight." Meryl Streep in *Out of Africa* never looked better.

Sawyer's Parisian rendezvous with Baryshnikov was also suffused with romance — deliberately, said Bednar, who bristled at the charge that their pieces were choreographed. "If the idea is to try to make this piece like Baryshnikov, who is romantic, then I don't think it's overproduced," Bednar said. This time, Sawyer and Baryshnikov were shown floating down the Seine at sunset, with Sawyer resting a glass of red wine against her knee. "Who is the most beautiful woman you ever saw?" she asked. One "PrimeTime" producer said he felt like walking up to his TV set, saying "I think you two would like to be alone now," and turning it off.

These were the most visible examples of a thread running through all of Sawyer's pieces — they were as much about her as about the story. This wasn't unique to Sawyer; viewers who tuned to "60 Minutes" and "20/20" did so, in part, to see Mike Wallace play prosecutor and Barbara Walters nuzzle up to her guests. But Sawyer was still trying to define herself, as millions watched. "I think she wanted to be Diane, queen of news," said a colleague. "She wanted to grace Baryshnikov and Africa with her presence."

It wasn't working. The trick in producing a magazine piece is to manipulate the viewers without seeming to do so. But Sawyer's calculations were transparent and her performances were mannered, as critic James Wolcott noted in a devastating appraisal in *Vanity Fair*. "Too often these days she seems to be playing a reporter rather than being one," he wrote. "And playing the role piously, as if she were applying for sainthood. It's sometimes painful to watch what a phony she's become."

Sawyer recognized the problem. She agreed that the Baryshnikov piece "got too beautiful." She resisted pressure from Roger Goodman to look like a well-coiffed anchor wherever she went. "People would secretly try to get hairdressers and makeup people to the shoots with me, and I kept refusing," Sawyer said.

But Sawyer had only herself to blame for her most embarrassing effort on "PrimeTime," an exclusive interview with Marla Maples, the girlfriend of New York developer Donald Trump. Maples was hiding from the networks and the tabloids, but Sawyer and booker Maia Samuel, working through Trump's people and Maples's family in Georgia, convinced her to do the interview, tracked her down in Atlantic City, and then eluded a horde of paparazzi who had latched on to Sawyer in hopes of locating Maples. During the interview, Sawyer brandished a *New York Post* headline that quoted Maples as saying that her affair with Trump was the "Best Sex I Ever Had" and asked, "All right, was it really the best sex you ever had?" This marked a low not only for "PrimeTime" but for all network news, and Sawyer later regretted leaving the question in the piece.

Knowing she could do better, Sawyer approached her work with even more than her usual intensity. She'd have dinner after the broadcast with Kaplan, Donaldson, and the senior producers, then go home to screen a videotape of "PrimeTime." Rarely did she find much to applaud in her own work or in that of others. "We'll have a great show," Kaplan said, "and she'll say, 'There is just nothing in here that's interesting,' and you want to punch her."

Producers admired her talent but found working with her a trial. She wasn't rude or unpleasant — to the contrary, she was considerate and almost never lost her temper. But Sawyer was so painstaking in her approach that she exhausted her colleagues, even those who understood that she was driven by a laudable desire to make the piece better. "Where she can exert control, she always will exert control," said a producer. "The stakes are very high for her every time she's in public, and she believes rightly that no one has her interests at stake as much as she does." But Sawyer could waste hours, even days, agonizing over decisions that others could make in minutes. "It's painful to watch her," said the producer. "She has a really hard time giving up things. She cannot make up her mind. It's a discipline, and she just doesn't have it." Often, she'd labor up until airtime on stories that had been in the works for months.

Like Sawyer, Donaldson was unhappy. He was dismayed by the evolution of "PrimeTime Live" — or "PrimeTime," as the program had come to be known — into a traditional magazine show. As more stories were taped and fewer pieces spun off the news, even the logo was redrawn, to shrink the word "live" down to tiny letters. One of the few remnants of the show's origins came when Donaldson signed off on Thursdays by exhorting viewers to "join us next week for another edition of 'PrimeTime LIVE'!" — with the emphasis, always, on "live." It was his good-natured way of reminding everyone that the new "PrimeTime" was not the show he wanted to be doing.

No one needed a reminder. Donaldson was a Johnny One-Note, a tiresome pain to colleagues who dreaded the staff meetings dominated by his complaints about the show's new direction. "Sam wanted to do 'This Week with David Brinkley' at ten o'clock on Thursdays," said a producer. "He literally wanted to bring in Tom Foley and do a live interview." Donaldson usually lost the arguments, but never without a fight. This was not the show he signed up for, he would say. "If Roone Arledge had come to me when I left the White House, and if he'd said, 'Sam, I want you to go on "20/20," in fact, you can be the co-anchor, and you have to do magazine pieces,' I would have said, 'Roone, we've got to find something else,' " Donaldson said.

Donaldson's reluctance was understandable. His strengths were covering breaking news, doing live interviews, and taking apart George Will on the Brinkley show, not crafting magazine pieces. A creature of Washington, he loved politics and government — subjects that were a hard sell in prime time, because they were thought to bore viewers — and he had no appetite for exposing petty scandals. "I don't want to catch the butcher," he said. "I want to catch the senator." Beyond the news, his interests were narrow. He knew very little about Hollywood, popular culture, or sports. "Who is Greg Louganis?" he asked at one staff meeting.

Donaldson struggled with the rhythms of a weekly program. He liked hard news and deadline work, and he did not like producers to spend weeks preparing his stories; he wanted to do the reporting himself. "Sam was a fish out of water," Kaplan said. "Sam was still trying to crash the weekly piece, and his pieces were the worst pieces in the show. And he was not willing to listen." For his part, Donaldson felt that no one listened to him. People rolled their eyes or snickered when he pushed for live Washington pieces, and even if he didn't see the smirks, he saw that his ideas were ignored. Other ideas, some from young producers who seemed to Donaldson to know very little about news, ideas that he thought were bad ideas — those were the stories that were getting done.

His daily routine also drained him. Although ABC rented a New York apartment for him, Donaldson commuted to the city by shuttle almost daily so he could spend his nights at home in Washington with his wife, Jan. "He was just hell on wheels, and he was unhappy and he didn't want to be here," Kaplan said.

Six months into the first season, Donaldson worried that he would be dumped from the show and blamed for its failure. Despite the contract guarantees he'd fought so hard to get, his fears had come to pass — he was being turned into a supporting player because Arledge wanted to showcase Sawyer. "It looked like Sam not only was never going to contribute to the program, but that he was hurting Diane," Arledge said. "A lot of it was his behavior. Everyone was so worn out from dealing with Sam."

Naturally, Arledge's disapproval vexed Donaldson. "It attacks your confidence," Donaldson said. "Ego is the one thing you have to have in this business, and what goes along with that is self-confidence." Under constant criticism, Donaldson said, "you don't do your best work."

As it happened, it was not Donaldson, but Rick Kaplan who nearly lost his job. Kaplan, who'd been such an able commander at "Nightline," could not get control of "PrimeTime." He'd wait until the last minute to throw the program together, needlessly upsetting everybody. "It was chaos getting the show on the air," he admitted. By the spring of 1990, Sawyer, thoroughly exasperated, approached Arledge to say that she had lost confidence in Kaplan, that he was taking too long to fix the show. Arledge agreed. They decided that the solution was to rehire Phyllis McGrady, the original executive producer who had left when her mother became ill.

McGrady was tempted. After "PrimeTime Live" premiered, people had told her that she was lucky to have avoided the fiasco. "No," she would say, "the truth of the matter is that I really wanted to do the show." Now she had another chance. She turned it down only because she had just decided to move to Hong Kong with her boyfriend, an ABC News producer. Her decision saved Kaplan's job.

When Kaplan heard about the coup attempt, he was distressed but said he didn't blame Sawyer. "You're talking about someone who gave up '60 Minutes,' who is coming over and getting trashed in the press, and has been promised the world, and is getting shit left and right, and nothing is working out," he said. "I'm the one who made her sit there on Thanksgiving, right? And don't think that she doesn't remember that."

It was at this point that, at Sawyer's behest, Arledge finally asserted himself. In May 1990, he arranged to have dinner after the show at Il Valleto with Kaplan, Sawyer, and Donaldson, in an effort to get them all on the same track.

Everyone was frustrated, they agreed. Life was too short to work so hard on a show that brought so much aggravation and so few rewards. Arledge expressed his own disappointment.

"If we were doing a program that was getting a thirty share of the audience, but we weren't proud of the program, that would be one thing. It would be an accomplishment of sorts — a commercial accomplishment," Arledge said. "If we were doing a great program that we were really proud of, and it was getting a ten share, that is another accomplishment. We'd probably be more proud of that, but maybe other people wouldn't. We're not doing either one. We're doing a program that is no good, and we're getting fourteen, twelve, sixteen, thirteen shares, and we must change it."

Arledge dissected the problems. The remaining live segments were not working. The pieces lacked consistency. There was no chemistry between Donaldson and Sawyer.

Pointedly, he turned to Donaldson and said, "There's this continuing problem of what you do. What is it you do?"

Donaldson was taken aback. He felt that he was being invited to leave the show. Instead, he offered to leave town. He realized that his battle to save the live format had been lost, and he suggested that he go back to Washington and do pieces.

"Diane should work alone," he said. "She works better when she doesn't have to share the stage." It wasn't personal. In fact, Donaldson said later that he was grateful for Sawyer's support "when others were willing to dispense with old Sam."

The others agreed to a separation. Without fanfare, Donaldson returned to Washington. He felt greatly relieved to be home and, more important, he began to generate lively magazine pieces. "I started getting with the program," he said. Over the next few months, as the show began its second season, Donaldson did an insightful profile of Colin Powell, the chairman of the Joint Chiefs of Staff; he exposed savings and loan crook Don Dixon; and he did a newsworthy interview with U.S. Supreme Court Justice Thurgood Marshall. With investigative producer Sheila Hershow, Donaldson ambushed congressmen on a taxpayer-funded Caribbean junket and videotaped them playing tennis, cavorting in the surf, and consorting with influential Washington lobbyists.

Meanwhile, Sawyer forged a valuable partnership with a talented, strong-willed producer named Robbie Gordon, whose specialty was investigative pieces, often using hidden cameras. Working with Sawyer and using a camera hidden in a purse, Gordon produced a vivid exposé showing abuse and neglect of patients at a Veterans Administration hospital in Cleveland. Together, they proceeded to do a series of high-impact investigations, notably a story that took hidden cameras into day care centers in New Orleans to show how children were neglected; the story demonstrated that centers were understaffed and workers untrained, and blamed a lax system of regulation. These stories were prime-time journalism at its best, original reports that uncovered social problems; because they reached a big audience, they often prompted reforms. These pieces were also ideal for Sawyer — they were serious, and yet they allowed her to display a full range of emotions, from sympathy to outrage. They also satisfied her desire to do meaningful work. "There's nothing more energizing than a story that can make a difference," Sawyer said, although she hardly needed energizing. She always worked at a backbreaking pace.

Everyone on the show was getting better. Chris Wallace unmasked shady goings-on at the Vancouver Stock Exchange. Judd Rose profiled Texas politician Clayton Williams and the king of Tonga. Producer David Doss's moving tale about a priest who ministered to children with AIDS in Rumania brought a huge viewer response. "We discovered there was no secret formula," said senior producer Marc Burstein. "We found out that magazine pieces, well executed and fully formed, with a good story, worked." The ratings began to improve.

No magic had been required — "60 Minutes" and "20/20" had learned those lessons years before. But what was needed was the right mix of anchors and correspondents, producers who had mastered a style of dramatic storytelling, and the willingness to concede that, in the end, "PrimeTime" was not going to be breakthrough television. The program succeeded when everyone decided that they would rather be good than be different.

The other necessities were patience and persistence. Kaplan had retained just enough faith in his talents to hang in there even when he had lost the support of Arledge and his anchors. Then, as success bred more success, Kaplan regained his equilibrium and competitive fire. Arledge, too, had stuck with "PrimeTime" even when the program was pulling modest ratings, hemorrhaging money, and, worst of all from his standpoint, embarrassing him and ABC News. The two-year commitment he had won from Cap Cities had proved invaluable.

Now all the new, improved "PrimeTime" needed was a spark to catch the audience's attention. The ultimate prime-time live event — a war in the Persian Gulf — would provide that and more.

Chapter Seventeen

ABC GOES TO WAR

THE FIRST BOMBS fell on Baghdad at 6:35 P.M., Eastern time — five minutes into the network evening newscasts. On ABC's "World News Tonight," Peter Jennings cut away to a live report over the telephone from Gary Shepard, ABC's man in Iraq.

News that the Persian Gulf War had begun was brought to millions of Americans not by the president of the United States or the secretary of defense but by a network correspondent who described the view from his room in the Al-Rashid Hotel.

"Peter, I'm looking directly west from our hotel now," Shepard said, "and throughout the entire sky there are flashes of light.

"Something is definitely underway here. Something is going on. The whole sky is lit . . .

"Obviously an attack is underway."

So was the television drama. The other networks were close behind, but ABC News had been first to report the onset of war. Not until twenty minutes later did White House press secretary Marlin Fitzwater announce solemnly that "the liberation of Kuwait has begun," which, by then, was old news.

Roone Arledge watched from the control room in New York. He had been preparing ABC News for war ever since Iraqi dictator Saddam Hussein invaded Kuwait on August 2, 1990. Two weeks later, Ted Koppel and his "Nightline" crew scored an extraordinary worldwide scoop when they became the first Western journalists, print or broadcast, to reach Baghdad and talk to the Iraqis. When American troops were deployed to Saudi Arabia, ABC's video brigades followed, and when President Bush visited the soldiers, Arledge and Jennings took their own presidential tour of the front. Arledge wanted to see the lay of the land before deploying his own troops.

His biggest decision involved Jennings. Although CBS and NBC would send their top anchors to the Gulf, Arledge kept Jennings in New York. "We decided that the story of the war was too diverse and that Dan Rather, even though he was doing some hot stories from aircraft carriers, was really out of position," Arledge said. Jennings agreed that the story was unfolding in so many places — Saudi Arabia, Iraq, Israel, Washington, the U.N., and elsewhere — that his best vantage point was New York. Otherwise, he said, "I would have been at the end of a tether." Having two world-class anchors afforded Arledge the luxury of casting Jennings as his stable anchor and dispatching Koppel to follow Operation Desert Storm to the Gulf. Both could call upon a lifetime of experience covering the Middle East.

Arledge was also ready — in a sense, his entire career had prepared him for this moment. He had become the master of live television, the producer and executive who more than anyone else had harnessed the power of the medium to capture unfolding human drama. Now, nearly twenty years after Munich, the Gulf War would present the ultimate human drama, a life-and-death conflict with an ending still to be written. The video technology of the 1990s — satellites, portable uplinks, cellular telephones, and lightweight cameras — meant that Arledge could telecast the action live into every living room in America, indeed, to homes around the world.

As the war began, Arledge took his place in the control room, behind executive producer Jeff Gralnick and director Roger Goodman. Watching the wall of monitors displaying the network broadcasts, Arledge liked what he saw. Once-mighty CBS was stumbling. NBC was suffering from its weak bench. It looked as if the night would belong to ABC.

Then came a scary moment. From Baghdad, Shepard was describing how the antiaircraft fire lit up the night sky "like the fireworks on the fourth of July, multiplied by a hundred" when his phone went dead.

"Gary Shepard, do you hear us?" Jennings asked. Urgently, he repeated, "Gary Shepard, do you hear us in Baghdad? Well, we have lost him for a second, at the very least."

For an instant, the same thought crossed everyone's mind: had Shepard's hotel been hit by a bomb?

A glance at the monitors brought relief. There, from the same hotel, Bernard Shaw, Peter Arnett, and John Holliman were safe as they reported for CNN.

Shepard was safe too, but he would do no more reporting from Baghdad. The Iraqis had pulled the plug on the telephone lines and herded foreign correspondents into an air raid shelter in the hotel basement. Shepard would be sent to the border the next day.

Only CNN remained on the air. Months earlier, the cable network had persuaded the Iraqis to install a dedicated phone line that permitted CNN to operate independently of the local system. "CNN got its edge because they had paid the Iraqis, in effect, to open a bureau in Baghdad," Gralnick groused. It didn't matter. For sixteen long hours, when America was riveted by the first night of the first true living-room war, the only place to get news from Iraq was CNN.

Now it was Bernard Shaw who was telling his viewers, "This feels like we're in the center of hell." The CNN trio of Shaw, Arnett, and Holliman became the first journalistic stars of the war.

Arledge was shell-shocked. While ABC turned in an outstanding performance — its first "special report" was the longest in its history, lasting forty-two hours and thirteen minutes — CNN was winning the public-relations war. Some broadcast stations abandoned their network coverage to show CNN, and Secretary of Defense Dick Cheney and Colin Powell, chairman of the joint chiefs, praised CNN during their press conferences after the air strikes. Newspapers and magazine headlines called the coverage "CNN's War" and "CNN's Triumph."

Worst of all, CNN stayed with the war after ABC was forced to resume its schedule of sitcoms and game shows.

For Arledge, this was an unexpected setback. By all rights, he thought, this should have been ABC's war and his triumph. He had built the strongest news organization in television. He had beaten CBS. He had beaten NBC. Now his news division was being overshadowed by CNN, a cable operation which, he knew, was no match for ABC News.

To Arledge, CNN was one brilliant idea — all-news, all-day on cable — and a mountain of public relations. People didn't realize that the CNN audience was tiny and that its anchors, reporters, and producers were no better than adequate when measured against their counterparts at the Big Three. Arledge found it revealing when Mary Alice Williams, one of CNN's biggest stars, went to NBC News and virtually disappeared; she was no Barbara Walters or Diane Sawyer, that was for sure. In Arledge's view, CNN didn't have any stars, and it didn't have any programs, and its organization was neither strong nor deep. "It bugged me," he said, "because I want ABC News to be the most important news organization in the world by every measure." But the critics had already begun to anoint Ted Turner as the television hero of the war. Ted Turner! It was almost too much for Roone Arledge to bear.

Over time, Arledge thought, quality will out. In the end, he believed, the muscle of ABC News would be felt. He had faith not just in his anchors but also in the talents and experience of his producers and correspondents — Brit Hume at the White House, Bob Zelnick at the Pentagon, John McWethy at State, Dean Reynolds in Israel, and in the Gulf, such battle-scarred veterans as Bill Blakemore, Barrie Dunsmore, and Mort Dean. Behind the scenes, ABC News could rely on such experienced people as Fabrice Moussus, the photographer who delivered to the world the first pictures of the bombing in Baghdad, green-tinted images of an exploding night sky. The CNN team was not nearly as talented or as deep.

Eventually, Arledge's confidence was borne out. In competitive terms, ABC News excelled during the Gulf War and CNN faded. ABC News did more original reporting and innovative programming than its rivals, and, among the anchors, Jennings best resisted the temptation to become partisan. Nevertheless, ABC's war coverage failed in significant ways to serve the public, who, when the fighting ended, had missed much of the story. The strengths as well as the flaws of the coverage could be traced back to Arledge.

It was Arledge, for example, along with his aide Joanna Bistany and Ted Koppel, who gave ABC correspondent Forrest Sawyer the approval he needed to circumvent restrictive Pentagon censorship and work independently in Saudi Arabia. Sawyer, a bright, aggressive reporter hired by ABC after an unhappy stint at CBS News, obtained the first pictures of the border between Saudi Arabia and Kuwait, flew on a bombing raid in a Saudi F-15, and became the first network correspondent to get video of the ground war onto the air. His feats stood out because so little enterprise work was done by others. "Everybody else was sitting around reading the paper in the Dharan International, waiting for their pool to be called," said Tom Yellin, ABC's top producer in Saudi Arabia during the ground war. Arledge paid Sawyer his highest compliment, saying, "He graduated from being a newsreader who could be a local anchor or a weekend anchor. He became a star."

In terms of programming, Arledge came up with several creative ways to compete with CNN in spite of the fact that, even in wartime, ABC could not turn itself into an all-news network. To assure ABC viewers that they could watch "Oprah" or "Roseanne" without fear of missing significant war news, Arledge and his aide Dick Wald created a series of round-the-clock forty-five-second "Gulf War Updates," broadcast every hour. To help explain the war, ABC News presented two prime-time specials called "A Line in the Sand" that located events, geographically and historically, for viewers who knew little about the Gulf; the first hour, on the eve of the war, became the highest-rated ABC News special since a 1978 telecast called "The World of the Supernatural." To deal with the questions and fears of children, ABC News presented a ninety-minute Saturday morning special, anchored sensitively by Jennings, that ran in place of cartoons.

More than anything else, what distinguished Jennings during the war was his refusal to play to public opinion, which was overwhelmingly pro-war. This was a war during which CBS's Rather literally saluted America's boys in the Gulf and NBC's "Today" turned patriotism into self-promotion by broadcasting video "postcards" from soldiers. On ABC, Barbara Walters, on "Nightline," blurred the lines between the press and the government by referring to "our side" and "the enemy." Sounding more like a military officer than a journalist, Walters asked, "How does this change our strategy? This means we can't bomb. It means we have to be very careful about the areas we attack, if we do attack."

Jennings, in contrast, remained above the fray, avoiding the use of "we" and "they" to refer to Americans and Iraqis. "It's not the journalist's role to be in one section of the stands or another," said Jennings, who was reflecting his Canadian roots as well as his professionalism.

Arledge himself was not a partisan, but he was partial to a certain style of coverage: live, visual, compelling, and high-impact. Over the years, by insisting that worldwide crises be covered live by ABC News, Arledge, more than anyone else, had generated the expectation that they would always be covered that way. As the other networks followed suit, viewers came to expect instant news from anywhere as a matter of right. Nothing less would satisfy them during the war.

The demand for immediacy turned the war into the ultimate stress test for television news. Live coverage, by nature, tends to short-circuit thought; the quality of journalism necessarily suffers when news has to be reported and shown immediately. "Journalism, after all, is not the training of a camera on an event live," said Ted Koppel. "Journalism lies in the editing and sifting out of what's important from what's irrelevant. And to the degree that even the best journalists require a little bit of time to consider what's important and what's not, doing things live reduces that to its bare minimum." Before the war, correspondent Barrie Dunsmore said, "We haven't given any serious thought to the consequences of reporting a war live."

On the war's second night, one of the dangers of instant coverage was vividly illustrated when all the networks broadcast rumors that, with time, could easily have been disproved. Reports that an Iraqi missile carrying chemical weapons had landed in Tel Aviv and that Israel was about to enter the war alarmed the huge prime-time audience. On ABC, Jennings said, "There are some reports that the Israelis are already in the process of retaliating against the Iraqis, and there is one report from ABC's Dean Reynolds in Jerusalem, quoting very high government sources, that some Israelis have been affected by nerve gas." This was not as reckless as NBC's Brokaw, who leaped ahead to denounce Iraq's use of chemical weapons as "crude and ruthless and almost unthinkable," but Jennings had failed to exercise proper restraint. Later, he apologized on the air for disseminating the false report.

Hours of live coverage created a demand for images as well as information. The networks turned to the Pentagon for footage, with the result that they literally presented a misleading picture of the war. Pentagon video of so-called smart bombs, which pierced elevator shafts and sliced through bridges with what Jennings described as "astonishing precision," obscured the reality that the laser- and radar-guided bombs and missiles made up just 7 percent of the explosives dropped on Iraq. High-flying B-52s carried most of the tonnage, conventional bombs that frequently missed their targets. Similarly, the oft-repeated video of Patriot missiles intercepting Iraqi Scuds created the misimpression that the Patriots provided a near-perfect antimissile shield. "Bull's-eye!" said Sam Donaldson, while screening one Patriot hit. "No more Scud!" Not until after the war was the inaccuracy of the Patriot exposed.

Other stories remained untold because there were no pictures to tell them. This was a sanitized war, a Nintendo war, because death never made an appearance on the home screen. As Ted Koppel told a reporter, "I'm not sure the public's interest is served by seeing what seems to have been such a painless war, when 50,000 to 100,000 people may have died on the other side. Obviously, this was done so they could maintain the closest possible control over public opinion, to increase support for the war." ABC's Bill Blakemore was more direct when he said, "Did I succeed in showing you the suffering of the Iraqis? No. Did others succeed in showing you the suffering of the Americans who died? No. It was a massive journalistic defeat."

The most basic problem with ABC's coverage, though, grew out of the packaging of the war as a television event. Once the fighting began, the story line revolved around a single question: Who's winning? This framework set off the parade of military analysts with their narrow focus on weaponry, tactics, and strategy; it cut short debate over the purpose, politics, or morality of the war. The effect was to turn upside down the observation that war is too important to be left to the generals — on the networks, coverage was dominated by military men who offered color commentary about the battles but paid scant attention to the history and politics of the region. Presenting the war as a clear-cut battle between good and evil made it easily digestible and dramatic, especially when the coverage was heralded with portentous theme music and heart-pounding graphics of tanks and planes.

This was true at all the networks, of course, but the case could be made that Arledge at ABC, with his appetite for drama, action, and immediacy, and his emphasis on production values, had more than anyone else created the climate that shaped television's war coverage. Arledge knew how to package and sell the news; given his television history, it was no surprise that the war came across as the ultimate spectator sport. "There's a tendency to treat the war like a football game," observed Michael Schiffer, a media analyst with the Center for War, Peace and the News Media in New York. "There's a scorecard, whether you're keeping score in tonnage, or in body counts, or mapping out plays with tanks and little arrows." Television presented the war as a spectacle because many news producers had come to think of their viewers as passive spectators, couch potatoes who needed to be entertained, rather than as active citizens who wanted to be informed. This new conception of the audience reflected a profound shift in values from the days when network news people saw themselves as serving a public. Now they were more likely to play to the crowd.

Certainly ABC News's war coverage turned out to be a crowd-pleaser. It was remarkable, in fact, how the audience migrated to ABC at key junctures, from the first night of the air war, to the opening of the ground war, to the day when the allied forces liberated Kuwait

City. Each time, viewers who flicked around to compare the networks' coverage settled on ABC News, which won the Nielsen ratings decisively. ABC's programs also thrived, as "World News Tonight" widened its ratings lead, "Nightline" outdrew Johnny Carson, and "PrimeTime Live" reached more viewers as it became more substantive.

But there were no victory parades for Arledge. The Gulf War had brought glory to ABC News, but not peace. Not-so-civil wars between shows and stars divided the news division. And Arledge was fighting his own quiet war with Dan Burke of Cap Cities, who had watched ABC lose millions of dollars in the Gulf because of added coverage costs and lost commercial time. Burke feared that he could no longer afford Roone Arledge.

Turf wars had become a way of life at ABC News. Competition, not cooperation, prevailed. "As Roone will never fail to deny, he fosters that kind of an atmosphere," Ted Koppel said. So long as the competition was healthy, Arledge figured everyone would benefit — people would work harder, and the shows would improve. Unhealthy competition was another matter, but that, too, was tolerated by Arledge because he hated to step into the middle of fights.

Occasionally, he had no choice. The night the Gulf War began, Koppel returned to Washington from the Middle East only to be told that Arledge had suggested that he might be weary from his travels and willing to skip "Nightline" so that Peter Jennings could stay in the anchor chair. Koppel exploded in his quiet but insistent way, shifting into what a colleague called "His Tedness" mode and leaving Arledge "sitting there between his 840-pound gorilla and his 790-pound gorilla." Koppel prevailed, with no hard feelings. He competed with Jennings, but they liked and respected each other.

Not as friendly was the rivalry between "Nightline" and Rick Kaplan's "PrimeTime Live." Some of the ill will dated back to Kaplan's departure from "Nightline." "Ted felt that I screwed him," Kaplan said. "That when I came over here, I raped 'Nightline' of its staff." That wasn't quite true, since several "Nightline" people went to "PrimeTime" before Kaplan, but Koppel said, "Rick pretty much cleaned the place out."

It didn't help that Kaplan disliked Dorrance Smith, who replaced him as "Nightline" executive producer. Smith's laid-back style had worked at the Brinkley show, but he lacked the energy, the force of personality, and the creativity needed to drive "Nightline." Nor was he willing to challenge Koppel. As a result, "Nightline" too often became little more than a rehash of the day's top story. "There was no creative spirit, no creative drive," a producer said. Koppel later admitted, "The show was getting predictable and boring."

In that unhappy environment arose a series of conflicts. "Nightline" and "PrimeTime" clashed over who would cover a gala birthday party for publisher Malcolm Forbes and over who would interview South African leader Nelson Mandela. They fought most harshly over a powerful interview that an ABC producer named Bob LeDonne had done with Ryan White, the Indiana teenager who was dying of AIDS. The interview, Koppel believed, belonged to "Nightline," but Kaplan used it on "PrimeTime." Dorrance Smith accused Kaplan of obtaining the footage under false pretenses, a charge strenuously denied by Kaplan.

Koppel was incensed. "I thought that was dishonorable," he said. "It offended my code of behavior." Believing that he had been lied to by a friend, Koppel sent a letter to Kaplan severing their professional relationship. "The bottom line of my letter," Koppel said later, "was that if I can do anything for your family, that's one thing, but don't come to me and ask for any professional favors." Soon after, when "Nightline" celebrated its tenth anniversary with a Washington party presided over by Arledge, Kaplan — who had once felt a brotherly closeness to Koppel — did not attend. "I didn't want to be in a room with Dorrance and Ted at that point, because I was really pissed," Kaplan said. Not until Yom Kippur, the Jewish day of atonement, did Koppel call his old producer to begin a reconciliation. Eventually, the two men rebuilt their friendship.

The most bitter rivalry pitted "PrimeTime" against "20/20." As the two shows grew more alike, they inevitably bumped up against each other. "We are out there competing for the same guests and the same stories," said Barbara Walters. But Walters fueled the rivalry, not deliberately but because she was "by far the most competitive and ruthless person in this industry," a competitor said. What's more, Walters had become obsessed by Diane Sawyer and the attention she was getting from Arledge.

It was nothing personal. Walters understood the pressures on Sawyer; she even threw a party for the "PrimeTime" stars at her country-style home in Los Angeles before an ABC affiliates meeting. "We are friends. We are buddies," Walters would say, when asked about Sawyer. "Would I rather get an interview ahead of Diane? Sure. But if it's a question of Diane getting it ahead of CBS or NBC, I'll fight like crazy to have Diane get it." Walters meant it, but she was so fiercely competitive that she was unnerved whenever Sawyer landed a high-profile interview ahead of her. Even then, Walters found it hard to let go.

Examples abounded. Once, Walters called Katharine Hepburn to ask her to cancel an interview with Sawyer and talk to her instead, even as a crew from "PrimeTime" was in Hepburn's apartment setting up the shoot. After Patricia Bowman, the woman who accused William Kennedy Smith of raping her, agreed to talk with Sawyer, Bowman's lawyer asked "PrimeTime" to promote the interview on the air to get Walters off his back. Walters also lodged a vehement protest when Sawyer pursued an interview with Syrian president Hafez al-Assad.

Walters set off an especially unseemly turf battle when she interceded after hearing that "PrimeTime" had convinced John Hinckley Jr., the man who tried to kill President Reagan, to talk to Sawyer. ABC News and Mark Lane, Hinckley's lawyer, had gone to court seeking permission for the interview from St. Elizabeths Hospital, where Hinckley was confined, when Walters called Lane and got him to switch the interview to her. Walters, who had interviewed Hinckley's parents, defended her action by saying she'd had a long-standing request in for John Hinckley Jr. But Sawyer was livid, especially after Arledge would not intervene. Rick Kaplan said, "We got screwed on the Hinckley situation. She trashed us and tried to steal it." The court ultimately ruled against ABC, so no one got the interview.

Publicly, Arledge denied that there was friction between his leading ladies. When a reporter asked what it was like to be caught between Walters and Sawyer, he replied, "Very pleasant. It fulfills all my fantasies."

Reality intruded rudely when Walters and her agent, Marvin Josephson, began serious negotiations with CBS News in 1991. Somehow, ABC News had allowed its exclusive renegotiation period with Walters to lapse, an oversight that later appalled the Cap Cities people. What, they thought, could be more important than keeping tabs on a superstar like Walters? In their eyes, this was more evidence that ABC News was poorly managed.

Walters was also disquieted. At an affiliates meeting, she sat with Arledge and "he never mentioned my contract," she said. "He wasn't returning Marvin's calls. Maybe there were other things that were on Roone's mind. But I had no feeling from Roone that he wanted me."

To Walters, the handling of her contract was symbolic. "My problems weren't money," she said, "but sometimes feeling less than part of the team. I felt I was being neglected in News." In a sense, she was being penalized for her success. "We all felt on '20/20' — all of us — that 'PrimeTime,' because it was new and struggling, got all the attention, the ads, the promotions," said Walters. "I was bringing in all this money, and I was sort of taken for granted."

At CBS, chairman Larry Tisch and Howard Stringer, president of the CBS Broadcast Group, offered Walters her own prime-time show. Star anchor Connie Chung would be one correspondent, and CBS wanted to hire Maria Shriver from NBC to be another. The money was mind-boggling — about $4 million a year, more than any other news star was paid. CBS executives believed that the network could pay Walters twice that and still make a profit on her show.

Walters was tempted, but she knew firsthand how traumatic it could be to leave one network for another. "I couldn't bear to go through that again," Walters said. "I knew I would probably end up on magazine covers, which would say, 'Why are they paying her this when they're firing the guy in the Hong Kong bureau?'"

She signed on for five more years at ABC. Her salary is a well-kept secret, but network insiders believe that she earns more than $3 million a year. ABC also purchased the rights to her library of celebrity specials, a deal worth millions more to Walters.

Her feelings for Arledge also came into play. "Roone was almost the reason that I left and, in part, he was the reason I stayed," Walters said. Arledge could be exasperating, she said, but "Roone and I have a relationship that we feel in our gut. I am deeply fond of him. He is deeply fond of me. I don't understand why this whole thing happened, but I also knew that I wanted to stay with him."

Not that she didn't have periodic doubts. Some time later, at an elegant birthday party for Walters at Le Cirque where the guests included Stringer, Tisch, and Dan Burke, Arledge delivered a toast. Pulling out a line he'd used in the past with David Burke and Frank Gifford, Arledge said that if he were locked up in a Turkish prison, the first person he would call would be Barbara, because she would get him out. "Roone," she replied, without missing a beat, "I'd be happy if you just returned my calls here in New York."

Roone Arledge hated corporate meetings. Sometimes he skipped the monthly meetings of senior Capital Cities management and sent an aide in his stead. Other times, no one from ABC News would show up. This irritated Dan Burke; he found it discourteous, if not arrogant.

"The Cap Cities people have a perception that Roone does whatever he wants, that he doesn't live by the rules," said an ABC News insider. "And to some extent that's true — but you can't run this place if you're sitting in seventeen million meetings a day."

Given Arledge's disdain for meetings — especially meetings that focused on the budget, which was never his favorite subject — it came as no surprise when the war between Arledge and Dan Burke burst into the open during a meeting over costs.

The session had gone badly from the start. Burke had assembled the top people from ABC News and from Broadcast Operations and Engineering (BO&E), a network division responsible for technical people and equipment, to enact a number of cost-cutting measures. But Arledge, Dick Wald, and Irwin Weiner did not seem prepared, and Arledge treated the issues at hand as trivial. His attitude came across as cavalier.

When Burke tried to pin him down, Arledge "dodged and weaved around the questions on the table," an executive said. Sounding exasperated, Arledge said, "I have no idea why things of this relative unimportance are being decided at this level." Some in the room thought he was about to leave.

Burke exploded.

"Roone," he said, in a voice that seethed with anger, "unless you're present, nothing ever gets decided, and these issues demand resolution."

Burke went on to chew out Arledge at length. "I can see you're not even paying attention to what's being decided here," he said, "because you're not writing anything down." Arledge, he went on, was wrong to believe that he, Burke, was not a friend of ABC News. But Burke said it was long past time that Arledge begin to live by the rules that govern everyone else at Cap Cities.

"You News guys think you're special," Burke said in an accusatory tone.

He also pointedly reminded Arledge that the corporation had just given him a lucrative new contract.

"It's time for you to start giving something back," Burke said.

Dick Wald sat nervously. When he grew tense, he pursed his lips in a way that made it look as if he were smiling. Burke, glancing his way, thought he was being mocked.

"Wipe that smirk off your face," Burke thundered. "This is not funny to me."

Arledge and Wald were silent. Only Weiner defended ABC News, saying that it was unfair for Burke to berate the news people after all ABC News had done for Cap Cities.

The meeting broke up, uncomfortably, a few minutes later.

Onlookers had never seen Burke so angry. "This was about a seven on the Richter scale," said one. Later, Burke denied he had lost control. "I wasn't angry, but I was absolutely determined to seize that moment to make my point," he said. After the meeting, he was actually pleased. Dan Burke believed in confronting problems openly and honestly. For the first time in the five years since the Cap Cities takeover, he said, people realized that ABC News was going to be asked to submit to the same disciplines as the rest of the company. Burke blamed himself for being too forgiving of Arledge's idiosyncrasies in the past. Now everyone knew Arledge was in the penalty box.

In truth, Dan Burke was both awed and appalled by Roone Arledge. He admired what Arledge had done for ABC News, and he recognized that Arledge's news operation, unlike those at CBS and NBC, was making money — about $70 million in 1990, by the news division's accounting. Burke, as a sports fan, cherished the time he'd spent with Arledge in the control room during the 1988 Calgary Olympics. "I'd just sit on a chair and watch him for two or three hours," Burke said. "There's tension and noise and confusion and hurt feelings and all kinds of things, and there's an unexplainable art to what he does. It's much more than directing a classical orchestra. It's an experience that I treasure and will never forget." Arledge's grasp of world events also impressed Burke, who recalled Arledge saying during the Gulf War that "this is just a sideshow" and that "the greatest event since World War II will unfold in Russia and Eastern Europe." Months later, Communism collapsed. "When somebody tells you something like that," Burke said, "and it is so prescient, you don't dismiss their instincts casually. There are some people who just have the capacity to look out over the horizon and understand, and Roone is one of them." Personally, Burke was fascinated by Arledge — by his unexplained comings and goings and his life as a single man in New York.

Their belief in Arledge's value had led Murphy and Burke to reward him in 1990 with a five-year, $3-million-a-year contract — more money than either of them earned from Cap Cities. They believed that, whatever his flaws, nobody was better able to run ABC News. They also felt that the contract ought to go a long way toward making

Arledge feel secure and toward easing what seemed to be his perpetual worry that the Cap Cities people were not on his side. That spring, at an industry dinner, Tom Murphy cast a public vote of confidence in Arledge by saying that his greatest personal satisfaction at ABC came when "you see the ABC logo and it says under it, 'More Americans get their news from ABC News than from any other source.' " Generously, Murphy invited Arledge to stand and described him as "the genius behind the great ABC News operation." The tribute was heartfelt.

So, however, were the frustrations that the Cap Cities men felt about Arledge's stubborn unwillingness to adjust to their ways of doing business. The Arledge problem moved close to the top of Dan Burke's list of worries when he replaced Tom Murphy as CEO of Cap Cities in June 1990, just as the television business entered another downturn.

Burke's biggest worry was the recession. A sluggish economy severely curbed the demand for advertising, as network shares continued to slide. "The network business is a very perilous, terribly difficult business," Burke said. Cap Cities stock, which reached a high of $633 shortly after Burke took over, tumbled to a low of $360 in December 1991.

By then, Burke had become resigned to the fact that ABC's revenues were unpredictable — they fluctuated with the ratings, with the economy, and with the advertising market, none of which the network could control. All that ABC could manage was its costs. Since 1986, Cap Cities had cut about eighteen hundred jobs from the corporate and network staff, the owned stations, the sports division, legal, public relations, and other departments. ABC News had shrunk too, but not to the same degree. "That Roone was untouched was the feeling in the rest of the company," a corporate executive said.

Burke was obsessed by costs. While Arledge glided around Manhattan in his chauffeur-driven Jaguar, Burke made a show of his own frugality, walking to work in the rain and then boasting about it. More to the point, Burke was an unstoppable force during budget meetings, which he used to remind people that "anyone in charge of anything shouldn't get too big or important to forget the details," an executive said. Even the ABC News people were impressed by the way Burke could get to the nub of an issue. "He just kept digging and digging and digging," said Dick Wald, "and showing you where the faults in your logic were, and pushing and pushing until you got down to the barest bones of what exactly it was you wanted, exactly why you wanted it, exactly how much it would do for you, and how much it would cost."

Elsewhere at ABC, Burke saw progress. "It's been gratifying beyond belief to hear people say things like, we really ought to nurse these hundred and fifty tape machines through another fifteen months because they're going to be obsolete eventually," he said. "They begin to take their share of the responsibility, instead of feeling that either (a) nobody is watching, or (b) some Big Brother is watching and will decide these things. You download a sense of responsibility." Burke believed strongly that "the companies that really succeed over an extended period of time are those that inculcate a feeling of maturity and responsibility about costs as far down in the organization as possible."

That wasn't happening at ABC News. Burke wanted the executive producers, the field producers, the desk people, and everyone else to strive for efficiency. But Arledge, who set the tone for the news operation, had no commitment to cost cutting — his passion was programming. Arledge failed even to keep a close eye on his budget. That sent exactly the wrong message, Burke thought.

One time, Burke watched Arledge in action when a big story broke, and while he couldn't remember the story, the scene stuck in his head. "People were coming in and out in a state of excitement," Burke said. "They were chartering jets in Europe and trying to reposition people, and Roone was reminded where camera crews and on-air people were. He'd make decisions and it was amazing to watch him do it." Impressed as he was by Arledge's generalship, Burke worried. "As I listened to him, I could just hear thousands and thousands of dollars being spent," he said. Nobody had even asked about costs.

Arledge, however, thought the Cap Cities people were so intent on cutting costs that they lost sight of what mattered most in television: the programs. "You can never get away from people's perspectives," he said. "You can have somebody who will look at the Sistine ceiling and say, 'I would have used a different kind of plaster. Or 'How much did the plaster cost and why do we need a scaffold?' It's frustrating." Arledge could not believe that Burke could be unhappy with him and so taken with penny-pinching managers like Dennis Swanson, who'd lost a bundle of money on the NFL while running ABC Sports, and Phil Beuth, who spent millions in a failed effort to develop a hit to follow "Nightline." In the world of Cap Cities, Arledge thought, the frugal executive seemed to be valued more than the successful one.

Philosophically, Arledge believed that a narrow focus on costs stifled risk taking. "If you are going to grow in an economy that is becoming global, and becoming bigger, you have to invest," he said. "There would not be an ESPN today if somebody had not been willing to invest in an idea that was going to lose money. There would not be a 'PrimeTime Live' if I hadn't spent all that time over everybody's objections trying to get Diane Sawyer."

Nothing bothered him more than the rap that ABC News was out of control. "What Roone resents is this assumption that we're bad managers," said Joanna Bistany, his trusted aide. "We are the leanest management. We run the largest operation. We bring the company prestige, and we make money for them. These people who say, 'Roone's a genius but he's a terrible manager' — I don't know how you can equate that with a successful news division. This news division did not become profitable by accident."

Despite his new contract, Arledge felt unappreciated. He didn't think he could count on the support of Dan Burke, just as Burke didn't think he could rely on Arledge to manage efficiently. This lack of trust complicated their dealings and hampered everyone's efforts to develop new programs for ABC.

An overnight news program, for example, got caught in the crossfire between Burke and Arledge. Burke wanted an overnight program, which he saw as a way to serve ABC's affiliates, compete with CNN, and, most important, use as an entry into the growing overseas markets for news. Arledge did not oppose the idea, but he worried that the money needed to mount a quality program would not be forthcoming from Cap Cities. Nevertheless, before a budget had been set, Dick Wald flew to a meeting of local TV news directors in San Jose, California, in September 1990, to announce that an overnight service would begin in January. He did so at a breakfast meeting, but returned at lunch to put the program on hold. Arledge, at the last minute, had decided that the show was underfunded. "He wasn't exactly looking for a Cadillac," Wald said, "but he was looking for an Oldsmobile, and we were trying to design a Buick or a Chevy." Aside from the embarrassment of announcing and postponing a program on the same day, everyone saw the delay as unfortunate. Had the program gone on as scheduled in January 1991, ABC News would have been on the air overnight during the Gulf War. "It's very much to be regretted that we didn't cut our teeth on that program at that time," Burke said. Instead, overnight news was not launched until January 1992, after NBC had begun its own overnight service.

Other new projects also languished. Inside the news division, producers and correspondents developed ideas for a Saturday morning children's program, for a prime-time show about relations between men and women, for a Sunday news-of-the-week-in-review show, and for a magazine show about popular culture. None could get Arledge's attention or enthusiasm, and the feeling spread that he was not as willing to take risks as he once had been. This was almost surely true, if only because Arledge felt constricted by an environment in which failure exacted a high price. The go-go days when he could spend freely on new ideas were over; the press could be harsh; and his personal reputation was established, so he had less to gain from new successes.

When Arledge did bring new programs to Cap Cities they were rejected. Late in 1987, Arledge had just about persuaded Larry King to leave CNN to do an interview show for ABC News after "Nightline" when the idea was shot down abruptly by Cap Cities' sales and stations people, who said King would not reach the younger viewers they wanted. "Larry King was a missed opportunity," Arledge said. "He was ready to come, and I just could not get it seriously considered." Another time, Arledge and Phyllis McGrady tried to sell the network on a moody, late-night talk show with Tom Snyder, called "Voices in the Night," but that, too, was turned down. On those occasions, Murphy and Burke were doubting Arledge's instincts as a programmer — which was unwise, given his track record. The company was paying a price for the fact that Arledge and the Cap Cities people had been unable to forge strong bonds.

What bonds did exist were strained further after the Gulf War, which proved enormously costly. By Burke's accounting, spending on news coverage had exceeded the budget by $30 million during 1990 and another $30 million during 1991 — and that was only part of the problem. Special events programming forced ABC to cancel revenue-producing entertainment shows. And as the recession deepened, advertisers used the war as an excuse to renege on earlier commitments to buy time. Burke had been unstinting in his support for ABC News during the war, but afterward he was determined to see to it that News operate prudently.

Burke wanted deep cuts in the News budget, which had climbed to about $375 million by 1991. He let it be known that the goal should be to cut $50 million, well beyond what News executives believed prudent. In response, Arledge put his budget chief, Irwin Weiner, in charge of a new budget commission, which put Weiner in a tough spot — while the pressure from Cap Cities was unrelenting, he knew that Arledge had no real stomach for budget cutting. "I worked for Roone," Weiner said, "but I also felt I had to service Cap Cities." The executive producers and anchors also fought for their shows.

Under pressure from Cap Cities, Arledge reluctantly approved another round of spending cuts. About a hundred positions were eliminated from a work force of about 1,250, and bureaus in St. Louis, Rome, Frankfurt, and Hong Kong were shut. Closing St. Louis, a midwest hub, left ABC News with only a handful of people between New York and Denver. Closing the three foreign offices meant settling for less original reporting from overseas, although ABC still devoted more attention than CBS or NBC to foreign news.

But Arledge stopped well short of where Weiner's commission wanted him to go. The commission proposed, for example, that the staff of "Nightline," which was split between New York and Washington, be consolidated in Washington, a logical idea that Arledge nevertheless resisted because he wanted the executive producer near him in New York, rather than under Koppel's sway. The two-city arrangement cost more than $1 million for extra staff and control rooms — wasted money, many thought. Arledge's budget plan put off consolidation until January 1993, and the Cap Cities people did not believe the move would take place even then.

Weiner's commission also wanted to merge the staffs of the weekend and weekday editions of "World News Tonight," to save another $2 million. Weekend news, the commission said, could be run by Paul Friedman's staff in New York. But Arledge opted to keep separate staffs and executive producers, to spur competition and preserve the weekends as an outlet for people who could not get onto the weekday show.

Ultimately, Arledge approved what he claimed would be $7 million worth of cuts for 1991 and another $25 million in savings for 1992. He took the package to Dan Burke.

Burke didn't buy it. "There was some substance to the commission deliberations, but there was a lot less substance than they were representing to me," Burke said. He thought that Arledge had nipped around the edges, sparing big-ticket items that were protected by show producers and star anchors. "Roone dislikes confrontation more than almost anybody I've met," Burke said. "He is really uncomfortable with it." Worst of all, Burke didn't believe the numbers. "No department was more capable of self-delusion than News," he said. "I never could be sure they knew what the hell they were talking about.

"The worst thing in business is to be working with numbers in which you lack confidence," he added.

A story he heard that summer troubled him. Traveling to London, Arledge, Bistany, and ABC consultant Judith Kipper had notified the bureau to send a car to the airport. Playing it safe, the bureau ordered three cars — so the two executives and Kipper rode into the city in what amounted to a presidential motorcade.

In some very real ways, Burke thought, ABC News had yet to be joined with Capital Cities. He concluded that Arledge, like many great thinkers, was a visionary but not an administrator. "I find that the courage and the talent, the intelligence, the energy, and the spirit that make great entrepreneurs frequently preclude a patience with detail and a patience with routine," Burke said. "Roone has to this day never developed a great appetite for that."

Burke felt impelled to act.

He had opened channels to key News executives, including Paul Friedman and Bob Murphy, and he'd heard the same thing from them — that Arledge had erred by not replacing David Burke. His underlings complained that Arledge himself was inaccessible and unwilling to delegate. Peter Jennings, now secure in his anchor job, was among those who told Dan Burke that Arledge was a great leader but an inattentive manager. Later, Jennings said, "One reason the knights rebelled against the king was that the king wasn't paying attention. When he pays attention, he's fabulous." When Arledge later heard that Jennings and Friedman had talked frankly to Burke, he felt betrayed.

In September 1991, with Arledge in Moscow producing the historic ABC News interviews with Mikhail Gorbachev and Boris Yeltsin, Burke made his move. He approached Stephen A. Weiswasser, a Cap Cities lawyer and executive vice president of the network, to see if he would be willing to tackle a tough assignment — to go to work inside ABC News and, with Burke's support, impose budget and management discipline on the division. Weiswasser was more than willing; he saw the job as a chance to prove that he had the management skills to run the entire company if all went well. His mandate was to transform ABC News from a fiefdom of Roone Arledge into an integral part of Capital Cities/ABC.

"It was important," Dan Burke said, "to get someone in there to articulate and communicate the principles that have been more quickly embraced in the other parts of the company."

Burke wanted the best of both worlds — he wanted Arledge so the network could reap the benefits of his vision and creativity, and he wanted ABC News managed the Cap Cities way.

The only risk was that Arledge might quit. After five years of living with his News president, that was a risk that Dan Burke was willing to take.

Chapter Eighteen

ON THE BRINK

WHO was running ABC News?

That was the question on the minds of the senior executives and producers who were summoned by Roone Arledge to a hastily called meeting on the first Tuesday in October 1991.

It was a question no one would have asked before. For the past fourteen years, as president of ABC News, Arledge had exercised complete control. Every major decision that affected programs, personnel, coverage, scheduling, budgeting, or promotion required his approval. He kept a hand in countless minor matters too — from choosing the photographs to hang on the walls to reviewing seating arrangements at ABC News functions. "The analogy to an absolute monarchy is not inapt," a veteran producer said.

That morning, rumors of a palace coup had swept through the news division. Some had Arledge resigning. Others predicted a shake-up, perhaps involving the removal of his closest aide, Joanna Bistany.

Entering the room only after everyone was seated, as usual, Arledge told his top people that the network would announce that afternoon that Steve Weiswasser had been appointed the executive vice president of ABC News.

He cast the news in a positive light.

"I'm confident that this will be good for all of us," Arledge said. "This will be good for ABC News."

As Arledge explained it, Weiswasser would be responsible for the budget and the day-to-day management of ABC News. Weiswasser would not, however, be involved in editorial and programming matters.

The idea, Arledge said, was to allow him to spend less time going to meetings and worrying about the budget so that he would be free to concentate on programs.

"It will lift a great load," Arledge said. "For better or worse," he added dryly, "you will all have me on your head more than you've had."

Arledge repeated that Weiswasser would have no say over editorial matters. "You'll all be meeting Steve soon," he said.

He was remarkably calm. Several of Arledge's executive producers were impressed with how gracefully he handled the situation.

Everyone knew that Roone Arledge had just been humiliated.

No other conclusion could be drawn. The most benign explanation for Weiswasser's appointment — one that ABC's spin doctors sold, with little difficulty, to the press — was that Arledge had hired him to improve relations between ABC News and Capital Cities.

No one in the room believed that for a minute. Arledge, they knew, would not voluntarily give up power. And even if he had chosen to hire an executive vice president, he would never have picked Steve Weiswasser. Weiswasser was a corporate guy whose loyalties flowed to Cap Cities.

But Arledge had no choice. Dan Burke had shoved Weiswasser down his throat. Cap Cities was finally taking over ABC News.

Everyone also knew that the distinction Arledge had tried to draw between Weiswasser's financial duties and his own authority over the editorial product was an artificial one. Budgetary decisions were nearly always editorial decisions too. No wall could be erected between them.

So many questions came to mind. Who would decide how many crews to send to a breaking story? Or whether ABC needed bureaus in Chicago or Hong Kong? Who would say whether ABC could interrupt regularly scheduled programming for a special report, and for how long? And who would decide how much to pay anchors, reporters, and producers? Every one of those decisions was financial, and yet each affected news programming. No one knew whether such decisions would be made by Arledge or Weiswasser. No one knew who was in charge.

Arledge did not invite questions after his announcement, but a few people spoke up. Victor Neufeld of "20/20" asked who would handle contracts with his producers, but stopped himself when he realized that the question might embarrass Arledge. Arledge simply said the contracts would be settled soon.

The meeting was adjourned. No one wanted to prolong the agony.

It had already been a brutal day for Arledge. Just before breaking the news to his staff, he had come out of an uncomfortable meeting with Weiswasser.

With ABC executives Sherrie Rollins and Patricia Matson, who handled the press, Arledge had gone to Weiswasser's Cap Cities office to review the ABC announcement of the appointment — a document that had been drafted with the utmost care in an effort to spare Arledge public embarrassment. The press release said, for example, that Arledge had "announced" the hiring, but it did not say who had put Weiswasser in his new job. That, of course, had been Dan Burke's doing.

As Arledge read the release, he casually suggested that it be reworded to say Weiswasser would report to him.

Calmly, Weiswasser demurred.

A bit later, Arledge repeated the suggestion. This time, Weiswasser suggested they take up the matter in private.

"Never mind," said Arledge. "Let's leave it out."

Nothing more needed to be said.

Afterward, as the story spread through ABC, many who heard it could not help but be amazed. Right up to the end, even after the uncomfortable truth had been made abundantly clear to him, Roone Arledge desperately wanted the world to believe that he remained the sole ruler of ABC News.

While ABC said nothing publicly about the reporting relationship between Arledge and Weiswasser, Weiswasser's title of executive vice president implied that he would serve as Arledge's deputy. The press release quoted Arledge as saying, "I am pleased that he is willing and able to help us in the important and challenging work ahead." Neither man did interviews, and the press treated the story as a routine appointment.

In fact, Weiswasser reported not to Arledge but to Dan Burke. Those were the only conditions under which he would take the job. "I'm not here to work for Roone, and wouldn't," he said. Nor was Arledge working for him. In theory, they were supposed to work together, with the understanding that any irreconcilable disputes would be taken to Burke. Tom Murphy and Dan Burke, two Harvard MBAs who prided themselves on their management skills, had created an unwieldy co-presidency of ABC News.

Inside ABC, the power-sharing arrangement, which created some initial confusion, gradually became understood. Weiswasser took over Dick Wald's office and ordered that a door be built to give him a direct and private entry into Arledge's office. Weisswasser insisted that the gesture was innocent, but others saw it as a power play. "I thought it was kind of silly, but to him it was very important," Arledge complained. "It became a symbol of Steve's ego that he had to have this access." Some time later, when Charles Gibson, the anchor of ABC's "Good Morning America," wondered at a meeting whether Arledge would support plans to improve coordination between "GMA" and ABC News, Phil Beuth, the Cap Cities executive in charge of "GMA," told him, "What you don't understand, Charlie, is that Roone Arledge is not in charge of ABC News." The word was out that all the big decisions at ABC News had to be approved by Weiswasser, who functioned, in essence, as an occupying general.

It was a challenging assignment, but Stephen A. Weiswasser, fifty, welcomed the chance to demonstrate his toughness and management skills. The son of a Michigan county prosecutor, Weiswasser had practiced law for eighteen years with Wilmer, Cutler, and Pickering in Washington, D.C., before Murphy and Burke hired him as their first general counsel during the ABC merger. He made a strong impression on people — he was six feet two inches tall, his early-morning jogs left him trim and energetic, and he spoke with all the certainty of a Harvard-educated partner of a high-powered Washington firm. Weiswasser's assignment to News was a test of his management skills. He was destined for bigger things, many thought, and he told people that he would work at ABC News for a year or so, fix up the place, and then move on.

His arrival ended Irwin Weiner's ABC career. Weiner, fifty-two, quit on the spot rather than report to Weiswasser; he was cut loose by Arledge, whom he'd served for twenty years. While Weiner got a generous financial settlement, it wasn't the ending he'd wanted. "I would have hoped that I had an Irwin Weiner protecting me, rather than a Roone Arledge protecting me," Weiner said. "I've taken better care of people I don't even know."

Weiswasser, meanwhile, began to carry out the mandate that Dan Burke had given him — to manage ABC News more efficiently, without damaging the quality of programming or losing Arledge. He listened to lots of people, but he also brought the message that the culture of ABC News had to change.

"Roone created a structure that was designed to do what it does extraordinarily well, which is to produce programming," Weiswasser said. "But it didn't have the management concepts or structures that are needed to be sure that things are not only done well, but done efficiently. People around here understood that the important thing was to get the show on the air and not be in a position where it wasn't done right because you could get into trouble for that. They knew that if the cost was a little over budget, they wouldn't have to worry about it."

Now, Weiswasser told people, "Part of your job is to think of ways to run your show that cost less than the way you did it yesterday. We save money because of the thousands of individual decisions made by people all over this place every day."

Weiswasser made some changes on his own. For starters, he carried out nearly all the proposals of the Weiner Commission, including those resisted by Arledge. "Nightline" was consolidated in Washington. Throughout ABC News, fewer editing rooms and control rooms were used. More Washington stories were covered by "pool" crews, allowing the costs of news gathering to be shared by all the networks. And producers for the magazine shows were given tighter shooting and editing schedules.

Layoffs followed in January 1992. While only about thirty jobs were eliminated, this was the third wave of staff cuts at ABC News in fifteen months. Washington correspondents Jed Duvall, Jeanne Meserve, and Steve Shepherd were among those let go, as was the veteran Sander Vanocur, Arledge's first hire at ABC News. "Business World," the weekend show anchored by Vanocur, later was canceled.

Weiswasser tallied up the savings and figured he had cut more than $25 million from the 1992 news budget — money that Arledge claimed he would have wrung out on his own. Weiswasser doubted that, and he believed that even more budget cuts were needed. Like Dan Burke, Weiswasser saw hard times ahead. "The cost profile of the news division and the network requires massive changes over the next decade," he said. "In a world in which revenues don't go up, the guy who succeeds is the low-cost provider."

Arledge strongly disagreed — success, he thought, was driven by hit shows, not by cost-cutting measures — but he was willing to let Weiswasser immerse himself in the budget. He held out a faint hope that Weiswasser could be made into an ally. "It might not be the most comfortable thing for everybody, or even for me," Arledge said. "But Steve has the clout to get some things done with the network." So long as Weiswasser's austerity campaign did not damage his shows or affect his stars, Arledge felt he could live with him, if not like him.

Besides, Arledge was unexpectedly confronted with a much more serious problem than Steve Weiswasser. A few months after Weiswasser's arrival, he was diagnosed with prostate cancer. He entered the Johns Hopkins Hospital in Baltimore, where doctors performed surgery on April 22, 1992, successfully removing the tumor. Chemotherapy was not required, but Arledge needed weeks to recover before he could resume work in the office.

Returning to his Park Avenue apartment, Arledge conducted some business over the phone, but he felt cut off. "What he feared desperately was that Weiswasser was going to change the locks," an aide said. Worried that he was losing control, Arledge asked that senior staff meetings be held in his living room — an idea resisted by Weiswasser, who thought it wasteful and proposed instead that Arledge be hooked up by phone. Eventually, Arledge prevailed, and he presided over a few meetings in his bathrobe from an easy chair, still connected to a tube. But aides saw a man whose frailty only underscored how his standing had been weakened at ABC.

Arledge had reason to worry about his waning influence. A case in point was his desire to hire CBS News anchor Connie Chung. He wanted Chung to anchor one of two new programs in the works at ABC News — either a Sunday night prime-time magazine or a show that would become "Turning Point," about personal and historical turning points, which was the brainchild of producer Phyllis McGrady.

Chung would lend star quality to either show. She was not of Diane Sawyer's caliber, Arledge thought, but she was promotable, a hard worker, and well liked by the viewers. Arledge called Chung and her agent, Alfred Geller, and she met with Arledge and other ABC News people four or five times in hotel suites and restaurants. Throughout their discussions, Chung expressed loyalty to CBS, which had given her time off to try to conceive a child with her husband, Maury Povich. But Chung liked McGrady and seemed intrigued by "Turning Point." Arledge was inclined to press on with serious negotiations. With the right offer — $2 million or $3 million a year — Chung might be pried loose from CBS.

Weiswasser, however, was unenthusiastic. The Cap Cities people envisioned the Sunday show as a low-cost, low-risk vehicle, one that did not require a name anchor, and McGrady's show would not debut for at least another year. Rather than spend a fortune on Chung, Weiswasser wanted to test Arledge's dictum that every show needed a star. "The way you do shows in this environment is not to go find somebody else's talent," Weiswasser said. He noted, with approval, that CBS News had made a hit of "48 Hours," a show which despite Dan Rather's incidental presence was not star-driven and cost far less than "20/20" or "PrimeTime Live." And he was not even willing to credit Arledge for bringing Diane Sawyer to ABC. "Maybe by hindsight if we had passed on Diane Sawyer, 'PrimeTime Live' wouldn't be where it is. But maybe it would," Weiswasser said. "We haven't ever tried to do it the other way."

The disagreement became moot when Chung decided to stay at CBS before Arledge went into his full-court press. But the experience dispirited Arledge, who felt thwarted. "Losing Connie Chung was a major thing," he said.

Arledge and Weiswasser also fought over scheduling the Sunday program, which would become "Day One." Dan Burke had said in January 1992 that he wanted the program by summer or fall, a timetable Arledge felt was unrealistic. "I kept telling people that I did not believe we had a program yet," Arledge said. Tom Yellin, the executive producer, agreed, saying, "It's not possible to do a program that quickly unless you want something that isn't good." But Weiswasser insisted that further delay was wasteful. "In a properly organized, properly run division, there's no reason why it could not have gone on the air, especially since the company's expectation was not that it would go on the air perfect," he said. "I was prepared to force it on the air because I had the view that that was the only way to get it going." Dan Burke, too, vowed that the show would go on — or else. Arledge avoided a showdown only because Cap Cities unexpectedly decided to renew the entertainment show "Life Goes On" for Sundays, rather than lose it to NBC.

Arledge complained, justifiably, that Cap Cities had given him a mandate to create new programs without the freedom to produce them his own way.

Those quarrels were minor by comparision to the battle that unfolded over Sam Donaldson. Burke and Weiswasser were convinced that Donaldson was overpaid. The contract he had extracted from Arledge before going on "PrimeTime" gave Donaldson a $1.7 million annual salary, as much as Peter Jennings; they vowed to bring him down a notch or two.

Burke said it was nothing personal, although others suspected that Sam Donaldson was just not Dan Burke's kind of guy. Weiswasser insisted that the sole issue was money. "It is not fair," he said, "to force the burden of cost cutting and efficiencies to fall solely on the shoulders of the people who make the least."

This was the case Weiswasser made to Donaldson when they sat down over lunch in March. He liked Sam, he said, but the days of bloated paychecks for every anchor were over. The company wanted him to take a 50 percent cut in pay.

"Steve," he said, "that's not even a basis for a negotiation."

Weiswasser urged him not to take it personally. "I've got a job I have to do," he said.

"Well," Donaldson replied, "I appreciate that, but I'm not going to accept any cut in pay. Not one penny."

His pride was wounded. "If you had come to me and said, 'We want a twenty percent cut in pay, fifteen percent,' I would not have accepted it, but I would not have felt as I feel today," he went on. "You have simply insulted me."

Weiswasser tried to soothe Donaldson. He climbed into a taxi to ride with him to the airport and even walked him to the gate, all the while trying to assure him that he was wanted at ABC.

Donaldson was unmoved. The money, by itself, was not the issue. He could absorb a pay cut and still live well. But Donaldson, who was already unhappy about his secondary role on "PrimeTime Live," refused to allow ABC to ratify his second-class status by cutting his pay. Besides, "PrimeTime" was climbing in the ratings and making money. Why should he take a hit? "It's unjust," he said.

Believing that Cap Cities would not back down after putting such a big pay cut on the table, Donaldson began talking to other employers. In his mind, he prepared to leave ABC.

Arledge, however, girded for battle. After his surgery, he invited Donaldson to his apartment to tell him that he would back him against Cap Cities. This was a turnaround for Arledge. "Of all the people there, I had a personal reason to want to screw Sam," Arledge said. "There's nobody before who refused to take my word, or would act ornery and foolish and then look dumb on the air because he wouldn't listen." But Arledge thought that Donaldson was vital to "Prime-Time" and told him so. "They don't understand talent," he said to his anchor. "They don't understand the value you have, over and above a piece you do here or a piece you do there. It's the feeling people have about ABC News. You're part of that feeling. They don't get it."

The stakes, for Arledge, were enormous. He had never lost a major star. He was worried not only about "PrimeTime" and the Brinkley show but about how losing Donaldson would be perceived. Within the network, the lines had been drawn — people knew that Arledge wanted to keep Donaldson and that Cap Cities was willing to lose him. He had to keep Donaldson not only to save Sam but to save face.

On Friday, May 29, Arledge returned to ABC News for the first time since his operation for a decisive meeting with Burke and Weiswasser. They debated the issue for two hours. Arledge argued that "when you have a show that has just turned the corner and become successful, to go break it up over a relatively small amount of money is crazy." Weiswasser finally broke the impasse by proposing a compromise: a one-year contract that would allow Donaldson to match his current salary provided that the ratings held steady for "PrimeTime." The one-year term and the ratings contingency were both highly unusual. In effect, they put Donaldson, a twenty-five-year employee of ABC News, on probation, and challenged him to prove he was worth the money. Reluctantly, Arledge accepted the proposal — it was the best he could do. With mixed emotions, Donaldson signed the contract and resolved to prove himself again in the months ahead.

At "PrimeTime Live" everyone felt relief. "Roone knows that when your watch is working, you don't take a part out of it," Rick Kaplan said. "Without Roone, they would have cut Sam's salary and he would have left."

The Donaldson issue had not been resolved, however — it had only been postponed. No one came away pleased, and ABC had nearly lost a valuable star.

By this time, it was evident that the power-sharing arrangement between Arledge and Weiswasser that looked good on paper to Dan Burke had become a power struggle. Weiswasser called it "a power struggle over policy and direction," but others saw the conflicts in personal terms.

The fundamental problem was that Roone Arledge and Steve Weiswasser had nothing in common. They had no shared values or shared history, as well as no common vision about where to lead ABC News.

They could not even agree on what had worked before, since Weiswasser believed that the success of Arledge's ABC News had little or nothing to do with the way the place had been run. "In many cases," he said, "the creative successes of people have been in spite of, not because of, the system. If you bring really smart people, really creative and talented people together, eventually they will do some good things." In his view of history, Arledge had become a bystander, if not an obstacle to success.

Their personalities didn't mesh either. Weiswasser came to work early and liked attacking problems in a logical, lawyerly, timely way. He believed in management systems, accountability, and chains of command. Arledge worked late, postponed decisions, and used delay to avoid conflict. He was emotional, intuitive, fluid, unwilling to be pinned down, and loath to take risks. His leadership style was intensely personal.

About all these two men had in common were their oversize egos, and that was another problem. It mattered to Weiswasser, as it did to Arledge, who got to stand in receiving lines at ABC functions. Once, Arledge fumed when Weiswasser was asked to appear at a photo session with ABC News stars. "There are no blowups, but there's a constant visible strain," said a news executive. Another griped, "The conflict is just maddening. Instead of things getting done, they get tied up in politics." An anchor said, "Roone is engaged in guerrilla warfare." Everyone knew it couldn't last.

It didn't. Weiswasser was impatient; he wanted to fix ABC News and get on to something else. The issue went beyond costs, to more fundamental issues of management, decision making, and long-term planning. In those terms, Weiswasser had concluded, Arledge was failing.

No single instance moved him to act, but Weiswasser was visibly upset by a donnybrook involving Sam Donaldson, Barbara Walters, and presidential candidate Ross Perot just before Election Day, 1992. The incident said a lot about the values shaping ABC News.

The problems began when Walters did something she'd never done before — she turned down a chance to interview the president. She was too busy to see George Bush, she told White House aide Margaret Tutwiler. Besides, she had secured an exclusive interview with Arthur Seale, the man who'd kidnapped and murdered a New Jersey oil company executive in a highly publicized case. Walters recalled telling Tutwiler, "I know this is going to sound very strange, Margaret, but I've got to do this kidnapper and killer on Tuesday. I cannot go with the president." Besides, she'd already interviewed Bush during the campaign, and he was talking to CNN's Larry King, "Today," and "Good Morning America." Arthur Seale was a bigger draw.

The White House then offered Bush to "PrimeTime Live" and Sam Donaldson, who accepted eagerly, explaining that he would also extend invitations to Bill Clinton and Perot. When Clinton agreed to come on, Donaldson stepped up his efforts to get Perot; he hoped to generate a television event, the closest thing viewers would get to a fourth debate. Donaldson called, wrote, and faxed Perot, who finally agreed to an interview — not on "PrimeTime" but with Barbara Walters on "20/20," who was also in hot pursuit. Unlike Bush, Perot was still a hot property.

A series of missed signals followed. Perot agreed to talk to Donaldson, but he changed his mind when he was told that he could not do both "20/20" and "PrimeTime." Traveling in London, Arledge was caught out of position, and he did nothing to resolve the conflict. As a result, Donaldson — who desperately wanted to prove that he could be a major player on "PrimeTime" — lost his chance to have Bush, Clinton, and Perot on the show.

Most people blamed Walters, first for interfering and then for not doing more to steer Perot onto "PrimeTime." Rick Kaplan, among others, said that Walters "should have done whatever she had to do to make sure it happened." Her selfishness cost Donaldson, her friend and longtime supporter, the opportunity to anchor a high-profile show. But relations between "PrimeTime" and "20/20" had become so poisoned by their long-running competition that neither show had any inclination to help the other.

ABC News and its viewers were the losers.

The way Steve Weiswasser saw it, the system fostered by Arledge was at fault. "The dominant mode of this place is competition," Weiswasser said. He could see that Arledge was unwilling to confront hard issues or hard people, like Barbara Walters, and that by disengaging himself, Arledge sanctioned all manner of competition, fair and unfair. Neither of ABC's prime-time shows was being guided from the top — there was no effort to coordinate them, mediate between them, or even differentiate them, so that they could compete in a world where a dozen or more prime-time news hours were on the air. That was symptomatic of the problems at ABC News, Weiswasser thought. Decision making was crisis-oriented and haphazard, at best.

"I saw an organization that I thought was teetering on the edge of serious calamity," Weiswasser said. "How can you survive competitively in this business if you've got nobody sitting there able to plan much beyond the day after tomorrow."

He was sure there was a better way.

"I hate to put it this way," he said, "but childish behavior requires discipline. . . . There are no management people here."

After a year of living with Steve Weiswasser, Roone Arledge described the world around him at ABC as "Kafkaesque." He felt unappreciated and undermined and second-guessed. It was as if all his accomplishments meant nothing.

ABC News was not only profitable but admired. Why else had Ferdinand Marcos called for elections in the Philippines on the Brinkley show? How else could "Nightline" have done path-breaking television in South Africa and the Middle East? Why else would Gorbachev and Yeltsin, in the midst of tumult in the Soviet Union, agree to a joint interview with Peter Jennings?

Where Weiswasser saw a poorly managed and wasteful operation that was unprepared for a difficult future, Arledge saw a news dynasty. He focused, as always, on the programs. His fifteen years of effort had yielded a rich harvest.

ABC's "World News Tonight" enjoyed continued success under Jennings and Paul Friedman, easily winning the ratings competition in 1993 for the fifth consecutive year. A thirty-second commercial on the broadcast sold for about $55,000, roughly 25 percent more than a spot on CBS or NBC, enabling the show to turn a profit of more than $50 million a year. Jennings knew it, and so when his contract expired in 1992, he was in a powerful negotiating position. Setting aside their austere public faces, Steve Weiswasser negotiated and Dan Burke approved an astonishing five-year, $35 million contract for Jennings — the most lucrative contract for a news anchor in the history of television. Their only consolation was that not a word of the deal leaked to the press.

More important, "World News" remained the most serious and thoughtful of the three network newscasts, despite the ever-present temptation to grab viewers with tabloid-style fare. Few newspapers outside New York and Washington treated the news as seriously as ABC. As White House correspondent Brit Hume put it, "The truth is that all three television networks are a hell of a lot more serious in their news programming than anyone would have a right to expect, given the mass audience to which they are trying to appeal."

"World News" also stood as the most influential of the evening broadcasts, if only because those in charge were willing to exercise the clout that came with a program that reached 14 million viewers every night. They defined "news" broadly, moving farther away from the day's events and closer toward their own views of what Americans needed to know. Jennings embraced causes, such as education and AIDS, and he used the broadcast to spotlight them; with Arledge's approval, he also continued to fight for coverage of foreign news. Proof that ABC News took a more global worldview than its broadcast competitors came when war broke out in the Balkans, and "World News" devoted far more time to the story than the evening newscasts on CBS or NBC. In 1993, Jennings traveled to Bosnia because he believed that too many journalists, and Americans, were turning their backs on the killing there. This willingness to highlight certain issues, Friedman said, "grows out of an arrogant idea that we are not in this business to simply report events. We're in this business to shape what people pay attention to." Their reporting was generally fair-minded, but by choosing which problems to explore and which to ignore, "World News" was making political judgments as well as news judgments. The straight-ahead, wire-service tradition upheld for many years by men like Walter Cronkite and Frank Reynolds had become only a memory.

"Nightline," too, was less tied to day-to-day events and more experimental than it had been when Dorrance Smith was nominally in charge. Smith had resigned from ABC News in March 1991 to take a job in the Bush White House, and it was a measure of his limited impact that he was permitted to remain executive producer of "Nightline" for several weeks before departing. He was replaced by Tom Bettag, forty-seven, the former executive producer of the "CBS Evening News," who had been forced out in a dispute with CBS management. Bettag, a soft-spoken, thoughtful, and exceptionally hardworking executive, was an inspired choice; he reinvigorated Koppel and "Nightline" with his ideas and enthusiasm. "The fact that CBS let Tom Bettag go is one of the great blunders of all time," Koppel said. "He's a born leader." Koppel himself did a great service to "Nightline" by finally shutting down his production company, KCI. "I just couldn't do both anymore because the hours were too long," Koppel said.

With Bettag and Koppel devoting all their energies to the show, "Nightline" blossomed. When major news stories broke, "Nightline" remained the place to turn for the freshest, most intelligent news coverage and interviews on television. Otherwise, the broadcast became delightfully unpredictable. "Nightline" did investigations, half-hour documentaries, mood pieces, and stories that took viewers behind the scenes of major events, such as the Los Angeles riot and the final hours of the Clinton campaign. "I've done this for eleven years," Koppel said. "There is no joy in doing the same thing night after night after night." On the story known as Iraqgate, about U.S. support for Saddam Hussein before the Gulf War, "Nightline" was way ahead of everybody else. "I don't think the show has ever been better," Koppel said.

"Nightline" was ideally positioned to capitalize on the turmoil in late-night television triggered by Johnny Carson's retirement and David Letterman's defection from NBC to CBS. By the end of 1993, "Nightline" usually reached more viewers than Jay Leno's "Tonight" show on NBC and slightly fewer than Letterman's new show on CBS. ABC also took steps to encourage more stations to clear "Nightline" live, with encouraging results. "Nightline" was already solidly in the black, earning about $20 million a year for ABC.

"This Week with David Brinkley," meanwhile, remained a Sunday morning fixture and a ratings winner, despite efforts by CBS and NBC to enliven their political talk shows. Brinkley himself was unchanged — in fact, as the years passed, he became more hidebound than ever — but the weekly matchups between Donaldson and Will still gave off sparks. The proceedings were also enlivened by Cokie Roberts, a Washington correspondent who divided her time between ABC News and National Public Radio. Roberts became the first woman to win both a regular spot on the panel and the acceptance of Donaldson and Will, which she once explained by saying, "I have children. It's good experience for a lot of things."

While "World News," "Nightline," and "This Week" were Arledge's prestige vehicles, "PrimeTime Live," "20/20," and his new program, "Day One," were unashamedly market-driven. By 1993, "PrimeTime" dominated its Thursday night period and occasionally climbed into Nielsen's weekly top ten shows. The ratings growth was gradual and steady, although the show became a hit around the time Diane Sawyer obtained the first, highly publicized interview with Patricia Bowman, the woman who accused William Kennedy Smith of raping her in Palm Beach, Florida. The audience, up to then the biggest ever to watch "PrimeTime," had to be impressed with Sawyer's sensitive yet pointed handling of the interview.

By then, "PrimeTime" was clicking. Sawyer was undeniably the star, presenting high-impact investigations into televangelism, mammography, and tainted supermarket meat, as well as high-profile interviews. Her power grew, and she was able to get the best producers and command airtime for her stories at the expense of others. While Sam Donaldson chafed at playing second fiddle, his stories continued to improve: he did a hard-hitting piece about the Tailhook scandal and exposed a military base on Bermuda as little more than a vacation retreat for top brass. "PrimeTime" also specialized in stories using tiny hidden cameras, which, in skilled hands, could generate pictures that actually showed wrongdoing to the audience. The best "PrimeTime" story ever may well have been a piece by Sawyer and producer Mark Lukasiewicz that used hidden cameras to illustrate the effects of racism on a black man and a white man as they shopped, looked for work, and tried to rent an apartment. "Many people thought racism would be impossible to capture on camera," Sawyer said, "but we were able to show the little outrages that black people are exposed to every day." But the use of hidden cameras raised prickly questions about privacy and fairness. For a Sawyer story about fathers who refused to pay child support, "PrimeTime" surreptitiously taped confrontations between children and their delinquent fathers — confrontations arranged by ABC producers. While the emotions were genuine, the scenes had been stage-managed by "PrimeTime."

"PrimeTime," "20/20," and "Day One" were shaped by entertainment values that bore scant relation to the traditional news judgments that had once guided decisions about which stories to tell. This was probably unavoidable, since these programs had to compete against dramas and sitcoms for viewers, but the upshot was that they presented an even more skewed version of reality than the one seen on the nightly news. Guided by Victor Neufeld, "20/20" sometimes had an unmistakably tabloid feel, as it explored lurid murder cases, battered women who fight back, the minds of rapists, courtroom killings, post office killings, hotel crimes, and a Soviet serial killer. These sensational stories were mixed with traditional investigations; self-help, medical, and lifestyle features; and Walters's newsmaker interviews.

Neufeld was guided by a time-honored approach: give the people what they want. "20/20" steered away from breaking news that had been seen elsewhere and provided minimal coverage of the economy, government, politics, the cities, foreign policy, the environment, and high culture. "Our obligation is not to deliver the news," Neufeld said. "Our obligation is to do good programming." The formula was spectacularly successful. During 1992–93, its fifteenth season on ABC, "20/20" was ranked the number thirteen show on television — a level it had never before reached. Even as the networks' hold over prime-time viewers weakened, "20/20" had steadily gained audience share ever since Neufeld took over. At an anniversary celebration for the show, Arledge called him "probably the best executive producer" ever at "20/20."

A similar philosophy prevailed at "Day One," a third prime-time magazine introduced by ABC News in March 1993. With Forrest Sawyer as anchor, "Day One" went after stories that touched the emotions — most of its early episodes dealt with sex or violent crime, and a full hour was devoted to a profile of serial killer Jeffrey Dahmer. This time, though, the viewers turned away — after starting strong, the ratings slid, and Sawyer fought with executive producer Tom Yellin about where to take the program, which barely escaped cancellation by ABC. A fourth magazine program, Phyllis McGrady's "Turning Point," was expected to debut early in 1994, in large part because the prime-time news programs had become money machines for Cap Cities. "20/20" delivered a hefty $40 million in annual profits, while "PrimeTime" earned between $10 million and $15 million, because its costs were higher and ratings slightly lower. Over time, the two new magazines were expected to post similar results.

All in all, Arledge and his people had built a formidable lineup of programs that either of the other networks would have killed to own. NBC News, for its part, struggled to break even and repair a reputation battered by years of cost cutting and on-air bumbles, most dramatically when the prime-time show "Dateline" admitted staging a fiery crash of a General Motors pickup truck. In the aftermath of that scandal, Michael Gartner was replaced as NBC News president by Andrew Lack, a CBS producer. Lack inherited a solid anchor in Tom Brokaw, the morning "Today" franchise, and not much else — no depth of talent, no innovative programs, and no tradition of excellence. CBS News was in stronger financial and journalistic shape, thanks to "60 Minutes," "48 Hours," and a proud history that still counted for something. But the CBS News president, Eric Ober, exhibited little creative spark or journalistic leadership. And when Dan Rather's "CBS Evening News" lost viewers, Connie Chung was named his congenial co-anchor and the broadcast took on the feel of local news, with cutesy features and reporters who strolled along as they did their closing stand-ups. As for CNN, the cable network remained a valuable service, especially during crises, but it was unable to regain the high profile it enjoyed during the Gulf War.

Measured against such competition, Roone Arledge, the onetime outsider who many feared would destroy the values and traditions of network news, had become the senior statesman of the industry. He was the most respected and admired executive in broadcast news — and deservedly so.

No wonder he could not fathom what was happening to him inside ABC. In his mind, he was an enormous success. Yet Steve Weiswasser was treating him as if he were a failure.

The last and most bitter struggle between Roone Arledge and Steve Weiswasser was almost entirely personal. It was not about the programs or the anchors or the budget, but about Joanna Bistany, Arledge's top aide and devoted friend. Arledge wanted her promoted. Weiswasser wanted her out of ABC News.

Bistany's future was put into play during a reorganization of ABC News management that was forced upon Arledge by Weiswasser. His goal was to impose a rational structure on the division, one that would dilute Arledge's power by granting decision-making authority to a new group of vice presidents. The new structure, Weiswasser said, was designed to expedite the decision-making process and develop a cadre of bright, committed executives who could focus on long-term as well as immediate problems.

Arledge thought it was mostly foolishness. For weeks, he ignored the proposal; then he resisted it. Weiswasser was acting like a lawyer, he complained, trying to "put people into boxes" and creating a wasteful new layer of management. To trusted aides, he worried that the new structure was designed to isolate him at the top, in a figurehead position.

But Arledge was forced to yield. He was being pressed not only by Weiswasser but also by Dan Burke, who told him over a long business dinner that the reorganization was critical to the future of ABC News. "Dan wanted a system to be in place so that the news division isn't depending on Roone's idiosyncrasies," said an aide to Burke. Once again, Burke tried to reassure Arledge that he was highly valued as a programmer, to the point where he dangled the prospect of a new contract before his news chief. But he made clear that the reorganization would have to be completed first.

Once Arledge agreed to the plan, he and Weiswasser set out to fill the new jobs. They agreed that Paul Friedman should leave "World News" to take on the most critical post: executive vice president of ABC News. They also agreed that Bob Murphy, a low-key executive who had been in charge of news coverage, was the best choice for the job of senior vice president for hard news; in his new role, Murphy would oversee "World News" and "Nightline," as well as coverage. Both Friedman and Murphy had managed the neat trick of winning the approval of Weiswasser and Dan Burke while keeping Arledge's confidence. Privately, though, both new vice presidents were Cap Cities loyalists.

Friedman, especially, thought that change was urgently needed at ABC News. In fact, he agreed to become Arledge's second-in-command and heir apparent only after getting assurances from Cap Cities that he would have significant decision-making power. He'd grown impatient with Arledge and had no desire to be his errand boy; instead, he would try to persuade Arledge to focus on programs and leave the day-to-day operations to him. "The more he's involved with programs, the better off we'll be," Friedman confided to a colleague. "And the less he's involved in making the news division run, the better off we will be." Some insiders thought that Friedman was in too much of a hurry to take over. "Paul has felt that Roone is absolutely on the skids and that he can take advantage of that," said an ally of Friedman's. Whatever his misgivings about Friedman, Arledge had a compelling reason to accept him and go forward with the rest of the reorganization: it was the only way he would get rid of Weiswasser, who refused to leave until the restructuring was complete.

The third senior vice presidency — a job overseeing the news magazine programs — provoked the battle over Bistany, who had become a controversial figure inside ABC. She was a conduit for those who could not get to Arledge, she stroked the anchor stars, and she could be counted on in a crunch; Sam Donaldson called Bistany, not Arledge, to alert the company when his producer, David Kaplan, was killed by sniper fire in Sarajevo. Most of all, she was the one person who had Arledge's complete trust; she was his guardian, screening his calls and deciding who could get in to see him. As Arledge's confidante, Bistany saw herself as the latest in a line of executives that included David Burke, Dick Ebersol, Don Ohlmeyer, and Bob Iger, all of whom had gone on to assume powerful jobs in network television.

Few others, however, put Bistany in their class. She was well liked but not widely respected; critics dismissed her as Arledge's lackey, and even her supporters acknowledged that she lacked experience in production and journalism. As the struggle over her promotion escalated, Walters and several executive producers tried to lobby on her behalf with Weiswasser. But Jennings, among others, dumped on her, saying that she was too close to Arledge, and Paul Friedman made it clear that he did not want to see her elevated. "It is simply wrong to think that she is anything other than Roone's mouthpiece," said an influential ABC insider. Weiswasser agreed. He was determined not to see her advance, driven, many thought, by a desire to undermine Arledge. "In Steve's mind, Joanna represented the bottleneck and the excuses that Roone could hide behind," said a colleague. While Arledge was entrenched, Bistany was vulnerable.

Arledge went to the wall for Bistany. "The three programs that she was deeply involved with were '20/20,' 'PrimeTime,' and 'Nightline,' all three of which are at their all-time high," he argued. He sought help from Bob Iger, who had become president of the network in December 1992, and pleaded with Dan Burke, to no avail. Arledge was furious with Cap Cities. How could the president of ABC News be denied the right to choose his own management team? "That was a sexist, visceral, venal, nasty action," Arledge said. Weiswasser was the villain, he felt, but Dan Burke was culpable too. "Dan ended up buying it," Arledge said with some bitterness.

Arledge was forced to accept Alan Wurtzel, who was then running ABC's audience research department, as his senior vice president for magazine programs. Wurtzel had even less news experience than Bistany, and in an earlier era, he would have been deemed wholly unsuitable for a top job in network news. But Wurtzel's ability to understand the audience was seen as extremely valuable to the task of guiding the prime-time programs. A bright, straightforward, and personable executive, Wurtzel was welcomed into the news division.

Inside ABC News, Bistany's failure to get the job was seen as another slap at Arledge. When Iger, Weiswasser, and Friedman all tried to find her a position elsewhere in the company, that, too, was interpreted as an attempt to weaken Arledge. "I see a further isolation of Roone Arledge in terms of his ability to run ABC News," said an anchor. "If he loses Joanna, he loses his gatekeeper, the confidante, the one person he can trust."

Arledge felt like he'd suffered another ill-deserved blow. His friends commiserated with him, and one, David Burke, gently suggested that he consider leaving ABC News and end the constant squabbles with Cap Cities. Burke lamented, "This is a guy who led the D-Day landing at Normandy fighting a skirmish in a small village in France." But Arledge found it hard to acknowledge his weakened state even to friends.

With Weiswasser gone, he had hopes of regaining control. He had a good relationship with Iger, who had worked for him in Sports and valued the contribution that News made to ABC. Iger, though, shared the view held by senior Cap Cities people that Arledge was a gifted programmer but an inattentive executive. "It was clear that a management structure was desperately needed," Iger said, because the news division had grown so much. He was determined to support Friedman, Murphy, and Wurtzel — if need be, at Arledge's expense.

Still, Arledge managed to win a few victories. When Sam Donaldson's one-year contract expired in the spring of 1993, there was no battle about whether to re-sign him. After consulting with Iger, Arledge offered the anchor a four-year contract with no reduction in pay, which Donaldson readily and happily accepted as a sign that he was back in the fold. "I was not just the seventh guy at the end of the picture," Donaldson said. "I was once again one of the boys." With Dick Wald, Arledge also negotiated a wide-ranging programming agreement between ABC News and the BBC that gave ABC access to BBC coverage around the world. That would help ABC and the BBC compete worldwide against CNN. And, even under the new structure, Arledge retained ultimate authority over many key decisions affecting ABC News. It was Arledge, for example, who along with Peter Jennings picked Emily Rooney, a news director for a local station in Boston (and the daughter of "60 Minutes" star Andy Rooney), to replace Friedman as executive producer of "World News Tonight." She became the first woman to become executive producer of an evening newscast at one of the Big Three networks.

On day-to-day matters, though, Arledge played a reduced role. "ABC has moved on, past the days when Roone was the supreme head," one of his anchors said. Arledge's absences became more frequent, particularly during warm weather. "When Roone gets cornered, he just goes golfing," complained a Cap Cities executive whose attempts to reach Arledge often proved fruitless. As always, Arledge skipped meetings and canceled appointments on a whim; he'd sometimes disappear for the rest of the day after stopping in to monitor the meeting of top management convened each morning by Friedman. "Roone has checked out. Period," said an aide who saw his comings and goings on the fifth floor. Others were more measured in their assessments, and Arledge denied that he was working any less than usual. But his energy and enthuasiasm had waned. He turned sixty-two during the summer of 1993.

In some respects, Friedman ran the place, with help from Wurtzel and Murphy. They installed loyalists in key positions on all the shows, so that the executives at the magazine programs, Rooney at "World News," and, to a lesser extent, Bettag at "Nightline" went to them first with problems. Friedman and his deputies also put together the news division's $425 million spending plan for 1994 on their own. While Arledge had to sign off on the budget, he'd played no part in shaping its priorities.

Even when it came to programming — the last realm where he was acknowledged by even his critics to have a gift — Arledge's role diminished. He opposed, for example, a proposal from Wurtzel to have former ABC anchor Linda Ellerbee produce and anchor an hour-long special on breast cancer for the network; in the old days, the program could never have been mounted without Arledge's backing. But Wurtzel and Friedman persisted, and Ellerbee went forward with her show, which garnered favorable reviews and made a profit of more than $1.5 million. Here, the new structure was working to benefit ABC News.

Often, though, ABC News suffered because of Arledge's waning influence and inattention. For one thing, his battalions did not respond as aggressively anymore to big stories; the division reacted slowly, for example, when U.S. troops landed in Somalia, and it provided significantly less coverage of the inauguration of President Clinton than either CBS or NBC. Arledge's old approach to breaking news — send in the troops, and then see if a big story develops — had given way to a cautious, cost-conscious style. Arledge also did little about the problems at "Day One," which struggled during its first months on the air and suffered because executive producer Tom Yellin and anchor Forrest Sawyer could not stand one another. Things got so bad that the show was nearly canceled by Iger in May 1993. "There was almost criminal neglect of that program," an insider said.

Worse, Arledge and his senior staff sometimes worked at cross purposes. "On paper, the structure plays to his strengths and shores up his weaknesses," said a senior executive. "In reality, it doesn't work." Key openings took too long to fill — the news division functioned for more than a year without a bureau chief in Washington because Arledge and Friedman could not agree on a candidate. Getting Arledge to focus was as hard as ever, a key aide said after a frustrating experience trying to get him to sign off on staff changes at

"World News." Arledge, this aide said, "is having absolutely no positive impact" on the division. Friedman himself struggled, suffering occasional sleepless nights and going to a doctor when a rash appeared on his face; stress, he was told, was the probable cause.

Behind the scenes, there were more signs that ABC's news dynasty was fraying around the edges. Several talented young producers left for other networks, as did the veteran Jeff Gralnick, who defected to NBC to run "Nightly News," in part because of his disaffection with Arledge. Jennings threw Gralnick a party that brought a teary-eyed farewell from the anchor; no team had ever covered special events better than they did them at ABC. Gralnick's absence was soon felt when Israel and the PLO signed a peace agreement in September 1993, in ceremonies at the White House. Director Roger Goodman's pictures were evocative, as always, but Jennings hogged the airtime and spoke far too much during the speeches, evidently trying to show off his knowledge of the Middle East. He was blasted by TV critics and deservedly so, said ABC insiders. Gralnick might have been able to get his anchor to pipe down for a moment.

Jennings was understandably distressed, and not just by his bad press. Some months earlier, after receiving an anonymous call, his wife, Kati Marton, confronted him in the newsroom with the charge that he was having an affair with a thirtysomething producer at "World News." In August 1993, they announced through syndicated columnist Liz Smith that they were separating after fourteen years of marriage. "Kati and Peter," she wrote, "have asked us to stress that there is no third party involved on either side." That was misleading, and several publications subsequently reported Jennings's affair with the producer. All of this only added to the tension at "World News," where Emily Rooney ran into opposition from veterans who did not like reporting to an outsider with no network experience; she struggled gamely to gain control.

The Cap Cities people worried a lot about ABC News. Dan Burke, as always, had conflicting feelings about Arledge. As Burke began to plan for his retirement in February 1994, he wondered whether he had made a mistake by not getting rid of his news president. Sometimes, he regretted not firing him. But Burke always came back to his bedrock belief that even a flawed Roone Arledge had value to ABC. Bob Iger was more certain that Arledge was worth keeping, and he made that case to Burke. Arledge, he thought, still had a fresh eye for programming, when he was willing to apply himself. As an executive-star, Arledge also brought a certain cachet to ABC News —

no other news division president was on a first-name basis with former presidents and world leaders. What's more, Iger knew, Ted Koppel and Diane Sawyer would soon begin contract negotiations and Barbara Walters wanted to reopen her deal. They all remained loyal to Arledge. Assessing Arledge, Iger said, "The news division is a wildly successful division right now. Sometimes, in order to hold on to an important asset, you have to accept some liabilities."

What Burke and Iger needed was a way to hold on to Arledge, at least for a while, without undermining Friedman, whom they saw as the future of ABC News. They decided to offer Arledge one last lucrative contract as president of ABC News — a contract that would pay him well over $3 million a year. The new agreement replaced a contract that expired in May 1995, and, at least in theory, it would keep Arledge in place through July 1996. He would then become the chairman of ABC News, a grand title that would permit him to consult on programming but, as a practical matter, would remove him from power. There was a catch, though — if Burke or Iger chose to move Arledge up to the chairman's job early, they could do so without financial penalty. That gave them leverage to insist that Arledge play by their rules. And Friedman was assured that he had their full support.

To no one's surprise, Arledge agonized before signing the deal. Ultimately, he did so — the money was a lure, as was the title that would make him feel important even after he stepped down. Much as he hated to think that ABC News could survive without him, Arledge had begun to reconcile himself to the idea that it was time for him to go.

CONCLUSION:
THE HOUSE THAT ROONE BUILT

RIGHT TO THE END, everything about Roone Arledge was out-size: his ego, his ambition, his achievements, his vanity, and his failure to adapt as the world changed around him. Arledge had always cast himself as a victim — as a lone figure struggling against the great gray mass of men who lacked his boldness and vision — and, in his last days at ABC, that was the role he was given to play. He was no longer the unchallenged master of the house he had built. He was the magician stripped of his powers or, as his detractors might say, the Wizard of Oz, exposed as a mere mortal when the curtain was pulled back. But Arledge's wizardry was no illusion.

No matter how his story ended, Roone Arledge would go down in broadcasting history as a giant. First in sports, then in news, he had transformed the way events were presented on television. He was a creature of television. He seized its possibilities. And he loved its impact. And, while he was as much a showman as a journalist, he took his responsibilities seriously.

His most valuable talent was his ability to sell the news, even serious news, to a mass audience that was impatient and prone not to care. He always thought about the audience. How could they be persuaded to watch? Would they understand? How could they be made to care? The audience and the show: those were what mattered most to Arledge. He was literally a show man, a product guy, not an MBA or a manager but a producer who, like all great producers, knew how to grab the audience's attention and keep it, by packaging the news in an engaging and dramatic way.

His triumphs were not his alone, of course. Arledge surrounded himself with creative people and fostered a culture that drove them to perform at peak levels. He could be an aloof and exasperating boss, but his gifted executive producers respected his judgment and valued his approval. Most important, they knew he was watching.

As a casting director, Arledge's record was imperfect — he had once preferred Max Robinson to Ted Koppel, and to the end, he was oddly reluctant to take chances on unknowns. He was obsessed with fame. But, perhaps because he valued stars so much, Arledge had no equal as a star-maker. His ABC stars knew they were in good hands with Arledge. The Hollywood maxim that television is a business of hits and stars applied to Arledge's ABC News. In a celebrity-driven age, he was an ideal television news executive.

In other ways, too, as he led ABC News during the late 1970s and early 1980s, Arledge was a man for his time. Because the network was immensely profitable, he had the money to recruit people and erect a first-class news organization. As technology advanced, he knew how to use television news to make the global village a reality. And, as the networks faced fierce competitive pressures, Arledge, unencumbered by tradition, created a news division that without compromising its principles could compete in a tabloid world.

But as times changed, the forces he had harnessed so adroitly turned against him. His stars became independent powers, who no longer had to take direction from the boss. His free-spending ways drove salaries so high that they became a burden. And technology bypassed the over-the-air networks, so that a twenty-four-hour-a-day cable channel became the place to turn for the crisis coverage that had been ABC's trademark. With its worldwide reach, CNN became the local channel of the global village.

In the ultimate irony, Arledge fell victim to the idea that network news could and should make money — an idea that had once been his alone. He had made ABC News profitable, but his failure to generate greater profits for Capital Cities brought his comeuppance. Instead of buying him autonomy, the expectations he created cost him his authority.

Arledge's character and personality also ensured that his story would not have an entirely happy ending. A complex man whose inner self remained hidden even from close associates, Arledge ran ABC News the only way he knew how — from a distance. His selfishness left him oblivious to the needs of others and, as a result, he built few strong bonds with those around him. Over time, his insecurities drove him to inflate his role in ABC's triumphs and to evade responsibility for its failures, traits that did not endear him to colleagues. And his technique of playing people against each other wore thin. In the end, Arledge commanded attention, respect, admiration, fear, and occasional loathing from those who worked for him, but he had few friends at ABC News.

This, of course, was not the standard by which he wished to be measured. He had not set out to make friends. He had set out to do one thing: to build a great news organization that would leave his imprint on broadcast news and on the world. That he had achieved. The ABC News he built served him well. It served the stockholders of Capital Cities/ABC well. Most important, it served the public well — not always, of course, but more often than not. "Nightline" was the jewel in the crown of broadcast news. "World News Tonight" was serious and substantive. "This Week with David Brinkley" made politics an entertaining sport. And even the prime-time programs, "20/20" and "PrimeTime Live" and "Day One," which were primarily engines of commerce, often presented original and enterprising journalism that served the public. The defects of ABC News were evident — the journalism was sometimes shallow, pictures overshadowed words, the range of ideas expressed was narrow, and drama, more than enlightenment, shaped some stories — but these flaws were common to all television news. Given the limits of the medium and its unceasing commercial pressures, Arledge's ABC News was a class act.

The question that remained, as Arledge's career drew to a close, was whether ABC News would thrive without him. Cap Cities would undoubtedly manage the division efficiently, but some signs were not encouraging: Arledge's ABC Sports, once the standard-setter in sports television, had withered after his ouster, a victim of plodding management and market forces that left the television sports business reeling. Fortunately, ABC News was far stronger. It was built upon a solid foundation of popular programs and boasted a surplus of bright, creative, and energetic people. But even the most successful programs need constant reinvention, and creative people need a special brand of leadership. And nowhere on the horizon was there another leader like Roone Arledge.

SELECTED READINGS

Alter, Jonathan. "America's Q&A Man." *Newsweek*, June 15, 1987.

Alter, Jonathan. "TV Women: Give Us Some Air." *Newsweek*, July 22, 1985.

Auletta, Ken. *Three Blind Mice: How the TV Networks Lost Their Way*. New York: Random House, 1991.

Baldo, Anthony. "CEO of the Year: Dan Burke." *Financial World*, April 2, 1991.

Bark, Ed. "Sam Donaldson." *Dallas Morning News*, November 19, 1989.

Bedell, Sally. "Can Roone Make the Double Play at ABC?" *TV Guide*, June 10, 1978.

Blum, David. "Up From 'Club Thirteen': The Rise and Rise of Peter Jennings." *New York*, November 30, 1987.

Boyer, Peter. "The Light Goes Out." *Vanity Fair*, June 1989.

Capuzzi, Cecilia. "The ABCs of Making News Profits." *Channels of Communication*, March 1989.

Carter, Bill. "Tender Trap." *New York Times Magazine*, August 23, 1992.

Collins, Nancy. *Hard to Get: Fast Talk and Rude Questions Along the Interview Trail*. New York: Random House, 1990.

Davis, L. J. "Can This Marriage Work?" *Channels of Communication*, July/August 1986.

DeParle, Jason. "Long Series of Military Decisions Led to Gulf War News Censorship." *New York Times*, May 5–6, 1991.

Diamond, Edwin. *The Media Show: The Changing Face of the News, 1985–1990*. Cambridge: MIT Press, 1991.

Downs, Hugh. *On Camera: My 10,000 Hours on Television*. New York: G. P. Putnam's Sons, 1986.

Flander, Judy. "Women in Network News: Have They Arrived or Is Their Prime Time Past?" *Washington Journalism Review*, March 1985.

Friedman, David. "In Her Prime Time." *Newsday*, August 1, 1989.

Goldberg, Robert, and Goldberg, Gerald Jay. *Anchors: Brokaw, Jennings, Rather and the Evening News*. New York: Carol Publishing Group, 1990.

Goldenson, Leonard H., and Wolf, Marvin J. *Beating the Odds: The Untold Story Behind the Rise of ABC*. New York: Charles Scribner's Sons, 1991.

Graham, Ellen. "ABC News Improves, But Ratings Still Lag, Under Arledge Regime." *Wall Street Journal*, April 26, 1978.

Greenfield, Jeff. "The Showdown at ABC News." *New York Times Magazine*, February 13, 1977.

Greider, William. "Terms of Endearment: How the News Media Came to Be All the President's Men." *Rolling Stone Yearbook*, 1984.

Gunther, Marc, and Carter, Bill. *Monday Night Mayhem: The Inside Story of ABC's Monday Night Football*. New York: William Morrow, 1988.

Halberstam, David. "Roone Arledge." *Fame Magazine*, December 1988.

Hirsch, Alan. *Talking Heads: Political Talk Shows and Their Pundits*. New York: St. Martin's Press, 1991.

Husock, Howard. "Siege Mentality: ABC, the White House and the Iran Hostage Crisis." Kennedy School of Government, 1988.

Kalter, Joanmarie. "I Don't Think He Will Ever Be Totally at Peace with Himself." *TV Guide*, January 3, 1987.

Kaye, Elizabeth. "Peter Jennings Gets No Self-Respect." *Esquire*, September 1989.

Klein, Edward. "True Grit." *Vanity Fair*, June 1992.

Klein, Edward. "Winning Diane." *New York*, March 13, 1989.

Macarthur, John R. *Second Front: Censorship and Propaganda in the Gulf War*. New York: Hill and Wang, 1992.

Matusow, Barbara. *The Evening Stars: The Making of the Network News Anchor*. Boston: Houghton Mifflin, 1983.

Matusow, Barbara. "How Frank Reynolds Viewed the News, Networks and Notoriety." *Washington Journalism Review*, September 1983.

Matusow, Barbara. "Top Gun: A D.C. Lawyer Is Helping Roone Arlege Run ABC News." *The Washingtonian*, March 1992.

McKay, Jim. *My Wide World*. New York: Macmillan, 1973.

Milloy, Marilyn. "Fadeout." *Newsday Magazine*, March 19, 1989.

Oppenheimer, Jerry. *Barbara Walters: An Unauthorized Biography*. New York: St. Martin's Press, 1990.

Peer, Elizabeth. "Barbara Walters: Star of the Morning." *Newsweek*, May 6, 1974.

Piantadosi, Roger. "Roone Arledge." *Washington Journalism Review*, May 1982.

Powers, Ron. *Supertube: The Rise of Television Sports*. New York: Coward-McCann, 1984.

Rather, Dan, with Herskowitz, Mickey. *The Camera Never Blinks*. New York: Ballantine, 1977.

Rivera, Geraldo. *Exposing Myself*. New York: Bantam, 1991.

Sanders, Marlene, and Rock, Marcia. *Waiting for Prime Time: The Women of Television News*. Urbana: University of Illinois Press, 1988.

Schwartz, Tony. "Why TV News Is Increasingly Being Packaged As Entertainment." *New York Times*, October 17, 1982.

Shales, Tom. "Uneasy Lies the Ted That Wears a Crown." *Washington Post Magazine*, February 26, 1989.

Simon, Roger. "No Longer Invisible." *TV Guide*, December 2, 1978.

Smith, Desmond. "Is This the Future of TV News?" *New York*, February 22, 1982.

Smith, Desmond. "The Wide World of Roone Arledge." *New York Times Magazine*, February 24, 1980.

Spence, Jim. *Up Close & Personal: The Inside Story of Network Television Sports*. New York: Macmillan, 1988.

Trescott, Jacqueline. "Max Robinson Signs Off." *Washington Post*, June 1, 1978.

Unger, Arthur. "Ted Koppel: A Journalist's Contribution." *Television Quarterly*, Volume 24, Number I, 1989.

Unger, Arthur. "Barbara Walters: I Can Ask Them But I Can't Answer Them." *Television Quarterly*, Volume 24, Number III, 1989.

Waters, Harry F. "The Wide World of Roone Arledge." *Newsweek*, February 6, 1984.

Westin, Av. *Newswatch: How TV Decides the News*. New York: Simon and Schuster, 1982.

Williams, Huntington. *Beyond Control: ABC and the Fate of the Networks*. New York: Atheneum, 1989.

Yagoda, Ben. "Friends in High Places." *Channels of Communication*, January 1987.

Zoglin, Richard. "Star Power." *Time*, August 7, 1989.

ACKNOWLEDGMENTS

WRITING any complex work of nonfiction is a collaborative task. Many people helped me with this book — friends, family, colleagues, the staff of Little, Brown, and the men and women of ABC News. I cannot thank them all here, but they have my gratitude.

I began my work by reading others. Many are listed in the Selected Readings; the books by Ken Auletta and Barbara Matusow were especially helpful. Ed Tivnan, a writer who worked briefly for "20/20," kindly shared with me an unpublished manuscript that provided a vivid account of the show's early days. This book contains some quotations that first appeared in print elsewhere, but in each instance I sought to check the quotes for accuracy.

Most of this book is based on interviews. I did nearly 300 interviews with 165 people, most face-to-face and many tape-recorded. I came away with an increased respect for the talents, energies, and good intentions of the people of ABC News. Most strive to serve their audience in the best way that they can, and many struggle against the boundaries imposed by commercial television.

I want to give special thanks to Roone Arledge. Predictably, he was hard to get — it took a year to arrange our first interview, with the help of his unfailingly pleasant assistant Nancy Dobi — but we eventually met eight times, often over lunch at his favorite hangout, Cafe des Artistes, and never for less than two hours. No reporter has ever been granted as much access to Arledge.

Other present and former employees of Cap Cities/ABC who were especially helpful include Tom Bettag, Joanna Bistany, Dan Burke,

David Burke, Marc Burstein, Mike Clemente, Sam Donaldson, David Doss, Mike Duffy, Paul Friedman, Bob Frye, Richard Gerdau, Marion Goldin, Roger Goodman, Jeff Gralnick, Brit Hume, Peter Jennings, Rick Kaplan, Ted Koppel, Deborah Leff, Ene Riisna, Judd Rose, Bob Siegenthaler, Dorrance Smith, Dick Wald, Irwin Weiner, Steve Weis-wasser, Betsy West, and Av Westin. Every major anchor at ABC News talked to me, for which I am grateful. And I benefited from the friendly and efficient help of the Cap Cities/ABC public relations staff, including Patricia Matson, Sherrie Rollins, Liz Noyer, Janice Grete-meyer, Teri Everett, Lucy Kraus, Rena Terracuso, Arnot Walker, Laura Wessner, Maurie Perl, and Scott Richardson. In an effort to be fair and accurate, I provided portions of the manuscript to about fifteen key people at Cap Cities/ABC who were kind enough to respond with comments.

At Little, Brown, I could not ask for a better editor than Fredrica Friedman. Her perceptive guidance, criticism, and suggestions prod-ded me to work harder and better than I thought I could. I'd also like to thank associate editor Catherine Crawford and editorial as-sistant Eve Yohalem, of Little, Brown. My agent, Esther Newberg, has been a valued advocate and adviser.

My friends Chuck Palmer and Bill Carter read portions of the manuscript and offered sound advice. My mother and father, Irene Weinstock and Edgar Gunther, and my brother Andrew Gunther were supportive, as always. Thanks also to Heath Meriwether, John Smyn-tek, Ann Olson, and Peggy Castine of the *Detroit Free Press*, who granted me two leaves of absence to work on the book, and to my researchers and transcribers, Jeannie Shatter, Monica Yant, Judy Minard, and Lisa Estreich.

My brother Noel Gunther has been a great friend and sounding board, as well as a tireless editor; he read every word of the manu-script, including many thousands that do not appear here.

Finally, there are the women who, mercifully, never let me forget that there was more to life than ABC News. My wife, Karen Schneider, yet another gifted editor in my life, and my daughters, Sarah and Rebecca, sustained me with their love and affection.

INDEX